NEW EVERY
Morning

NEW EVERY

Morning

365 DAYS OF WORSHIP

CREATED AND COMPILED BY
PHIL BARFOOT

B&H
PUBLISHING
NASHVILLE, TENNESSEE

Contents

WEEK 4

WEEK 5

WEEK 6

WEEK 7

WEEK 8

WEEK 9

WEEK 10

WEEK 11

WEEK 12

WEEK 13

WEEK 14

WEEK 15

WEEK 16

WEEK 17

may

WEEK 25

WEEK 26

WEEK 27

WEEK 28

WEEK 29

WEEK 30

WEEK 31

Jul

WEEK 35

WEEK 36

WEEK 37

WEEK 38

WEEK 39

Aug ## WEEK 40

WEEK 41

WEEK 42

WEEK 43

WEEK 44

WEEK 45

WEEK 49

WEEK 50

WEEK 51

WEEK 52

Preface

New Every Morning was created by 118 premiere worship pastors, ministers of music, and Christian university professors across America!

First and foremost, I am humbled and grateful to count each of them as my friends and want to express my deepest appreciation that they would take the time out of their hectic schedules to contribute to this book of unique and dynamic devotionals.

From the bottom of my heart, I say a huge "Thank You" to each of these contributors. Your spiritual insight and godly encouragement will make this book a blessing to many.

One of the unique features of this book is its flexibility to be used as a private devotional book or as a group devotional. I encourage choirs, praise teams, orchestras, Sunday school classes, and all types of groups to read through the devotions on the same schedule corporately as each one does individually during private study and personal devotional time.

Reading these devotions on the same schedule also opens up the opportunity to share and discuss each other's thoughts together in small or large group settings.

Another feature of the book is included on Wednesdays and Sundays. On each of these days, there are always a few thoughts aimed at those in music and worship ministries. These Wednesday and Sunday devotions are designed to read to your choir or group and ask the questions included in each devotion to encourage discussion.

Whether you utilize this devotional book in your daily private time with the Lord or with your choir or ministry groups, my prayer is that God would use its truths and spiritual insights to *inspire, encourage, uplift,* and *bless* all who read it.

God's *BEST* to you as you experience His mercies *New Every Morning!*

Dr. Phil Barfoot, Editor

Attitude Is Everything

About midnight Paul and Silas were praying and singing hymns to God, and the other prisoners were listening to them. Suddenly there was such a violent earthquake that the foundations of the prison were shaken. At once all the prison doors flew open, and everyone's chains came loose.

Acts 16:25–26 (NIV)

We have a choice. Every day in every situation and circumstance, we have a choice. We can follow the naysayers and negative whims of the masses, OR we can come with thankful and grateful hearts and attitudes to face even the most overwhelming and challenging situations.

If Paul and Silas would have responded negatively to their imprisonment, having been beaten, stripped of their clothes and put into jail with their feet in shackles, you would never have heard this story. It would have been just another unremarkable night in that Philippian prison.

However, Scripture tells us that at midnight they "prayed and sang praises to God." That's right—they didn't whimper and complain. They praised God in their dire situation.

God honored their "attitudes of gratitude" along with their thanksgiving and praise in the midst of those dark and desperate circumstances. God truly inhabited the praises of Paul and Silas that night! In fact, they prayed, praised, and sang until, suddenly, an earthquake shook the foundations of the prison, all the doors were opened, and EVERYONE'S chains were loosed. Not only were Paul and Silas delivered, but all the prisoners were!

The jailer rushed in and fell trembling before Paul and Silas and asked, "Sirs, what must I do to be saved?" (v. 30). Paul and Silas then sealed the deal by explaining he must "believe in the Lord Jesus Christ and you will be saved—you and your household" (v. 31). The jailer and his entire family were then saved!

Today, you will be faced with a choice. I encourage you to choose thanksgiving in *every* circumstance.

1. What are some steps that I can take to change my attitude to trust God at all times in every situation?
2. When faced with a choice, how can I confidently learn to *believe* rather than *doubt*?

~

Lord Jesus, help me to choose the "attitude of gratitude" when faced with challenges and overwhelming situations today. In the almighty name of Jesus I pray, Amen.

Dr. Phil Barfoot
President / CEO
Celebration Concert Tours International / CCT Music, Franklin, TN

Our Real Calling

*"Of all the commandments, which is the most important?" "The most
important one," answered Jesus, "is this: 'Hear, O Israel: The Lord our God,
the Lord is one. Love the Lord your God with all your heart and with all
your soul and with all your mind and with all your strength.'"*
Mark 12:28b–30 (NIV)

The answer Jesus gives this religious teacher to this all-important question sets the purpose, priority, and plan of our lives here on this earth. Jesus is clearly saying that
WORSHIP is the greatest commandment!

It's what's going on in heaven now and for all eternity and what *should* be going on in
each of our lives as believers. Worship is heaven's highest occupation and the earth's greatest
privilege. The Westminster Shorter Catechism says it this way, "The chief end of man is to
glorify God and enjoy Him forever."

Revelation 4:11 (KJV 2000) puts it like this, "You are worthy, O Lord, to receive glory
and honor and power: for you have created all things, and for your pleasure they are and
were created."

In other words, we were created to please the Lord. We *please* Him by *praising* Him.

I encourage you today to consider your *AVOCATION*. We all know what our
VOCATIONS are—plumbers, electricians, teachers, nurses, accountants, ministers, business owners, etc. Our *AVOCATION* is to be ministers *to* and worshipers *of* Almighty God.

First Peter 2:9 calls us "a chosen people, a royal priesthood, a holy nation, a people
belonging to God, that you may declare the praises of him who called you out of darkness
into his wonderful light" (NIV).

As you go about your day, let me simply encourage you to fulfill your *AVOCATION*—
the greatest commandment of loving the Lord your God with all your heart, soul, mind,
and strength . . . *WORSHIP!* In doing so, you will satisfy the purpose to which we have all
been called . . . worshipers of our awesome, almighty, loving Father.

1. What are some practical steps I can take to *love* and *worship* the Lord in a deeper
   way?
2. How can my *avocation* be reflected in my *vocation*?

~

*Lord Jesus, help me to focus on my real calling and purpose today . . . to be a minister
to and worshiper of Almighty God. May YOU be my priority and the focus of all my
time and attention and purpose today. May I please You in all I do. May I glorify
You and enjoy Your loving presence. In the strong name of Jesus I pray, Amen.*

Dr. Phil Barfoot
President / CEO
Celebration Concert Tours International / CCT Music, Franklin, TN

Worship as an Act of Sacrifice

I urge you, brothers, in light of God's mercy, to offer your bodies as living sacrifices, holy and pleasing to God—this is your spiritual act of worship.
Romans 12:1 (NIV)

In our day and age, there seems to be a big push for making worship services as consumer-friendly as possible. I would even go out on a limb and say that many of us have joined churches based on the style of music, worship service schedule, or what the church had to offer our family or us. While these concerns may seem to be fully legitimate in today's culture, they directly contradict a key word in our Scripture passage—sacrifice.

According to the apostle Paul, the correct attitude in worship is one of sacrifice. When we sacrifice, our individual wants become secondary. When we worship, we should strive to become more Christlike, who "humbled himself" and became "nothing" for the sake of mankind (Phil. 2:5–8). So how does this translate in real terms? It means that when there's a congregational song that is not in the style that I personally like, I sing it anyway because that song is ministering to someone else in the congregation. It means that a grandparent should be willing to sing a song that ministers to his/her grandchild—and vice-versa.

When we sacrifice our personal agendas, God takes His rightful place at center stage. I cannot come to church with the expectation that corporate worship will replicate my private time with God. That would be self-serving.

1. What are some hindrances that prevent me from truly sacrificing my personal preferences in corporate worship?
2. What results from worship bring joy to God's heart?

Dear Lord, help me to not be self centered in my worship. Help me strive to become more like Jesus and willing to sacrifice my personal preferences when I come together with others in corporate worship. In Jesus' name, Amen.

Carlos Ichter
Minister of Music and Worship
Tallowood Baptist Church, Houston, TX

1. When I focus on those who are uninterested in worship. Acting as if they need to be entertained.
2. When He is the main attraction, then He inhabits our praise.

Built to Last?

*So then you are no longer strangers and aliens, but you are fellow citizens with
the saints, and are of God's household, having been built on the foundation of the
apostles and prophets, Christ Jesus Himself being the corner stone, in whom the
whole building, being fitted together, is growing into a holy temple in the Lord, in
whom you also are being built together into a dwelling of God in the Spirit.*
Ephesians 2:19–22 (NASB)

If you've grown up around the church, you've probably heard songs with "cornerstone" in the title. Today, the cornerstone is a masonry stone of dedication and remembrance that is unveiled at the dedication of a building. In earlier days, the cornerstone was the very first masonry stone that was laid. It determined the direction and layout of the entire structure. If the cornerstone was not laid precisely, the building was not built according to plan.

Jesus should be the Cornerstone of our lives and the place where the Holy Spirit dwells. Everything about our lives should be built on Jesus as revealed in Scripture. But what if we've messed up? The good news is that when we repent and ask, Jesus forgives and forgets. Today, take in God's Word. Talk with Him. Pay attention to what He is doing in and around you. Today, let your life be built on the Cornerstone that will never lead you away from the very best that God has for you.

1. What do you need to tear down and let God rebuild?
2. What do you tend to substitute for THE Cornerstone?

*Lord, may You be the foundation of who I am and everything I do. Show me what You
see and show me where I need to rebuild to be in line with You. May it be obvious, due
to the presence of the Holy Spirit, that my life is built on the Chief Cornerstone.*

Mark Blair
Minister of Music
Bellevue Baptist Church, Memphis, TN

Handling Life's Interruptions

"I will ask the Father, and He will give you another Helper, that He may
be with you forever; that is the Spirit of truth. . . . In that day you will
know that I am in My Father, and you in Me, and I in you."
John 14:16–17a, 20 (NASB)

Interruptions are simply a part of life. Some interruptions are mild irritants, like noticing a flat tire on your parked car in the driveway or receiving a telemarketing robocall on your smartphone. Other interruptions, like losing a job, fighting cancer, or surviving a devastating accident, can instantly alter the trajectory of one's life.

In a CBS televised interview on *60 Minutes*, newly-elected Canadian Prime Minister and boxing enthusiast Justin Trudeau remarked, "People think boxing is about how hard of a punch you can throw, but boxing is really about how hard a punch you can withstand and keep fighting."

Our best response to life's interruptions is depending on Christ to work *through* us. If Christ is living in me through His Word, it will shape my responses. If I try to manhandle the situation without Christ, it's likely I'll fail and make a mess in the process. Christ allows me to withstand life's interruptions and keep fighting.

For those who have been called to serve God, who are seen by others as ambassadors of Christ, it is not enough to have an effective plan for our life and ministry. We must also respond well to the interruptions that can derail the best-made plan, not just for our own benefit, but for those who look to us for guidance, wisdom, and strength.

1. Visualize your name written on the outside of a small envelope. Then visualize sealing your envelope into a larger one with the name of *Jesus* written on the outside of it. Then place both of these envelopes within a larger one with *God—The Father* written on the outside.
2. Now, reread John 14:20.

Lord, give me the wisdom to remember I cannot control when interruptions impact my life. I can only control my response to them by knowing and applying Your Word. Thank You for the assurance that You live in me and are guiding me always. In Jesus' name I pray, Amen.

Dr. D. Doran Bugg
Chair of Music Department
Belhaven University, Jackson, MS

The Basics

You brought my inner parts into being; You wove me in my mother's womb. I will praise You, for You made me with fear and wonder; marvelous are Your works, and You know me completely. My frame was not hidden from You when I was made in secret, and intricately put together in the lowest parts of the earth. Your eyes saw me unformed, yet in Your book all my days were written, before any of them came into being.

Psalm 139:13–16 (MEV)

I often see people who seem blessed beyond what the average human deserves. I can't help but notice when a new colleague has a new CD out, was published, or got a promotion. My first reaction usually isn't excitement for them. It's usually more like, "Why do *they* get all the attention?" or "I'm better than him, why does he get all the cool gigs?"

When these thoughts creep into my mind, I try to go back to the basics. God made me who I am: the good, the bad, and the ugly. I know it seems basic, but I have to constantly remind myself that I am made to be who I am because the Master Creator molded me this way. Read and reflect on Psalm 139.

God placed me where I am. We are not in our positions because of our skill, talent, or education. God placed us in positions of influence no matter where we fall on the worldly scale of success. Mary and Joseph didn't just happen to be in the room where the angels appeared. It was no accident that Joseph was in that pit. Moses wasn't on a joyride down the Nile. God ordained every one of these events. The same is true for us. Whatever it is you are doing today, God has placed you there for a specific purpose and reason.

God loves me the way I am. Sometimes, we can begin to believe that God made us, but He must not *like* us. Not true! God adores you. When God looks at you and me, He sees a wonderful, intimate act of creative genius. "I will praise You, for You made me with fear and wonder; *marvelous are Your works, and You know me completely.*" Did you get that? "Marvelous are Your works." You are His handiwork. The next line says, "and You know me completely." That means even the stuff you don't want anyone to know about, He knows and still thinks you're pretty great.

God uses the good and the bad. Think about David, a "man after God's own heart," who made some stupid choices. Some of us feel like God has limited our success because of past failures or mistakes we have made. While I believe God molds us, He does not punish us because of our mistakes. We must allow our mistakes and failures to be the things that sharpen us into the image of Christ. Turn your *failures* into *features*. Let Christ turn your *mess* into your *message* and your *mistakes* into your *mission*.

1. What are some of the beliefs you have about who God is that may be false?
2. How can your past mistakes mold your message today? What have you learned from past failures that you can turn into features to demonstrate God's goodness?

~

*Lord, help us use all of our experiences, both good and bad, to point people to You today. Help us make our **mistakes** our **message** and our **tragedy** our **testimony** today. Amen.*

Brent Dyer
Lead Worship Pastor
Champion Forest Baptist Church, Houston, TX

The Process of Worship

Then I heard the voice of the Lord, saying, "Whom shall I send, and
who will go for Us?" Then I said, "Here am I. Send me!"
Isaiah's Commission—Isaiah 6:8 (NASB)

Have you ever thought about what should take place in worship? Isaiah 6 gives us an exceedingly vivid picture of worship that should occur inwardly as we experience authentic biblical worship. We must be so consumed (vv. 1–3) by God's presence that we surrender ourselves completely in total abandonment in our adoration and praises to Him. We should be convicted (vv. 4–5) of our rebellion against God, humble ourselves, and confess our sins.

We should realize the importance of asking God to forgive us of our sins and cleanse (vv. 6–7) us from all unrighteousness. Then, we can be commissioned (v. 8). When we are a clean, pure, and authentic vessel, God can use us however He sees fit to advance the kingdom. Our Sunday worship should be a fragment compared to our worship throughout the entire week.

1. Are you truly preparing your heart for worship and asking the Holy Spirit to speak to you or are you simply going through the motions?
2. What are some worship experiences that have changed and impacted your life?

~

Father, we ask You to create in us a clean heart and renew a right spirit within us. Cleanse
us of anything that is not of You and may our spirits be consumed by Your presence,
convicted when dishonoring Your name and humbled enough to ask for forgiveness.

Tommy Quinn
Associate Pastor of Worship
First Baptist Church Tillman's Corner, Mobile, AL

The Value of Vision

Now to him who is able to do far more abundantly than all that we ask or think, according to the power at work within us, to him be glory in the church and in Christ Jesus throughout all generations, forever and ever. Amen.
Ephesians 3:20–21 (ESV)

Recently, my wife and I traveled to the coast. There is nothing like a morning stroll along a desolate beach just before the onslaught of crowds, chairs, and umbrellas. The chatter of hovering seagulls calls for a fresh perspective. Typical in popular beach communities, million-dollar residences peer over the sand dunes, each home boasting impressive views.

As we enjoyed our sunrise saunter together, a loud boom interrupted the solitude. To our amazement, a traditional beach house was being destroyed by a wrecking ball! As we watched, shingled walls, windows, and doors were being smashed into rubble and we both wondered why.

Later, we had a conversation with the demolition supervisor regarding the demise of this vintage bungalow. He explained that there was more value in this ocean view lot than in the actual building. Sometimes the view has more value!

As a leader in ministry, I've discovered that communicating a "spirit-led" vision is highly valuable. A compelling vision encourages others to join in. A healthy ministry vision aims and defines our impact to the glory of God! People are motivated when they sense that the vision is God-sized.

1. Do you have a captivating ministry vision for your specific area of ministry?
2. Are you effectively communicating God's vision to those you lead?

~

Lord, I desire a fresh ministry perspective and a God-sized vision for my life and ministry calling. Forgive me for thinking small or treasuring successes of the past more than seeking new revelation for effective ministry possibilities . . . until the whole world hears of YOU!

Rick Briscoe
Associate Pastor of Worship
Prestonwood Baptist Church, Plano, TX

Be Still and Worship

He says, "Be still, and know that I am God; I will be exalted
among the nations, I will be exalted in the earth."
Psalm 46:10 (NIV)

What is your most memorable moment in worship? We sometimes fall into the trap of equating our most meaningful moments in worship where there was a full stage, a full audience, just the right lighting, or just the right song. I, however, have found that it isn't always in the biggest, brightest, or most crowded settings that God speaks the loudest.

David reminds us in Psalm 46 that we can "know God" when we are still before Him; but this is one of the most difficult things to do, especially in ministry. Jesus told Martha in Luke 10:41–42, "Martha, Martha, you are worried and upset about many things, but few things are needed—or indeed only one. Mary has chosen what is better, and it will not be taken away from her." It is more important to sit at the feet of Jesus than to stay on my feet working for Him; listening to His voice instead of others listening to mine.

For me, it was a TRUTH concert in the mid-90s at a college beach retreat in a small banquet room with less than one hundred people. Halfway through the concert, the power of God fell on the room. It wasn't us, it was Him. We knew more songs but couldn't play. I always have words, but at that moment, I couldn't speak. It was in the stillness and the quiet that we all experienced the sweetest worship I can remember. I recall not even being able to open my eyes. God moved in and we moved out of the way.

1. When you review all the church services, rehearsals, retreats, concerts, workshops, small group gatherings, and private times with the Lord, is there one experience in worship that stands out above the rest? Why did it?
2. Is there something you need to change in your life or ministry so that you have time to be still and worship?

～

In the busyness of our lives, in the bigness of our worship settings—God,
slow us down, make us quiet, and show up so we can truly worship.

Jason Breland
Worship Pastor
Immanuel Baptist Church, Little Rock, AR

What Are They for So Many?

There's a boy here who has five barley loaves and
two fish—but what are they for so many?
John 6:9 (CSB)

We live in the era of the talent reality series. Whether it's *America's Got Talent*, or *The Voice*, or *American Idol*, we have a fascination with the process of discovering who has the most talent. I wish I could say it's not that way in the church, but sometimes it feels like it might be true there as well.

A person might think their voice is not good enough because they can't sing with the confidence or accomplishment of someone on the vocal team. They could easily say to themselves, "I'm not going to sing because it's not very good." Others make fun of themselves and say things like, "If I sang, it would empty the church." Nothing could be further from the truth.

The song made up of all the redeemed children of God has a quality about it that goes beyond the individual talents of the few. Because of this, talent of any kind is powerless to impact others in and of itself. God has repeatedly demonstrated that He confounds the wise with the simple; He specializes in taking the unlikely and ordinary and using it to glorify Himself.

The one thing to remember about the boy with the fish and loaves is that he had enough to feed himself. But when the Master asked for his lunch, he gave it. Everyone ate that day.

It's not the character or quantity of the food that mattered; it was the power of the Teacher to bless it after it was given to Him.

He can do the same with you.

1. What do you have in your hands that you can give to the Lord for His use in the Kingdom of God? *Teach, Counsel, Pray*
2. What are you holding on to because you think it doesn't have value? Why don't you release it to the Lord today?

Lord Jesus, forgive me for the things I have held on to because I was unwilling
to trust them to You. Help me surrender my talents, my resources, and my
ambition so that You can use my life for Your glory today. Amen.

Mike Harland
Director of LifeWay Worship
LifeWay Christian Resources, Nashville, TN

Mirror, Mirror, on the Wall

. . . bearing with one another, and forgiving one another; . . .
even as Christ forgave you, so you also must do.
Colossians 3:13 (NKJV)

Years ago, I had someone enter back into my life that I had once been very close to. I had purposely cut off all communication with this friend due to my own guilt and shame, but also because of a misperceived hurt. For years I played the victim by dragging my hurts and pain behind me like a beat-up, old U-Haul trailer.

As I began to examine all those old feelings, I realized that there were also the piles of endless, self-righteous tallies of wrongs (some belonging to this person) that had been done to me, or so I thought. There is no better experience that I have had than to make amends to a person I've hurt or who has hurt me. After apologizing to that person, my prodigal heart was embraced by one of the best friends I have today.

In this experience, I received a gift of untold value—a gift that changed my life in more ways than I can count. God gave me a mirror of unmitigated truth, and I saw myself more clearly than ever before. So much of my life had changed because of building walls between myself and others, but in that gift of the mirror I saw my true self—a child of God, more deeply loved than I am flawed.

1. Who is longing to hear from you and hoping to repair a relationship long broken?
2. What do you see when you look in that mirror?

~

Lord, may we seek to embrace others as You have embraced us,
without judgment, without condition. Amen.

Greg Crane
Worship Minister
First Baptist Church, Hendersonville, TN

A Lesson from Baseball

*Be very careful, then, how you live—not as unwise but as wise, making
the most of every opportunity, because the days are evil. Therefore
do not be foolish, but understand what the Lord's will is.*
Ephesians 5:15–17 (NIV)

I am addicted to baseball. What a game! The love of baseball came early. Growing up in Oklahoma, Dad and I would watch the "game of the week" while listening to another game on the radio. We did it all: summer league, Y-league, church league, and school leagues were at the top of my priority. When cable came to 3410 Pioneer in Oklahoma City, we made "America's Team" (the Braves) our team! Now, if you are wondering if the home of the Braves had anything to do with accepting the call to come to Georgia—let's just say, it didn't hurt!

Recently, the Braves beat the Nationals in what was a VERY long nine innings. I really needed to get to bed early considering the "to do" list that was waiting for me the next morning. I just couldn't pull away until the final out. Before I knew it, I had been watching this game for well over three hours.

I read a news article that was published many years ago regarding the actual time it takes to play a nine-inning game. Dick Wade, a Kansas City sportswriter, once decided to find out exactly how much "action" occurred in a baseball game. So, on June 21, 1956, he took a stopwatch to a game between the Kansas City Athletics and Washington Senators and counted the time it took a ball to leave the pitcher's hand until it arrived at home plate; then on all hit balls, he let the clock run until the batter was either out or safe. The total "action" during the 2-hour, 28-minute game was 8.5 minutes. Kansas City won, 15–6 (this story comes from online archives by Tom Peters in the *Philadelphia Inquirer*).

The baseball theme serves as a gentle reminder that the things that matter most can get lost in the things that matter least. Prayer, Bible study, fellowship, worship, and ministry engagement can be smothered by less important agendas.

I must admit that devoting three hours to a ball game ushered a hefty dose of conviction when measured against the time I spent in prayer last Tuesday night. As a fellow disciple on the road, may we all be encouraged to revisit our priorities. We can still root for the Braves!

1. How much time do you spend in prayer and Bible study through any given week? 2 hrs
2. What are three things you could remove from your list of daily activities that would free up time spent with the Lord? Phone, TV

Dear Lord, You are timeless, eternal, and sovereign. As awesome as it is to think of Your greatness, I live in utter amazement that You would want to spend time with me. What a joyous thought. Thank You for showing such love and mercy as to allow me into Your presence to simply commune with Your child. May I slow down and spend time with You. May I be still and hear from Your Word. Thank You for Your presence in my life and for the joy of praising You for all eternity.

Jon Duncan
Lead State Missionary of Worship and Music Ministry
Georgia Baptist Mission Board, Duluth, GA

The Power of Praise

When I pondered to understand this, it was troublesome in my sight. Until
I came into the sanctuary of God; then I perceived their end.
Psalm 73:16–17 (NASB)

Clarity is something that can be difficult to find. The world and how we perceive it is EVERYTHING in life. EVERYTHING. It affects what you believe about yourself, your relationships, your career, and the list goes on. Our intellect can only take us so far. Our emotions can wreak havoc if we allow them to be the only thing that informs us about a circumstance or situation. I've learned that I can rarely depend on my emotional state from day to day. Totally unreliable. I am constantly needing a "reset" or a "fresh" perspective.

The same was true for Asaph in Psalm 73. His perspective had been completely turned upside down from his belief system. The psalmist doesn't say why or how it happened, but it's not hard to believe; it often happens to me. However, I am grateful for the rest of Asaph's story. In the last part of Psalm 73, he found his perspective. He found the truth once again. He decided to spend some time focusing on God instead of his circumstances. He began to praise God. He came into the presence of God and entered His sanctuary. And it all became clear to Asaph once again: God's got this, I just need to trust Him. Oh yeah . . . God really is who He says He is. Total perspective change.

1. Are you facing a difficult circumstance?
2. Have you been relying on your emotional state this week? Take a "reset" and praise God. It's powerful!

~

Father, I praise You today that I can come into Your presence, and it can completely change
the way I look at my life and circumstances. I ask You right now to renew my heart and
mind. May I see the world through Your eyes. I praise You for giving me new life.

Larry Harrison
Pastor of Worship Ministries
Crossings Community Church, Oklahoma City, OK

A Blind Sacrifice

"How I wish one of you would shut the Temple doors so that these worthless
sacrifices could not be offered! I am not pleased with you," says the LORD
of Heaven's Armies, "and I will not accept your offerings."
Malachi 1:10 (NLT)

That is a chilling verse of Scripture! God's people had decided to take some shortcuts and were offering blind, lame, or otherwise imperfect animals. God was offended with their gifts and said, "Try giving gifts like that to your governor, and see how pleased he is!" (Mal. 1:8 NLT).

I think we can extract truth from this story and apply it to our modern-day music ministries. First of all, as leaders, I think we need to take the necessary time to be well prepared and bring our very best to every rehearsal and every worship service. We should be very serious and intentional, because there's no question about how serious our offerings and sacrifices are to God.

I also think we should continually remind our choir members that their musical preparation is also an act of worship. They should faithfully attend rehearsals with a happy heart, staying all the way to the end, and not leaving early just because they might be tired.

First Chronicles 21:24 records King David saying, "I will not present burnt offerings that have cost me nothing" (NLT). I think we would be wise to adopt that same mantra, as God deserves nothing less than our very best!

Our friend Derric Johnson says, "If better is possible, good is not enough!"

1. What are some other ways we can offer a worthy sacrifice to God?
2. What are some things that we might unintentionally do that are perhaps an unworthy offering to God?

~

Father, thank You for Your provision! We ask that You help us make
right choices and bring worthy offerings to You, for Your glory.

Marty Hamby
Minister of Worship and Music
First Baptist Church, Roanoke, VA

Know Who You Are

Therefore, if anyone is in Christ, he is a new creation; old things
have passed away; behold, all things have become new.
2 Corinthians 5:17 (NKJV)

I read a story about Christian Herter who was running for governor of Massachusetts in the 1950s. After a long day of campaigning and not eating, he went to a barbecue where the lady passing out chicken gave him one piece. Extremely hungry, he asked for another piece of chicken and the lady replied, "Sorry. Only one piece per person."

Usually unassuming, he decided to try a different route and replied, "Do you know who I am? I am the governor of this state!"

She replied, "No, but I know who I am. I am the lady in charge of the chicken. Move along."

When you know who you are, you can stand in that authority.

In Christ, we are forgiven, accepted, redeemed, complete, free from condemnation, established, anointed, hidden with Christ in God, and can do *all* things. (There are Scripture references for every one of these!)

When we sin, we are operating like something we are not. When we know our identity in Christ, our lives align with that belief. We will always have people around us who will try to label us with their opinions, but we can choose to reject those opinions in favor of God's truth about us. God's truth always supersedes man's opinions.

1. Make a list from the New Testament of each instance where the Bible says, "In Christ." These are also readily available online.
2. Read those Scriptures as daily affirmations of your identity in Christ.

~

Lord, thank You that I am not what someone has said about me. I am who
YOU called me to be and who YOU say that I am. Thank You for Your
forgiveness and for making me a person after Your own heart.

Ken Hartley
Executive Pastor of Worship
Abba's House, Hixon, TN

Renewed in God's Presence

*"Abide in me, and I in you. As the branch cannot bear fruit by itself, unless it abides
in the vine, neither can you, unless you abide in me. . . . Whoever abides in me and
I in him, he it is that bears much fruit, for apart from me you can do nothing."*
John 15:4–5 (esv)

Fully devoted followers of Christ make a habit of spending time daily with the Lord. As servants of the Most High God, it is imperative that we meet with our Father daily to ensure that our plans follow His agenda. The psalmist said, "In the morning, O Lord, You will hear my voice; in the morning I will order my prayer to You and eagerly watch" (Ps. 5:3 nasb). Hearing God's voice at the start of our day is crucial for several reasons:

1. I am a sinner, and I need to be reminded that His mercies "are new every morning" (Lam. 3:23 esv) and that the accusations of the enemy have no power over me.
2. In His presence there is fullness of joy, and when I see Him at the start of the day, He will "make known to me the path of life" (Ps. 16:11 esv).
3. When I am quiet, I become more attuned to His voice and am able to better distinguish it from the surrounding noise. "Be still, and know that I am God" (Ps. 46:10 esv).

When we spend time in the presence of the Lord, we will be changed by the encounter. When Moses spent time with God, "his face was radiant" (Exod. 34:29–35), and the Israelites knew that he had been with God. Not only are we different on the inside when we spend time alone with God, but we are also different on the outside. The people around us can tell that we have been with the Lord when we reflect His glory.

1. How does being still help a person know that God is indeed God? *peace*
2. How would you describe someone who radiates God? *exhibits faith*

*Lord, help me to develop an abiding awareness of Your presence in my life. Give
me joy in Your presence so that I may exhibit the fruit of the Spirit (love, joy, peace,
patience, kindness, etc.) and bring Your light into the lives of those around me.*

Steve Holt
Worship Minister
Central Baptist Church, College Station, TX

An Irresistible Community

"By this all people will know that you are my disciples, if you have love for one another."
John 13:35 (ESV)

As human beings, we share the fundamental need to belong. The collective aspect of a spiritual community is where we find rich relational resources that encourage us throughout our lives. We are members of many types of communities (our families, our office groups, etc.), but no "tribe" brings more reinforcement than the village we find in the church! This is where we find comfort in our sorrows, celebration in our wins, and advice in our decision-making. The Reverend Martin Luther King Jr. put it this way: ". . . all life is inter-related. All men are caught in an inescapable network of mutuality."[1]

As a pastor of choral worship, I can testify that there's no more extraordinary community than that found in a worship choir! A choir of the redeemed, worshiping in harmony, is the most powerful metaphor there is for community. Something supernatural takes place when the choir ceases to be a group of individuals and becomes one unified voice of passionate praise unto God.

I often remind our choir that people listen more with their eyes than with their ears. It's true! The best recruitment tool for growing a worship choir is to collectively display a passionate love of Jesus and a committed and enthusiastic love for one another. That's a song that's truly irresistible!

1. In what ways are you personally encouraged by your community? *Calls, Words*
2. How do you see the love of Jesus expressed through community? *Food Bank*

God, give me a faith and a passion for You that is truly irresistible to others. Thank You for the community You have blessed me with. I pray the love of our community, put on display, will be a supernatural magnet for those needing community and a spiritual family.

Rick Briscoe
Associate Pastor of Worship
Prestonwood Baptist Church, Plano, TX

Bankrupt Revival

*But the Holy Spirit produces this kind of fruit in our lives: love, joy, peace, patience, kindness,
goodness, faithfulness, gentleness, and self-control. There is no law against these things!*
Galatians 5:22–23 (NLT)

In a sea of change and a season of political headliners, most of us are legitimately concerned about our country and where our culture is headed. Politics has become nasty, bitter, and has caused great dissension in our nation. If you eat from that plate, you will dine on a constant diet of poison.

But *we* are the element of change. That's what we're called to do. So, we pray for revival in our nation. And we pray for revival in our churches. We come on Sundays asking God to "fill this temple."

And yet, I believe we're missing an important point. God doesn't desire to send revival or fill the temple. He desires to bring revival to me—to fill me up as His holy temple! He desires to see His church on fire for Him with you and me filled with the Holy Spirit. That's it!

Galatians 5 is a pretty clear picture of what a follower of Jesus looks like. They bear fruit. That's it! Fruit—tangible and obvious: *love, joy, peace, patience, kindness, goodness, faithfulness, gentleness, self-control.*

Signs of a flesh-filled life: sexual immorality, impurity, sensuality, idolatry, sorcery, enmity, strife, jealousy, fits of anger, rivalries, dissensions, divisions, envy, drunkenness.

It's time we stop praying for God to send revival in our nation or church and ask God to send revival in me. Me—not him or her or them. Me! It's time we start bearing good fruit and holding each other accountable. Then we can call out the bad for what it is.

Are you ready for that? It's our choice. A spirit-filled life is the way of Jesus. It's what we were made for!

1. When is the last time you examined what your life is producing? *daily*
2. Do you bear the marks of a follower of Jesus, filled with the Spirit? *yes*

*Father, put a revival in me. Fill me with Your Spirit and give me a hunger to know
You and follow You. I surrender my will and submit myself in total obedience.*

Jeff Lawrence
Executive Pastor
Lifebridge Church, Orlando, FL

Walking in the Light

Thy word is a lamp unto my feet, and a light unto my path.
Psalm 119:105 (KJV)

When my dad was just a little boy, he and my grandfather were walking up the steps to their front porch after working in the fields all day. My grandfather said to my dad, "Harold, go down to the barn and make sure the door's shut." My dad instinctively turned to obey, but as he looked down toward the barn he hesitated and said, "But Daddy, it's dark down at the barn!" So, my grandfather took a lantern, lit it, and gave it to my dad and said, "Take the lantern and when you get there, there will be light at the barn."

So, Dad held the lantern up a little higher, looked down at the little circle of light around his feet, and took that first step in the light that he had. When he did, he discovered that there was enough light to take the next step, and the next, and then the next, and before he knew it he was standing at the barn door and had walked step by step in the light the entire way.

On the path of life, God's Word will be a "lamp unto your feet" to show you where you are, and it will be a "light to your path" to show you where you are going. You will be amazed as you look back on your life and realize that God was leading you step by step and that you were walking in the light the entire way.

1. When we are anxious about the future, what does Philippians 4:6–7 encourage us to do?
2. How do Matthew 6:11 and 6:33–34 relate to our devotion today?

~

Father, help me not to worry so much about the distant destination. Give me enough faith to trust You for the next step and the next after that.

Dr. Gary Mathena
Director of Practica
Liberty University, Lynchburg, VA

Healing Power in Honest Confession

Is anyone among you in trouble? Let them pray. Is anyone happy? Let them sing songs of praise.
Is anyone among you sick? Let them call the elders of the church to pray over them and anoint
them with oil in the name of the Lord. . . . Therefore confess your sins to each other and pray for
each other so that you may be healed. The prayer of a righteous person is powerful and effective.
James 5:13–14, 16 (NIV)

The elders with oil, the laying of hands, and prayer groups abounded. Our trial with cancer was real in Suzanne's body. A prayer group surrounding our property borders was arranged with 250 persons holding hands, praying and singing. What would neighbors think? Many came and joined in too, whether Christian or not. What was God about to do? It was a moment that shall never be forgotten by anyone. It was, and still is, talked about throughout the town.

As Suzanne and I studied this passage, we took each other by the hand, knelt, and laid face down in our living room to humbly confess our sins to one another and to the Lord Almighty that He would, in His mercy, spare Suzanne's physical life. We cried and wept for what seemed like hours hearing the prayers aloud of one another. Our hearts were purified and healed by this moment. It was so intimate with our loving Father above. I shared that story at the funeral.

A few weeks later a law enforcement officer spoke to me after worship and mentioned that he was working traffic at the funeral. He explained that he had listened and felt compelled to go home to his wife and have a similar confession. It was a miraculous healing in their lives. The prayer that had brought so much healing to our spirits brought the same to another couple.

1. Is there someone that needs to hear your honest confession today before them and the Lord Jesus? It brings eternal healing! Why wait?
2. What needs to be cleansed from your heart before God today?

~

O God, may You cause us to confess our sin and be made whole today! Amen.

Roger McGee
Pastor of Music and Worship
First Baptist Church, Alexandria, VA

Regard for One Another

Therefore if there is any encouragement in Christ, if there is any consolation of love, if there is any fellowship of the Spirit, if any affection and compassion, make my joy complete by being of the same mind, maintaining the same love, united in spirit, intent on one purpose. Do nothing from selfishness or empty conceit, but with humility of mind regard one another as more important than yourselves; do not merely look out for your own personal interests, but also for the interests of others.
Philippians 2:1–4 (NASB)

As you minister alongside your senior pastor and fellow staff members, you are bound to have differing opinions and even instances where someone's personality may conflict with yours. In ministry, certainly our most important relationship is with the Lord, but how we relate to others is also vitally important.

As we have a Christlike attitude toward each staff member, it will promote a wonderful God-glorifying culture. Each person has a unique perspective to bring and a unique way of expressing it. With humility of mind, look out for their interests, pray for them and hold them in high esteem. This is a choice you make; choose to maintain the fellowship of the Spirit, the same love that Christ expressed and the unity of the spirit. This releases God to work not just in your staff, but in the whole church. It's a contagious thing.

1. What are some ways you can promote the fellowship of the Spirit in your staff?
2. Are there some decisions to be made among the staff where applying this Scripture might make a difference?

~

Father, let me walk, filled with Your Spirit, so that I might have the attitude of Christ toward each of our staff members. Show me where I have my own agenda and where I may be selfish in looking out only for my own interests. As we walk together, give us a unity of mind and spirit that You would be glorified in all we do.

Gary Rhodes
Worship Pastor
First Baptist Church Woodway, Waco, TX

Sharpening the Tools

For the word of God is living and active. Sharper than any double-edged sword,
it penetrates even to dividing soul and spirit, joints and marrow;
it judges the thoughts and attitudes of the heart.
Hebrews 4:12 (NIV)

It is like nails on a chalkboard when I'm mowing my grass and the engine starts to choke down because the grass is too thick for my dull blades to cut. I can't stand having the right tool for the job but it not being in proper condition to manage the task. This is how it is for all of us when we try to do ministry without the power of the Word of God. We are like dull blades bogging down trying to cut through the thick grass and weeds.

Even as a believer, it was years before I realized the definitive impact that the Word of God could have on my life and ministry. It is true that God reveals His Word to us as we are able to understand it, and the more we read, the more we want to read. When we commit to this process, the Word of God begins to shape and change our actions, thoughts, and decision-making process. Our leadership capacity will be increased by the time spent reading God's Word and understanding its principles. "Spiritual leaders of every generation will have a consuming passion to know the Word of God through diligent study and the illumination of the Holy Spirit."[2]

1. Am I allowing the Word of God to penetrate and permeate my thinking and my everyday activities?
2. Do I often feel like a dull blade bogging down when trying to maintain my ministry "yard"?

~

Lord, Your Word informs me of the attitude, motive, and actions of my days; it
sharpens me and equips me for my purpose and calling. Father, help me use the
opportunity of being in Your Word so that I can know You and Your ways; and as I do,
sharpen me so that I can lead and love Your people the way You designed me to.

Daniel Morris
Worship Minister
Brentwood Baptist Church, Brentwood, TN

Storms

Then Jesus got into the boat and started across the lake with his disciples. Suddenly, a fierce storm struck the lake, with waves breaking into the boat. But Jesus was sleeping. The disciples went and woke him up, shouting, "Lord, save us! We're going to drown!" Jesus responded, "Why are you afraid? You have so little faith!" Then he got up and rebuked the wind and waves, and suddenly there was a great calm.
Matthew 8:23–26 (NLT)

When I was a boy and visiting my cousins who lived near the Gulf Coast, I awoke one morning to find I had slept through a hurricane! As I walked out of the house that morning, I saw thirty pine trees lying flat on the ground, but out of all of them, only two struck the house. Amazingly, no one was hurt.

Storms of this nature are always going to be a part of this world. The storms of life sometimes take on different forms. Sickness, divorce, death of a loved one, loss of a job, etc., come into all of our lives at some point. Someone has said that some of us are either approaching a storm, in a storm, or just coming out of a storm.

Fortunately, we have a Savior who sees us through whatever life may throw at us. He can speak peace into any situation and bring hope to every desperate heart.

1. What storms has God brought you through?
2. Do you need God's help with a storm right now?

Lord, thank You for never abandoning me when I come to a storm. Help me to trust Your never-failing love and power no matter what I am facing. Thank You for always hearing my cries for help. I know You will answer me and rescue me. In Jesus' name, Amen.

David Oliver
Worship Pastor
Crossgates Baptist Church, Brandon, MS

God Hears the Heart, Not the Voice

*Let the peoples praise you, God; let all the peoples praise you. Let the nations rejoice
and shout for joy, for you judge the peoples with fairness and lead the nations on
earth. Selah. Let the peoples praise you, God, let all the peoples praise you.*
Psalm 67:3–5 (CSB)

I have a friend named Tim. He has been a member of our local church choir for more than thirty years and has never missed a rehearsal—not once. He's faithful and committed. He does his homework and prepares to lead worship every Sunday with excellence. In so many ways, he's the model choir member.

There is one intriguing tidbit about Tim that may surprise you: he doesn't sing very well. For decades, he has been hidden away in the back row, strategically placed right between two stronger singers, pouring out his heart before the Lord with passion.

You can imagine the wave of astonishment that swept over the choir loft when Tim stepped forward to sing a solo one Sunday morning. Quiet murmurs trickled across the sanctuary. Tim shared a brief word of testimony about how the Lord had delivered him from years of very deep and private bondage. Then, he began to sing the classic Gaither Vocal Band favorite "Beyond the Open Door" and the Holy Spirit began to move. By the time Tim finished the song, the altars were lined with people.

This powerful moment was a reminder to me that when it comes to the praises of His people, God hears the heart, not the voice. The Holy Spirit honors the depth and integrity of our discipleship, not musicianship.

1. Throughout the Bible, there are stories about God using the weakness of man to accomplish great things. What are a few of these instances?
2. What makes someone effective as a worship leader?

*Lord, help us to remember that the praises we sing are postured by the condition
of our hearts. We read in Your Word that You are seeking worshipers. May
we be found as people who are more devoted to Your Word than we are to
musicality. Uncover Your glory among us—even in our weakness.*

Craig Adams
Creative Director of LifeWay Worship
LifeWay Christian Resources, Nashville, TN

The Confession

*Be gracious to me, God, according to your faithful love; according to your abundant
compassion, blot out my rebellion. Completely wash away my guilt and cleanse me from my sin.*
Psalm 51:1–2 (CSB)

I remember the night well. I sat with my family and told them a story—or, actually, I made a confession.

His name was Leroy. He was six years old, and I was too. He was my neighbor—and a good friend. One day, Leroy and I were playing on a rickety old board that spanned a mud-filled ditch. I was wearing a brand-new pair of jeans that my mom had just told me not to get dirty. The board slipped, and I fell in. My jeans were covered in mud.

But that's not the story I told my mom. Instead, it was all Leroy's fault. He had pushed me in. Leroy denied it, of course, and our moms even joined the quarrel. (It was not pretty!) Needless to say, Leroy and I didn't play together much after that, and a year later my family moved.

Since that day, my lie—and its consequences—has haunted me. But, somehow, the act of confessing it to my family (and to my God) helped bring me peace and restoration.

God calls us to confess our sins to Him. He also calls us to confess our sins to one another. When we admit our failures, we experience healing and restoration as we are pointed to the forgiveness that only a sinless, perfect Savior can provide.

1. Can you recall occasions where confessing your sins has brought you peace, healing, and restoration?
2. Do you have unconfessed sins that are hindering your relationship with God or with others?

～

*Father, thank You for promising forgiveness when we confess our sins.
Forgive me for the following sins: _____.*

Scott Shepherd
Worship and Music Specialist
Tennessee Baptist Mission Board, Henry, TN

Who's in Charge Here?

There are many plans in a man's heart, Nevertheless the Lord's counsel—that will stand.
Proverbs 19:21 (NKJV)

In my opinion, the book of Proverbs contains some of the greatest truth in all of Scripture. During my senior year of high school, I was walking through our den. A Billy Graham crusade was on the TV, so I stopped for a moment to listen. I heard Dr. Graham say, "You may think you have your life all figured out, but God has the final say." I thought, "Right!" Because like most high school seniors, I had my life all figured out!

I enrolled in college as a music major. At the beginning of my sophomore year, I met my future wife, also a music major. She was a preacher's kid; my family didn't even attend church. But, we began dating and nevertheless fell in love. We began to discuss marriage. She asked me if I had ever thought of being a minister of music. I told her, "never," to which she replied, "Good, 'cause I'll never marry one!" This coming May we'll celebrate forty-three years of marriage and forty-three years of music ministry. God is so good!

There are people who seemingly never make plans. This isn't what the passage teaches. In fact, many other Proverbs speak to the benefit of careful, diligent planning. So, examine and evaluate your life's situation and, by all means, make plans. But, before acting on them, pray. "Let the wise listen . . . let the discerning get guidance" (Prov. 1:5 NIV).

1. What is your process for making important decisions in your life? What role does faith/confidence in God play in those decisions?
2. Are you open to the possibility of God giving you a new ministry direction/calling for your life?

Father, we give you praise that You guide us and use us for Your kingdom's purpose. Help us to always seek Your wisdom before making our plans.

Joe Estes
Minister of Music and Worship
First Baptist Church, Trussville, AL

Creation Inspires Praise

The heavens declare the glory of God, and the expanse proclaims the work of his hands.
Day after day they pour out speech; night after night they communicate knowledge.
Psalm 19:1–2 (CSB)

A few years ago, I read a story about a famous violinist who went incognito into a metro station in Washington, D.C. For forty-five minutes he played six Bach pieces on his $3.5 million instrument. Only a handful of people stopped to listen, and while a few threw money in his case, he went largely unnoticed. A few days prior to his metro station performance, Joshua Bell sold out a large concert hall where tickets averaged more than $100 per person.

This experiment says a great deal about our culture. We rush through life without stopping long enough to appreciate something truly remarkable.

We live amid the glory of God's creation every single day. How often do we pause to be astounded by it? Paul tell us in Romans 1:20 that God has revealed Himself so clearly to the world through creation that all people are without excuse when it comes to acknowledging His "eternal power and divine nature" (CSB). Creation continually testifies to His power and His glory and so should we!

1. When was the last time you stopped to praise God for something beautiful in creation?
2. How will you take time today to be in awe of the great Creator?

~

Lord, I thank You for putting Your power and glory on display in all You have made. All I have to do is look around to find reasons to praise You. Help me take time to be aware of Your presence and power today. In Jesus' name, Amen!

Jonathan Tyner
Minister of Music
Olive Baptist Church, Pensacola, FL

A Proposal for Complete Worship

*"Love the Lord your God with all your heart, with all your soul,
with all your mind, and with all your strength."*
Mark 12:30 (CSB)

When I proposed to my wife, Laura, I was both *intentional* and *emotional*. I say I was *intentional* because I had a specific goal in mind, and I was focused on communicating to her why marrying me would be a great idea! I was also *emotional* because I have a deep love for her that I wanted to convey and because my heart leapt at the very idea of spending my life with her (and it still does!).

When we lead worship, we must be both *intentional* and *emotional*. We have a clear calling to lead people to bring praise to God. We should take that very seriously, and we must be purposeful as we approach this weighty task. Many times, we have the opportunity to use music to point an unbeliever to salvation through faith in Jesus. This is also a serious consideration—their eternity is at stake! We should not approach it casually but with a deep sense of responsibility.

Most of us would agree with the above, but then some of us get frightened by the "e word": *emotional*. But the same people who are afraid of getting emotional about God get emotional about their spouse, their kids, their parents, their team, or their truck, or their country . . . Why would we not get emotional about a God who loves us so much and who gives us so much? For example, He gave us our spouses, our kids, our parents, and so much more. So next time you stand to lead in worship, make it *intentional* and *emotional*!

1. Why do you think some people are afraid to include emotion as a part of their worship?
2. What are some specific ways we can be intentional in our worship leading?

~

Lord God, You created us as whole beings, with a heart, a mind, and a body . . . may we hold nothing back from You. May we offer every part of ourselves to You through our worship.

Clay Owens
Pastor of Worship Ministry
Emerald Coast Fellowship, Lynn Haven, FL

Trusting God's Sovereignty

Joseph said to them, "Do not be afraid, for am I in God's place? As for you, you meant evil against me, but God meant it for good in order to bring about this present result, to preserve many people alive. So therefore, do not be afraid; I will provide for you and your little ones." So he comforted them and spoke kindly to them.

Genesis 50:19–21 (NASB)

Joseph was sold into slavery by his own brothers and later put into prison for a crime he did not commit. He could have easily become bitter and focused on revenge. Instead, he trusted God. It protected his heart from bitterness, and God, in turn, prospered Joseph in whatever he did. God also was able to use Joseph to save many lives from the famine that was to come. In the end, Joseph chose to forgive his brothers and dealt kindly with them.

You may have walked through times in your own life where someone wronged you, or you were betrayed in a deep, hurtful way. You can't control what people do or say. Instead, trust in God's sovereign hand, and deal kindly with those who have offended you. God will be your Defender. He will protect you from bitterness and put you in a place to receive His blessing, and God will use you to fulfill His purposes.

1. How did God bless Joseph as a result of him trusting God?
2. How did God use Joseph to accomplish His purposes?
3. How does this apply to your life?

Lord, I choose to trust in You, even in the midst of difficult circumstances. You are sovereign, Lord! I choose forgiveness toward those who have hurt me. Thank You for being my Defender. Let me see Your hand in my life. Use me for Your glory in all that I do.

Gary Rhodes
Worship Pastor
First Baptist Church Woodway, Waco, TX

Dealing with Death

*"'He will wipe every tear from their eyes. There will be no more death' or
mourning or crying or pain, for the old order of things has passed away." He
who was seated on the throne said, "I am making everything new!" Then he
said, "Write this down, for these words are trustworthy and true."*
Revelation 21:4–5 (NIV)

The reality of death, whether it be our own or a family member, is something we all will encounter. I just lost my brother Bobby (who had Down's Syndrome) to Alzheimer's this past week. We made the decision to remove all fluids knowing that he would only have a few days left to live. At the end, he went seventeen days without water. That just doesn't happen according to Google! I had planned his funeral due to family being able to travel, and the day we had it he was still with us.

We questioned why God would allow this to go on. Tears were shed and hurt was experienced. Then, at his passing, one hour before I was to leave for Africa on a mission trip, we realized God had done this so that we could fully see that He was in control. He had a place for Bobby that was far greater than this life.

The realization that God had completely healed Bobby was overwhelming. No more Alzheimer's, no more Down's, no more suffering; Bobby was in the presence of God, and the knowledge that Jesus makes all things new brought such joy to our hearts. Tears of sadness were replaced with tears of joy.

1. Are you hurting or struggling with the death of a loved one?
2. Does your family know Christ? If not, pray that God would give you opportunity to share the gospel with them.

~

*Lord, Your Word says that this world is not our home. Give us a passion to live each day
for You, being mindful of eternity. Help us to see that You are in control of all our days.
May we always be pointing people to Jesus, the Author and perfecter of our faith, Amen.*

Dale Wilbur
Worship Arts Pastor
The Heights Baptist Church, Colonial Heights, VA

Living the Song

May the words of my mouth and this meditation of my heart be
pleasing in your sight, LORD, my Rock and my Redeemer.
Psalm 19:14 (NIV)

It is not that difficult to sing a song to or about the Lord. Living out the text of a song for the Lord, on the other hand, is a more formidable challenge.

Assuming the music we sing in our worship gatherings is based on God's Word, as followers of Christ we are called to live out the truths of these songs in our everyday lives. Allow me to pose this question: What would happen if we lived out, to the word, the truth of just one worship song for one week? Can you imagine?!?

The practice of connecting our corporate worship practice to our daily life, from a mental and spiritual standpoint, might be referred to as "dangerous worship." When we sing phrases to the Lord such as, "I surrender all," "Wherever He leads I'll go," or "I lay my life down at Your feet," do we really mean it?

If we intend to live our songs, here are two things we can do:

1. Think about the words as we sing. *Words matter!*
2. Practice spiritual disciplines all day, every day. *Moments matter!*

Write the title of a worship song you sang this week: *I NEED Thee Every Hour...*

Consider the text of this song. With the Holy Spirit's help, write down three things you can do today to live these words:

1. *Reflect on His Power*
2. *Surrender*
3. *Worship Him*

Lord, please help me refrain from mindlessly worshiping You or casually
singing my commitments to You. Remind me that the words I sing to You
matter to You. May my life song bring pleasure to You today. Amen.

Dr. Herb Armentrout
Minister of Music
Broadmoor Baptist Church, Shreveport, LA

Temptation Happens

*Then Jesus said to him, "Away with you, Satan! For it is written, 'You shall worship the L*ORD *your God, and Him only you shall serve.'" Then the devil left Him, and behold, angels came and ministered to Him.*
Matthew 4:10–11 (NKJV)

In today's world, temptation is everywhere. From television to social media, Satan tries his best to influence Christians, seeking to destroy lives. In today's reading—Matthew 4:10–11—we read about Satan tempting Jesus in the wilderness.

How did Jesus respond to temptation? How should Christians respond? Let's HEAR from God.

(**NOTE:** I use the acrostic H.E.A.R., developed by Robby Gallaty, the founder of Replicate Ministries (replicate.org), to assist me in my daily Bible study and journaling.)

HIGHLIGHT (*highlight a passage from the daily reading that speaks to me*)

Then Jesus said to him, "Away with you, Satan! For it is written, 'You shall worship the LORD your God, and Him only you shall serve.'" Then the devil left Him, and behold, angels came and ministered to Him. (Matt. 4:10–11 NKJV)

EXPLAIN (*write out in my own words explaining what the passage is saying to me*)

According to verse 1, God just led Jesus to the wilderness to be tempted by Satan. After Jesus had fasted forty days and nights, He was hungry. Satan then approached Him and tempted Him three times with food, life, and power. Verses 10–11 are Jesus' responses. Jesus overcame what Satan was tempting Him with by quoting Scripture. Then He rebuked Satan, told him to leave, and said that He was only going to worship and serve the LORD God. Satan left, and the angels came and ministered to Jesus.

APPLY (*how does this apply to my life?*)

Temptation is not sin. Yielding to temptation is sin. If Jesus defeated Satan's temptations with Scripture, so can we. *Memorize this:* F+O=V (*Faith + Obedience = Victory*).

RESPOND (*a simple prayer to God*)

Lord Jesus, thank You for YOUR example for all Christians to follow when we too are tempted by Satan. Because of You and Your power living in us, we too can overcome Satan. Hallelujah Jesus!

Scott C. White Sr.
Woodstock, GA

Stretching to Serve

Forgetting those things which are behind and reaching forward to those things which are ahead, I press toward the goal for the prize of the upward call of God in Christ Jesus.
Philippians 3:13b–14 (NKJV)

Have you ever experienced those times where it almost seems impossible to keep up with all the demands of life, family, and ministry? We are pulled in so many directions that we can sometimes feel like a rubber band getting ready to snap. While stretching, reaching, and pressing are actually athletic terms, rubber bands are designed to be pliable and resilient.

Rubber bands come in different sizes, shapes, and colors. They must be stretched to be effective. Similarly, our personalities, talents, and gifts are different, and we are not effective unless we are stretched. Our spiritual journey will cause us to run, headlong, toward many goals, dreams, and visions.

God will never call us to a task or ministry that He will not also provide the ability to accomplish the call. Sometimes stretching does not come naturally; most of us need to be motivated to stretch. It is through these experiences that we see God doing His greatest work in our lives. Don't ever look back. Keep reaching and pressing forward, moving toward God's call on your life. Be faithful to the task and persevere to the end.

1. Why don't you stretch? Fear? Uncertainty? Vulnerability?
2. Are you willing to allow God to stretch and mold you into His likeness for His glory?

~

Dear God, I present my life to You today as a sacrifice of praise. Help me to worship You in the midst of all my life's demands.

Terry Williams
Music and Worship Consultant
Florida Baptist Convention, Jacksonville, FL

Holding on to Me

But as for me, I trust in You, O Lord, I say, "You are my God." My times are in Your
hand; Deliver me from the hand of my enemies and from those who persecute me.
Psalm 31:14–15 (NASB)

I remember my dad's hands being so big that they would swallow up mine when held in their grasp. Looking back, I know it was because my hands were those of a child, small and tender. My dad's hands were the strongest I knew; strong enough to hold me and keep me safe and strong enough to restrain me when I would try to pull away. As an adult, I remember holding hands with my dad as he was in his last days.

Even then, there was security in his grasp. It just all seemed better when my hand was in my father's. I am thankful that my life and my times are in the hands of my strong and mighty Father in heaven, the One who will never let go and never forsake me.

1. Are you able to trust, knowing that you and your times are in His hand?
2. Whose hands do you need to hold to lead them to Christ?

Lord Jesus, thank You that I am held in Your hand. Thank You for holding
on to me even when I am tempted and try to go my own way. Help me to
rest in You and serve You, knowing that my times are in Your hand.

Mark Blair
Minister of Music
Bellevue Baptist Church, Memphis, TN

Empowering Your Song

Have mercy on me, O God, according to your unfailing love; according to your great compassion blot out my transgressions. . . . For I know my transgressions, and my sin is always before me. . . . Create in me a pure heart, O God, and renew a steadfast spirit within me. . . . Restore to me the joy of your salvation and grant me a willing spirit to sustain me. Then will I teach transgressors your ways, and sinners will turn back to you. . . . The sacrifices of God are a broken spirit; a broken and contrite heart, O God, you will not despise.
Psalm 51:1, 3, 10, 12–13, 17 (NIV)

First, let me acknowledge that this Scripture addresses the totality of our spiritual pilgrimage. It speaks to the shortcomings of humankind and on what terms we can return to God. David penned it following his encounter with the prophet Nathan, dealing with David's affair with Bathsheba. He was broken and convicted, and desired to be reconnected to God.

It is while in this state that David reveals to us the wonderful formula that renders us useful to God: *Confession leads to Restoration, and Restoration leads to Utilization.* The order is not accidental. If we are out of favor with God, then we will undoubtedly be out of fellowship with God and not be in a position to be used by God to the fullest: a separation caused by some sin in our life. In addition to our Christian walk in general, I believe this also holds a valuable lesson for us as worship leaders, choir, orchestra, and praise team members.

Step one . . . *Confession.* Until we agree with God about what's not right in our life, we will be impotent. We'll be able to think of nothing else (*My sin is always before me*), and that alone will hold us at bay spiritually.

Step two . . . *Restoration.* The good news is that once we confess our wrongdoings, our fellowship with God can be restored (*Restore to me the joy of your salvation*). And like so many other *broken things mended*, we have the prospect of enjoying an even deeper relationship with God.

Step three . . . *Utilization.* Here is the payoff, both for God and us. Once we've confessed and been restored, it's then that God will use us for His glory (*Then will I teach transgressors your ways, and sinners will turn back to you*). We're now in a position for our effectiveness for God to skyrocket!

Do we want our song to be empowered to the fullest? Here are questions to ask to know how to make that happen.

1. What in your life stands in the way of your effectiveness for God?
2. What is keeping you from giving that area of your life over to God, and allowing Jesus' grace to take it from you?

~

To You, forgiving Savior, do we bring our faults and shortcomings. And not just today, but each day as we commit new sins. We pray that as You cleanse us and make us whole again, that You would bring us back into Your fold, allowing us to be used for Your purpose as never before. Help us to "let go, and let God" as a lifestyle, that it might be as natural a thing to us as breathing. Amen.

Bob Morrison
Minister of Music
First Baptist Church, Pensacola, FL

Seeing Clearly through Blind Spots

Each time he said, "My grace is all you need. My power works best in weakness." So now I am glad to boast about my weaknesses, so that the power of Christ can work through me.
2 Corinthians 12:9 (NLT)

Though I didn't realize it at the time, I was a really chubby kid. Surviving evidence supports it; I'm bigger than other kids my age in old photos, I exclusively rocked "Husky" pants from Sears, and I've never met a dessert I didn't like. Add coke-bottle glasses to the mix, and you have a vivid mental image of my early years. The thing is, as an only child nurtured within a loving home, I was completely unaware of what others saw. Now obvious in hindsight, it was a *blind spot*.

A *blind spot* refers to something people would view as being out-of-character with the sum of one's behaviors or beliefs. What can seem innocent or naive can morph over time into something damaging.

The awkwardness of adolescence is behind me (thanks to a welcomed growth spurt in middle school, fewer cookies, and contacts). As a Christian (husband, parent, minister, friend, etc.), there are spiritual *blind spots* others see that void the value of my education, experiences, and desire to serve God honorably. The best defense against any threat, known or unknown, is total reliance on God. If my objective is to serve the Lord and be faithful to His Word, His power will dominate my weaknesses.

Thank the Lord He has never seen me, or judged me, as the chubby, nearsighted kid others saw. My devotion and obedience to His calling is what He sees.

1. What is your biggest blind spot?
2. If you need clarity, ask a few trusted people around you what they see as your greatest strengths and weaknesses, but don't ask them unless you are ready to move forward, having been influenced by their honesty.

~

Lord, thanks for seeing me differently than others see me, or even the way I often see myself. Thank You for choosing to use me in spite of my shortcomings. May the confidence I need today come from my dependence on Your wisdom, grace, and love. In Jesus' name I pray, Amen.

Dr. D. Doran Bugg
Chair of Music Department
Belhaven University, Jackson, MS

The Invisible Man

I will praise you, for You made me with fear and wonder; marvelous
are Your works, and You know me completely.
Psalm 139:14 (MEV)

"For I know the plans that I have for you, says the LORD, plans for
peace and not for evil, to give you a future and a hope."
Jeremiah 29:11 (MEV)

I have a confession to make. I'm about to be transparent. The words I'm about to say will allow you to see right through me.

Sometimes I feel . . . *invisible.*

It seems no matter how many goals I achieve, no matter how much "success" I attain, how much is in my bank account, how many people work for me . . . there are times I feel invisible. For years, this feeling of "invisibility" made me do crazy things. It was the driving force in my life. I needed to be "seen." Only, I didn't *know* I felt invisible.

Looking back, I realize this feeling was safe. I liked this feeling because it allowed me to expose only the parts of me I wanted seen. The only problem is this isn't how God intended me to live. Jesus didn't die so I could hide from people around me. I wasn't created to be invisible. God didn't paint me with disappearing ink, and I wasn't saved to build walls.

The Bible says I am "fearfully and wonderfully made." The Bible tells me God has plans to "prosper and not harm" me. The Bible reminds me God is "for me, not against me" and that I am a "child of the King and an heir to the throne."

You are not invisible, either. Don't believe the lies Satan whispers in your ear. Your value is not determined by the size of your paycheck. Your worth is not equal to the square footage of your home. You are called, equipped, blessed, and worthy. You are a child of the King, an heir to the throne.

Want to hear something ironic? The more transparent I become with people, the less invisible I feel. The more I tear down the walls I've built around my heart, the more that space is filled with genuine relationship, acceptance, and love.

Let's live authentic lives of transparency and love. Let's let others see the good work Christ began in us as He faithfully completes it.

1. Do you ever feel invisible? If so, why? Write down the things that trigger those feelings.
2. Who does the Bible say we are? How does Jesus describe our identity?

~

Lord, help us remember we are made in Your image. Help us see ourselves and those
around us the way You see us. Give us the strength to be transparent, vulnerable,
and real with our families, friends, coworkers, and churches. Amen.

Brent Dyer
Lead Worship Pastor
Champion Forest Baptist Church, Houston, TX

"Be-Attitudes" for Life and Ministry

But the Holy Spirit produces this kind of fruit in our lives: love, joy, peace,
patience, kindness, goodness, faithfulness, gentleness, and self-control . . .
Galatians 5:22–23 (NLT)

I just completed my thirtieth year as worship pastor at my church. It has been my greatest joy to serve the wonderful people of this fellowship. I was asked to share with our leaders some of the things I had learned over the past thirty years about life and ministry. I call these my "Be-Attitudes" for life and ministry.

#1   Be Devoted—First, be a fully devoted follower of Christ. Whether it's life or ministry, this is the foundation of your existence. Also, be devoted to your spouse and family. This is critical to your success.

#2   Be Diligent—Work hard. Show up on time (or even early) and set the pace for others. Strive for excellence in everything you do. Don't just be "good enough." Give the best you can offer!

#3   Be Loyal—Be supportive of those in authority over you. Love them and always have their back.

#4   Be Faithful—Lead by example . . . people are watching. "The Holy Spirit produces this kind of fruit in our lives: love, joy, peace, patience, kindness, goodness, faithfulness . . ."

#5   Be Humble—It's not about you! Our job is to make God famous! "God sets Himself against the proud but gives grace to the humble" (James 4:6).

#6   Be Kind—Love people and treat them with respect. Let your speech be gracious. Look for the best in others.

#7   Be Optimistic—Lead with a positive attitude . . . it's contagious. People love to follow optimistic leaders.

1. What additional "Be-Attitudes" would you add to this list?
2. Which "Be-Attitudes" are the most difficult for you?

∼

Lord Jesus, let my life be a living example of Your love. Let the
fruit of the Holy Spirit be seen in me today. Amen.

Ron Cochran
Former Executive and Music Pastor
Portland Christian Center, Portland, OR

Resonating Worship

He put a new song in my mouth, a song of praise to our God. Many
will see and fear, and put their trust in the LORD.
Psalm 40:3 (ESV)

Most worship leaders, musicians, and technicians are quick to notice a room's natural reverberation and the organic transfer of vibration through a space. We're weird like that. The atmosphere is a critical component when considering the dynamic projection of music and sound. A room's capacity, based on seating, humidity levels, and warm bodies filling that space, seriously impacts the ambience or atmosphere.

Did you know that our personal worship also has a resonating quality? Webster defines the word *resonate* as "to produce or to be filled with a deep, reverberating sound." Most church choirs and orchestras spend hours of rehearsal perfecting the "product" part of that definition, and quite possibly making the "being filled with deep reverberation" part less of a priority.

As our platform song is prepared with crafted skill, our SOUL must first resonate more profoundly in the process! Secondly, our SONG is enhanced by the "story" of our soul. In other words, your journey with Jesus must be heard in your declaration. Finally, our SOUL and SONG are put on display through our SERVICE to His glory!

The psalmist resonates from a desperate place: "O God, you are my God; earnestly I seek you; my soul thirsts for you; my flesh faints for you, as in a dry and weary land where there is no water" (Ps. 63:1 ESV).

1. What do the vibrations of your soul communicate to those who know you best?
2. Are others spiritually impacted by more than just your musical skill?

~

Lord, my sincere desire is to resonate a magnificent song with my life. Like
the psalmist, may the reverberation of my musical gifts joined with a soul that
reflects the character of Jesus resonate a sincere heart of worship for You.

Rick Briscoe
Associate Pastor of Worship
Prestonwood Baptist Church, Plano, TX

He Finds You Wherever You Are

*"Suppose one of you has a hundred sheep and loses one of them. Doesn't he leave the
ninety-nine in the open country and go after the lost sheep until he finds it?"*
Luke 15:4 (NIV)

We once had a chocolate lab named Mousse. He was obsessed with going, getting, and bringing back. You would think a ball was his favorite, but no, plain rocks were his choice. He would stay with you all day and night chasing after any rock you would throw. Rocks!!!

One night I thought I would test him. I found a rock about half the size of a baseball—just an average run-of-the-mill plain rock. I rolled it over in my hand a little and then threw it about ten to twelve feet in the dimly lit part of the backyard. Mousse ran after the rock in the general direction I had thrown it and sure enough, he found it. He immediately brought it back and dropped it at my feet, ready to go again. This time I threw it a little further with the same result. He was ready to do this all night long!

After a couple more throws, I was way past ready to turn in as it was past ten by now. "One more time, old buddy," I stated, and I threw it way up into the woods behind the house. Off he went in a full run in the direction I threw it. I heard him snorting and sniffing trying to find the rock in pitch darkness. I chuckled to myself and knew he would be there for hours and probably never find it. To my surprise, out of the dark he came, headed back in my direction with the rock in his mouth. It was indeed the very same rock I had thrown. With those results, my scent on the rock had to have been the clue in his search.

His desperate pursuit of that rock reminded me that Jesus searches for us in the very same way. We have the scent of our Father on us and He pursues us in the darkness. When I stray and find myself in the dark, wooded wilderness, my Shepherd always pursues His rocks. Yep, I'm just a plain old run-of-the-mill rock, but Jesus sees me as a special rock, worthy of fetching. As my loving Father, He will search all night long if that's what it takes.

1. Have you wandered so far into "the woods" that it might take weeks to find you?
2. Do you have that "holy smell" about you?

~

Lord, I have wandered into a desolate place. Please come and find me and bring me home!

Greg Crane
Worship Minister
First Baptist Church, Hendersonville, TN

He Sees You and That Is All That Matters

God is our refuge and strength, a very present help in trouble. Therefore we will not fear.
Psalm 46:1–2a (NKJV)

This powerful expression was the theme of Martin Luther in which he based his famous hymn "A Mighty Fortress Is Our God." This psalm is a wonderful testament to God's love and provision. "Sometimes the Lord calms the storm. Sometimes He lets the storm rage and calms His child" (unknown source).

Fear is real. All of us remember the devastation of Hurricane Katrina. No one was prepared for the massive destruction that took place. We have seen the effects of natural disasters, but the psalmist reminds us that even though the "earth be removed" and the waters "roar" (vv. 2–3), there should be no fear because of the amazing stability of God. I don't believe God *causes* such storms as much as He allows such to happen so that we can discover true refuge in God's unchanging nature. Not all storms, however, are natural disasters. Ugly weather can be found in troubled homes, at school, work, or even church. These fearful moments can paralyze us mentally and emotionally. Regardless of the source of the turmoil, we discover great news from the psalmist in verse 7. "The LORD of hosts is with us!"

This declaration is one of victory over all fear. The One who created everything will overcome all evil and destruction. Sometimes we just need to recognize our Source of deliverance. This is what it means to take a "leap of faith."

One night a house caught fire and a young boy was forced to flee to the roof. The father stood on the ground below with outstretched arms, calling to his son, "Jump! I'll catch you." He knew the boy had to jump to save his life. All the boy could see, however, was flame, smoke, and blackness. As can be imagined, he was afraid to leave the roof. His father kept yelling: "Jump! I will catch you." But the boy protested, "Daddy, I can't see you." The father replied, "But I can see you and that's all that matters."[3]

Faith is knowing that the "Lord is with us." He sees you and cares for you. The fears we experience are real but the source of our deliverance is always there. When the fear of violence, divorce, racism, loneliness, or some other threat clouds your view, remember that our Refuge—the Lord, is with you. He is ready to catch you if you will take a leap of faith. He sees you and that's all that matters.

1. In what ways have you personally seen God's hand in the midst of a storm?
2. Do you know of someone going through a storm whom you can share your story of deliverance?

~

Dear Lord, You are creator and redeemer. As Creator, You are in control of nature and all issues of life. As Redeemer, You have saved me. I am now part of Your family. When struggles, fear, or even disaster befalls me, I will trust my heavenly Father. May my response to the storm only serve to bring glory to You. May I always remember that there is no crisis so great as to take me from Your love and care. Thank You for being my refuge and deliverer. Amen.

Jon Duncan
Lead State Missionary of Worship and Music Ministry
Georgia Baptist Mission Board, Duluth, GA

Ministry Seasons

There is a time for everything, and a season for every activity under the heavens.
Ecclesiastes 3:1 (NIV)

Early on, I was bluntly ignorant to the application of seasons to my ministry and life. I felt that if my ministry was not growing then something was wrong. Looking back, I realize how foolish I was to not apply this simple teaching from God's Word. We are never in perpetual growth. God created seasons with a purpose.

I'd like for you to consider that all of us are in one of these life or ministry seasons:

- *Season of Growth or Addition*—This season is exciting and energetic!
- *Season of Organization and Training*—This season is necessary if we want to see lasting growth.
- *Season of Rest*—This season often naturally occurs right after or before a major period of transition.
- *Season of Discovery*—A time to think through and reestablish our values, mission, strengths, and weaknesses.

These seasons are not in any particular order, and a combination of different seasons can happen at any given time. All of these seasons, working together, bring about a holistic environment of growth and change. Every season is necessary and helps prepare for the next. When experiencing a season of growth, enjoy it! Know that it will not last forever and that it comes with a price. Growth without any intentional change will only lead to burnout, frustration, and missed opportunities.

1. What season(s) do you think that your ministry might be in?
2. How can identifying the season you are in help you look at the over-all picture and stage of the journey that your ministry is in right now?

⌒

Father, Your ways are always best. You know exactly what we need and when we need it.
Thank You for providing seasons for us to enjoy and benefit from the long-haul of fulfilling
our purpose on the earth. Please give us wisdom to know what season we are in and help us
to navigate this season with trust and assurance that You are preparing us for the next one.

Daniel Morris
Worship Minister
Brentwood Baptist Church, Brentwood, TN

The Power of Remembering

Yet this I call to mind and therefore I have hope: Because of the LORD's great love we are not consumed, for his compassions never fail. They are new every morning; great is your faithfulness.
Lamentations 3:21–23 (NIV)

God has given us one of the most under-celebrated faculties—an ability to remember or "call to mind." In fact, throughout Scripture, we find that our ability to remember is encouraged and identified as a primary way to find encouragement and hope on our journey with God. Abraham built memorials to remember; God gave the children of Israel many festivals and celebrations to remember. Passover for the Israelites has become communion for New Covenant believers so that we continually and consistently "call to mind." God knows us pretty well. He knows that we can forget things easily, very important things.

Jeremiah had been faithful to preach and prophesy to Jerusalem. It was a tough message: repent or else. We know the story—the same story that has played out time and time again. Jeremiah struggled as he saw God's judgment. It was horrific, worse than what he could have imagined. In fact, he wrote a whole book in the Bible to help him deal with his grief. Yet in the midst of his struggle, he found hope by remembering.

Through God, we have the power to overcome anything we face. Part of that process is to remember His great love, His faithfulness, and His goodness to us.

1. Have you spent time today remembering all He has done for you? Make a list. Hope is close by.
2. Build a memorial in your heart and mind.

~

Father, open the eyes of my heart that I might see You, Your power, and Your provision. Help me to remember ALL that You have done in my life. I give You thanks today for Your goodness and love. Great is YOUR faithfulness.

Larry Harrison
Pastor of Worship Ministries
Crossings Community Church, Oklahoma City, OK

River or Reservoir?

But do not forget to do good and to share, for with such sacrifices God is well pleased.
Hebrews 13:16 (NKJV)

I was recently in Israel at the Dead Sea. The water in that sea (it's technically a large lake) is known for its healing properties, and people come from all over the world to soak in it. There are many skin care products produced every year from the minerals in the Dead Sea.

When you get into the water, it is impossible to sink. Because the salt content of the water is so dense, it pushes you upward and makes you float. It is also extremely dangerous to put the water in your mouth. If you drink a few ounces of water from the Dead Sea, it will kill you.

Why?

Because at 1,300 feet below sea level, the Dead Sea is the lowest point of land on planet Earth. During rainy season in Israel, rainwater pours downward from Jerusalem and other high points in Israel and floods the roads and pours into the Dead Sea and there is no outlet. It only takes water in. It's just a large reservoir.

If you go north of the Dead Sea, you'll see that the Jordan River flows into it. This is the same river where Jesus was baptized. That same water provides life for people in Israel. Rivers allow water to flow through them. Reservoirs do nothing but take in. As leaders, we should be rivers, not reservoirs.

1. Who mentored or poured into you? When is the last time you thanked them? If you can, contact them today and tell them how much you appreciate them.
2. Who have you poured your life into? Ask God to help you identify those into whom you can let your experience and knowledge flow.

~

Father God, make me a river of Your grace and show me those whom I can pour into today.

Ken Hartley
Executive Pastor of Worship
Abba's House, Hixon, TN

Quit Your Belly-Achin'

. . . but God shows his love for us in that while we were still sinners, Christ died for us.
Romans 5:8 (ESV)

We've all been told, "quit your belly-achin'." That's usually when we're whining about something that we have no reason to whine about—like when we don't get what we want, are required to do something we don't like, or assume someone else has it better than we do.

In his book *Heart of the Artist*, Rory Noland makes an obvious, but often ignored, statement: "Music in the New Testament is no longer priestly and professional. It has become social, congregational, even 'amateur.' The work of the ministry is no longer relegated to a few full-time professionals. It is the responsibility of EVERY spirit-filled believer to do the work of ministry" (paraphrased) (1 Pet. 2:5, 9).[4]

Let's apply this to the music portion of a worship service. Isn't it about time we quit belly-achin' about:

My favorite this . . .

I don't like that . . .

I don't sing well enough . . .

I'm afraid someone will hear me . . .

Also, about today's verse—Christ's love for us was extremely PUBLIC and extremely PASSIONATE (read Rom. 5:6–11). Shouldn't we take every opportunity to loudly praise (sing/play) the One who saved us from eternal night and transferred us into glorious day?! (Rhetorical question, of course.)

Our excellence isn't what He's after; it's our hearts! For all Christ did for us, shouldn't our worship be PUBLIC and PASSIONATE?

So, quit your belly-achin'.

Rejoice! We have eternal life through Jesus Christ our Lord! There's nothing to whine about!

1. Are you rejoicing in the finished work of Christ in you? Publically? Passionately?
2. How can this extend to all parts of your worship, other than singing in church?

~

Father, thank You for Your Son, Jesus Christ, and the debt He paid for me! Forgive me when I don't proclaim that. Help me not to make ME the center of my worship, but YOU!

Ken Atkinson
Worship Pastor
First Baptist Church, Daytona Beach, FL

Burdened with Busyness

"Come to me, all who labor and are heavy laden, and I will give you rest. Take my yoke upon you, and learn from me, for I am gentle and lowly in heart, and you will find rest for your souls. For my yoke is easy, and my burden is light."
Matthew 11:28–30 (ESV)

We live in a culture that is moving at an ever-increasing, hectic pace. One of the weapons that the enemy often uses against us is, simply, busyness . . . moving from one task to the next and never taking the time to rest. Satan doesn't even mind that the things I am doing are good things. His goal is simply to keep me from spending intimate time with my Lord. I find that most people like to stay busy. In fact, we sometimes even take pride in letting others know how busy we are and don't stop to realize that our busyness is keeping us from intimate fellowship with God. At creation, God gave us the example of resting from labor and He has commanded us to "remember the Sabbath day, to keep it holy" (Exod. 20:8 ESV).

When I do not take the time to address my own soul, in a short period of time I will inevitably become barren and dry, with very little in my spiritual reservoir for myself or to offer those who need my help. We must remember that when we abuse our body it affects our soul, and when we neglect our soul it will affect our body. While on the earth, Jesus made it a habit to withdraw from the stress and give Himself the opportunity to regain His physical, emotional, and spiritual strength. If we desire to be available to God for a lifetime of kingdom service, we must take care of ourselves as He intends.

1. What does it mean to keep the Sabbath holy?
2. What is one thing you can let go from your schedule in order to give you greater margin to cultivate greater intimacy with the Lord?

~

Father, I desire to live a life that is guided by You instead of one that is consumed with busyness. Help me to regularly slow down and find true rest in You so that I may be physically, emotionally, and spiritually renewed.

Steve Holt
Worship Minister
Central Baptist Church, College Station, TX

Danger of the Routine

From the rising of the sun to its setting, the name of the LORD is to be praised!
Psalm 113:3 (ESV)

Routine often dulls us to the majestic and beautiful. That which we see and enjoy on a daily basis succumbs to the certainty that it/he/she will always be there. We often take for granted those who are closest to us until It's too late.

This summer, while at the beach, I played in the sun until I got burned. Then I sat in the shade complaining about the heat and sunburn and wishing I had a little respite from the singe of the sun's rays.

Then came the winter. I longed for just a flicker of heat, the feel of the sun on my face and its steady warmth to sooth my pale soul. I was homesick for the very thing in the summer that I wished would wane.

Every day we've had on this earth, the sun has risen and set in its path. We set our clocks by its course and we live out our schedules completely tethered to the sun's timetable. We just take it for granted.

Recently, we watched as the sun was eclipsed. For a moment, it went dark. The routine was interrupted. When she peeked her head back out from behind the moon, we let out a sigh of relief and gave thanks for His grace that gives us a second chance.

Choose to push back against routine. Allow the wonder of this day to take your breath away. Praise Him for His good gifts, for the Word tells us His day of judgment that will darken the earth will surely come!

1. What has become routine for you? What do you take for granted?
2. When is the last time you felt wonder that left you breathless?

~

Father, today, teach me to love and be grateful for the gift of this day. Help me to be grateful for what I have. Help me overcome the numbness of routine.

Jeff Lawrence
Executive Pastor
Lifebridge Church, Orlando, FL

Losing Jesus

Supposing Him to have been in the company . . . went a day's journey.
Luke 2:44 (NKJV)

In Luke's account of the boy Jesus at the temple, it is interesting to note that *Jesus was lost to the strangest people—His very own*. He was lost to the ones who loved Him the most. I have always marveled at John 1:11 that says, "He came to His own, and His own did not receive Him."

Jesus was lost in the strangest place—the House of God. Jesus has become lost in the midst of all our religious activity and ecclesiastical efficiency. Like the Ephesian church in Revelation 2:4, many have left their "first love." Jesus, standing outside His church, pleads with us, "Behold, I stand at the door and knock. If anyone hears My voice and opens the door, I will come in to him and dine with him, and he with Me" (Rev. 3:20 NKJV).

Jesus was lost in the strangest way—simply by neglect. Jesus' parents "supposing Him to have been in the company . . . went a *day's* journey" (Luke 2:44, emphasis added). How many times have we, in the excitement and chaos of the moment, gone a day's journey only to discover that we have left Jesus behind? Like Joseph and Mary, we become frantic and confused and simply have to go back to the place where we left Him. We who serve Christ vocationally in the local church stand in the greatest danger of losing Him in all the hectic hurry and scurry of ministry.

1. What are some ways we can "lose Jesus" in our work and ministry if we are not careful?
2. What are some safeguards we can put in place to keep that from happening?

～

Lord Jesus, help me to hear Your gentle knock, and Your still, small voice,
inviting me to turn aside from my clamoring calendar and my insistent
itinerary to commune with You and worship at Your feet.

Dr. Gary Mathena
Director of Practica
Liberty University, Lynchburg, VA

The Fire of Cleansing

That the genuineness of your faith, being much more precious than gold that perishes, though it is tested by fire, may be found to praise, honor, and glory at the revelation of Jesus Christ.
1 Peter 1:7 (NKJV)

It was a day of celebration. I, not being known as a handyman, an instruction follower, or a patient builder, had just finished creating a gas grill after following the "simple" instructions. Even though it took me all day, it was ready for dinner. We were in our brand-new house, on our brand-new deck, and I had found the perfect spot for my creation: under a little roof extension on the deck, next to the house.

"Burgers tonight!" I declared to my wife and three daughters. I started up that "baby," went inside to collect the utensils and burgers and proceeded back to the deck. To my amazement, the perfect placement of the grill had caused the vinyl siding to melt right off the brand-new house. The vinyl was dripping off the wall like melted cheese, revealing the wall itself.

Sometimes, I wonder if God allows the heat of life in our lives so that the "vinyl" can be burned away and the only thing people see is His character in our lives. When hard and difficult things happen that get our attention, do we receive these as God's attempt to purify our soul? I have found that stress brings out my worst: anger, lack of patience, and the opposite of the fruit of the Spirit. May I guard my heart so only Jesus is seen in me.

1. What are some areas that need to be purified in my life?
2. How will that purification make me a more effective worship leader?

~

Jesus, as a worship leader, I want people to see You. Burn away the junk in my life so only You are seen in me. Amen!

Dr. Gary Matthews
Pastor of Worship and the Arts
Christ Memorial Church, Holland, MI

WEEK 8—MONDAY
The Joy of the Lord

Though the fig tree does not bud and there are no grapes on the vines, though the olive crop fails and the fields produce no food, though there are no sheep in the pen and no cattle in the stalls, yet I will rejoice in the LORD, I will be joyful in God my Savior.
Habakkuk 3:17–18 (NIV)

My wife, Suzanne, was dealing with terminal cancer. We heard words of encouragement as one might expect from their Christian friends, but we also heard statements from those that are outside of the church that reminded me of the lost-ness of humanity such as: "I wish I could have a faith that strong," or "I hope your faith works for you."

It's so easy to project our joy in the Lord when all is well; but what about when things aren't so rosy? Would our very expressions of praise to God be amplified in the face of great trial? Verse 19 says, "The Sovereign LORD is my strength; he makes my feet like the feet of a deer, he enables me to tread on the heights."

Habakkuk's feelings were not controlled by events around him but by faith in God's ability to give him strength. Take your eyes off of your difficulties and praise and thank Him for His power and deliverance. Habakkuk had asked God why evil people prosper and the righteous suffer. God's answer—they don't! Not in the long run. We see our own limitations in contrast to God's unlimited control of all the world's events. God is alive and HE is at work. Stress NOT! We cannot see all God is doing or will do, but we can be assured that He is God and will do what is right. That gives me great confidence. How about you?

1. Repeat after me, "the joy of the Lord . . . is my strength."
2. Now go and live it today!

~

O Father, You are my strength and salvation, and I rejoice in You today! Amen!

Roger McGee
Pastor of Music and Worship
First Baptist Church, Alexandria, VA

Wise Counsel

Listen to my instruction and be wise. Don't ignore it.
Proverbs 8:33 (NLT)

When I was just starting my working life, I found myself in a mess. Taxes, bills, deposits, school loans, car repairs . . . it was all overwhelming and new. I wondered why I hadn't been taught how to make all these things work out. In my frustration, I turned to my dad for help. He helped me work through all the details and laid out a financial plan for me that I still use today. The last thing I said to my dad was, "Why didn't you teach me these things earlier?" I laid the blame at his feet. His response was sage. "Until someone really wants to know something, it's hard to teach them anything."

His words struck home. I had been the typical teenager who thought my parents knew very little. I did not take advantage of learning from them the things that might have helped me avoid mistakes.

All of life doesn't have to be trial and error. There is wisdom and knowledge that can be found if we just have a teachable spirit and seeking heart. God gives us Scripture, the Holy Spirit, and sometimes more experienced people to speak into our lives and guide us.

1. Do you have a teachable spirit?
2. In what areas could you use some wise counsel?

Lord, please give me a teachable spirit that will bring You glory. Guide me with Your Word to be more pleasing to You. Put wise people in my path that I can learn from. In Jesus' name, Amen.

David Oliver
Worship Pastor
Crossgates Baptist Church, Brandon, MS

Praise Comes First

After consulting the people, the king appointed singers to walk ahead of the army, singing to the LORD and praising him for his holy splendor. This is what they sang: "Give thanks to the LORD; his faithful love endures forever!"
2 Chronicles 20:21 (NLT)

I discovered the story of King Jehoshaphat when I directed a children's musical called *Fat, Fat Jehoshaphat.* The part of Jehoshaphat's life that is retold in this musical involves the crisis he faced when many enemy armies were coming together to attack Israel. The most surprising thing I read in the script was that by God's direction, the Israelite army was led into battle by the CHOIR!

After I read that, I went directly to the Bible and discovered that the script was entirely accurate! But how on earth could the Israelites be expected to win a battle against a vast army with the singers leading the way?! I recommend you read the whole story in 2 Chronicles 19–20. The bottom line is this: by following God's instructions, the Israelites were victorious, led by the singers' declaration of praise.

So, here's the lesson for us: the Israelites praised God *before* the battle. So often, we praise Him after things have gone our way, but when we praise God beforehand, we are recognizing His faithfulness and goodness—no matter the outcome.

Whether your battle involves illness, joblessness, broken relationships, or sinfulness, praise Him right now for who He is! Nothing you're facing is too big for Him. The battle is His. Believe this truth, then stand back and watch Him fight for you.

1. What battles are you facing in your life?
2. Why is it so hard to praise Him in spite of the outcome?

~

Sovereign Lord, I thank You that You are going before me in the battle I face. Help me to trust You and raise my voice in praise even before I know the outcome. In Your mighty name I pray, Amen.

Tempa Bader
Music Minister/Women's Ministry
Crossroads Christian Church, Gray, TN

Mentor

Imitate me, as I also imitate Christ.
1 Corinthians 11:1 (CSB)

"How's your walk?" It was a probing question, and to be honest, it bothered me. I remember thinking: *Who does he think he is? My walk with Christ is my business.* It was Christmas break during my sophomore year of college, and I had decided to visit my high school chorus director, Mr. Strickland. I looked forward to chatting with him, but I certainly didn't expect him to question me about my spiritual health.

In hindsight, I shouldn't have been surprised. You see, Mr. Strickland was so much more than a teacher. He was a mentor. He helped shape me during my most formative and impressionable years. He provided an example for me, not just musically, but spiritually. He pointed me to Christ. Without Mr. Strickland, I would not be the man I am today.

Mentors certainly aren't a novel idea. Jesus mentored the twelve disciples. Paul mentored Timothy. And in his letter to Titus, Paul instructed older women to mentor younger women. In fact, this pattern of faith perpetuation fills the pages of Scripture.

Mentors are a crucial part of God's plan for passing down the heritage of faith. May we live in light of those who have passed the legacy of faithfulness to us, and may we continually pass the torch to others as well.

1. Who were the mentors in your life? Who are your "Mr. Stricklands"?
2. Who are you mentoring now? Who is going to look back in twenty-five years and recall the impact you made on his or her life?

Father, thank You for mentors who helped shape me as a follower of Christ.
Please lead me to have an eternal impact on those You call me to mentor.

Scott Shepherd
Worship and Music Specialist
Tennessee Baptist Mission Board, Henry, TN

Not Growing Weary

Let us not lose heart in doing good, for in due time we will reap if we do not grow weary.
Galatians 6:9 (NASB)

Paul may be using the word "reap" to reference the blessings of eternal life that will come one day. He is encouraging the reader that, in due time, things will get better! Farmers go about four months between planting and harvesting. I lived in a farming community twice during my early ministry. It was always fascinating to watch the process from planting to harvest and see a bountiful crop grow from just a seed. After watering and fertilizing, the farmer always waits to enjoy the benefits of his or her labors.

The same can be said for many parents who have loved and nurtured a child through the years only to experience heartache and frustration with what seems to be a rejection of those same values for a period of time. Paul encourages us not to be weary and to keep praying and loving them. Many times, our good deeds on this earth go unnoticed, but God is waiting to reward us in heaven. The key is to not give up! Even when we are discouraged, know that things will get better. Thomas Edison, the inventor of the light bulb stated, "I have not failed. I've just found 10,000 ways that won't work." Sometimes when our plans don't work out the way we *want*, it brings us closer to where God *wants* us. And that's really where we ultimately need to be.

1. Who can you pray for who needs extra encouragement right now?
2. Think of a time you were discouraged and how God brought you through that time. Praise Him and thank Him for that.

~

Father, thank You for encouraging my spirit today through Your Word.
Help me not to be disappointed when things don't go as planned, but to
know that You have everything under control. Thank You, Lord!

Tom Tillman
Director of Music and Worship
Baptist General Convention of Texas, Dallas, TX

Repentance Ignites Praise

Who perceives his unintentional sins? Cleanse me from my hidden faults. Moreover, keep your servant from willful sins; do not let them rule me. Then I will be blameless and cleansed from blatant rebellion. May the words of my mouth and the meditation of my heart be acceptable to you, LORD, my rock and my Redeemer.
Psalm 19:12–14 (CSB)

Two of my three children were adopted from Ethiopia. About a year after our adoption was finalized, I returned there to do some work for our adoption agency. As I told my then five-year-old about the trip, I explained that I would be visiting his former orphanage. He gave me a puzzled look and said, "What's an orphanage?" As I explained it is a home for boys and girls who don't have parents, his little face fell, and he said, "Oh, that is so sad . . ." and then he went on his way. I was quite taken aback by his response because he had lived in an orphanage just a year earlier. But now, the thought of it was completely foreign (and even a little shocking) to him.

Wouldn't it be wonderful if, when we come to Christ, the old way we lived would become almost unthinkable to us? We should allow God to remake us so fully that the old man or woman is unrecognizable, and the old life is unimaginable.

In Psalm 19, David repents of his hidden and willful sins. He then surrenders his all to the Lord and finally praises Him—his Rock and Redeemer!

1. Recall the time you repented of your sin and gave your heart to Christ.
2. What are you holding onto that is keeping you from being fully surrendered to the Lord?

Lord, I thank You that when I came to You, the old me passed away, and You made all things new. Help me to be quick to confess sin when it creeps in and continue to learn to live under Your lordship. As I do, renew a heart of praise within me. In Jesus' name, Amen!

Jonathan Tyner
Minister of Music
Olive Baptist Church, Pensacola, FL

God Is at Work

For God is working in you, giving you the desire and the power to do what pleases him.
Philippians 2:13 (NLT)

Years ago, a wonderful Christian composer by the name of Fred Bock adapted this verse and published it in Bill Gaither's *Hymns for the Family of God*. You've read the verse and not really noticed the importance of what it says?

Paul tells us in Philippians 2 that God is "working in us"—not only giving us the *desire*, but also the *power* to do what pleases Him. Ephesians 3:20 further says that God "is able to do immeasurably more than all we ask or imagine, according to his power that is at work within us" (NIV).

When Satan tells us that we can't have victory in the Christian life and are not worthy to lead people in worship, we only have to remember that we are not alone. It's the power of Almighty God within us, giving us the desire and ability to do what pleases Him. In those times when Satan accuses us, we can throw this back at him and say, with Paul, that all the glory goes to Christ Jesus, the author and finisher of our faith (Heb. 12:2 KJV) who is working in us. He is not finished yet. Let's give Him the glory today as we lead others to join us and praise His name!

1. How does this verse apply to your attitude toward your personal music ministry?
2. Have you ever felt inadequate to lead because you don't seem to be spiritual enough? How does this verse change your perspective?

⁓

Father, help us to never forget how much we need You every day to work within each of us in fighting Satan's lie that we can do this on our own. We ask You to come in with Your Spirit's power and show us the victory and joy of knowing and watching Your work in our lives. Amen.

Don Marsh
Associate Professor of Music and Worship, Songwriting
Liberty University, Lynchburg, VA

He Sings Over Me

The LORD your God is in your midst, a mighty one who will save; he will rejoice over you with gladness; he will quiet you by his love; he will exult over you with loud singing.
Zephaniah 3:17 (ESV)

It is a beautiful and comforting image to think of God rejoicing and singing over us, but in context (earlier in the chapter), God first enacts His holy judgment over Jerusalem and the backslidden nations, removing the elements that are not honoring God. However, as the fire burns away the chaff, the meek, humble, and lowly are spared. For Jerusalem, even during God's holy anger, He is merciful. And the Almighty meets them with rejoicing and exultation. What blessings!

If we apply this directly to ourselves, we can see God's merciful correction in our lives. We are often directed by our sinful nature, and correction is hardly ever comfortable. But, when we desire God's correction and submit to His will, the Lord is waiting with a soothing, beautiful song to sing over us.

1. Do you know what it sounds and feels like to hear the Lord singing over you?
2. What can you do to discern the sound of the Lord's voice when He is singing over You?

～

O God, I pray that I would find peace in Your mercy. In Your holy judgment, will You correct me where You see fit? In Your holy correction, will You sing songs of peace over me? Will You rejoice over me with gladness?

Austin Neal
Worship Pastor
Champion Forest Baptist Church, Jersey Village, TX

Be Prepared

*Then the king said to me, "What do you request?" So, I prayed to the God of heaven. And
I said to the king, "If it pleases the king, and if your servant has found favor in your sight,
I ask that you send me to Judah, to the city of my fathers' tombs, that I may rebuild it."*
Nehemiah 2:4–5 (NKJV)

Preparation is important in all areas of life. Athletes train, teachers plan, students study,
musicians rehearse, and the list goes on. For the Christian, we prepare our lives daily
through prayer and Bible study. In today's reading—Nehemiah 2:4–5—we read about
Nehemiah's desire to "rebuild" the wall of Jerusalem and how he was prepared to do so.

How was Nehemiah prepared? What did he do? Let's HEAR from God.

(**NOTE:** I use the acrostic H.E.A.R., developed by Robby Gallaty, the founder of
Replicate Ministries (replicate.org), to assist me in my daily Bible study and journaling.)

HIGHLIGHT (*highlight a passage from the daily reading that speaks to me*)

> Then the king said to me, "What do you request?" So, I prayed to the God of
> heaven. And I said to the king, "If it pleases the king, and if your servant has
> found favor in your sight, I ask that you send me to Judah, to the city of my
> fathers' tombs, that I may rebuild it." (Neh. 2:4–5 NKJV)

EXPLAIN (*write out in my own words explaining what the passage is saying to me*)

When Nehemiah heard about the walls in Jerusalem being destroyed, he was sad and
felt a burden to go and repair them. To do so, he needed permission, supplies, and support
from the king. He was "prepared" to DO what God had put in his heart when the King
asked him why he was sad. His response? He prayed to God and then replied to the King.

APPLY (*how does this apply to my life?*)

Prayer must be *first* and not last. We can go to God first with any need. *Where God
guides, He provides.* Prayer and Bible study are "key" to being prepared every day for the
Christian life. *Memorize this:* F+O=V (*Faith + Obedience = Victory*)

RESPOND (*a simple prayer to God*)

*Lord, I love You. Please lead me where You want me to go and do what
You want me to do. Thank You for Your presence, Your power, and
Your provisions in my life. All praise to You, Lord Jesus!*

Scott C. White Sr.
Woodstock, GA

Doxology

. . . to him be glory and dominion . . .
Revelation 1:6 (ESV)

"Worthy are you, our Lord and God, to receive glory and honor and power . . ."
Revelation 4:11 (ESV)

". . . to the Lamb be blessing and honor and glory and might . . ."
Revelation 5:13 (ESV)

*". . . Blessing and glory and wisdom and thanksgiving and
honor and power and might be to our God . . ."*
Revelation 7:12 (ESV)

What will heaven be like? Streets of gold? Big mansions?

This, of course, is the wrong question. The focus is on our earthly concerns of wealth and possessions. The focus of heaven is not the what, but the WHO, and once we arrive there, the schedule is pre-determined.

Revelation explains our activities in heaven. Preachers will be out of a job. We won't have to study the Word, because the Living Word will be there to see! There will be no prayers of supplication or intercession. No more tears, sorrow, death.

But there will be worship—day after day, worship in the presence of Christ. The musicians and singers will still have plenty to do. We will truly "sing like never before (O my soul)."

Doxology is defined as a formula of praise to God. A series of verses in Revelation are doxologies, and they increase in number and intensity. Chapter 1 is a two-fold doxology, ascribing "glory and dominion" to the Lord. Chapter 4, a three-fold doxology. In chapter 5, four-fold. And in chapter 7, the perfect seven-fold doxology!

Musically, this is a crescendo—a crescendo of doxologies.

The most important thing we do today is what we'll be doing for eternity: worship. Live your life in an ever-increasing crescendo of doxologies to God, acknowledging His presence and work in your life and giving Him the praise that He alone deserves.

1. How is your worship different when you're walking through a valley?
2. When you're leading people, does your worship differ from your private, personal times of worship? How?

~

*Thou art worthy, O Lord, to receive glory and power and praise,
for You created all things for Your glory. Today, regardless of my
circumstances, make my life a crescendo of praise to You. Amen.*

Kevin Batson
Worship Pastor
Taylors First Baptist Church, Taylors, SC

Watching Words

Watch your words and hold your tongue; you'll save yourself a lot of grief.
Proverbs 21:23 (MSG)

We live in an age like no other when it comes to communication. Social media, texting, and email are the main mediums of communication of our day. Though we have all these tools to communicate, we seem to have lost the art of talking to people face to face or directly on the phone. It has become too easy for us to say something without much thought about how it will affect a relationship or be viewed by the masses.

However you choose to use these means of communication, I believe it is always important to stop, pray, think, and reconsider before writing or responding to any text, tweet, post, or email. I say this because I have learned the hard way. All too often, I have read into messages something that wasn't there or responded to things that, when looking back, needed no response. Communication is so important in the ministry. When confronted with political rants, false information, and personal attacks, sometimes it is just better to hold your tongue!

1. What could you have said or not said yesterday that would have saved you some grief?
2. What is your plan when dealing with social media in the future?

⁓

Lord, knowing that You have called us to be Salt and Light to this world, help me today and every day to watch what I say and how I say it. Forgive me for those I have hurt with my words and help me to stop, pray, and think before I respond. May the words of my mouth and the meditations of my heart be pleasing to You, O Lord.

Dale Wilbur
Worship Arts Pastor
The Heights Baptist Church, Colonial Heights, VA

Remember Your Calling

I, therefore, the prisoner of the Lord, beseech you to walk worthy of the calling with which you were called, with all lowliness and gentleness, with longsuffering, bearing with one another in love, endeavoring to keep the unity of the Spirit in the bond of peace.
Ephesians 4:1–3 (NKJV)

There is something uniquely divine and supernatural when you are called into a spiritual ministry. The decision to follow is life altering, sacrificial, and fundamentally holy. Regardless of the outward interferences, our response should be a laser-like focus to prepare spiritually and musically to fulfill the call.

Many interruptions can distract your motivation, dreams, and goals. The enemy desires to derail and destroy any attempt to follow. If God has called you to sing or play a musical instrument, place your confidence in His ability to guide you to the right place to serve and provide all you'll need to accomplish the task.

In ministry, if you're not careful, you'll develop a misplaced identity. You are *not* WHO you are, but rather, you are WHOSE you are! Your calling started with your willingness to say: "Here I am Lord, send me." Responding to God's call is never free; it will always cost something, however, the reward is certainly eternal.

Being fully committed as a singer or musician in a worship ministry has the potential to be the greatest experience in the world. Using your God-given talent in worship creates an atmosphere of unity where God's presence is felt, the lost are redeemed, the hurting are healed, and the oppressed are delivered. Never underestimate what God can do through a fully devoted worshiper. He is worthy of your greatest expression and sacrifice of praise.

1. What has God been saying to you regarding your spiritual calling?
2. Are you prepared to fulfill that call?

Lord, help me focus on Your call to become a faithful worshiper, using all You have provided in my life as a tool for ministry.

Terry Williams
Music and Worship Consultant
Florida Baptist Convention, Jacksonville, FL

Keep Swinging!

He gives strength to the weary and increases the power of the weak. Even youths grow tired and weary, and young men stumble and fall; but those who hope in the LORD will renew their strength. They will soar on wings like eagles; they will run and not grow weary, they will walk and not be faint.

Isaiah 40:29–31 (NIV)

The most meaningless statistic in a football game is the score at halftime. It's not over till it's over! You might have experienced a recent setback or what you might consider a failure. You're not alone. All of us have at many points in our lives.

The very thing that you might consider a barrier or hindrance might actually be a doorway or an opportunity to move ahead. What looks like a curse might actually be a blessing in disguise.

Consider this:

- In his search for natural rubber, Thomas Edison had 50,000 failures. After 50,000 experiments with no positive results, he did not lose hope. He simply viewed this as valuable research eliminating 50,000 things that wouldn't work. Quitting was not an option.
- Henry Ford's largest investor sold his stock in 1906, giving up on Ford's "wild dreams."
- After many failed attempts, Colonel Sanders was seventy when he discovered his secret KFC recipe.
- Babe Ruth hit 714 home runs and struck out 1,330 times. During a slump, he was asked how he kept from getting too discouraged. His answer was simple, "I realize the law of averages will catch up if I just keep swinging."
- After years of frustration and "detours," Moses was eighty years old when he led 3,500,000 people out of captivity.
- Caleb was eighty-five when he said, "Give me that mountain."

When we face setbacks, the best thing that we can do is get up, dust ourselves off, try to understand what lesson the Lord has for us in it, and *KEEP SWINGING!* Remember, we're in a marathon, not a sprint. It doesn't matter where you start; it's where you end up that counts!

1. How can I strengthen my faith in the Lord and learn to trust Him more with my future?
2. What dream or goal is before me that I know is God-ordained?

~

Lord, You alone are my strength and my song. My help comes from You alone. Help me to hold on to Your unfailing hand as I do what You have called me to do today. In the powerful name of Jesus, Amen.

Dr. Phil Barfoot
President / CEO
Celebration Concert Tours International / CCT Music, Nashville, TN

Sound Check

I will sing with the spirit and I will sing with the mind also.
1 Corinthians 14:15b (NASB)

I've had several conversations with church members about rapidly changing music styles. There's no doubt that it's true, but other than them wanting to repeat some phrases in the lyrics, I can't recall objections about rapidly changing "lyrical content." The concern was always more so the musical style.

One pastor even stated,

> *"There are several reasons for opposing [new music]. One, it's too new. Two, it's often worldly . . . there are so many new songs that you can't learn them all . . . It puts too much emphasis on instrumental music rather than godly lyrics . . . It's a money-making scheme and some of these new music upstarts are lewd and loose."[5]*

The pastor was William Romaine in 1723, writing primarily about Isaac Watts. For fun, I utilized CCLI (a copyright company) to research the most popular hymns today. Of the 38 most popular, 31 of them were written after 1835—112 years *after* Romaine's letter regarding NEW music. Aren't you glad the church kept writing music? One thing is certain—music styles change, God's Word doesn't.

There are occasional unscriptural lyrics, and it's the music leader's job to filter through God's Word. That can be problematic at times, because some of our "filters" aren't healthy. Pray for those who select music to maintain unity. Ask Jesus to help your leaders emphasize the *soundness* of music sung, and not the *sound*. God rejoices to hear His Word; I'm not so sure about guitar or organ.

1. What are some ways you can help the congregation focus more on the *soundness* than the *sound*?
2. How do we establish stronger "filters" using the Word of God?

~

Heavenly Father, help me worship You today in truth. Remind me that when I help lead others to worship You, the sound of what we sing isn't what impresses You, but rather, singing in spirit and in the truth of Scripture with a heart that's cleansed and clinging to Your presence.

Mark Maier
Pastor of Worship
First Baptist Church, Rogers, AR

O Be Careful Little Eyes . . .

Therefore, since we have so great a cloud of witnesses surrounding us, let us also lay aside
every encumbrance and the sin which so easily entangles us, and let us run with endurance
the race that is set before us, fixing our eyes on Jesus, the author and perfecter of faith.
Hebrews 12:1–2a (NASB)

Late in her life, Fanny Crosby, a poet and songwriter who was blind since an early age, was receiving an award. The presenter was D. L. Moody. In the process, he asked her to share one of her poems. At the time, it had not been set to music and was very personal. She said it was her "soul's poem."

> "Someday the silver cord will break,
> and I no more as now shall sing;
> but oh, the joy when I shall wake
> within the palace of the King!
> And I shall see Him face to face,
> and tell the story—saved by grace!"[6]

Today, we have to be so careful what we allow our eyes to see. Many have foolishly thought that it doesn't matter, but time has shown that it definitely does matter. We take for granted the beautiful things of the Lord that we can see and, at the same time, let down our guard on what we allow to pass through our lens.

Fanny Crosby saw "seen" things that most can barely grasp but had never seen with physical eyes. She cherished the fact that the first thing she would truly see would be the face of her Savior.

1. What have you seen recently that reminded you of the goodness and greatness of God?

2. What do you need to see more of and less of in order to have a deeper relationship with Jesus?

~

Lord, open my eyes to see only what You would have me see. May
Your Word filter all I see so that I may be closer to You.

Mark Blair
Minister of Music
Bellevue Baptist Church, Memphis, TN

What a Jerk!

Create in me a clean heart, O God, and renew a steadfast spirit within me. Do not cast me away from Your presence and do not take Your Holy Spirit from me. Restore to me the joy of Your salvation and sustain me with a willing spirit.

Psalm 51:10–12 (NASB)

I've seen it happen in relatives, friends, even mentors. Joy fades to unhappiness. Hope slowly becomes cynicism. Generosity degrades into selfishness or jealousy, leaving someone unrecognizable by the end of a career or a life. I call it the *jerk complex*.

It's one of my biggest fears—slowly becoming less of a person Christ can use, rather than continually growing into the full potential God created me to be. It helps to know our fellow musician, David, had similar concerns. He unapologetically asked God for renewal and restoration.

Below is a list of helpful reminders God has shared with me along the way—sometimes personally, sometimes through others. They keep me joyful, hopeful, and generous toward others.

- Talent alone is never enough. (My dad told me this; John Maxwell later agreed.)
- Change is inevitable; growth is optional. (John Maxwell)
- Think less about what I cannot control and more about how I can make a positive impact.
- Empathy is fundamental to my calling.
- Being effective and appreciated feels better than just being right.
- I can take God's love personally.
- The person most aware of his sin is also most aware of his Savior. (Robert Jeffress, pastor)
- A time-out can change the course of a game. (ESPN commercial)
- People with different opinions are not my enemy; Satan is.

The takeaway always comes back to God. He is the source of life and the sustainer of abundant life. Any ability I possess or opportunity I am given is for His glory, not mine. In the process, He sustains me and keeps my heart pure toward poisonous people and each of life's obstacles.

Everyone has personal strengths and weaknesses that distinguish us from others.

1. What is/are the biggest way(s) Satan has tried to diffuse your effectiveness?
2. What are some ways Satan has tried to destroy your joy?

~

Lord, thank You for showing me the ultimate example of persevering through adversity. You proved it when You lived a perfect life, then died for my sin before defeating death. If You can love me, I can love others until You rescue me to eternity. In Jesus' name I pray, Amen.

Dr. D. Doran Bugg
Chair of Music Department
Belhaven University, Jackson, MS

Paul's Definition of Worship

Therefore, I urge you, brothers and sisters, in view of God's mercy, to offer your bodies as a living sacrifice, holy and pleasing to God—this is your true and proper worship.
Romans 12:1 (NIV)

On the subject of worship, in Romans 1, Paul gives us the greatest clarity on what worship is and how it should be seen in the life of the believer. First, we should live our lives everyday sacrificially to God, holy to God, and pleasing to God. "A living sacrifice" simply means that we do not live for the flesh anymore, but we live like a poured-out vessel by yielding all of our passion and desires to the LORDSHIP of Christ in our lives. Second, we must live a holy lifestyle. The Hebrew word for holy is *qodesh,* that literally translates, "otherness, transcendent, or set apart." This means that in order to live a holy life, we must not live in the ways of the world but live in the LIKENESS of Jesus Christ. Third, to live a life of worship, we must be "pleasing" to God, that is to be and do things to His LIKING.

Worship is more than just music and praise. It's more than just a "worship service" one day a week. It is living every single day of our lives BY HIS LORDSHIP, IN HIS LIKENESS, and TO HIS LIKING.

1. What are some ways we pour ourselves out on a daily basis as an act of worship?
2. If God desires us to live to His liking, what are some ways we can bring God pleasure with our church, friends, and in our home?

Lord Jesus, let me see that You desire for me to worship You more than just one day a week. I want to live by Your lordship, in Your likeness, and to Your liking. May I worship You with all that I am. In Your name I pray, Amen.

John Bolin
Minister of Worship and Arts
Houston's First Baptist Church, Houston, TX

What's That Smell?

In fact, God thinks of us as a perfume that brings Christ to everyone. For people who are being saved, this perfume has a sweet smell and leads them to a better life.
2 Corinthians 2:15–16a (CEV)

There is a "wax-melt thingy" in my office. I'm sure that's not the official name, but you know . . . the little thing you put wax blocks in, they melt, and it fills the room with a particular fragrance. Some people like fruity smells. Some like the smell of roses and flowers. They even have cologne scents that are supposedly more "manly." What could be manlier than melting fragrant wax?

When you first put in the wax, the smell can be overwhelming. The entire office complex will smell, not just my office. The smell overtakes everything in its path. It is all consuming. These smells eventually left me with a question.

What do we "smell" like?

I have to be honest. Sometimes I smell like pride. Sometimes I smell like fear. Sometimes the scents of jealousy, anger, and insecurity are so strong in my life, I'm pretty sure the people around me wish they could turn me off for a little while to let the air thin.

The problem is that I am supposed to have the aroma of "Christ's offering to God." When people walk into my life, just as when they walk into my office, the aroma of Christ should be so thick, overwhelming, and all-consuming that they can't help but notice.

Ephesians 5:2 says, "walk in love, just as Christ also loved you and gave Himself up for us, an offering and a sacrifice to God as a fragrant aroma" (NASB). Our *lives* should be a "sacrifice to God as a fragrant aroma." How do we become fragrant? How does our life become a living sacrifice that smells sweet to both God and those around us?

Pursue Jesus. Often, I find myself pursuing my career, an achievement, accolades, etc., and Jesus becomes an afterthought. We must make the pursuit of Christlikeness our first priority. We can't smell like the aroma of Christ if we don't know Him and experience the fullness of His riches. Memorize Scripture. Spend time in private worship. Get on your knees.

Love People. Most of us have a morning routine. We shower, fix our hair, put on deodorant, etc. To look and smell good takes effort. If we neglect our personal hygiene, we will begin to stink, but the scent does not matter if there is no one there to smell it. For us to smell like the aroma of Christ to the people around us, we must spend time with those people, invest in them, and really love them. These relationships will be our legacy.

1. What do you smell like today?
2. What are some things you can do today to be a sweet-smelling and fragrant offering to Christ?

~

Lord, help me be a fragrant aroma to those around me today. Show me how to love well, lead well, and smell like You. May my aroma be life-giving, encouraging, and help others see Jesus. Amen.

Brent Dyer
Lead Worship Pastor
Champion Forest Baptist Church, Houston, TX

Getting Used to the Family of God

Behold, how good and how pleasant it is for brethren to dwell together in unity!
Psalm 133:1 (NKJV)

No matter how you read it or whatever translation you read it from, obviously it is good for us to get along. Life is just too short for the church to be quarreling with each other.

How many *Peanuts* fans are out there? Linus was watching TV one morning when his sister Lucy walked in and demanded he change the channel. She even threatened him with her fist. "What makes you think you can walk right in here and take over?" asked Linus. Lucy replied, "These five fingers!" as she held out her hand. "Individually they are nothing. But when I curl them up like this into a single unit, they form a weapon that is terrible to behold!" she said, as she shook it at her brother. Linus immediately gave in and asked her, "What channel do you want?" Then he looked at his fingers and said to them, "Why can't you guys get organized like that?"

Why do you suppose that the psalmist is so intent on telling us how good it is to get along? When the church is divided, it will surely fall. When you and I go out every Sunday morning to lead in triumphal, God-honoring praise, there is a battle taking place. The enemy does not want us to succeed and will use everything at his disposal to upset our heart for worship. We need to be united each and every week. We lead the front line of the battle. The musicians always went out front in Old Testament accounts.

Consider the snowflake. It's one of nature's most fragile creations. One flake by itself isn't much, but just look at what they can do when they stick together!

1. Who is that one person who gets under your skin on a weekly basis?
2. When is the last time you prayed for that person and asked God for a great relationship?

~

God, give me the ability to be united with the body and with You as I lead each week.

Greg Crane
Worship Minister
First Baptist Church, Hendersonville, TN

The Tree Psalm

He will be like a tree firmly planted by streams of water, which yields its fruit in its season and its leaf does not wither; and in whatever he does, he prospers.

Psalm 1:3 (NASB)

The majority of my adult life has been spent in Oklahoma. Having grown up in the tall pines and broad, tall oaks of southern Arkansas, I never knew how bad I could miss trees until I moved to the plains of Oklahoma in my late twenties. Now, the sunsets are unparalleled in Oklahoma because there's nothing to obstruct your view. The trees, however, are hard to find and the ones in this region don't tend to grow very tall or large. They are called "Scrub Oaks" for a reason. The red soil is dry and doesn't nurture an environment for trees.

However, there is one place where you can find large, tall, and flourishing trees in Oklahoma: next to streams and rivers. You can look across the plains as far as you can see and when you spot a group of flourishing trees, you know there's water flowing nearby. Typically, these trees are located on the banks of these streams and in some cases, they are even in the middle of the streams.

David's metaphor of a tree that flourishes and yields its fruit in its season is a powerful picture. Like a tree, I must be planted near the stream of God's Word—consistently, methodically, and desperately.

1. Are you drinking from the stream of His Word today?
2. When did you last take a drink? We need some tall and flourishing trees in our world today. Plant yourself deep in the stream of God's Word.

Charles Stanley said, "It's impossible to live a godly life with a closed Bible."[7]

~

Lord, give me a thirst for Your Word. Open my eyes to see that it is my source for life. Just as water is to a tree, so is Your Word to my soul. Make me a tall and fruitful tree for You.

Larry Harrison
Pastor of Worship Ministries
Crossings Community Church, Oklahoma City, OK

What to Do When You Have Lost Your Song

By the rivers of Babylon—there we sat down and wept when we remembered Zion. There we hung up our lyres on the poplar trees, for our captors there asked us for songs, and our tormentors, for rejoicing: "Sing us one of the songs of Zion." How can we sing the LORD's song on foreign soil?
Psalm 137:1–4 (CSB)

You don't hear many sermons or songs written using Psalm 137. It's tough—written as God's people remember their time in captivity. This lament paints a picture of when all hope was gone, and they had given up. They put their instruments of praise down and closed their mouths—they wept. Been there? Can you identify in some way when you faced a time when your song was silent and the only sound coming from your heart and soul was a cry of desperation?

In these times, and most of us have them; do what these people did in their time of despair. They remembered to worship. Jerusalem (Ps. 137:6) was their holy place of worship where they met in community. They also remained faithful. They had hope even when they had no song. They had faith in God even when they had fear. They understood the day but prayed and trusted God to act on their behalf.

In the New Testament, James gives us an encouraging word: "Is anyone among you suffering? He should pray. Is anyone cheerful? He should sing praises" (James 5:13 CSB).

Maybe it's time to lift your head, warm up your voice, and pick up your instrument of praise to the Lord. He may just be waiting to hear your song.

1. Have you experienced a time when you had no hope or song of praise?
2. How can you encourage someone who has lost their way and their song of praise?

～

God, even in my time of need I acknowledge that You are my only hope. You are the giver of life and hope. Beginning today, let me see You working in my life and hear Your voice. Then, let me lift my song of praise to You once again.

Dr. Randy C. Lind
Worship and Music Specialist
Baptist General Convention of Oklahoma, Oklahoma City, OK

The "As If" Principle

So we do not lose heart. . . . For this light momentary affliction is preparing
for us an eternal weight of glory beyond all comparison, as we look not to
the things that are seen but to the things that are unseen. For the things that
are seen are transient, but the things that are unseen are eternal.

2 Corinthians 4:16–18 (ESV)

Christians must become proficient practitioners of walking by faith and not by sight. In the same way that we cannot see the spiritual forces with whom we do battle, our circumstances in life do not always reflect spiritual realities. The promises given to us by God are eternally true, and we must live and act accordingly in those promises, even when we don't see the evidence of those promises. This can be called the "*as if*" principle, and it is the essence of faith and obedience. Moses "persevered because he saw him who is invisible" (Heb. 11:27 NIV). Paul told the Ephesians to "serve wholeheartedly, as if you were serving the Lord" (Eph. 6:7 NIV).

When facing life's challenges, we must choose to take charge of our emotions and attitudes, bring them under the control of the Holy Spirit and refuse to act according to our feelings. We must base our actions on God's Word instead. When we fix our eyes on Jesus and choose to give Him thanks and praise, very soon the "things of earth grow strangely dim in the light of His glory and grace."[8] As followers of Christ, we must strive to reflect His character and live a life that gives evidence of our faith in God. We cannot always control our circumstances, but when we choose to live "*as if*," we can control our attitudes in the midst of those circumstances.

1. How can you train yourself to walk not by what you see, but by the promises in Scripture?
2. As you have walked through difficult times, what about God or the Bible has caused you to hold confidently and courageously to your faith?

~

Dear God, I want to walk in faith and not in fear. I will build up my faith today
by reading Your Word and choosing to respond in obedience to Your direction when
facing the challenges of life. Thank You for Your promises and Your grace.

Steve Holt
Worship Minister
Central Baptist Church, College Station, TX

He Restores My Soul

He restores my soul.
Psalm 23:3 (esv)

Recently, I watched a show called *Fixer Upper*. The stars of the show take a run-down dilapidated house and restore it. They take the old and make it new. When we, as a TV audience, are given a glimpse of the house in the "before" condition, there is no way most of us could visualize a pathway where this out-of-date, run-down, aged, tired house becomes a work of art.

But it does!

And you know why? Because someone with the power to transform sees potential. When everyone else says, "tear it down," these architects of renewal say, "we can make it new."

Have you ever looked in the mirror and gazed at a reflection that feels out-of-date, run-down, aged, and tired? Or you feel useless and valueless. You just can't see the potential anymore. Regardless of your age, you might just feel like the house that simply is what it is: worn, weary, and spent. Your soul is tired, and your heart has lost its passion.

God is the architect of transformation. He sees us as we are and offers a full restoration. A transformation. A revival!

It's more than paint and spackling. It's not cosmetic but foundational. He longs to rebuild your walls, shore up your foundation, and add new features. He sees you as a masterpiece, even before the work has begun. He sees the end result way before the job has broken ground.

Today, if this is you, then you need a restoration. It all begins with a view of what He sees. The journey begins with a tiny glimpse of the plan from the Grand Architect. See you as He sees you. You are a pearl of great worth. You are a masterpiece under construction.

The completion date is after your spirit escapes the bounds of this life! Make sure you're there for the unveiling!

1. How do you really see yourself?
2. Do you feel or see the value God says you are?

~

Lord, restore my soul. Bring me Your peace!

Jeff Lawrence
Executive Pastor
Lifebridge Church, Orlando, FL

Commit to Faithfulness

What you have heard from me in the presence of many witnesses
entrust to faithful men, who will be able to teach others also.
2 Timothy 2:2 (ESV)

This is Paul's last letter. He is passing the baton to his apprentice Timothy, who is taking over the churches Paul had started. In Paul's final words we find incredible godly wisdom in principles of leadership. "Entrust to faithful men . . ." The KJV says, "*commit* to faithful men." Commit/entrust the gospel ("the things you have heard from me in the presence of many witnesses") to faithful men who will be able! They will be—they may not be now, but if they are faithful, they will be! In our ministries, sadly, we often look for ability before faithfulness. We look for the person who can play or sing the high notes, or the best to sell a song, or get the best mix in the sound. But Paul says that's backwards! Faithfulness leads to ability.

I've seen many great, naturally gifted musicians who take their gift (or gifts) for granted and never work to develop any further. In contrast, I've seen others not as gifted, work harder, practice longer, be on time, put in the hours, and become much better. The diligent and the faithful become able!

Paul's wisdom doesn't stop with the ability. It goes on to say, "able to teach others also." What will they teach? That faithfulness leads to ability! And THAT ability leads to teaching others . . . the gospel! (What you have heard from me in the presence of many witnesses.)

1. Do I commit to faithful people first or able people?
2. How can I be more faithful with the gifts the Lord has given me?

～

Lord, help me be faithful, first to You, and then to those around me. Help me
commit to faithfulness and encourage character and then, ability and skills. Help
me teach that to others as I share the gospel faithfully. In Jesus' name, Amen.

Dr. Steve Bowersox
Chair, Department of Worship and Technology and Assistant Professor of Worship
University of Mobile, Mobile, AL

Called to Worship

But you are a chosen generation, a royal priesthood, a holy nation, His own special people, that you may proclaim the praises of Him who called you out of darkness into His marvelous light.
1 Peter 2:9 (NKJV)

A fire chief was training some new recruits, barking orders, and making assignments. He assigned one man to polish the bell, another to tend the hoses, another to wash the truck, and another to cook. He continued until all the jobs were filled. After he made the assignments, he went back to the first man in line and asked, "Now, what's your job?"

The young rookie timidly replied, "To polish the bell, sir." Upon hearing that the chief put his nose against the nose of that young fireman and shouted, "No! That is not your job! Your job is putting out fires!"

The point was well made. There are many necessary duties that must be tended to in the course of our ministry—many occupations that occupy our time—but we must never allow our occupations to take precedence over the vocation to which we have been called—the worship of God.

We have been *created* to worship (Isa. 43:7 NKJV). We have been *commanded* to worship (Mark 12:30 NKJV). And we have been *called* to worship (1 Pet. 2:9 NKJV). The study of Christian worship is critical, therefore, because it is the essence of all we are in Christ and all we do for His glory.

1. How is it possible that our "occupation" can take precedence over our "vocation" to which we have been called?
2. In what ways can we structure our lives and ministry to demonstrate that we have been created, commanded, and called to worship God?

~

Father, help me not to become so busy doing things for You that I neglect my relationship with You.

Dr. Gary Mathena
Director of Practica
Liberty University, Lynchburg, VA

Singing When There Are No Words

*Blessed be the God and Father of our Lord Jesus Christ, the Father of mercies, and God of
all comfort; who comforts us in all our tribulation, so that we may be able to comfort those
who are in any trouble with the comfort with which we ourselves are comforted by God.*

2 Corinthians 1:3–4 (JUB)

The soloist, a young mother, walked to our chapel stage in a memorial service for her
grandmother. She carried one of her small children in her arms to keep him calm. Her
solo was "His Eye Is on the Sparrow." Though not formally trained, she began with simple
beauty . . . *"Why should I feel discouraged, why should the shadows come?"* Nearing the end of
the first verse, her emotions took over and she began to weep, unable to sing another note.

She hugged her child, wiping away her tears . . . the piano continued to play softly
and suddenly one by one the audience joined, *"I sing because I'm happy, I sing because I'm
free. For His eye is on the sparrow and I know He watches me."* While we sang, she regained
her composure and picked up at the next verse, *"Let not your heart be troubled . . ."* finishing
the song with strength. What a picture of the people of God coming alongside someone,
bearing a burden, picking up the song of life, and bringing encouragement through a tough
time! The audience gave the words when the singer couldn't. We often need those that love
us to pull us through, for our own struggles have prepared us to bear one another's burdens
(Gal. 6:2).

1. I have experienced this support in my song of life. Is it hard to let others pick up
   your song for you?
2. Can you think of someone who needs help in their life song where they are
   speechless with despair?

~

Jesus, be my song of joy, my song of truth, and my song of life. Amen!

Roger McGee
Pastor of Music and Worship
First Baptist Church, Alexandria, VA

How to Conquer a Tough Situation

And when they began to sing and praise, the LORD set an ambush against the men of Ammon, Moab, and Mount Seir, who had come against Judah, so that they were routed.
2 Chronicles 20:22 (ESV)

It was an overwhelming problem they were facing. A vast enemy army was approaching, and it was so large that defeat seemed inevitable. Everyone was looking to the king for a solution. In the middle of this crisis, the king made a good decision. He would PRAY! "O God, we don't know what to do, but our eyes are on You."

God answered, "Do not be afraid and do not be dismayed. Tomorrow go out against them, and the LORD will be with you" (v. 17). The king and the people believed God. So much so that they appointed singers to praise the Lord and give thanks to Him even before the victory had actually happened, and guess what? As they began to praise and thank the Lord, God fought for them and their enemy was defeated!

God has a victory plan. Pray. Believe. Praise!

1. What obstacles are you facing today?
2. Have you tried God's victory plan?

~

Lord, help me to understand and believe how powerful You are and how much You love me. Help me to trust You with even my most overwhelming circumstances. Let my praise rise to You before, during, and after You win the victory for me. In Jesus' name, Amen.

David Oliver
Worship Pastor
Crossgates Baptist Church, Brandon, MS

Why Am I Holding Back?

*David retorted to Michal, "I was dancing before the LORD, who chose me
above your father and all his family! He appointed me as the leader of Israel,
the people of the LORD, so I celebrate before the LORD. Yes, and I am willing
to look even more foolish than this, even to be humiliated in my own eyes! But
those servant girls you mentioned will indeed think I am distinguished!"*
2 Samuel 6:21–22 (NLT)

We all know the story. Earlier David had failed to bring the ark of the Lord into Jerusalem. This time was different. When the ark finally reached Jerusalem, David was overjoyed. In fact, he began to worship without thought or reservation. He danced!

I confess that there have been many times through the years when I have wanted to shout, lift my hands, and even fall on my face during our worship times, but held back because of what I thought others would think or say. I didn't want to offend anyone. I didn't want to scare anyone off. I was more concerned about how they would view me than allowing myself to fully express my love for my Savior. There was one part of the passage above that stood out to me while I was preparing to share with our worship team. It had to do with the servant girls. David's wife was afraid of what they would think. David said that they would respect him even more. We tend to stop at the first part of verse 22, but the second part is just as important. May we all remember that expressing our worship to God should trump everything.

1. When is the last time you felt totally free to worship the Lord?
2. What do you need to ignore so you can be free to worship the Lord this week?

~

*Father, You deserve better. Today I choose to change and give You
all of my worship without restraint. To You be all praise.*

Chip Leake
Worship Pastor
Thompson Station Church, Thompson's Station, TN

Adopting Grace

*Pure and undefiled religion before God the Father is this: to look after orphans
and widows in their distress and to keep oneself unstained from the world.*
James 1:27 (CSB)

You received God's Spirit when he adopted you as his own children.
Romans 8:15 (NLT)

My wife was weeping. She isn't normally the emotional sort, but this morning was different. In between sobs, she shared the testimony of a mom who recently adopted a precious little girl. My wife's words to me that morning are forever etched in my mind: "I don't know what God is calling us to do, but He's calling us to do something."

Soon, we knew exactly what God was calling us to do. Eighteen months later we adopted Grace, a beautiful four-year-old little girl from China.

I was unprepared for the spiritual truths God would reteach me during our adoption journey. I saw in a fresh way how radically adoption changes one's life. Before we adopted Grace, her name was Shi Yi Wei. She had been abandoned—likely due to her cancer. She lived in a spiritually dark nation, had no family, and no inheritance.

When we adopted Grace, that all changed. She was given a new name: Grace Shiyi Wei Shepherd. She has a new family, a new inheritance, and regularly hears the gospel of Jesus Christ. To top it all off, she is now 100 percent cancer free!

When we are adopted into God's family, our transformation is even more radical. We are new creations. May we live continually in the light of our new identity as sons and daughters of God.

1. What are some ways children's lives are impacted when they are adopted into a new family?
2. What are some ways Christians are transformed when they are adopted into God's family?

~

*Father, thank You for adopting me into Your family and making me one of Your
children. Help me live continually in light of my identity as Your child.*

Scott Shepherd
Worship and Music Specialist
Tennessee Baptist Mission Board, Henry, TN

Waiting

Wait for the LORD; be strong and let your heart take courage; yes, wait for the LORD.
Psalm 27:14 (NASB)

Generally, we do not like to wait. We are impatient by nature! But there are reasons we need to wait. God is at work. He's also trying to teach us things during the waiting period. I hate waiting at stoplights. I want to get to where I'm going, but I also realize everyone else on the road wants the same. While I'm stopped at the light, the folks at the intersection are allowed to progress in an orderly fashion with every person taking their turn. It's no different with our spiritual lives.

While we are waiting, God is working out details that need to occur before we can go to the next step in our journey. As Moses was summoning Joshua to succeed him, he said, "The Lord is the one who goes ahead of you; He will be with you. He will not fail you or forsake you. Do not fear or be dismayed" (Deut. 31:8 NASB). Pray today that throughout the day, you realize that waiting is an important part of life's process. Check out Hebrews 6:15. While you are waiting, use that opportune time to talk to God about what He is trying to teach you.

1. What are you waiting on God for right now?
2. What can you do during that time of waiting to be a blessing to others?

~

Father, help me to be still and know that You are God. When I am restless, calm me.
When I'm impatient, remind me that Your timing is perfect and God-ordained.
Thank You for Your powerful, encouraging Word! In Jesus' name, Amen.

Tom Tillman
Director of Music & Worship
Baptist General Convention of Texas, Dallas, TX

True or False Worship

"Yet a time is coming and has now come when the true worshipers will worship
the Father in spirit and truth, for they are the kind of worshipers the Father seeks.
God is spirit, and his worshipers must worship in spirit and in truth."
John 4:23–24 (NIV)

In John 4, Jesus teaches the Samaritan woman everlasting principles regarding the worship of God. The first time I read this passage, I assumed that if Jesus went to the trouble to describe "true" worshipers, then there must be such a thing as a "false" worshiper. The assumption begs a question. What's the difference between the two?

The passage answers many questions:

Who do we worship? *THE ONE TRUE GOD*

When do we worship? *NOW*

Where do we worship? *ANY TIME, ANY PLACE*

Who worships? *ONLY TRUE WORSHIPERS*

How do we worship? *IN SPIRIT AND IN TRUTH*

Who is looking for true worshipers? *GOD IS*

Who's help do we need to worship? *THE HOLY SPIRIT*

Can we worship our own way? *NO, WE CAN ONLY WORSHIP GOD'S WAY.*

I have come to believe that true worshipers and false worshipers can sit right next to each other in church, stand next to each other in the choir loft, and give money in the same offering plate. They can wear the same clothes, carry the same Bibles, and sing the same worship songs. The difference is not a visible difference on the outside, but it is a difference found in the very heart of the worshiper.

I cannot worship God in my flesh. Only when I am empty of myself can I ascribe to God His true worth. I always tell the worship team that it is a good thing we have to walk over the altar on our way to the stage. We should stop and check our heart before assuming the role of a true worshiper.

1. Am I a true worshiper of God?
2. When God is seeking worshipers, does He ever look past me?

~

God, help me to never assume that I am the kind of worshiper You are seeking. Help
me be a TRUE worshiper every day of the week, whether or not I'm at church.

Jason Breland
Worship Pastor
Immanuel Baptist Church, Little Rock, AR

The Word Instructs Praise

The instruction of the LORD is perfect, renewing one's life; the testimony of the LORD is trustworthy, making the inexperienced wise. The precepts of the LORD are right, making the heart glad; the command of the LORD is radiant, making the eyes light up. The fear of the LORD is pure, enduring forever; the ordinances of the LORD are reliable and altogether righteous.
Psalm 19:7–9 (CSB)

Anyone who desires to be a worshiper must also be a faithful student of God's Word. In Psalm 19:7–9, David gives several descriptions of the Scriptures: instruction, testimony, precepts, commands, ordinances. He also attaches benefits to each of these words. The idea is we can trust the Word of God and, in keeping it, we will reap blessings.

The Bible renews life! The Bible imparts wisdom! The Bible gives us joy! The Bible enlightens us! The Bible endures forever and is completely righteous! And God has given His Word to us to help us know Him. The more we know of God's Word, the more we will want to worship Him. The more we know His Word, the more we will know *how* to worship Him appropriately.

1. Are you committed to daily time in God's Word?
2. What is something God has recently taught you from His Word?

Lord, I praise You for Your Holy Word! Thank You that You have revealed Your heart and Your plan to me. Help me to make it the final authority in my life. Make my time in Your Word life-giving each and every day. Instruct me today in the way I should live and worship. In Jesus' name, Amen!

Jonathan Tyner
Minister of Music
Olive Baptist Church, Pensacola, FL

Let God Lead

Trust in the LORD with all your heart, and do not lean on your own understanding.
In all your ways acknowledge him, and he will make straight your paths.
Proverbs 3:5–6 (ESV)

Do you ever feel inadequate or feel like you don't have the gifts to lead a ministry, skills to lead others, or even the knowledge to lead a family? I struggle with this all the time. There are days that I have no clue how to move forward. I so often try, in my own strength, to move into the day, and so often I make a complete mess of it.

Merriam-Webster's definition of *trust* is "the belief that someone or something is reliable, good, honest, effective." Hallelujah, my God is all of these. How much better to give Him the keys to start your day than to rely on your own abilities. How much better to lean on the One who, by His very Word, can straighten your path and make a way. Put this Scripture on your desk, your phone, your computer, and most importantly, on your heart. Find strength today by acknowledging Him and letting Him lead.

1. What is your biggest struggle in front of you today?
2. Where do you need God to work most in your life today?

~

Lord, let me rest in You completely today. Help me to fully and completely
rely on You for wisdom and direction in the decisions I make. May others
see in my life that You are the Way, the Truth, and the Life. Amen.

Dale Wilbur
Worship Arts Pastor
The Heights Baptist Church, Colonial Heights, VA

Last Words

> *Now the days of David drew near that he should die, and he charged Solomon his son, saying: "I go the way of all the earth; be strong, therefore, and prove yourself a man. And keep the charge of the LORD your God: to walk in His ways, to keep His statutes, His commandments, His judgments, and His testimonies, as it is written in the Law of Moses, that you may prosper in all that you do and wherever you turn."*
>
> 1 Kings 2:1–3 (NKJV)

There's an old saying, "You will never see a hearse pulling a U-Haul." When a man dies he cannot take anything with him. There is no need for a U-Haul. However, when a man is dying and knows it, his last words are of great importance to those closest to him. In today's reading, 1 Kings 2:1–3, we read about David's instructions to Solomon (his son) just before he dies. David's last words.

What did David say? What was important to him? Let's HEAR from God.

(**NOTE:** I use the acrostic H.E.A.R., developed by Robby Gallaty, the founder of Replicate Ministries (replicate.org), to assist me in my daily Bible study and journaling.)

HIGHLIGHT (*highlight a passage from the daily reading that speaks to me*)

> *Now the days of David drew near that he should die, and he charged Solomon his son, saying: "I go the way of all the earth; be strong, therefore, and prove yourself a man. And keep the charge of the Lord your God: to walk in His ways, to keep His statutes, His commandments, His judgments, and His testimonies, as it is written in the Law of Moses, that you may prosper in all that you do and wherever you turn."*
> (1 Kings 2:1–3 NKJV)

EXPLAIN (*write out in my own words what the passage is saying to me*)

King David was about to die, and these were his last words to his son, Solomon. He charged Solomon to keep the ways of the Lord his top priority, and then he would prosper.

APPLY (*how does this apply to my life?*)

When you know you are dying, you want to speak to your loved ones. In this case, David was laying the foundation for his son Solomon to serve as king in his place. His #1 request? Be faithful to God and His Word. Now, that is a good word from a dying father to his son. These last words of David were not about himself, finances, or material things. These words were a charge for Solomon to be strong, obey God's Word (law), and then he would prosper. *Memorize this:* F+O=V (*Faith + Obedience = Victory*).

RESPOND (*a simple prayer to God*)

> *Lord, help me to die the way I live, faithful to You and Your Word. Help me to influence my family with these principles through my daily life and with my last words.*

Scott C. White Sr.
Woodstock, GA

Only My Best Is Good Enough for God!

*"When you bring injured, crippled or diseased animals and offer them as
sacrifices, should I accept them from your hands?" says the LORD.*
Malachi 1:13b (NIV)

One of my co-ministers has a reputation of always planning ahead and doing nothing
halfway. She always signs her e-mails with the phrase, *"Only My Best Is Good Enough
for God!"* And does she ever personify that statement!

The first two chapters of Malachi are a scathing indictment of the prevalent attitude
toward worship among the priests in Israel. Evidently, they had lost the vision that God is
worthy of our best offerings. It became so bad that God makes a shocking statement: "'Oh,
that one of you would shut the temple doors, so that you would not light useless fires on
my altar! I am not pleased with you,' says the LORD Almighty, 'and I will accept no offering
from your hands'" (Mal. 1:10 NIV).

We live in a fast-paced world, and it can be so easy to fall into the trap of not preparing ourselves for worship. How does this lack of preparation manifest itself?

If you are a worship pastor, as I am, it's easy sometimes not to put the time and effort
into corporate worship planning. It can be tempting to choose only music that is popular
at the given time instead of prayerfully considering song offerings that compliment the
pastor's message.

1. If you sing in the choir or play in the band, are you really giving God your best
   when you don't spend adequate time beforehand in rehearsal? If you are a congre-
   gant, how do you prepare yourself prior to worship?
2. Are you engaged in the singing? Do you bring offerings to God that reflect your
   best?

God is worthy of our very best and nothing else.

~

*Dear God, please forgive me for my contempt toward You. Please bring to mind
ways that I can worship You with excellence. In Jesus' name, Amen!*

Carlos Ichter
Minister of Music and Worship
Tallowood Baptist Church, Houston, TX

Obedience Is . . .

And Jesus said to them, "Follow me, and I will make you become fishers of men." And immediately they left their nets and followed him.
Mark 1:17–18 (ESV)

Fishing was very familiar to Simon and Andrew. It was their trade and livelihood. It was how they provided for their families. Leading up to this interaction, these men had already heard about Jesus, but there came a moment of decision where their lives would intersect with the living Christ and never be the same. It was at that moment when the trajectory of their lives changed to becoming fishermen of the kingdom of God. The eleven words, "follow me, and I will make you become fishers of men," brought such conviction and were delivered with such authority, that the men immediately left what they were doing and followed Him. Simple obedience was enough. He would take care of the rest.

Growing up, I was taught that obedience is doing exactly what I'm told to do, when I'm told to do it, and with the right heart attitude. Simon and Andrew exemplified this type of obedience when they immediately left their nets and followed Christ. He called them and promised to equip them. When God is calling us to move on something, we should act instantly with wholehearted trust that His ways are better than ours. I've often heard that delayed obedience is disobedience. Don't delay. Obey today.

1. Is there an area in your life where God is calling you to act and obey?
2. What are those steps of obedience, and are you willing to trust Him?

Lord, align my heart with Yours and direct me to move when You say to move. Give me courage and faith. Help me to become a fisher of men and to look for ways to share Your story wherever I go today and throughout my life, until I see Your face.

Travis Blye
Worship Pastor
Longview Point Baptist Church, Hernando, MS

Never Alone

"Peace I leave with you; my peace I give to you. Not as the world gives do I give to you."
John 14:27a (ESV)

Suppose you were to sit back and recall your most meaningful worship experiences. Where would it be? Who was with you? How did it come and under what circumstances? Please understand that I'm not talking about your average experience here. I'm talking about a "way out there" God moment. A holy ambush that left you weak in the knees and stuttering for words. Speechless. Confounded. Beautifully torn to pieces.

When was that for you? How was it for you?

A holy visitation is not something we soon forget, nor is it something we want to see slip away. Rarely does it come at predictable contrived moments and rarely does it come in groups. When we're awash in a God moment, it rarely precedes our emotions, but instead leaves our emotions overflowing like a Spirit-filled tsunami. It's a heart-racing, wide-eyed stoppage of the time continuum when Yahweh taps you on the shoulder.

Once the tide has subsided and you begin to collect yourself, a new supernatural peace transforms everything. You just know everything will be okay. True worship brings true peace. It's a type of peace that the word *peace* doesn't adequately define or describe. Calm, cool, and collected, the peace of God is a piece of Christ. Worship refines our sight and senses to the spiritual and re-tunes our heaven-bound spirit. Then, a glimpse over our shoulder leaves us astounded to see Jesus right there, to the very end.

"And behold I am with you **ALWAYS**, even to the end of the age" (see Matt. 28:20). You have never been, nor will we ever be . . . alone!

1. What was your most memorable worship experience?
2. What lasting effect did it have? Did it leave you longing for more?

~

Jesus, help me to see You in the tough times and when things are blurred. Give me courage to follow You even when it's hard to know You're there. Give me Your peace!

Jeff Lawrence
Executive Pastor
Lifebridge Church, Orlando, FL

By All Means, Sing!

I will sing to the LORD as long as I live; I will sing praise to my God while I have being.
Psalm 104:33 (ESV)

A few weeks ago, I attended the funeral of a sweet lady and neighbor of ours. It was there that I was reminded of the power and purpose of the songs of the church. My soul was encouraged as I was able to unite with believers whom I've never met, and to sing and be encouraged by the hope we have in Christ, even (if not especially) in death.

The song of God's people is woven throughout the entirety of Scripture, starting in Exodus and ending in Revelation. The song gives wings to our praise in our seasons of joy, serves as the voice of our sorrows when our lips are unable to speak, and imprints the truths of Scripture on our hearts and memories unlike anything else.

God designed the song for our benefit and for His glory. That is why we sing every Sunday. Music in worship goes much deeper than stylistic preferences or soaring melodies. It becomes the vehicle by which God's Word connects with our emotions, minds, hearts, and souls. When our hearts are consumed with the things of God, He is truly magnified, and worship has taken place.

So, when you join others for worship on Sundays, sing! Put aside your preferences and remember that your singing is giving God glory, is helping you faithfully live the Christian life, and yes, even preparing you for death. By all means, sing!

1. Describe a time in your life when a song pointed you to Christ and helped you through a very difficult situation.
2. With this discussion in mind, why is it incredibly important that our songs' lyrics be saturated with the truth of God's Word?

~

Father, thank You for the gift of song! Let me not be a passive observer
in corporate worship, but an active worshiper who sings in spirit and in
truth, knowing that it's for Your glory and for my good. Amen.

John Brewer
Associate Pastor of Worship
First Baptist Church, Mustang, OK

The Sacrifice of Praise

Therefore by Him let us continually offer the sacrifice of praise to God,
that is, the fruit of our lips, giving thanks to His name
Hebrews 13:15 (NKJV)

Watchman Nee said, "We must not only raise the note of praise when we stand on the summit and view the promised land of Canaan, but we must learn to compose psalms of praise when we walk through the valley of the shadow of death. This is truly praise."[9]

Paul and Silas were beaten within an inch of their lives and cast into the darkest, dankest part of the dungeon. With their feet clamped in leg irons, battered, bloodied, and bruised, they lifted their voices at the midnight hour in a concert of prayer and praise for all the prisoners to hear. As a result of that midnight worship service, the earth quaked, prison doors were opened, chains were loosed, and the jailer and his entire family came to faith in Christ.

Indeed, it is easy to praise God when all is well and life is grand, but real praise—praise that is sacrificial—is praise offered at the midnight hour. There is nothing quite as impressive to a lost world as sacrificial praise. It is a powerful witness and a worthy offering to the Lord.

1. How can trials and difficulties make us more effective witnesses for Christ?
2. How can we use our sorrows to minister to others and bring glory to God?

~

Father God, when faced with trouble and trials, I pray that You would put more in me than the devil can put on me. Remind me that even though this world is full of tribulation, You have overcome the world. Help me to worship You sacrificially.

Dr. Gary Mathena
Director of Practica
Liberty University, Lynchburg, VA

Remembering and Forgetting!

"For I will forgive their wickedness and will remember their sins no more."
Hebrews 8:12 (NIV)

Y ou learned a choir anthem two years ago and your minister of worship decides to sing the piece again. As soon as the music begins, the memory comes flooding back; in a flash, the text, the notes in your voice part, the dynamics and the inflection of the text are immediately brought forth and you sing!

Our minds are a wonderful computer of memory. We don't forget very much! Our minds are often flooded with memories, both good and bad, like fondly remembering family holiday celebrations, the smell of food triggering a particular memory or making a song easy to prepare again for the service.

It is those bad memories that can keep us from living, as John 14:20 says, ". . . you [the choir member] are in me [Jesus] and I [Jesus] am in you [the choir member]" (NIV). Our old mind often leads us away from living out Christlike lives. That's why in Romans 12:2 we are compelled to "be transformed by the renewing of your mind" (NIV). Our minds don't forget!

The Father promised us a new heart. Ezekiel 36:26 says, "I will give you a new heart and put a new spirit in you . . ." (NIV). He never promised us a new mind! That we must do on our own, renewing it daily, in the Word of God.

Don't remember the alto who dismissed your comment or the tenor who said something that offended you. Let it go! Remember and imitate the words of the Father: "I, even I, am he who blots out your transgressions, for my own sake, and remembers your sins no more" (Isa. 43:25 NIV).

1. Are there memories that need to be forgotten in order for me to move forward with a renewed mind?
2. How will "transforming my mind" be translated into renewing my mind?

Father, wipe clean from my mind the things I remember that lead me away from You. Amen.

Dr. Mark Deakins
Worship Minister
Broadway Christian Church, Lexington, KY

Waiting Is Worship

*Wait for the LORD and keep his way, and he will exalt you to inherit the land.
You will watch when the wicked are destroyed. I have seen a wicked, violent
person well-rooted, like a flourishing native tree. Then I passed by and noticed
he was gone; I searched for him, but he could not be found. Watch the blameless
and observe the upright, for the person of peace will have a future.*
Psalm 37:34–37 (CSB)

I don't know about you, but I struggle with patience. Waiting on God to move can be impossible at times.

Perhaps you find yourself in a season of waiting. Be encouraged today! If you simply keep your focus on living a holy life—consecrated and surrendered—you can be sure that the Lord is working (at times above and beyond your comprehension) and He will move.

Bear in mind that waiting is an act of worship. It is in waiting that we recognize God's sovereignty. When we act out of haste and move ahead of the Lord, we remove Him from His rightful throne in our lives. Resting with humility keeps our gaze fixed on His will, not our own.

So, keep praying. Keep trusting. Keep walking the pathway of the righteous. His ways and timing are absolutely perfect. You can trust His heart—even when you can't trace His hand!

1. Can you think of a moment in your own life when you moved ahead of the Lord? What was the outcome?
2. Share an example in Scripture of someone who waited on God. What was the outcome?

~

*Father God, we admit to You that we lack patience—especially when
circumstances get difficult. We acknowledge that we need You—we know Your
ways are higher than ours. So, we surrender our own desires and will to Yours.
As a deliberate act of obedience in worship, we wait for You to move.*

Craig Adams
Creative Director of LifeWay Worship
LifeWay Christian Resources, Nashville, TN

Undignified Worship

Yes, and I am willing to look even more foolish than this,
even to be humiliated in my own eyes!
2 Samuel 6:22a (NLT)

Second Samuel 6 is an amazing account of King David's worship of the Lord. I can't help but compare our worship experiences to what I read of King David's.

First, I think about David's full-out, all-in, engaged and with complete abandon worship of God. Verse 14 says David was dancing before the Lord with all his might. Think about what that might look like! How much is "all his might"? I am sure there were others along with Michal, Saul's daughter, who were watching and despised him for (as *The Message* puts it) "exposing himself to the eyes of the servants' maids like some burlesque street dancer."

But I love David's reply, "In God's presence I'll dance all I want to. Oh yes, I'll dance to God's glory—more recklessly even than this" (MSG). The NIV says, "I will become even more undignified than this!" I love that. David was more concerned about touching the heart of God in celebration than he was concerned about what others thought of him.

Sometimes I wonder if we have become so dignified in our worship that we have structured and programmed God completely out of our worship of Him. You can expect criticism anytime worship happens apart from the expected "norm." I believe things should be done decently and in order, but I also think there is much room for authentic, upward and undignified celebration, praise and worship.

1. Has there ever been a time when you experienced this level of freedom in worship?
2. What would have to change to experience this kind of freedom?

~

Lord, help us to worship You with full abandon. Help us to remember we are
worshipers before we are worship leaders. May we lose ourselves in exuberant
worship as we declare the matchless worth of who You are. Amen.

Terry Hurt
Executive and Worship Pastor
Great Hills Baptist Church, Austin, TX

Counterintuitive

"Give, and it will be given to you. A good measure, pressed down, shaken together and running over, will be poured into your lap. For with the measure you use, it will be measured to you."

Luke 6:38 (NIV)

The message Jesus offered in this passage is counterintuitive and goes against the grain of popular cultural thinking. Our society encourages this ideology:

"Take and then take some more. Once you think you have enough, pack it down and stuff in even more. If you don't look out for yourself, you will never have everything you want. If you wait for others to give things to you, they will disappoint you, for they are trying to get things for themselves."

Jesus admonishes us to give and give generously—no strings attached (2 Cor. 8). We are commanded by the Lord to give to others our time, talents, and finances (Rom. 12:5–8). If we give all we possess, we will be blessed immeasurably (2 Cor. 9:8).

The blessings we receive as a result of our generosity are most often spiritual in nature—the joy of serving as Jesus' hands and feet, the satisfaction of sacrifice, and a legacy of righteousness. Make kingdom investments today.

A good friend of mine keeps a $100 bill folded up in the back of his wallet. When an opportunity to help someone presents itself and the Holy Spirit moves in his heart, my friend gives the money to the one in need. By God's providence, that $100 is replaced, usually within a day or two, and the process continues. God has called us to be a conduit through which His love and grace can flow into the lives of others (John 7:38).

What are you holding on to that God may be calling you to release?

1.
2.
3.

What can you give away today that will demonstrate the evidence of God's love?

1.
2.
3.

~

Father, provide many opportunities for me to give freely today. I resolve, with Your help, to let go of things that don't matter and invest Your love and my life in others. Amen.

Dr. Herb Armentrout
Minister of Music
Broadmoor Baptist Church, Shreveport, LA

A Holy Fear

But I, through the abundance of your steadfast love, will enter your house.
I will bow down toward your holy temple in the fear of you.
Psalm 5:7 (ESV)

One morning in my first-grade year, I was late to school due to sickness. I was so fearful of my elementary school principal with his deep, loud voice and glaring gaze, that I ran around the building and entered through the back, so he wouldn't see me. The problem was that it was pouring down rain, so I was even more mortified when my teacher sent me to the office to borrow clothes, which happened to be three sizes too big for me!

The "fear" spoken of in Psalm 5:7 is not this type of fear. I remember a seminary professor that I respected and "feared" so much that I wanted to be in his class every day because of his spirit, his wisdom, his inspiration, and his care. His love for God and the students just poured out of him. His character deserved awe and respect.

Psalm 5 is calling us to be so amazed and blown away by the mercy of Christ and His work in us that we cannot help but pour out our worship to Him. Only He can make a way for us! Only He can bridge the impossible gap between God and man. Only this Savior deserves my honor, respect, and worship!

(Oh, and for the record, my principal was actually a very godly man, active in our church, and loved his family. He ran a tight ship at school, for sure!)

1. What is the difference between "holy fear" and "worldly fear"?
2. How can my worship demonstrate a reverential awe for God?

~

Lord Jesus, I am in awe of You! Thank You for the sacrificial and amazing price
You paid for my soul. It is my desire today to reflect a life that is constantly
aware of who You are, and that You are worthy of all my praise.

Jeff Askew
Worship Pastor
Liberty Baptist Church, Hampton, VA

Your Walk or Your Talk?

*By faith Enoch was taken up so that he should not see death, and he was not found,
because God had taken him. Now before he was taken he was commended as having
pleased God. And without faith it is impossible to please him, for whoever would draw
near to God must believe that he exists and that he rewards those who seek him.*

Hebrews 11:5–6 (ESV)

What did you want to be when you grew up? As a young boy growing up in the Dallas/
Ft. Worth area, all I wanted to be was a sports star. It didn't matter if it was for the
Cowboys, Rangers, or Mavericks, I loved sports, and I wanted my reputation to show that
I was great at any sport I played. Now, that's pretty normal for most young boys, but as I
grew older and realized that my 5-foot 6-inch frame was more than likely not going to star
for any of my favorite teams, I had to rethink what my reputation was going to say.

Hebrews 11:5 states that Enoch was commended as having pleased God. What a
reputation! That far exceeds my original desire of being a sports star. As a worship pastor,
I hear many opinions. I received a compliment many years ago that has stayed with me. I
was told that my reputation offstage matched my reputation onstage. In other words, my
walk matched my talk. Shouldn't that be the goal for all of us? My goal now is that my walk
pleases God.

1. What is my testimony to the outside world?
2. When people see me, do they want what I have?

~

*God, when people see my life, may they not see me or anything I want to be, but help them to
see You and what You have transformed me into. Help us to be a light in a dark world. Amen.*

Chris Copeland
Worship Pastor
Central Church, Collierville, TN

The "Luv" Chapter

If I speak in the tongues of men and of angels, but have not love, I am a noisy gong or a clanging cymbal. And if I have prophetic powers, and understand all mysteries and all knowledge, and if I have all faith, so as to remove mountains, but have not love, I am nothing.
1 Corinthians 13:1–2 (ESV)

Years ago, our family took a mission trip to a large country in Asia. Our job was to teach English in an unnamed city. Our goal for our last day there was to offer a "cultural exchange day." They would share their holidays and traditions and we would share ours. Dad allowed us to share about our two greatest holidays: Easter and Christmas. I even got to read these two stories straight from the Bible to two hundred faculty and students! Surprisingly, we were accomplishing His work in this unique setting. Our team used the words of our Lord, which are living and able to change lives. It is only when we are finally home with our heavenly Father that we will know the impact His words made that day.

Back to "cultural exchange"—the teachers showed us the art of calligraphy and challenged us to give it a go. Giggling at our feeble attempts, they offered to give us gifts of calligraphy to take home. They asked, "What are valuable, important words in your culture?" Our team scrambled to find meaningful words that would also leave a lasting impression. We agreed on three simple words: faith, hope, and love.

These three words in calligraphy hang framed on my office wall today as a reminder to seize every opportunity He gives, no matter how sudden or out of the ordinary and to share His love.

1. How has the Spirit uniquely surprised you, asking you to share His love?
2. How did you respond?

~

Father, ours is not to question, but to be obedient. Give us the vision to see where You are at work, and the fortitude to obey.

Ken Atkinson
Worship Pastor
First Baptist Church, Daytona Beach, FL

The Great Adventure

*The LORD is my light and my salvation; whom shall I fear? The LORD
is the stronghold of my life; of whom shall I be afraid?*
Psalm 27:1 (ESV)

The Christian life is a life of faith. We begin our walk by faith according to Ephesians 2:8–9, and then the great adventure begins. Jesus said in John 10:10 that He came to give us abundant life. How many people miss out on abundance, joy, and adventure simply because they are crippled by fear and insecurity? Instead of pursuing God without reservation, a life of safety, ease, and little risk become the norm. In essence, the reward just isn't worth the risk!

Hebrews 11:6 reminds the believer that, "without faith it is impossible to please God" (NIV). The difference between seeing seas part, the dead rising, walls crumbling, armies overcoming, and every other mighty miracle on display in Scripture and the average life is one word—*faith*! The choice belongs to every believer. One can either accept the common or seek the extraordinary, it only requires faith.

The most radical experience isn't the adventure itself, it is the process of wholeheartedly trusting and believing God to do the impossible. With God, all things are possible. The life of faith allows us to arrest fear and embrace the great adventure of God—abundant life!

1. What fear is crippling you from abundant life?
2. What adventure has God given you, and are you fully trusting Him?

~

*Lord, You are my life and salvation! I cast all my cares on You and
wholeheartedly believe and trust in You. Thank You for abundant life.*

Matthew Slemp
Minister of Music
First Baptist Church, Indian Trail, NC

A Work of Art

For we are God's handiwork, created in Christ Jesus to do good
works, which God prepared in advance for us to do.
Ephesians 2:10 (NIV)

I love art. I am often drawn to Medieval and Renaissance church art. It is so rich in symbolism, and every detail is intentional. In Renaissance art, for example, particular items identify the four Gospel writers. With all four writers you will see a book or quill in their hand. With Matthew you will also see a winged angel, with Mark a winged lion, with Luke a winged ox, and John is seen with an eagle. You can tell who the artist is depicting by what is seen around him.

Did you know that we are God's works of art? Ephesians 2:10 says, "For we are God's handiwork, created in Christ Jesus to do good works, which God prepared in advance for us to do." The word *handiwork*, often translated into *workmanship*, is the Greek word *poiema*. We are His "work of art."

We are God's creation, made to show the "incomparable riches of his grace" (v. 7) to a world that is in desperate need of God's love and grace. When the world sees you, make sure they can clearly see Jesus!

1. Do others see Jesus when they see you?
2. What are some ways you can demonstrate Christ's presence in your life?

Father, thank You for Your amazing grace! Thank You for creating me to
do good works that You have already laid out for me. Help me be more like
You so that others may see in me Your great love and grace. Amen.

Don Barrick
Worship Pastor
The Wooodlands First Baptist Church, The Woodlands, TX

Singers Lead the Way

People have seen your procession, God, the procession of my God,
my King, in the sanctuary, Singers lead the way.
Psalm 68:24–25a (csb)

E veryone loves a good parade. And the best parades are the ones that have some sort of parade marshal or honoree that everyone looks forward to seeing sometime near the end of the festivities. The anticipation builds and builds until finally, there he or she appears.

In Bible times, the procession of a conquering hero was common, and the psalmist uses that imagery in this psalm. The meaning here is not lost on us. We have a conquering hero and worship Him every time we gather. Christ is the reason we gather—the reason we worship.

We all desire for His presence to be felt in our times of worship. We want to hear His voice and know His presence is with us. We understand as Christians that He comes to live *in* us, but we also want to experience His presence *with* us as we gather in community. You could even say it this way: our worship gatherings are a procession of our conquering King.

The next time you think the singing of the church doesn't matter, remember this verse, "Singers lead the way." Our singing actually becomes the welcomed announcement of the arrival of our hero.

Join the song. Sing your heart out. The King is coming.

1. Does the singing in your church announce the presence of our King? Is it befitting the arrival of our conquering hero?
2. In what way do the "singers lead the way" in your church? How does the singing of the leaders impact the congregation?

~

Lord Jesus, thank You for being our King and our conquering hero! Help us to
sing in anticipation of Your work among us every time we gather. Inspire the
singers to lead the joyful procession every time we sing in worship! Amen.

Mike Harland
Director of LifeWay Worship
LifeWay Christian Resources, Nashville, TN

Dependence

GOD, I'm not trying to rule the roost, I don't want to be king of the mountain. I haven't meddled where I have no business or fantasized grandiose plans. I've kept my feet on the ground, I've cultivated a quiet heart. Like a baby content in its mother's arms, my soul is a baby content. Wait, Israel, for GOD. Wait with hope. Hope now; hope always!

Psalm 131 (MSG)

Sunday comes every seven days.

For worship pastors, these words haunt us every Monday morning. We need the perfect song, a fresh transition, a new twist on an old hymn, better musicians and singers, and ALWAYS more time to rehearse. No matter your profession, there is some aspect of your work that can bring an overwhelming pressure to do something better, to perform at a higher level than what you've done before. The desire for approval can bring poor habits and unholy motives.

Writer Barbara Brown Taylor puts it this way: "Behind my heroic image of myself I saw my tiresome perfectionism, my resentment of those who did not try as hard as I did, and my huge appetite for approval."[10]

John Wesley began the practice when greeting a parishioner of asking, "How is it with your soul?" We often ask, "How are you?" and get impatient when someone actually decides to tell us how they are doing. A question about our soul forces us to give an account of the health of our inner self, which often leads to admitting that we may not be doing as well as we want others to think.

So, how is it with your soul? Caring for your soul, recognizing your dependence on God, and keeping your relationship with Him fresh is foundational for every believer.

1. Do you ever seek man's approval over God's approval? In what areas of your life?
2. How is it with your soul today?

~

Lord, You are more interested in my heart than my performance. Help me today to be with You before I do for You. My hope is in You. Amen.

Kevin Batson
Worship Pastor
Taylors First Baptist Church, Taylors, SC

The Cost of His Glory

As He was passing by, He saw a man blind from birth. His disciples
questioned Him: "Rabbi, who sinned, this man or his parents, that he was
born blind?" "Neither this man nor his parents sinned," Jesus answered.
"This came about so that God's works might be displayed in him."
John 9:1–3 (HCSB)

Jesus and His disciples encountered a man who was blind from birth. A common belief in their day was that blindness was a form of punishment for a sin committed by his parents or by the man, himself, before he was even born. When asked, Jesus gave the disciples the reason for the man's affliction: so that God's works might be displayed.

Imagine being this man. The reason he had never seen anything until he met Jesus was so that God's glory could be shown through his healing. If I were that man, I would have asked, "Couldn't God's glory have been shown another way? Was it really worth the price I paid?" Yes, it could have been—and was—revealed in other ways, and yes, it really was worth the cost.

God's glory, revealed to the world, is worth any price we must pay. It is not only for when it is convenient, or when we feel like it, or when it benefits us. God is worthy of being glorified at all times, in all circumstances.

1. What are some ways God's glory is revealed in and through our trials?
2. Have you ever focused on what life's troubles have cost you, rather than how God can be praised in those times of hardship?

Lord, help me keep my eyes on Your glory instead of my circumstances. Use me to
reveal Your greatness to those around me. May I always glorify Your name.

Michael Cole
Associate Pastor of Music and Worship
Morrison Heights Baptist Church, Clinton, MS

True Worship

*"But the hour is coming, and is now here, when the true worshipers will worship
the Father in spirit and truth, for the Father is seeking such people to worship him.
God is spirit, and those who worship him must worship in spirit and truth."*

John 4:23–24 (ESV)

This passage discusses the account of the Samaritan woman Jesus met at the well just before the triumphal entry. She began the conversation by recognizing the wall that separated the Samaritans and the Jewish people, comparing/contrasting how they worshiped. She discussed ritual, practice, and methodology. Jesus saw through this and began a discussion about what true worship looks like. Often, discussions on religion begin with the differences of how we worship. We can often become preoccupied with personal preferences and methods.

This is a way of keeping God at a distance. Jesus cut through human thinking to get to the heart of the matter. It is in this passage that Jesus defines authentic, genuine worship. He says, true worshipers will worship in *"spirit and in truth."* The word *spirit* recognizes the intangible part of every human, God created us with a spirit. God is also spirit and we have a relationship with His Holy Spirit when we worship Him. Second, we worship Him well when we learn and understand His truth, the Bible. True worship contains the powerful words through Scripture. We worship with greatest authenticity when we worship Jesus through the connection of our spirit with the Holy Spirit and through the powerful foundation and truth of God's Word.

1. As you go to worship, what consistent objection floods your mind and heart and stalls your worship?
2. Lay that before the Lord today and confess your focus on Jesus.

*Lord, I want to worship You in spirit and in truth. I want to focus my attention today on
Your Holy Spirit's work inside of me. I recognize my need of a Savior and claim anew that
You are the Lord of my life. I do not want to be dominated by my own rituals and selfish
preferences. I want to worship You by examining Your Word and taking up Your example of
worship. Order my life in Your powerful and unmistakable authoritative Word. Amen.*

Jeff Brockelman
Worship Pastor
Anderson Mill Road Baptist Church, Moore, SC

Humble Yourself

Therefore humble yourselves under the mighty hand of God,
that He may exalt you at the proper time.
1 Peter 5:6 (NASB)

We live in a time when building one's name and brand is a priority. Just the other day, I was in a meeting where someone was encouraging students to always be thinking of pushing who they are and their talent out for recognition and impact. Although I agree with the desire for impact, the greatest cause of impact is not to push or exalt our own name over others. It is, rather, to humble our heart, actions, and spirit and let the Lord push us into the direction He wants us to go.

Humility is all about perspective. When we truly get a glimpse of who God is, we see who we are, which enlightens our understanding of our complete and utter dependence on Him. When we see what God gives, we see that everything that is good and perfect comes from Him. When we see what God does, we see His handiwork in and through all things. Therefore, this right perspective gives us the right mind-set to humble ourselves, worship Him with all we are, and trust Him for the future.

There is no place that God could not send us if we accompany godliness, effectiveness, and excellence with the key ingredient of genuine humility.

1. Where is the place in my life where I find it the hardest to have a humble heart and spirit?
2. Are there some areas in my life that I am trying to build a brand or name for myself instead of letting God do it?

~

Lord Jesus, I want to have the right perspective of who You are, and who I
am in You. Cultivate in me a hand that is righteous, a mind that is pure,
and a heart that is always humble. In Your name I pray, Amen.

John Bolin
Minister of Worship and Arts
Houston's First Baptist Church, Houston, TX

I Shall Not Be Shaken

I have set the LORD always before me; because he is at my right hand, I shall not be shaken.
Psalm 16:8 (ESV)

In difficult times, it is easy to become overwhelmed with what is staring you in the face! Even Peter faced this when he was in the storm with Jesus, walking on the water and took his eyes off Jesus (Matt. 14:30)! In Psalm 16:8, David tells us that he has kept his mind and purpose upon the Lord and His plans and providence. He is not using his fleshly eyes but rather his faith eyes, his trusting eyes. David is so confident of his God that whatever comes his way, David would not face it alone. God was with him, right by his side. And God is able, so He will not be shaken! God is bigger than anything I will face. I can trust Him! David does not even get worried. David knew his God and he personally trusted Him. I love H. C. Leupold's analysis of this passage: "If you hold to God, God will take care of you perfectly."[11]

This is such a powerful passage that Peter used it in one of his first sermons in Acts 2:25. If you study the rest of Psalm 16, it points to Jesus' resurrection. David was so caught up in *"the Lord before him,"* that he saw his future secure. He then prophesied of that security in our Savior's resurrection. Paul even quoted from this passage as well in Acts 13:35–38. If they studied this, maybe we should too!

1. How can I always keep the Lord before me?
2. What things distract me from trusting Him?

~

Lord, forgive me for being fearful and not trusting You. Help me keep You
before me in all things—to seek first Your Kingdom and Your plans; to meditate
on Your Word and Your truth. I know You love me and care so well for me.
I trust in You and will keep my eyes on You. In Jesus' name, Amen.

Dr. Steve Bowersox
Chair, Department of Worship and Technology and Assistant Professor of Worship
University of Mobile, Mobile, AL

Character Matters

For the LORD gives wisdom; from His mouth come knowledge and understanding.
He stores up sound wisdom for the upright; He is a shield to those who walk in
integrity, guarding the paths of justice, and He preserves the way of His godly ones.
Then you will discern righteousness and justice and equity and every good course.

Proverbs 2:6–9 (NASB)

There is an oil well valve and service company in Oklahoma City that made a dramatic turnaround when they began to focus on character. For many years, this company led the nation in "on the job" injuries, employee absences, theft, and poor morale. Revenues floundered, and the CEO was on the brink of an emotional collapse. The Lord revealed to him that lack of character was the root problem. Every category that the rules and regulations failed to fix were corrected when the employees and supervisors developed godly character.

Character is not one's religion, personality, or reputation; it is the inner sense of right and wrong with a passionate desire to do what is right regardless of the cost. Christ consistently exemplified good character. He is the one and only example worth studying. Even in the darkest hour before His crucifixion, Jesus, alone and abandoned, modeled obedience, self-control, meekness, and humility.

It has been said you are who you are when no one is looking. If you claim to be a Christ-follower, you are held to a higher standard. People are watching to see if your walk matches your talk. Living a life with godly character will draw others to Him. Live it for all to see!

1. Is your life rooted in godly character, represented in humility, forgiveness, self-control, dependability, flexibility, and truthfulness?
2. Are you bringing out the good fruit in others?

～

Father, may we follow the example of godly character found in Your Son, Jesus. May we strive daily to serve You and others well. May our lives lead people to You. For His Glory! Amen.

James Bradford
Minister of Music
Quail Springs Baptist Church, Oklahoma City, OK

With or Without

Therefore, I urge you, brothers and sisters, in view of God's mercy, to offer your bodies as a living sacrifice, holy and pleasing to God—this is your true and proper worship. Do not conform to the pattern of this world, but be transformed by the renewing of your mind. Then you will be able to test and approve what God's will is—his good, pleasing and perfect will.

Romans 12:1–2 (NIV)

God loves music, but He is more interested in worship. We should bring our worship to the music! This statement might surprise you, but I can worship with or without music! Worship is an internal experience, not an external one. True worship begins in the heart of a person—music or no music.

Then what should motivate worship? Romans 12 indicates that when the believer experiences the mercies of God, the response to these attributes results in pure worship! What produces true worship? I once heard Dr. John MacArthur say, "A grasp of the riches of salvation given to undeserving sinners like you and me produces true worship in us."[12]

What is necessary to reveal the truth about the riches of God? The living Word. As the heart is changed and blessed by truth, we experience real worship. We cannot respond in worship until God *reveals* Himself to us. We need music to encourage the mind of believers to know God through His Word. Sing the Word! The Holy Spirit uses the Word to minister. And when you lift up Jesus in song, you are exalting the very fulfillment of the Word!!

If there was ever a time for music in the church to be strategic, it's today! We don't need songs to merely sound good, we need musicians who live good. Do we actually believe the Levitical singers boldly marched ahead of the army of Jehoshaphat because they had a good song? These musicians were dedicated, holy servants of God who believed "His love endures forever!" God anoints singers, not songs.

So, sing the Word in the power of the Holy Spirit and magnify Jesus. He is our song! Remember, we don't sing because we can sing. We sing because we have the Song!

1. Should singing be more than performance?
2. How can we make worship meaningful to the believer?

～

Dear Lord, remind me that people observe my face before they hear my voice. Give me a countenance that is sincere and honest—a countenance that shines with Your glory. Let my face act as the surface of the moon—a reflection of the Son! In Jesus' name, Amen.

Rick Stone
Worship Pastor
Whitesburg Baptist Church, Huntsville, AL

Clear the Weeds

Do not present your members to sin as instruments for unrighteousness,
but present yourselves to God as those who have been brought from death
to life, and your members to God as instruments for righteousness.

Romans 6:13 (ESV)

The definition of a *weed*: a plant that is not valued where it is growing and is usually of vigorous growth; *especially*: one that tends to overgrow or choke out a more desirable plant (*Merriam-Webster*).

Weeds are tricky. Often mistaken for flowers, weeds can generally grow anywhere and require regular maintenance to keep from overtaking a garden. No matter how many healthy plants surround it, a weed requires an action plan from the gardener lest it take over the soil once designated for healthy plants.

Sin works in similar ways. It can typically spring up when our spiritual garden goes uncultivated and requires regular maintenance to be removed from our lives. Simply asking the Lord to remove it is not enough. While His forgiveness is assured for every believer in Christ, we need to take measurable steps toward removing sin. This is especially important as worship leaders.

Jesus called the religious and worship leaders of His day "hypocrites." "Well did Isaiah prophesy of you, when he said: 'This people honors me with their lips, but their heart is far from me; in vain do they worship me'" (Matt. 15:7–9 ESV).

May this never be said of us. Let us pursue the Lord with a passion for His glory and for His holiness.

1. What weeds in your life need to be removed from your spiritual garden?
2. In addition to what needs to be removed, what healthy habits have you recently neglected that need to be reincorporated into your spiritual disciplines?

~

Lord, You have called me to be holy as You are holy. Let me not be content
with an unkept spiritual garden. Help me to be so in love with Your glory
that I develop a holy hatred for my sin. Through the power of Christ in me,
give me victory in removing sin from my life. In Jesus' name, Amen.

John Brewer
Associate Pastor of Worship
First Baptist Church, Mustang, OK

Temptation

Therefore he had to be made like his brothers in every respect, so that he
might become a merciful and faithful high priest in the service of God,
to make propitiation for the sins of the people. For because he himself has
suffered when tempted, he is able to help those who are being tempted.
Hebrews 2:17–18 (ESV)

How many of you have ever been tempted? Come on now, ALL of us! I know that I have. I am a big Diet Coke drinker and nothing goes better with a Diet Coke than a Snickers bar. These two things were just made to go together. The sweet things have always tempted me, especially a Snickers bar. It seems like it is always the good-tasting things that we are not supposed to have that tempt us the most. Occasionally, I will give in to my temptations and get that Snickers bar to go with the Diet Coke. For me, it's the chocolate, the peanuts, and the nougat that are bad for me. Not from an allergy standpoint but just from a sugar and nut standpoint.

I can imagine that Jesus was tempted just as we are. Well, maybe not with a Snickers bar, but I am sure He was tempted in many other ways. Hebrews 2:17–18 tells us that He became like us so that as He Himself was tempted, He is able to come to the aid of those who are tempted. The devil will try each and every day to find those things that you love and enjoy and will tempt you to cause you to stray. Christ is there to aid and strengthen you in overcoming those temptations. He knows and understands temptation and tells us He is here for us each and every day. Stay strong, trust in the Lord, and He will provide for you. Maybe even a Snickers without peanuts!

1. What are things you are tempted by?
2. How are you overcoming that temptation?

~

Dear Father, I pray that as we are tempted each and every day that You would give us the
strength to call upon You for strength to make it through the temptations of each day.

Wayne Bridges
Traditional Worship Leader/Senior Adults
First Baptist Church, Ruston, LA

God's Song

"The LORD your God is with you, the Mighty Warrior who saves. He will take great delight in you; in his love he will no longer rebuke you, but will rejoice over you with singing."
Zephaniah 3:17 (NIV)

It's a special feeling when people sing to us. It may be in celebration of a birthday or anniversary. Maybe you've had a special someone sing to you, or dedicate a song in your honor. The common theme behind someone singing to you is . . . LOVE. How much more does a loving God want to show His affection for you? After all, He loves you more than you could ever imagine!

Zephaniah explains a time in the future when God will joyfully sing over His people, Israel, because they repent and follow Him. Verses 14–15 say God's people will sing His praise. Then God sings. Can you imagine what that song will sound like? Without a doubt, the most beautiful song and voice in all of history!

Jesus taught in Luke 15 that "there is joy before the angels of God over one sinner who repents" (v. 7). When we come to the Lord and accept His gift of salvation, there is REJOICING in heaven. The amazing reality is that God is with us. He loves us and cares for us. He offers us salvation through Jesus, and "takes great delight" in us when we follow Him. One day, the Lord will sing over His people. He delights in YOU today as you daily place your life in His hands and strive to be more like Jesus!

1. We can't imagine what the celebration must be like in heaven when a sinner becomes a saint. How does it make you feel knowing there is rejoicing in heaven over your decision to follow Christ?
2. Knowing this, does it inspire you to worship the Lord with renewed passion?

Lord, thank You that You are with me, You love me and care for me. Thank You for Jesus and my salvation. I am in awe that You delight in me, and what hope there is to one day hear Your song. Until then, may I continually delight in You!

David Butler
Worship Pastor
First Baptist Church, St. Charles, MO

Recognize the Voice of the Shepherd

"So Jesus again said to them, "Truly, truly, I say to you, I am the door of the sheep. All who came before me are thieves and robbers, but the sheep did not listen to them. I am the door. If anyone enters by me, he will be saved and will go in and out and find pasture. The thief comes only to steal and kill and destroy. I came that they may have life and have it abundantly. I am the good shepherd. The good shepherd lays down his life for the sheep."

John 10:7–11 (ESV)

This pastoral illustration is one that is often foreign to us in this twenty-first-century culture because most of us don't tend flocks. We don't really understand the nuances and best practices of being a shepherd. Jesus knew this very well. He was from Bethlehem, a place where sheep herding was normative for the culture. Jesus wanted to communicate His salvation in a way that people would identify. So, He used these terms to describe His care and shepherding qualities.

Whenever the shepherd was leading flocks to graze, they were often called to move through a gate into the next grazing pasture. The sheep heard the voice of the shepherd and trusted him to move them. Can you say the same? You can immediately identify areas of your life where you have allowed the enemy to "steal, kill, and destroy" by believing and following a message that should not have been trusted.

1. As you have listened to the heart of the Good Shepherd through this Scripture, take a minute to respond and write down an important area of trust that He is calling into greater clarity for your life.
2. Ask the Shepherd to help you stay in a position where His voice would be the clearest and most resounding one in your life.

~

Lord, we pray that Your voice would always be the most prominent influence in our lives. So often we support our own sinful nature and desires by following the advice of the world and this leads to destruction. Our tendency is to let other voices of this life overpower the "still, small voice" we know so well. Help us to focus on and respond to Your voice through Your Word. Amen.

Jeff Brockelman
Worship Pastor
Anderson Mill Road Baptist Church, Moore, SC

God in the Daily

But when Daniel learned that the law had been signed, he went home
and knelt down as usual in his upstairs room... He prayed three times
a day, just as he had always done, giving thanks to his God.
Daniel 6:10 (NLT)

I had a student once who knew beyond the shadow of a doubt that God had called him to be a worship pastor. His biggest life challenge, however, was also going to be his greatest career challenge—Brian was blind. This extremely bright and talented young man sailed through all of his classes. That is, until he got to choral conducting. That's when he discovered the importance of depth perception in the art of conducting.

No matter how hard he tried, he just couldn't establish a consistent rhythm. I was convinced that if Brian could only practice the precision of his conducting, he would eventually develop muscle memory and get it. So, I went to the local Toys "R" Us and picked up a toy xylophone. I removed the C, G, F, and E tone-plates and mounted them to a board in the exact place Brian would need to strike in order to have the perfect conducting pattern. With mallet in hand, Brian began to craft the art and accuracy of conducting. The more he practiced, the better he got. He not only got conducting, he got a job, and today, Brian is serving a church as a worship pastor/choir director.

Brian's story of hard work, discipline, and determination is similar to our faith journey. As we put into practice daily habits of devotion and spiritual disciplines, the more like Christ we become. If worship is our response to God's revelation, it only makes sense to read His Word daily so that we may know Him more. If God responds to the prayers of His people, then we, like Daniel, should make prayer a regular part of our day. God works in the routine. He moves in the midst of what we may consider mundane. So, "let us not become weary in doing good" (Gal. 6:9 NIV). God is in the daily.

1. Have I established a regular routine of Bible reading and prayer?
2. Am I making the most of available resources designed to help me become more systematic in my spiritual disciplines?

～

God, in my pursuit of deeper intimacy with You, teach me to
value routine and see You at work in the ordinary.

Scott Bullman
Worship Pastor
Thomas Road Baptist Church, Lynchburg, VA

Home

For we know that when this tent we live in—our body here on earth—is torn down, God will
have a house in heaven for us to live in, a home he himself has made, which will last forever.
2 Corinthians 5:1 (GNT)

I went home recently to visit with my parents, both in their eighties and Mom with Alzheimer's. We visited. Reminisced. Drove around town looking at the old home place. Sharing memories. Mom's are not always there.

We ate at a diner that was there when my parents were dating and was a hang-out during my formative years. As we drove around, it was easy to note that things had changed. My school. The house where I grew up. My church. This definitely wasn't "home" anymore!

Then it hit me . . . this world is NOT my home! My citizenship is in heaven (Phil. 3:20). That is where my true home is! This present "home" is changing constantly as reality changes and as our memories change and fade. But the home that is eternal, that will never change, awaits us once we pass through this part of life into the next!

1   Who can I tell about my eternal "home" today?
2.   How will I let the reality of my heavenly home impact my life today?

Dear Lord, please help me see . . . remind me . . . that "this world is not my home,
I'm just a passin' through." Help me to anticipate my home in heaven and to
remember that my eternal home has room for all of those I see today. Amen.

Keith Clutts
Worship Pastor
Grand Avenue Baptist Church, Fort Smith, AR

A Passionate Response

Shout with joy to the LORD, all the earth! Worship the LORD with gladness. Come
before him, singing with joy. Acknowledge that the LORD is God! He made us, and we
are his. We are his people, the sheep of his pasture. Enter his gates with thanksgiving;
go into his courts with praise. Give thanks to him and praise his name.

Psalm 100:1–4 (NLT)

When I was around ten years old, I became very passionate about basketball. I began to work hard every day on my dribbling and shooting skills: left hand, right hand, between the legs, spinning the ball on my index finger, and shots from the free throw line. It wasn't until later that I began to understand that my 5 foot 6 inches height and small frame might become a problem for this future NBA player. And so, my passions began to change.

What are you passionate about? The answer is easy. Look at your calendar and at your bank statement. Where we spend our time and money says a lot about our passion. It is so easy to direct our passion toward so many other things in life and then bring God the leftovers when we come to worship Him. Friends be reminded, once again, of how much God loves you and all He has done for you!

1. Do you worship the Lord with gladness?
2. Is there passion in your expression of worship? God wants you to bring your passion to public worship. God desires and deserves your passionate worship.

～

Father, may my worship be in proper proportion to Your grace. You
gave Your best. Now, may I give You mine through worship!

Rocky Gillmore
Worship Pastor
Crossroads Baptist Church, The Woodlands, TX

Don't Go It Alone

"If you are pleased with me, teach me your ways so I may know you and continue to find favor with you. Remember that this nation is your people." The LORD *replied, "My Presence will go with you, and I will give you rest." Then Moses said to him, "If your Presence does not go with us, do not send us up from here."*

Exodus 33:13–15 (NIV)

The presence of God was so important to Moses that he refused to move ahead without it. We need God's presence in our lives every day, every minute, and every hour.

How do we experience God's presence? One of the ways is through our worship. Here is my definition of worship: *worship is living a life fully aware of God's presence, all the time, experiencing God's presence in every part of our lives.* Whether we're praying, singing, speaking, leading, serving, working or encouraging, we must always be aware of His presence.

The Bible speaks of God's presence in two distinct ways:

1. God's presence is everywhere. He is omnipresent—that's universal.
2. God manifests His presence in the lives of His people—that's personal.

His presence imparts blessing, power, grace, wisdom, peace, patience, compassion, purpose, direction, and more. God wants us to be constantly refreshed by His presence. That's what worship is all about.

God's presence is described many times as a river. I think that is a good picture for us. We can stick our toe in and say, "Wasn't that amazing?" We can wade in knee deep or waist deep, or we can jump in and let the presence of God surround us and carry us where He wants us to go. Let's jump in!

1. How would you describe God's presence in your life?
2. What can you do personally to be more aware of God's presence?

~

Lord Jesus, I want more of You in every part of my life. I long to go deeper with You and sense Your presence in everything I do. I worship You as Lord of my life! Amen.

Ron Cochran
Former Executive and Music Pastor
Portland Christian Center, Portland, OR

Joyful Suffering

And when they had inflicted many blows upon them, they threw them
into prison. . . . About midnight Paul and Silas were praying and singing
hymns to God, and the prisoners were listening to them . . .
Acts 16:23, 25 (ESV)

When suffering, the natural response is to grumble, murmur, or complain. In this text Paul and Silas show us a different way to respond in a time of suffering. After a day of being severely beaten with rods, their garments torn, and being thrown into the inner parts of a stone wall jail with their feet uncomfortably fastened to stocks, they counted it an honor and chose to worship. The Holy Spirit filled their hearts with joy and praise.

God inhabits the praises of His people, and they experienced that powerful presence from the One who had promised to never leave them. The text then says ". . . and the prisoners were listening to them." Hearing singing in a situation like this isn't what people would expect, but their response alone points them, along with those who heard them, to the One who is greater than their circumstances.

John 12:32 says ". . . when I am lifted up from the earth, will draw all people to myself" (ESV). As Christians, we have to get to a place where no matter what the situation may be, we allow the Holy Spirit, who is always present with us, to fill us and help us. He will use our response as a tool to draw people to the One who holds all things together.

1. When was a time you were suffering and struggled to give praise to God?
2. What did you learn in that time about God and how can you apply that through the next storm?

~

Father, we know that You are a sovereign God, and You are with us in every situation. Help us to sing Your praises even in life's darkest moments. You are faithful. Praise Your holy name!

Travis Blye
Worship Pastor
Longview Point Baptist Church, Hernando, MS

Let Them See Christ in Me

He put a new song in my mouth, a hymn of praise to our God. Many
will see and fear the LORD and put their trust in him.

Psalm 40:3 (NIV)

As a worship leader and choir director, it is sometimes very easy to spend all of my energy and effort in getting the right *sound*. After all, isn't God worthy of my very best?

He absolutely is, and our attitude should be to only offer our best. But our best is so much more than just sound. God uses our worship leadership to draw others into His presence. I tell my choir all the time, "If sound was all that mattered, we could put in a CD and just play it on Sunday morning!" We could stay home on Wednesday night and not have to bother with practice, choir membership, and time away from home.

But this psalm tells me that the *testimony of a life expressing praise* is a demonstration of what is *alive* in me, and God uses it to show others how to worship Him. When they see our authenticity in expression, and our passion for the King of kings, they will be encouraged to put their faith in God for salvation and worship Him as their Lord and Savior!

So, devoted choir members and worshipers, know that your worship is making a difference in those you love and lead each week!

1. Why is it so easy to be satisfied with only the musical aspects on Sunday and nothing else?
2. How can I work on my expression of authentic worship, so others will "see" God and trust in Him?

Lord, let your Spirit in me keep my song, my life, my worship, my expression, and
my love for those I lead in a place that is fresh and authentic each week. May they
see my worship and the way I live my life as a testimony of Your presence in me.

Jeff Askew
Worship Pastor
Liberty Baptist Church, Hampton, VA

I've Got the Joy, Joy, Joy, Joy!

Rejoice in the Lord always; again I will say, rejoice.
Philippians 4:4 (ESV)

The book of Philippians has been called "the epistle of joy" because the words *joy* and *rejoice* are used at least sixteen times through its four chapters. Over the course of the letter, Paul talks about prayer, his imprisonment, the unity of the Philippian church, the example of Jesus, and specific instructions for believers. However, he always returns to the subject of joy. Is it because Paul is just happy? That's doubtful, since he told us in 2 Corinthians that he had been beaten, imprisoned, shipwrecked, and stoned; not to mention being in danger from heat, cold, starvation, thirst, and robbers. He even had to support his own ministry by working for a living!

The joy that Paul encourages us to seek is "in spite of" the circumstances of life, not "because of" them. On occasions when we experience sadness, frustration, or despair, Paul's words (rejoice, delight, take pleasure in the Lord) refocus us on our purpose for living. They "recall our calling." It's easy to allow the world to take away our happiness. Mainstream media thrives on bringing us bad news every day at 6:00 and 11:00. It's a Christian's privilege to reflect Jesus' love through our joy so that the world can experience "the peace of God which surpasses all understanding" (Phil. 4:7 ESV). This was so important to Paul he said it twice!

1. Are you allowing your circumstances to dictate your attitude or is your attitude influencing your circumstances?
2. What is your biggest "joy thief" and how can you use this passage to lock it away?

~

Father, through Your Son we have been given immeasurable joy. I pray today that I would decrease so that You could increase in my home, my job, my relationships, and my testimony. You are the source of joy and I love you. Amen.

Barry Cook
Minister of Music and Worship
First Baptist Church, Tifton, GA

Lamp or High Beam?

Your word is a lamp to my feet and a light to my path.
Psalm 119:105 (ESV)

Not too long ago I was up late watching a ballgame. After the game ended, an info-mercial came on television for one of those new, really bright, flashlights. Now, I can be a sucker for some of those late-night infomercials, but I've come to find out through experience that those products don't normally work as well as they say they do. This one fascinated me, though, because I do not like to be in the dark. When I drive at night, I have to fight the temptation to put my high beams on all the time. Why do I do this?

I do this because I'm not content only seeing a few feet ahead of me. I want to see the whole road! But when it comes to driving, I can't do that because I will blind the other drivers coming my way.

Psalm 119:105 clearly says that the Word is a lamp. It doesn't say that it's a high beam headlight. In other words, His Word shows us what we need to know at that time and asks us to have faith for what we cannot see. I don't know about you, but in my mind, I would rather see everything. God, however, clearly says He will light our path and remind us that we need to have faith in the unseen moments. The concept may be simple but following it can often be difficult.

1. Why do we feel like we need to see everything?
2. What is God teaching us when He asks us to wait?

~

Father, we love You and trust You. Please forgive us for not having enough faith for what we cannot see. Thank You for always providing what I need, when I need it. Amen.

Chris Copeland
Worship Pastor
Central Church, Collierville, TN

Stretch!

*Going on from that place, he went into their synagogue, and a man with a
shriveled hand was there. . . . He said to the man, "Stretch out your hand." So
he stretched it out and it was completely restored, just as sound as the other.*
Matthew 12:9–13 (NIV)

Someone once said, "Too many people confine their exercise to jumping to conclusions, running up bills, sidestepping responsibility, pushing their luck, and stretching the truth." While we certainly don't want to stretch the truth, stretching before exercise is very important. Stretching can increase circulation and flexibility, increase range of motion and reduce stress.

Just as it is important physically, stretching is important spiritually. Has Jesus ever asked you to stretch? Stretch out your faith? Stretch out of your comfort zone? Talk with someone about their faith? Maybe increase your giving and trust God to provide. There are innumerable ways to stretch.

Just as the man's hand extended as he stretched it out, God will give you strength as you stretch your faith, your giving, your witness, or whatever it is God has asked you to do.

The spiritual benefits parallel the physical benefits.

Increased circulation: God will allow you more opportunities to stretch your faith, more opportunities to give, more chances to use your talents as you use them.

Flexibility: You'll find that your spirit is not as rigid as you think when you watch what God is doing through and around you.

Reduced stress: As you exercise your faith, in whatever form that takes, you will become increasingly more comfortable with whatever you are doing for Him.

So, how about some spiritual exercise?

Jumping to do what God asks.

Running to finish the race before you.

Sidestepping excuses not to be involved.

Pushing past your comfort zone.

Stretching your faith.

You'll reap the benefits every day!

1. How is God asking you to stretch your faith?
2. What is your biggest obstacle to exercising your faith?

Lord, help us to be willing to stretch our faith and trust You.

Glenn Crosthwait
Worship Pastor
Johns Creek Baptist Church, Alpharetta, GA

Admirable

Whatever is true, whatever is noble, whatever is right, whatever is pure, whatever is lovely, whatever is admirable—if anything is excellent or praiseworthy—think about such things.
Philippians 4:8 (NIV)

Excellence is the quality of being outstanding or extremely good. When I read worship ministry job descriptions, mission statements, and ministry brochures, "pursuing musical excellence" is a phrase that's used frequently. It's rather hard to pin down whose standard of excellence will be used, and frustratingly, there always seems to be someone else who is "more excellent."

What if our goal in music ministry was first to be characterized as admirable and praiseworthy? Something admirable arouses respect and approval from others. When others observe our rehearsal and watch us relate to one another, do they admire what they see? In our music ministry, it is not *enough* to have a good heart, but it is MOST important.

Have you ever rooted for a team that had a hard time getting the win, but they had great character and good personal chemistry? You could tell that even though adversity knocked them down, they were always giving their best. You wanted them to win because they worked hard, and you knew that if they stayed the course . . . maybe next year would be the big one!

Our worship ministry has chosen to value the characteristic of being admirable and praiseworthy. We want to honor the Lord and one another in our process, practice, and performance. We may not hit a home run every Sunday, but we want people to see that we love well and are giving our best each week.

1. What trait in Philippians 4:8 is most valued in your ministry?
2. What compliment would you value more than, "That music was excellent!"?

~

Father, as we worship You, help us to prioritize the character
of our heart above the quality of our art.

Jonathan Ford
Minister of Worship and Arts
Forcey Bible Church, Silver Spring, MD

Anticipating Anxiety

Be anxious for nothing, but in everything by prayer and supplication
with thanksgiving let your requests be made known to God.
Philippians 4:6 (NASB)

This verse frequently appears on motivational posters and social media. It's also one that many of us have "hidden in our hearts," but Satan, the author of lies, would tell us that this applies to everything except our "pet struggle." We all have that "pet struggle" that immediately cuts us to the quick, like our finances, our health, our relationships, or our secret insecurities. We tend to think no one else has been in this same situation or has suffered quite to the same extent or same way we have. Fortunately, we are instructed to be anxious for nothing . . . absolutely nothing. There is no exception!

When we continue reading, we're reminded that, "the peace of God, which surpasses all comprehension, will guard your hearts and your minds in Christ Jesus" (Phil. 4:7 NASB). What a blessing to know that when we turn that sudden feeling of anxiety over to God, He will give us peace. Notice also that the peace we are given is His peace. There is nothing our all-powerful, all-knowing God worries or gets nervous about!

1. What things or situations instantly bring you anxiety?
2. Where can you place this verse to bring you God's peace?

~

Father God, thank You for Your forgiveness and the certainty of our salvation!
The certainty of our salvation reminds us that we can trust You with all our
other needs. Please help us to have the peace that passes all understanding today.
Help us to trust and not be anxious. In Jesus' name we pray, Amen.

Charles Darus
Worship Pastor
First Baptist Church, Kissimmee, FL

Not My Brother, Not My Sister, but It's Me, O Lord . . .

For You have been a stronghold for the helpless, a stronghold for the
poor in his distress, a shelter from the storm, a shade from the heat;
For the breath of tyrants is like a rainstorm against a wall.

Isaiah 25:4 (AMP)

How many times as a young boy did I disobey my parents in the simplest of things and then have to pay a big price? I remember going to a peanut farm one fall and picking up peanuts that had been left behind in the field. We picked up peanuts from sunrise to sunset. When we got home, I began helping myself to those green peanuts. Mom was quick to warn me about over indulging, but what did she know?

I remember how sick I got and how ashamed I was to tell my parents what I had done. The longer I waited to go to them, the worse I got. Funny thing was, I didn't have to tell them. They already knew and were ready to go to the medicine cabinet for help. That's so much like our heavenly Father.

I think nineteenth-century Scottish poet and minister George MacDonald summed it all up too well, "How often do we look upon God as our last and feeblest resource! We go to Him because we have nowhere else to go. And when we learn that the storms of life have not driven us upon the rocks but into the desired heaven."[13]

1. What is your greatest need in life right now?
2. Have you turned it over to our heavenly Father?

~

Heavenly Father, thank You for being a stronghold for the helpless
and for me. I need You every day to give me strength, help, and guidance.
Thank You, Lord, for what You are about to do in my life! Amen.

Paul Davis
Worship Pastor
Northcrest Baptist Church, Meridian, MS

Use Your Gifts as God Intended

As each has received a gift, use it to serve one another,
as good stewards of God's varied grace.
1 Peter 4:10 (ESV)

God has blessed each of us with at least one gift. Some have great singing voices, some are talented speakers, some are skilled with plans and logistics, some are athletic, and so on. God gave us gifts for a purpose: to serve each other and to be motivated by His grace.

We face the temptation of using our talents for our own gain, whether it is for recognition from others, gaining influence or some other advantage. God calls us to use our gifts to serve one another; to consider others more important that ourselves. You are called to bless others by using your talents for their sake, not your own.

Our motivation for using our gifts to serve others should be rooted in the awareness of God's grace toward us. We should bless others with the abilities God has given us because God has been merciful to us. God extends His grace to those around us and uses our faithfulness in serving Him to demonstrate that grace.

1. How are you tempted to use your gifts for your own gain instead of for others?
2. What specific ways are your gifts a blessing for other people?

~

Father, thank You for showing grace to me. Please help me to use the talents
You have given me to encourage others and for them to see You.

Michael Cole
Associate Pastor of Music and Worship
Morrison Heights Baptist Church, Clinton, MS

Empty Glory

*Do nothing out of selfish ambition or conceit, but in humility
consider others as more important than yourselves. Everyone should look
out not only for his own interests, but also for the interests of others.*
Philippians 2:3–4 (csb)

Pride comes in a variety of styles and colors; you can find one to fit your own personality. My personal choice is "humble pride." It is soft-spoken, tastefully adorned in understatement. It does not boast or even posture. It just meditates on self. It dreams about self. Like all forms of praise, the inner vision that drives it is not God or truth but self-glorification.

Self-pride is like lust. In the dark, privacy of our hearts, it can stimulate and energize, but when it is brought to the light and exposed in public, it is easily seen as a ridiculous lie. What had puffed us up now makes us hide and choke in shame.

When Satan tempts you to savor this empty glory, see it as the cheap imitation it is. Turn away from it and embrace your true glory, the presence of God Himself with you and in you. When I turn away from myself and look to God, it's as if someone has opened the windows of my mind and heart. Now the sun is shining, and the air is fresh.

Prayer and praise shed the light of truth on who we are. They keep life in perspective. They liberate us from the smallness of pride into the wide-open wonder of God's love.

1. How have I been prideful in my own life?
2. Who can I show gratitude to in my ministry today?

~

*Heavenly Father, thank You for being with me now and always. Give
my mind and heart strength to not be distracted by the enemy, so
that I can discover and enjoy the wonder of living in You.*

Chris Mason
Worship Pastor
First Baptist Church, Arnold, MO

Exalt the Humbled One

And being found in human form, he humbled himself by becoming obedient
to the point of death, even death on a cross. Therefore God has highly exalted
him and bestowed on him the name that is above every name.
Philippians 2:8–9 (ESV)

The archetype of humility is none other than Jesus, the Son of God. He, being God in every way, chose to become a man and demonstrate humility during His time on the earth. Imagine God-in-flesh, calming the Sons of Thunder when they wanted to obliterate a town for turning them away (Luke 9:51–56); or Jesus' careful response to religious leaders seeking to stone a woman for adultery (John 8:1–11). These moments of humility are impressive because the Maker showed restraint with His creation.

Jesus also showed tremendous humility in His last hours before the crucifixion. He, being God in every way, *chose* to die a horrific death for the sins of humankind. It is made clear through His prayers in the Garden of Gethsemane that Jesus did not have to follow through with this plan (Luke 22:39–44). He chose to be obedient to the will of God, the Father, and allowed His body and spirit to be broken. He chose to take our rightful wrath of God upon Himself.

This unmatched humility is greatly rewarded. This humble Savior became Victor over death. He has the name above all names. We praise Jesus for His humble death and His amazing resurrection. The Lord Jesus is well deserving of all praise.

1. Think on the example of humility Christ demonstrated for us. How has His example changed how you live?
2. How can you demonstrate your adoration for the Risen Savior to the world around you?

~

Thank You, Jesus, for living a humble life on the earth and dying a
humble death for my salvation and eternal hope. Help me to live in such
a way that those around me know that I exalt You. Amen.

Chris Diffey
Minister of Music and Worship
Lakeside Baptist Church, Birmingham, AL

What Are We So Worried About?

"And which of you by being anxious can add a single hour to his span of life?"
Matthew 6:27 (ESV)

The theme of productivity seems to stay at the forefront of our lives, as it should. We want to be productive in our work. We want our kids to be productive at school and with their homework. We want to be productive when we exercise. We want to be productive in how we disciple our children and watch them grow in their relationship with Christ. Sometimes, we even want to be productive on our vacations!

In the midst of our desire to be productive, there's one thing we're prone to do that is completely unproductive: worry. In fact, worrying has the complete opposite effect! It's often paralyzing as we worry about something in which we most likely have no control.

How does this apply to music and worship? I'm glad you asked! Have you ever been part of a worship service or a concert where your greatest hope was to just survive without any train wrecks? I sure have . . . and now, I look back and grieve at the opportunities I missed to truly worship the Lord in those moments. In fact, I would venture to say that it's impossible to worship the Lord when we are overcome with worry. If I'm worried about something, then I'm not trusting in the sovereign God who is in complete control of whatever it is that I'm worried about.

1. Does anything have you worried today that's keeping you from trusting in God?
2. Take a moment and look for verses and passages on this topic that might be good for you to memorize. They are certain to come in handy the next time you find yourself paralyzed by worry.

~

Father, help us to trust You with every day and every circumstance. Remind us daily of Your sovereignty and power. You are worthy of our absolute trust. Amen.

Cliff Duren
Arranger, Worship Pastor
First Baptist Church, Woodstock, GA

Singing with Jesus

While they were eating, Jesus took bread, and when he had given thanks, he broke it
and gave it to his disciples, saying, "Take and eat; this is my body." Then he took a
cup, and when he had given thanks, he gave it to them, saying, "Drink from it, all of
you. This is my blood of the covenant, which is poured out for many for the forgiveness
of sins. . . ." When they had sung a hymn, they went out to the Mount of Olives.
Matthew 26:26–28, 30 (NIV)

All of my life, the simple fact that Jesus and the disciples sang together after the supper was always mentioned as we closed the Lord's Supper, and we would sing a hymn together. Biblical scholars agree that it was likely that Jesus and the disciples sang Psalms 113–118, the "Hallel" from the Psalter. It was the custom for Jews to sing this on the first night of Passover. Jesus and the disciples followed this custom.

I am moved by these verses from Psalm 116. Imagine Jesus singing these words in the Garden of Gethsemane:

> Precious in the sight of the LORD is the death of his faithful servants. Truly I am
> your servant, LORD; I serve you just as my mother did; you have freed me from
> my chains. (vv. 15–16 NIV)

It is a powerful notion—Jesus was faithful to sing praise to God as He faced the most difficult task anyone has ever encountered. I believe Jesus is still inviting us to sing with Him, no matter the circumstances we face.

1. Am I faithful to sing praise to God in both good times and bad, or do I allow my circumstances to dictate my faithfulness in worship?
2. Can you think of a time that a song ministered to you in worship in a time of deep anguish?

~

Jesus, teach me to sing and worship in spirit and in truth
no matter the circumstances of my life.

Keith Ferguson
Associate Pastor, Worship Arts
First Baptist Church, Carrollton, TX

Placing My Trust in God Alone

Trust in the LORD with all your heart and lean not on your own understanding;
in all your ways submit to him, and he will make your paths straight.
Proverbs 3:5–6 (NIV)

We had just wrapped up a wonderful vacation in Oklahoma and were traveling across America on I-40 to our California home. After spending the night in New Mexico, we loaded back into our RV to continue our journey. My dad put his hand on the stick shift to put our RV in gear when he lost his ability to use his right hand. After putting the vehicle in park, he proceeded to experience a massive stroke right before my eyes. In front of me sat the strongest, most influential person in my life, and he had just lost his ability to move or even speak one word to me. I was fifteen years old and was confronted with "real" life. *Would my dad live? Would he be able to provide for our family?* All of these things and more raced through my mind. I felt lost and overcome with grief and a pain that I wasn't prepared for.

My dad had always taken care of my family and myself. I fully trusted in my dad, without question. To trust in the Lord in this situation meant that I had to let go of trusting completely in my dad or myself. I needed to wholly rely on God's wisdom, goodness, and His providence for my life and our family's future.

1. Is there someone or something that you are trusting instead of the Lord?
2. What is one step you can take today to move your trust to Him?

~

Father, sometimes it is hard for us to trust You instead of ourselves. When I start to trust in man, please use Your Holy Spirit to remind me that I am to trust You alone. Amen.

Jeff Elkins
Minister of Worship
First Baptist Church, Tulsa, OK

Praising with Your Whole Heart

With all my heart I will praise you, O Lord my God. I will give glory to your name
forever, for your love for me is very great. You have rescued me from the depths of death.
Psalm 86:12–13 (NLT)

When I contemplate the love God has for me, I am overwhelmed. His love for me is not based on my works, past, present, or future. His love for me is based on the final work of the Lord Jesus on that cruel cross that brought salvation to a lowly worm like me.

So, why shouldn't I praise Him "with all my heart"? "With all of my heart" has a new meaning to me. Back in April 2018, I watched and prayed a friend through the most difficult time of his family's life. A family of five, all of a sudden in just a six-week span, became a family of four. Their oldest daughter, Eliza Cait, ten years of age, was diagnosed with cancer. Over this six-week span, I saw this family crying out to God for answers and for healing. Our great God chose to bring Eliza Cait into His presence. At the funeral I watched this family, with overwhelming grief, praise the Lord with all of their heart.

As the father lifted his hands in worship, holding a stuffed animal of Eliza Cait's, I realized worship for me would never be the same. Oh, that I would worship and praise the Lord with all of my heart. Oh, that you, would worship and praise the Lord with all of your heart in the midst of whatever circumstances you face today and in the future. Know that even from the depths of death you have been rescued.

1. Do you praise God with all of your heart, or is there a portion of your heart that you keep from God?
2. In the valleys of your life, do you praise Him?

⁓

Lord, You are very great and I will glorify Your name forever. Thank You for
loving me with an everlasting love. Help me to trust You in every situation
of my life and help me to praise You with all of my heart. Amen.

Chris Ellenburg
Minister of Music
First Baptist Church, North Spartanburg, SC

The Cost of Worship

However, the king said to Araunah, "No, but I will surely buy it from you for a price,
for I will not offer burnt offerings to the LORD my God which cost me nothing."
So David bought the threshing floor and the oxen for fifty shekels of silver.

2 Samuel 24:24 (NASB)

David was called "a man after God's own heart," but his thoughts and actions often tend to mirror ours more than God's. He had been disobedient (again) and God had handed down his punishment. God eventually told him to erect an altar and offer sacrifices on Araunah's threshing floor. When Araunah tried to give his king the floor, oxen, and yoke for the sacrifice, David said, "I will not offer burnt offerings to the LORD my God which cost me nothing."

How many times have we neglected our preparation (musical and spiritual) only to arrive at a time of worship unprepared? Is rehearsal not an investment in a sound presentation? When we enter into a time of worship as leaders, we should be as ready as we can be to lead God's people into a time of transcending praise to the One who is worthy of our absolute best and nothing less. When our priorities in worship don't rest initially on getting ourselves ready to lead, we are—like David—faced with the choice of presenting a worthless song or an "offering" that actually costs us something. Isn't God worthy of that kind of sacrifice of praise?

1. How can we give God a sacrifice of praise that costs us something?
2. Do you remember a time when you felt God's presence as you prepared for worship?

～

Father, it is a comfort to know that You loved David even though his ways were so
like ours. As we seek to please You with a true sacrifice of praise, give us an awareness
of the great price You paid for us. May our worship delight You, O Father!

Barry Cook
Minister of Music and Worship
First Baptist Church, Tifton, GA

What? Me Worry?

"But seek first his kingdom and his righteousness, and all
these things will be given to you, as well."
Matthew 6:33 (NIV)

In 1988, Bobby McFerrin wrote and recorded a song with an infectious rhythm, a catchy melody, and a simple, encouraging title: "Don't Worry, Be Happy." It soared to No. 1 and was named both song and record of the year. Everywhere you went, the song was playing. Smiley-face pictures and posters abounded. McFerrin appeared on every major TV show. His concerts sold out. Pastors even "borrowed" the title for their sermon series!

Why did this song become such a phenomenon? It's probably because most of us are, in fact, worriers. It's not that we want to be. We just can't seem to help ourselves.

Worrying isn't new. One day, Jesus encountered a large group of worriers on a mountainside, and He knew what was on their minds. What would they eat? Where would they live? What would they wear? First-world problems. Then Jesus, knowing their bent to worry, offered them a substitute—faith in God. He assured them that the heavenly Father is keenly aware of our daily needs (v. 32b) and that if they will change their focus from worrying about receiving those needs to honoring the God who supplies them with their lives, He will indeed provide "all these things" and not just for them, but for all of us.

Today, honor Him with your life and be blessed with the reality of His provision.

1. Do you believe that God knows your every need?
2. Will you allow Him to meet your needs by seeking Him first?

～

Heavenly Father, thank You for being ready and able to meet my every need today.
Help me to seek Your kingdom first in everything I do. In Jesus' name, Amen.

Joe Estes
Minister of Music and Worship
First Baptist Church, Trussville, AL

Where Did the Bushes Go?

"I am the true vine, and my Father is the gardener. He cuts off every branch in me that bears no fruit, while every branch that does bear fruit he prunes so that it will be even more fruitful."
John 15:1–2 (NIV)

Think about springtime. The weather is beautiful, but you need to prune your bushes, flowers, trees, and so on. I remember one year pulling up to the church after lunch and saying to my pastor, "What happened to the bushes?" Someone had cut the bushes in front of the church, and it looked like there was nothing there but a few sticks in the ground. By summer, however, they were fuller and healthier than they were before the drastic cut.

So, my Father is like those men that came to church that day. He cuts EVERY branch in me that bears no fruit right off down to the ground, but for those branches that do bear fruit, He only cuts them back a little, so they can continue to grow even stronger.

Why are we so resistant to this process? This process is clear. Sometimes our Father must help us see things from a new perspective, which means He must EXPOSE the branches that are headed in the wrong direction or could cause the bush to die.

So, when we are going along, and things seem to be going better than ever and we face a setback, remember that this is just the pruning process. Our Father knows best what we need, and we need to let Him prune us. How often have we looked at setbacks as a punishment for something we did wrong when it could be the result of God pruning us by changing our perspective? In James, it says that we should have joy when we face trials because the testing of our faith produces perseverance!

1. Where did your bushes go?
2. Is your Father in heaven cutting off some dead branches so you can continue to grow stronger? God's design was for us to "bear much fruit," and fruit cannot bloom on a dead vine . . .

~

Father, do whatever it takes to prune my dead branches so I can bear much fruit and be who You called me to be. In the name of Jesus I pray, Amen.

Matt Fallin
Associate Pastor of Worship
Santuck Baptist Church, Wetumpka, AL

Real Change

Trust in the LORD with all your heart, and lean not on your own understanding;
In all your ways acknowledge Him, and He shall direct your paths.
Proverbs 3:5–6 (NKJV)

Why do we keep trying to do better only to end up failing yet again? It could be that we rely solely on our willpower and resolve; and if we somehow succeed, the glory goes to us. What if, instead of relying on willpower and resolve, we rely on the Holy Spirit working in and through us? God can give us the ability and strength to live a disciplined life. The best part is that when we succeed, the glory goes to God alone!

Do you want some real change in your life? Start here:

1. Read through the Bible—find a Bible reading plan and stick with it. It is not how many verses you read each day but that you read each day. Ask God to speak to your heart and pray to Him as you read.

2. Memorize Scripture—start with one verse a week. Try to do what the verse says while you are memorizing it. Once learned, make sure you review that verse once a week. Today's Scripture (Prov. 3:5–6) is a good place to start!

3. Thanksgiving list—make a list of all the things you are thankful for and pray through your list once a week. When God brings something else to mind, write it down.

~

Father, help me to rely on You for all things. I need some real change in
my life, and You are the only One I can depend on. Instead of trusting
myself, I am going to trust in You alone. Thank You Lord. Amen.

Chason Farris
Worship Pastor
First Baptist Church, Hendersonville, NC

We Are Messengers

Therefore, we are ambassadors for Christ, God making his appeal through us.
2 Corinthians 5:20a (ESV)

The Durens love basketball. April and I both played growing up, and now our kids are following in our footsteps. This is the first season where all four kids have played on different teams. It was busy, but we loved it!

We also watch a lot of basketball at home. When the NBA season ends, the off-season ends up being just as exciting as teams start trading players in order to improve their roster for the following season. It's always interesting to watch it all unfold.

Once the trades are made, the analysts go to work giving their opinion on who got the best end of the deal. In the end, only the next season will reveal who truly made the best trade.

Take a moment and read 2 Corinthians 5:17–21. David Jeremiah calls this passage "the greatest transaction in the history of the world." Jesus offering His perfect righteousness in exchange for our sin . . . and calling it an even trade. Unbelievable.

As Christians, we are not only receivers of this gift, but messengers to the world that they can have this same gift! "We are ambassadors for Christ, *God making his appeal through us.*" What a privilege to represent Almighty God in such a way.

As members of a music ministry, we have this opportunity every week as we share the gospel through song. Far beyond making beautiful music, our highest honor is making much of Jesus and the saving message of the gospel.

1. How do you currently view your role in music ministry where you serve? Does this passage change your mind-set?
2. Beyond the worship service, what are other opportunities you have each week to be an ambassador for Christ?

Father, thank You for the gift of Your Son and the incredible exchange of His righteousness for our sin. We are forever unworthy and forever grateful. In the saving name of Jesus we pray, Amen.

Cliff Duren
Arranger, Worship Pastor
First Baptist Church, Woodstock, GA

God's Infinite Creation

Let the heavens rejoice, let the earth be glad; let the sea resound, and all that is in it. Let the fields be jubilant, and everything in them; let all the trees of the forest sing for joy.
Psalm 96:11–12 (NIV)

How long has it been since you seriously considered the inconceivable enormity and the incomprehensible intricacies of God's infinite creation? It's a complex question but is even more a complex thought. A thoughtful visit to any zoo will thrust you into a visual and aural smorgasbord of color and sound that overwhelm the senses. Viewing the beautiful animals' coats of fur, the bold pigmentations of birds, or those in aquatic habitats reminds us of the majesty of Creator God. The grandeur of mountain peaks, the crash of waves from oceans deep, the palette of desert sands, and the lushness of forest glades all pay homage to God's magnificent creation.

"The heavens declare the glory of God; the skies proclaim the work of his hands" (Ps. 19:1 NIV). We glance into the sky to view a supermoon, millions of twinkling stars, a comet, or even experience an eclipse; virtually all have the power to take one's breath away.

It is a thrill to witness the birth of a child. The anticipation of learning if it is a boy or a girl, hearing its first cry, counting their fingers and toes brings tears to the eye and joy to the heart.

"Let all the earth fear the LORD; let all the inhabitants of the world revere him" (Ps. 33:8 NIV). Let all the universe and everything in it sing for joy!

1. Which facets of God's creation draw you closer to Him?
2. How do you express your adoration to God for the wonder of His creation?

~

Oh, Lord, our Lord, how majestic is Your name in all the earth. I bow humbly before You acknowledging You as Lord of all creation, Maker of heaven, earth, every living creature and even me. I stand in awe and exalt Your holy name for displaying the beauty, wonder, and majesty of Your infinite creation. In Jesus' name, Amen.

Joe Fitzpatrick
Worship and Music Pastor
First Baptist Church, Nashville, TN

Don't Fear the Wall

And Moses said to the people, "Fear not, stand firm, and see the salvation of the LORD,
which he will work for you today. For the Egyptians whom you see today, you shall
never see again. The LORD will fight for you, and you have only to be silent."
Exodus 14:13–14 (ESV)

Have you ever been down to the beach and felt the mist of the water spray your face and body? For most of us, it's a refreshing perk of being on vacation! This was not the case for the Israelites, as they found themselves standing at the banks of the Red Sea. With each crashing wave, the mist of the water reminded them that they had come to a dead end. Off in the distance they could hear and sense Pharaoh and his army approaching.

We can sense their fear and frustration as they begin to doubt Moses and God's plan. In verses 11–12, they are literally yelling at Moses for freeing them. In their eyes it would have been better to die as slaves than to be killed in the wilderness. To them the sea was a wall that could not be overcome.

Scripture doesn't say, but I often wonder if anyone in the crowd stopped to ask God to intervene, or was the uproar of the masses so loud that fear engulfed every person? Either way, chaos was in full force! With calmness and assurance, Moses tells the people to be quiet and to trust that the Lord will FIGHT for them. It wasn't long after this that God instructed Moses to part the sea using his staff.

1. Have you convinced yourself that a wall in your own life can never be moved?
2. When was the last time you stood silent and asked the Lord to FIGHT for you?

～

Lord, I need You to move this wall today! I trust in Your
Sovereign plan, and desire to see You fight for me!

Brett Fuller
Worship Pastor
First Baptist Church, Pelham, AL

Singing the Gospel into the Hearts of the People

But you are a chosen race, a royal priesthood, a holy nation, a people for his possession, so that you may proclaim the praises of the one who called you out of darkness into his marvelous light.
1 Peter 2:9 (csb)

Worship and evangelism walk hand in hand throughout the gospel. Today, as then, the message of a God who loves is often best remembered and told with a melody. This is certainly true of an experience that Glenn Boyd tells. At the time, Glenn and his family were music missionaries in—you guessed it—Africa. After months of training, one of the African men said that he must return to his village with the Good News. A few months later, Glenn and others visited the village and, to their delight, saw hundreds gathered for worship and teaching. When asked what the secret was, the leader responded that they simply "sang the gospel into the hearts of the people."

Our message and command are to "go and tell" the gospel story, but we also give others an opportunity to "come and see" (Ps. 66:5) the work of the Lord. Think of the time when Paul and Silas were in prison. As they sang and worshiped the Lord, the message of the gospel was heard. Wouldn't you have loved to hear what they sang? I'm guessing it was passionate, "full voice" praise to the Savior. They sang stories of hope and redemption. Certainly, it was loud enough for others to hear. Do you remember what happened? Those who heard asked a question that we all ask in our journey to Christ: "What must I do to be saved?" As you sing/play to the Lord, do it so that all might hear. You, too, have the opportunity to carry the gospel into the hearts of the people.

1. Do you have a "Paul and Silas story" of when you saw God move in the midst of worship?
2. What opportunities are available for you to share the gospel story through music or worship ministry?

~

God, thank You for giving me the opportunity to sing the story of Your love. Thank You for letting me share about a God that changed my life and will change others as they hear and believe. Amen.

Dr. Randy C. Lind
Worship and Music Specialist
Baptist General Convention of Oklahoma, Oklahoma City, OK

Staying Clean in a Dirty World

For God did not call us to be impure, but to live a holy life.
1 Thessalonians 4:7 (NIV)

I have a new black truck and I'm having a hard time keeping it clean. The truck is too long to park in the garage, so it stays in the driveway where the pine trees drop sap and all of the elements have free access to its body. I protect it by staying off of dirt roads, avoiding dirty environments, and keeping a good coat of wax on it.

You and I live in a very dirty world. Since we can't stay in the "garage" where it is safe and clean, we must be aware of the contaminants around us that can leave us dirty, marred, and stained. The cultural climate that we live in is moving in the opposite direction of Christ. We have to make a continual, conscious decision to walk in purity. Jesus Christ was the perfect example of staying clean in a dirty world. He never gave in to sin. So, how do we do it?

Second Corinthians 5:17 tells us that if we are in Christ, then we are a new creation; we are positionally pure. But we can only live this out if we are allowing Christ to reign and rule in our daily lives. It's like a good coat of "Jesus" wax that repels our sin-polluted culture.

1. Are you spending time daily with Jesus and in the Word to build up a good coat of protection against the evils of this world?
2. Are you compromising in areas that would not honor God and represent holiness? Be reminded of your position in Christ and strive to live it out practically.

~

Father, give me a desire to live a pure life and desire holiness. May my desire to be like You draw others into Your presence.

Rocky Gillmore
Worship Pastor
Crossroads Baptist Church, The Woodlands, TX

Grace Greater Than Our Sin

But God, being rich in mercy, because of His great love with which
He loved us, even when we were dead in our transgressions, made us
alive together with Christ (by grace you have been saved).
Ephesians 2:4–5 (NASB)

Do you remember when God spoke to you and called you to repentance and faith? I will never forget the day I opened my heart to His mercy and love. Even though I was deserving of His wrath and judgment, He lovingly drew me to Himself. All those arduous days of searching for real peace finally ceased when Jesus took up residence in my once vacant heart.

The apostle Paul reminds us of God's grace through faith that we have received through Jesus. Though dead in our trespasses and sins, Jesus' resurrection power has raised us up and made us alive with Him. We were underserving of His mercy and yet, from His own loving heart, Christ lavished His grace upon us to redeem us and to sustain us in all of life.

You and I have a new and living hope in Christ! Hallelujah! His grace is always at work, and the insurmountable trial in which you find yourself today is not a comment on His care or love for you . . . that was settled on the cross. Beyond the cross, there is an empty grave declaring His abiding presence and intercession for you (Heb. 7:25). Beloved, rejoice! The reality is that God's grace is greater than your sin, greater than your present situation, and He has promised to be your ever-present Help and the Sustainer of your life until the day of Christ Jesus.

1. How has God's grace sustained you in your current situation?
2. Who has God called you to share His love with today?

～

Heavenly Father, thank You for breathing new life in me and for the joy of
Your never-ending love and unrelenting grace. In Your name, Amen.

John Griffin
Worship Pastor
Calvary Baptist Church, Beaumont, TX

Our Souls Long for Eternity

For the invisible things of him from the creation of the world are
clearly seen, being understood by the things that are made, even his
eternal power and Godhead; so that they are without excuse.
Romans 1:20 (KJV)

Gustav Holst, the composer of *The Planets,* once said, "The enormity of the universe revealed by science cannot readily be grasped by the human brain, but the music of *The Planets* enables the mind to acquire some comprehension of the vastness of space where rational understanding fails."[14] Romans 1:20 gives us the kingdom perspective of the stars and planets.

Ecclesiastes 3:11 (NIV) opens our minds further to our desire for transcendence when rational understanding fails saying that God Himself has "set eternity" in our hearts. As we long for heaven, filled with the fullness of a loving God and our caring Savior, we must care for those in need and point them to eternity.

1. Do you delight in God's creation? Does your delight draw you to time alone with Him and a deeper awareness of God's goodness?
2. Do you remind those in your care of God's handiwork and His desire for relationship? (Rom. 1:20)

~

Father, I pray for those within my care. Help me to stimulate within them the desire
for eternity, for a picture of the pleasures and joys that await those who confess You
alone as the Lord, resurrected and reigning. Help me to encourage my flock to spend
time in communion with God. Help me to speak words of truth and life regarding that
eternity that awaits those who believe, and even more to those who struggle to see beyond
their meager existence. We await Your coming. Maranatha, Lord Jesus! Amen.

Dr. David Hahn
Chair, Department of Commercial Music
Liberty University, Lynchburg, VA

The Singer and the Song

Praise the LORD! Sing to the LORD a new song, and His praise in the assembly of saints.
Let Israel rejoice in their Maker; Let the children of Zion be joyful in their King.
Psalm 149:1–2 (NKJV)

Every year, thousands of people enter singing competitions. They endure discouragements, disappointments, and financial hardships, just for the chance to share their talent with the hopes of being recognized. Why is that? You see, for the dedicated vocalist, singing is so much more than the physical action of making a sound with your vocal cords. How could two small pieces of cartilage in your throat create such feelings of joy and beauty for the singer and then produce the same effect in those who listen? The answer is because this is how we were made.

When we use our voices, we are truly using a God-made instrument. For the believer, there is an added dimension. The believer's love of singing is a result of our love for our Savior, Jesus Christ. We have trusted in Christ for our salvation and accepted His gift of grace. This gives us a lot to sing about! We have a song in our heart for the Lord, not only as Creator, but also as our Redeemer and Friend. In Psalm 149 the people are admonished to "sing to the LORD a new song." We need to sing a new song because we have experienced new mercies, and the old ways of praising just aren't enough!

1. What is something new that you can thank the Lord about?
2. What are the benefits of joining in praise with other believers?

~

Lord, thank You for Your mercies, which are new every morning. Help me to have a new
song of praise in my heart for all that You have done and continue to do in my life. Amen.

Tobin Davis
Minister of Music
Shadow Mountain Community Church, El Cajon, CA

Pop Quiz—Who Among You Is Wise?

Who among you is wise and understanding? Let him show by his good behavior his deeds in the gentleness of wisdom. But if you have bitter jealousy and selfish ambition in your heart, do not be arrogant and so lie against the truth.
James 3:13–14 (NASB)

James, the half-brother of Jesus, is asking a rhetorical question to provoke his listeners to examine themselves. Scholars tell us this reference to a "wise" person would be someone who takes the knowledge of God's truth and applies it to their life. The word *understanding* in James' day would refer to someone who was becoming a specialist in some field of study. Putting the two together would result in the idea of someone becoming very skilled at applying God's truth to their life.

This process in someone's life will be evidenced by good behavior and humility or as James puts it, "deeds in the gentleness of wisdom." This carries the idea of power under control and can be illustrated by an appropriate dose of medicine. The correct amount would promote healing while too much could bring potential disaster.

Verse 14 warns that the opposite of wisdom and understanding is bitter jealousy and selfish ambition. If we have that in our hearts, we will become more and more arrogant as we justify sin in our own minds. We will scheme and rationalize as we seek power, recognition, and financial gain. We will lie to ourselves and deny God's truth.

Let us therefore seek to be wise and strive to apply God's truth to our lives every day.

1. Can you think of another example of power under control?
2. What is the default result if we do not strive to apply God's truth to our lives every day?

~

Father, thank You for the Bible. Help us spend time in Your Word daily; grant us Your wisdom and help us apply Your truth to our lives.

Marty Hamby
Minister of Worship and Music
First Baptist Church, Roanoke, VA

I Will Be with You

But now, this is what the LORD says—he who created you, Jacob, he who formed you, Israel: "Do not fear, for I have redeemed you; I have summoned you by name; you are mine. When you pass through the waters, I will be with you; and when you pass through the rivers, they will not sweep over you. When you walk through the fire, you will not be burned; the flames will not set you ablaze."
Isaiah 43:1–2 (NIV)

How many times has someone said, "*I will be here for you*"? It may have been a parent, friend, teacher, or spouse. How much more powerful are these words when God says, "*I will be with you*"? My family experienced this firsthand during the birth of our second child. In the delivery room, just before the excitement of welcoming another baby girl into our family, we received a phone call informing us that our house was on fire.

We were shocked and overwhelmed as we processed this news. My grandmother had passed away the previous day, so our hearts were already heavy. We began to receive encouraging phone calls and visits to the hospital. Shortly after the fire, a group of church members and neighbors gathered at our damaged home to pray. God's words to the people of Israel began to ring in my mind, "Do not fear . . . I will be with you . . . you are mine." Our tears of sadness turned to tears of joy as our second daughter was born just hours after that devastating phone call. We were reminded that the gift of life is far more important than a home or material possessions. When we face trials and unforeseen circumstances, we can rest assured that the Lord will *always* be with us.

1. Can you think of a time when you heard God say, "I will be with you"?
2. What causes you to feel overwhelmed?

~

Dear Jesus, thank You for walking with us through the storms, fires, and difficulties of this life. I give You my fears, doubts, and concerns. Thank You for Your redeeming love, and for loving us as a father loves his children. In the name of Jesus, Amen.

Mark Hill
Minister of Music and Worship
First Baptist Church, Garland, TX

A Chosen Vessel

*But the Lord said to him, "Go, for he is a chosen vessel of Mine to bear
My name before Gentiles, kings, and the children of Israel. For I will
show him how many things he must suffer for My name's sake."*
Acts 9:15–16 (NKJV)

What comes to your mind when you hear the word *vessel*? Does it bring images of large ships carrying cargo? Maybe you imagine a slender, hollow container that can carry liquid? In this passage in Acts, the Lord is referring to the apostle Paul as His "chosen vessel." Paul was given this distinction not because he was going to carry cargo or a liquid, but a message.

A fundamental principle of a good vessel is that it needs to be open to receive what it is intended to carry. If it isn't open to receive, it isn't a vessel at all. For the apostle Paul, this meant being open to the Lord teaching, instructing, and training him for the future. In Acts 9:16 the Lord says he will show Paul, "how many things he must suffer for My name's sake." This only happens because Paul has turned away from his old life and turned for instruction and direction from the Lord. When Paul is converted on the Damascus road, his response to Jesus is "Lord, what do you want me to do?" That's a great question for all of us to ask! That is the sign of an open heart to receive and mind to learn.

1. What are some of the unique ways that the Lord prepared Paul for his gospel mission?
2. What are other qualities necessary to be an effective vessel for the Lord?

*Lord, please give me open eyes, ears, hands, and heart to receive whatever You have for
me so that I may, in turn, be Your vessel to share with those around me. Amen.*

Tobin Davis
Minister of Music
Shadow Mountain Community Church, El Cajon, CA

Just Do You

Timothy, guard what has been entrusted to your care. Turn away from godless chatter and the opposing ideas of what is falsely called knowledge, which some have professed and in so doing have departed from the faith. Grace be with you all.
1 Timothy 6:20–21 (NIV)

In nearly everything of the Christian life, especially ministry, we do things together. Since the beginning, when God created Adam and Eve, this is what God intended. Think about all of the things we do together: marriage, work, church, ministry, friendships, parenting, and the list goes on. Sometimes we struggle with a feeling that some of those around us are not doing as they should. They're not contributing their share, or what they're doing, we feel, is wrong. For those of us who struggle with this feeling, this passage of Scripture from Paul is so freeing! Paul tells Timothy, "guard what has been entrusted to your care." In other words, you can only control that which you've been given control. Isn't it good to know that we must focus on doing the best we can only on that which we have control?

We also struggle sharing our feelings and thoughts about these issues that, at times, are more harmful than helpful. Although we sometimes need to share our struggles with others, it's often that this sharing can become "godless chatter." Do we need to share our struggles with others? Yes. Does that involve explaining every detail of someone else's faults and speaking negatively of others? Isn't it our struggles we're supposed to be sharing? Paul's last words in this passage are, "Grace be with you all." In this particular area, I know I need grace every day.

1. Have you ever wanted to control things you can't control?
2. Have you spoken "godless chatter" to someone recently?

~

Lord, keep me focused on what You've entrusted for me to do. Keep my words honoring of others and helpful for the future. Thank You for Your grace and mercy. Amen.

Brad Jett
Worship Pastor
First West, West Monroe, LA

Don't Start Down That Path

But when she brought them near him to eat, he took hold of her and said to her, "Come, lie with me, my sister." She answered him, "No, my brother, do not violate me, for such a thing is not done in Israel; do not do this outrageous thing. As for me, where could I carry my shame? And as for you, you would be as one of the outrageous fools in Israel. Now therefore, please speak to the king, for he will not withhold me from you." But he would not listen to her, and being stronger than she, he violated her and lay with her.

2 Samuel 13:11–14 (ESV)

Chapter thirteen of 2 Samuel is the chapter of shame and sorrows for the house of David. David's immorality had consequences far beyond his ability to control or even address. David, who always did the right thing in battle, was on a roller-coaster ride of sorrows that seemed to never let up. David's sons followed the example they had seen from their father, using subterfuge to get what they wanted.

When someone fails morally, this reveals their loss of proper personal discipline, but it also impairs one's ability to see clear warning signs of similar behavior. It is because of a tremendous guilt, a deep sense of regret, or a personal loss of moral authority that makes them believe they no longer have the authority to either make a judgment or intervene in a situation as they once could and would.

Proverbs 17:14 comes to mind, "To start a conflict is to release a flood, stop the dispute before it breaks out" (CSB). Moral compromise has the power to blind us to the immediate wrongness of a situation and then to bind us from acting with proper moral authority when related issues surface later. DON'T START DOWN THAT PATH!

1. Have you started down that path (even mentally) and had blinders on to the point that you couldn't see it?
2. What moral compromises have you made that you need to repent of today?

~

Heavenly Father, remove the blinders that might be in or around me to show me any moral compromises that might be occurring. Reveal to me the errors of my ways and restore me to a place of pursuing holiness and gospel-centeredness all because of Your amazing grace. In Jesus' name, Amen!

Ross Johnson
Worship and Music Pastor
First Baptist Church, Madison, MS

God's Perfect Rulebook

The instruction of the LORD is perfect, renewing one's life; the testimony of the LORD is trustworthy, making the inexperienced wise. The precepts of the LORD are right, making the heart glad; the command of the LORD is radiant, making the eyes light up. The fear of the LORD is pure, enduring forever; the ordinances of the LORD are reliable and altogether righteous. They are more desirable than gold.
Psalm 19:7–10a (HCSB)

I am no stranger to the law. My grandfather served in corrections, both of my parents worked in law enforcement for most of my adolescent and teenage years, and my brother has continued the family tradition through his work in a state prison. This close association to the law meant the concept of obeying rules was ingrained in me from a very young age. I came to see rules not as a hindrance but rather as a way of life.

When we examine Scripture, especially for the first time, the rules and laws given to us by God may seem a bit overwhelming or limiting, when in fact they are the opposite. God didn't establish His laws to bind us but instead He ordained them to uplift, clarify, enlighten, and inspire us. The laws of the Lord are perfect! They come from a Holy Father who loves us and wants the best for us. His laws set us free and light the pathway to righteousness and freedom from sin.

1. In what areas in your life are you refusing to be obedient to God's will?
2. Are you holding on to the empty promises of the world, or are you trusting that God has a plan for your life?

Dear Lord, I trust the plans that You have for my life and that Your laws are meant to refine me. Please help me to obey Your instructions and be joyful knowing that Your ways are perfect.

David Jones
Director of Music and Worship
Immanuel Bible Church, Springfield, VA

Fresh, Inspired Worship

Sing to Him a new song; play skillfully with a shout of joy.
Psalm 33:3 (NASB)

How many times have you entered into an organized time of worship only to see worshipers talking, texting, reading the bulletin, or just staring blankly into space? For that matter, how many times have others seen us doing those things when we worship? Psalm 33:3 tells us to sing a *new song* and to play *skillfully*. The "new song" refers to the conscious act of making every worship experience fresh as we come before our Lord and Creator. The actual song doesn't have to be "new" but the way we present it should be. After all, hasn't God blessed us in new ways since the last time we sang that song?

The word *skillfully* in this verse is the same word used to describe David's musical abilities to Saul when he was looking for someone to play in his court. David's playing was not only accomplished but *inspired* as well. God expects no less from us when we bring our worship before Him.

True worship requires the worshiper to be engaged in the process by offering a fresh (new) rendition of a song in an inspired (skillful) and energetic way. God delights in thoughtful and joyful worship!

1. How do you spiritually prepare yourself for a time of worship?
2. What are some practical ways that you can keep yourself focused during a time of corporate worship?

~

Lord, may my next time of worship with You be fresh and inspired. Remind me of Your "new every morning" goodness as I sing and You're "the same yesterday, today and forever" faithfulness as I play. May my worship be inspired AND inspiring. Amen.

Barry Cook
Minister of Music and Worship
First Baptist Church, Tifton, GA

Be Prepared

A final word: Be strong in the Lord and in his mighty power. Put on all of God's armor so that you will be able to stand firm against all strategies of the devil.
Ephesians 6:10–11 (NLT)

Reading through Ephesians 6, it is apparent that Paul wanted the church to be ready for the ensuing spiritual battles that Satan would bring against Christians. All believers need to be aware that they have a real enemy who is going to bring about spiritual warfare against them. You cannot avoid this, but you do not have to live in fear.

To be ready for war you need to be strong in the Lord's power . . . not your own. Ask the Lord to fill you with the Holy Spirit and subject yourself continually to His Scriptures.

Next, we need to put on the armor of God. No good soldier would go into battle without the proper gear. God has provided armor—put on the belt of truth, the breastplate of righteousness, the shoes of peace, the shield of faith, helmet of salvation, and take up the sword of the spirit, the Word of God.

Finally, stand firm . . . don't go looking for the battle, the battle will come, and when it does, make sure you're ready. It is clear that you must stand so that you will not be totally distracted by the enemy and continue in the work that God has set before you to do.

God is your commander-in-chief. He has given you instructions on how to prepare for the attack of the enemy.

1. What kinds of attacks do you think you will receive next?
2. How will you react when the next attack of the enemy comes your way?

~

Father, I know that I have a real enemy who wants to destroy my family and me. In Jesus' name, I resist the enemy by the authority of the name of Jesus and by the shed blood of Your Son on the cross. I will choose to walk in victory no matter how bad it may seem because I know that You have overcome all evil. Jesus, You have made me to be more than a conqueror. In Jesus' name, Amen.

Ray Jones
President and Founder
Radiance Ministries, San Antonio, TX

The Faith of a Child

*And he said, "Truly I tell you, unless you change and become like little
children, you will never enter the kingdom of heaven."*
Matthew 18:3 (NIV)

Recently my wife and I were keeping our five-year-old grandson, Judah, during a time when my wife's father was very ill. One day, we asked Judah if he would like to say the blessing before dinner, and he prayed, "Thank You, God, for taking good care of Papa."

We knew that God was indeed taking care of Papa through medical personnel, and many friends and family members, but what we didn't know was that in just a few days God would be taking care of him in the best way possible, by calling him home to live in heaven forever. Those phrases and concepts like "a child-like faith" and "a little child shall lead them" suddenly took on a much deeper meaning!

Is there someone or something that you need God to "take care of"? Do we have the simple "faith of a child" that innocently trusts God's goodness, faithfulness, and love for us? As the old hymn says, "God will take care of you."

God is good. He loves you. Trust Him, believe Him, and thank Him for His care for you.

1. What is it—or who is it—that causes you to worry or lose sleep at night?
2. What do you need to do in order to "let go of it" and trust God with it? Can you—will you—do that very thing today?

~

*Lord, thank You for loving us so much more than we can understand. Help us to accept
Your perfect love even though we can't understand it. Thank You for taking the best possible
care of us. Help me to trust You more with every aspect of my life. In Jesus' name, Amen.*

Randy Kirby
Worship Pastor
First Baptist Church, Simpsonville, SC

Fit for the Master's Use

In a large house there are articles not only of gold and silver, but also of wood
and clay; some are for special purposes and some for common use. Those who
cleanse themselves from the latter will be instruments for special purposes,
made holy, useful to the Master and prepared to do any good work.

2 Timothy 2:20–21 (NIV)

Assigned in the early twelfth century to protect the Holy Land, the Knights Templar fell to Saladin in just a few years. Their armor, supply networks, weaponry, and castle walls were far superior to that of Saladin. Their strength was also bolstered by a firm commitment to purpose and a constant flow of reinforcements. How could such an army fall in such a short time?

The Templar's defeat was attributed to compromise, corruption, decadence, and a breakdown of communication and supply lines that connected the castles. The group became obsessed with power. They moved toward cultural darkness and embraced cultic practices. This "holy" band displayed religious symbols but were corrupt on the inside. Their change of direction and purpose led to disaster. One by one the castles fell at the hands of the Turks. Some castles remain today and serve as reminders that not all defeats come from superior armies. The Templar lost purpose and became consumed with their power and influence, taking their eyes off what they were commissioned to protect.

In Paul's letter to Timothy, he admonishes to guard that which is within. Paul writes that in a great house there are "vessels of gold, silver, wood, clay; some to honor and some to dishonor." He goes on to say that we are to "be a vessel of honor, sanctified and fit for the master's use, prepared for every good work" (2 Tim. 2:20–21 KJV [paraphrased]). We are protectors of the "holy." Our purpose is to guard and display, with integrity, the Truth of our Message. We are to be known for obedience before fashion—truth before packaging—substance before style and conviction before preference.

Today, we face an army much greater than Saladin's. The foe we struggle against is not flesh and blood but the powers of darkness. American culture is pressing against the church to prioritize the consumer ahead of the Exalted Christ. We face the pressures of today's "Have It Your Way" theological practice that pushes a "whatever works" ethos into the life of the church body. The result can lead to compromise and a misplaced focus.

Our purpose is the Great Commission. My prayer is that we will not lose sight of this purpose. It is vital to remind ourselves that the One within—our Master—has called us to "make disciples." May we be vessels of honor that remain "fit for the master's use"—to fulfill our commission.

1. As worshipers, how can "truth" be compromised?
2. How can we focus our purpose to carry out the Great Commission?

⁓

Dear Lord, forgive us when we place style or packaging ahead of biblical
values and mandates. Help us to be diligent in our service and never take
our eyes off of You. Keep us humble and usable for Your glory. Amen.

Jon Duncan
Lead State Missionary of Worship and Music Ministry
Georgia Baptist Mission Board, Duluth, GA

Wait a Minute!

We wait in hope for the LORD; he is our hope and our shield. In him
our hearts rejoice, for we trust in his holy name. May your unfailing
love be with us, LORD, even as we put our hope in you.
Psalm 33:20–22 (NIV)

When we think of the ways that we worship, we immediately think of singing, playing instruments, clapping our hands, lifting our hands, reading God's Word, giving an offering, praying, shouting, and dancing. But there is one way for us to worship that we seldom use: waiting.

In our fast-paced lives, we hate to wait. We hate waiting in traffic. We hate waiting in lines. We hate waiting for the ENTIRE five minutes it takes for our microwave lunch to cook. But in most cases, we have no choice. We may not like it, but we just have to wait.

What about waiting on God? Sometimes, we pray and pray about something and may even begin to think God just isn't listening to us. In some of those cases we might even say, "I'm not waiting. I'll just take care of this myself." We all know how that turns out.

It takes a committed decision from us to say, "Your way is best, Lord. I'll wait on You." That decision is the realization that God is God and we are not. You know what we call that? Worship! Waiting. We hate to do it, but when we tell God that we will put our desires aside to wait on His way, I believe we are showing one of the purest forms of worship we could offer.

1. What past experiences have shown you how to wait on God?
2. What are you doing your way that you need to stop and wait on God?

Father, right now, I desire to worship You by waiting on You. I submit my will to Yours. Help me to be patient as I wait for Your perfect answer and timing. Amen.

Ryan Krivsky
Worship Pastor
Greenwell Springs Baptist Church, Greenwell Springs, LA

Looking at Love

Love is patient and kind; love does not envy or boast; it is not arrogant or rude. It does not insist on its own way; it is not irritable or resentful; it does not rejoice at wrongdoing, but rejoices with the truth.
1 Corinthians 13:4–6 (ESV)

This chapter is aptly titled "The Love Chapter" because it gives a beautiful illustration of what perfect love is all about. We must admit, however, that we fall short when it comes to living out this kind of love daily. I read years ago about a helpful test that will cause us to examine ourselves in light of these verses. First, read these verses out loud as they are written. Then read them again but insert *your name* in place of the word *love* or when the word *love* is implied.

How did it feel to say those altered verses out loud? Does it hurt a bit? The final test is to read these verses again but insert the name "Jesus." His name fits perfectly because Jesus is the embodiment of true love. Therefore, to be more loving, we need more of Jesus and less of ourselves. When we hear the world singing "all we need is love," it should be a reminder to us that what the world really needs is Jesus because it is only His love that can transform the human heart.

1. Think of the latest situation when you were not patient or kind and consider how Jesus would have responded.
2. We are very quick to notice when others don't practice love to us, but think of ways we can become more sensitive to times when we don't show love to others.

～

Father, we thank You for sending Jesus to show us how to love. Help us to be transformed by Your Spirit to love others as He did, especially when it may be difficult to do so naturally.

Clay Layfield
Associate Pastor, Music and Senior Adults
First Baptist Church, Eastman, GA

Open Our Eyes

And Elisha prayed, "Open his eyes, LORD, so that he may see."
2 Kings 6:17a (NIV)

God had been giving Elisha the plans of the king of Aram. Elisha shared that information with the king of Israel. The king of Aram sent his army to capture Elisha. The next morning Elisha's servant walked outside and saw they were surrounded by an army. He was afraid. Then Elisha told his servant not to be afraid because there "are more with us than against us." He asked God to open the eyes of his servant so he could see. God opened his eyes and he saw the army of the Lord. I'm pretty sure he wasn't afraid anymore.

One thing I noticed is that there is always more going on that we don't see with our own eyes. When we come together to worship, there is a spiritual battle that is raging all around us. Satan and his followers are always trying to interfere when the church worships. How many times do we find ourselves acting like Elisha's servant? How often do we live in fear?

I also noticed that Elisha could already see what his servant could not. Elisha knew that God's army was there. That is why he had the confidence to ask God to open the eyes of his servant. The army, however, was never called into action. Instead, Elisha showed God's love and compassion. Not a soul was killed and the army of Aram stopped raiding Israel's territory. Read the rest of the passage to see what happened.

1. Close your eyes. Picture your church. If God were to open your eyes, what do you believe you would see?
2. How can we approach worship with the confidence of Elisha?

~

Father, open my heart and my eyes so that I can be more aware of how You are always working in my life. Help me to live with power and understanding that can only come from You. Then, may I show love and compassion to those who are against me, so that You will be glorified in my life and in theirs. Amen.

Chip Leake
Worship Pastor
Thompson Station Church, Thompson's Station, TN

Five Priorities for Music Ministry

I will bless the LORD at all times; His praise shall continually be in my mouth.
Psalm 34:1 (NKJV)

I have been a worship pastor for more than thirty years. Every year, as we start a new season of ministry, I share with my choir and worship teams these five priorities:

1. *Priority of Wholehearted Worship:* We are not performers, but we are worship leaders. We exist to lead others into worship. God calls us to be worshipers at all times.

2. *Priority of Holy Living:* I will honor the Lord with the way I live . . . on stage and off. Our lives should be a declaration of God's living presence in us.

3. *Priority of Humility:* We are not competitors, but we are co-laborers with Christ. This is a hard one for musicians. We have been trained our entire musical life to compete for the spotlight. Remember, God sets Himself against the proud but gives grace to the humble.

4. *Priority of Prayer:* We need to be people of prayer—praying for the church and praying for each other—as we bear one another's burdens. We also should pray that God will use us for His glory, and that His presence will bring hope and encouragement to His people through us.

5. *Priority of Faithful Service:* We serve as the worship leaders of our church. We use our musical gifts and talents to welcome people into the very presence of God. We must be faithful to our calling as worship leaders.

1. What is the difference between leading in worship and performing worship music?
2. If everyone in this ministry was as committed to this as I am, how effective would we be?

~

Lord Jesus, I praise You today that You are a faithful God. I want Your priorities to become my priorities. Lord, have Your way in me this day. Amen.

Ron Cochran
Former Executive and Music Pastor
Portland Christian Center, Portland, OR

I Believe ... Help My Unbelief

"How can I know this?' Zechariah asked the angel. 'For I am
an old man, and my wife is well along in years.'"
Luke 1:18 (CSB)

Zechariah and Elizabeth were good and righteous people. Earlier on in this chapter, it is said that they walked blamelessly in all the commandments of the Lord. They desired to have a child and had probably been praying for quite some time that God would allow them to have a child. Yet, Zechariah doubted.

He didn't believe the angel's proclamation that they would be parents! The physical reality that they were old and past childbearing years was reason enough for him not to believe. Even in the very presence of an angel sent directly from God, he doubted.

I see myself in Zechariah. I'm ashamed to admit that I have doubted God. I have found it easy to believe God for the bigger promises such as the promise of salvation, grace, forgiveness, and love. Where I struggle is in the everyday things and in the daily grind of life. For example, the unexpected bill that I wasn't prepared for or the doctor's diagnosis that came out of left field; those are what get to me.

It is in these times I have learned to remind myself that God *promised* to never leave me; He *promised* that nothing is too hard for Him, and He *promised* that all things are working together for my good and for His glory.

1. Rest in God's promises and stop doubting. Believe Him. Trust Him. Pray and ask Him to reassure you of His promises to you and of His love for you.
2. What is it that is causing you to doubt God's love and faithfulness?

A simple prayer to pray in this situation is this: "Lord, I believe, help my unbelief."

Robert Maddox
Worship and Missions Pastor
Spotswood Baptist Church, Fredericksburg, VA

Hocus Pocus

Now when the apostles in Jerusalem heard that Samaria had received the word of God, they sent them Peter and John, who came down and prayed for them that they might receive the Holy Spirit. For He had not yet fallen upon any of them; they had simply been baptized in the name of the Lord Jesus. Then they began laying their hands on them, and they were receiving the Holy Spirit. Now when Simon saw that the Spirit was bestowed through the laying on of the apostles' hands, he offered them money, saying, "Give this authority to me as well, so that everyone on whom I lay my hands may receive the Holy Spirit." But Peter said to him, "May your silver perish with you, because you thought you could obtain the gift of God with money! You have no part or portion in this matter, for your heart is not right before God."
Acts 8:14–21 (NASB, emphasis added)

As the early church began spreading, Philip departed to Samaria preaching and performing miracles (vv. 5–8). These miracles caught the attention of a popular local magician named Simon. After witnessing the Holy Spirit enter believers through the apostles, Simon offered money to receive that same power. Peter vehemently denied him (vv. 20–21). Just like Simon assumed the power of God and praise of man could be purchased, every worship leader can be swayed to the same conclusion.

The temptation is thinking that our talent/technology is like some magic potion drumming up God's power. Let's be honest, if songs and media are performed "on cue" with excellence, impressing the masses, wouldn't God be as well? Like Simon, we can spiritualize sin (v. 19), "sharing our gift" on a platform when, honestly, we just crave attention. Any one musician who holds a microphone, sings in choir, or plays an instrument should guard against men's applause; it robs Jesus of the glory He alone deserves, and twists true spiritual worship.

No musical presentation, audio, video, or lighting display is of any value to Jesus, apart from His Spirit's leading. Like the hymn states, "all is vain unless the Spirit of the Holy One comes down." It's only when the Spirit of God works that true transformational worship occurs. Remember Zechariah 4:6, "'Not by might nor by power, but by my Spirit,' says the LORD Almighty" (NIV).

1. How can we pursue musical/media excellence before God, without putting our trust in man's efforts?
2. What is the best way to prepare our hearts and worship experiences so that God might show His power?

～

Heavenly Father, it's only You who changes the hearts of men. Help me to not trust in talent or technology. Jesus, You grew in wisdom, stature, and favor with both God and man. Help me to do the same for Your glory alone. In Jesus' powerful name, Amen.

Mark Maier
Pastor of Worship
First Baptist Church, Rogers, AR

In the Sanctuary

Until I went into the sanctuary of God.
Psalm 73:17a (ESV)

Take a moment and read the entire 73rd Psalm. This psalm is the fascinating testimony of Asaph, a worship leader during the reign of King David and King Solomon. Asaph found himself surrounded by unbelievers who were living sin-filled lives and seemingly getting everything they wanted. Not only that, they even mocked the one true God. At a low point, Asaph admits, "All in vain have I kept my heart clean" (v. 13). How sad to think that this man who had served in ministry for most of his life was now questioning if it was even worth it.

The turning point of Asaph's perspective is verse 17. From this point, it seems like we're reading the words of a different person. This man, who was ready to give up, was changed as he worshiped the Lord.

By verse 26, Asaph is more confident than ever that his God is the true God. "God is the strength of my heart and my portion forever." By the last verse, he is ready to minister once again, "I have made the Lord God my refuge, *that I may tell of all your works*" (v. 28).

Only God can change someone's outlook in an instant. I'm convinced that there are people just like Asaph in the room every time we gather to worship. People who are struggling. People who are questioning their faith . . . or who've never believed. It's the music ministry that they encounter first! What an amazing thought that God would use you and me to be a part of someone's defining moment like this.

1. When was the last time worship changed your perspective in a moment?
2. Does thinking about a worship service through the lens of Psalm 73 change the way you prepare?

~

Father, we recognize and celebrate Your power to change lives. May we approach every worship gathering with an expectancy for You to change us and draw us closer to You. Amen.

Cliff Duren
Arranger, Worship Pastor
First Baptist Church, Woodstock, GA

In the Grip of Grace

For I am persuaded that neither death nor life, nor angels nor principalities nor powers,
nor things present nor things to come, nor height nor depth, nor any other created thing,
shall be able to separate us from the love of God which is in Christ Jesus our Lord.

Romans 8:38–39 (NKJV)

I am, at my very core, a chump! If you are honest and transparent, I believe you will admit that you, also, are a chump. As a matter of fact, Scripture tells us that "our righteousness are like filthy rags" (Isa. 64:6 NKJV). So, clearly God doesn't love me because of what I bring to the table! He loves me because He created me and called me to be His child.

Oftentimes, we find ourselves in troubling situations. Sometimes these are of our own creation, sometimes they are brought on by the decisions of others, still other times they are the result of living in a fallen world. It is comforting to know that no matter the circumstance, God is faithful to His children. His enduring love is not changed by height, nor depth, nor any created thing!

Because of my acceptance of God's gift of salvation, I know I am His child. As such, I can trust in His love, His mercy, and His grace no matter the situation in which I find myself. God's love for us is not contingent upon our behavior or circumstance. Because of His steadfast love, we should strive to live in such a way that brings honor to Him all the while knowing that even when we fall, there is nothing that can separate us from the love of God that is in Christ Jesus!

1. Realizing God's love and grace is unchanging, how does it affect my daily action?
2. How does it change the way I show grace to others?

~

Father, thank You for Your great gift of salvation and never-ending
love. Thank You that Your generous grace exceeds my need. Help me to
live my life in such a way that others will be drawn to You.

Kenneth Martin
Minister of Music and Worship
First Baptist Church, Milton, FL

Creation's Praise

All you have made will thank you, Lord; the faithful will bless you.
Psalm 145:10 (csb)

On a Saturday morning in spring, I was walking through the woods near my home. At one point, a dead tree caught my eye. It was taller than the green trees around it, and its branches were high, close to the trunk, and pointing upward. Against the clear blue sky, the tree seemed to stand in solemn silence, lifting praise to God in an endless liturgy.

That one glimpse helped me see again that all creation is God's temple, quietly but constantly reminding us that He is here; He is great beyond our imaginations; He is love; He lavishes Himself upon us, holding nothing back.

When I look at creation and believe that He shaped it all for His purpose, I realize I am surrounded by many liturgies to God. Each tells us about Him in ways that are more universal, more lasting, and more tangible than human language. I look into the night sky and am awestruck by His vastness. I swing through the round of day and night, season after season and experience His unchanging faithfulness. Water drops to endless oceans paint Him as a fountain of rich, unbounded life, and every breath I take reminds me that He shared His eternal life, Himself, with me.

Creation reminds me that the purest faith, the most profound prayer, the deepest worship we offer God is not expressed in words. Such prayer is expressed in being and doing. It is not heard in church services or read in books. It is seen in the faithful lives of His people, living *for* God and *in* God day after day, age after age.

1. What can I praise God for today?
2. How can I praise God in a new way as I worship?

~

Heavenly Father, I want to be a part of that prayer. I want my whole life to sing, trust, praise, and love You faithfully and constantly forever and ever.

Chris Mason
Worship Pastor
First Baptist Church, Arnold, MO

WEEK 23—SATURDAY
Time

"[However, this kind does not come out except by prayer and fasting.]"
Matthew 17:21 (HCSB)

During my college days, I started a little routine at the end of every semester that became a precious time to get alone with God. On the day of my last semester exam, my wife Donnita would help me pack a little red and blue gym bag with enough clothes for two or three days. As soon as I finished the last exam, I would drive directly from school down to the Arbuckle Mountains, where I had reserved a room at our state youth campground. It was a precious time.

No television, no telephone, no people—just God and me. I would take my Bible and walk out into the hills where I had found a beautiful place by a little stream that ran through the middle of the encampment. There, I would talk to God, meditate on His Word and allow the Holy Spirit to recharge my batteries.

I have become intensely aware that I must spend more time in prayer if I am going to be the worship leader God wants me to be. Vance Havner said, "The devil is in constant conspiracy against a preacher who really prays, for it has been said that what a minister is in his prayer closet is what he is, no more, no less."[15] It is the height of arrogance to think that we can do God's work without God's power—and that power comes only by prayer.

1. How often do you get alone with God for extended times of fellowship with Him in prayer?
2. How dependent are you on prayer for the success of your ministry?

~

Dear Father, remind me that the work You have called me to do is not accomplished by might or power, but by the Spirit of God. Forgive me for relying on talent, skill, experience, and organization. Help me today to make prayer the priority in my life and ministry.

Dr. Gary Mathena
Director of Practica
Liberty University, Lynchburg, VA

The Power of Music

*I lift up my eyes to the mountains—where does my help come from? My
help comes from the Lord, the Maker of heaven and earth.*
Psalm 121:1–2 (NIV)

It's incredible how the power of music can kickstart our hearts and minds to remember
the greatness of our God.

Back in 2017, when the Sutherland, Texas, church shooting took place, there were an
overwhelming number of news reports covering the tragedy. One particular story focused
on an outdoor, community-wide prayer service held on the Monday evening after the
Sunday massacre. What was initially hard to comprehend was the fact that people were
singing. They sang, "What a beautiful Name . . . What a wonderful Name . . . What a
powerful Name . . . the Name of Jesus!"[16]

In those moments of heartache and despair, they were worshiping God. As they worshiped, there were tears shed, hands raised to heaven, and people embracing one another
in unity. Like the lyrics of the song, their singing was beautiful, wonderful, and powerful.
It certainly didn't erase the tragedy that occurred, but it brought them closer to God and
closer to one another. It gave them hope that healing could happen. It gave them strength
to carry on as they faced multiple funerals in the days to come.

Every time we gather to sing, it is beautiful, wonderful, and powerful. It draws us
closer to God and to one another. It offers us, and others, healing, strength, hope, and above
all else, it honors God.

1. What is your go-to song when life is difficult?
2. How does singing songs of praise give you a better perspective on your situation?

⁓

*Lord, thank You for the incredible gift of music. Thank You that, when trouble
surrounds us, and we are without words of our own, words of praise lifted
to You in song bring glory to Your name and healing to our hearts.*

David Butler
Worship Pastor
First Baptist Church, St. Charles, MO

My Passion for the Closeness of God

Draw near to God and He will draw near to you.
James 4:8a (NKJV)

We lived 0.7 miles from the door of the church to the door of our house. Half of the distance was the church parking lot. Following a Sunday morning of worship leading, I was going to take two of our daughters home while my wife took our infant home. Jodi (age 4) and Jessica (age 6) came from their Sunday school classes and jumped into the front seat with both wanting to sit next to me.

I admired the love, but after some pushing and shoving, I said, "Girls, girls, what would Jesus say to you about two people wanting the same thing?"

Jodi, in her second-born, peace-making, innocent, and repentant heart said, "I guess Jesus would tell me to let Jessica have the middle seat."

"Good, Jodi," I said. "That's what Jesus would say, I'm sure." "Jessica," I continued, now that I was on a spiritual-father-of-the-year roll, "what would Jesus say to you?"

"Well," Jessica replied, "if Jesus told Jodi that I should have the middle seat, then I guess I should have the middle seat!"

Not the best answer, but after clearing up that theology, I did reflect on the joy I felt seeing their deep desire to be close to me. Do I awaken each day with the desire and then the discipline to be close to Jesus? Do we seek after Jesus with all that we are? As a worship leader, we can't give what is not inside. We can't lead people to God in our singing if we are not close to Him in our living!

1. Right now, do I have a passion to draw closer to God?
2. If I do, what actions must I take to intentionally carry out this discipline?

~

*God, give me a passion to draw near to You. Help me lay down other
things in my life so that I take the time to be close to You. Amen!*

Dr. Gary Matthews
Pastor of Worship and the Arts
Christ Memorial Church, Holland, MI

Getting to Know Jesus

I want to know Christ and the power of his resurrection and the
sharing of his sufferings by becoming like him in his death.
Philippians 3:10 (NRSV)

L et us imagine that we are the closest friends Jesus has. We join Him in a garden for prayer. He leaves us for a while, praying in agony for deliverance from death. He returns, and we are asleep. He says, "So, could you not stay awake with me one hour? Stay awake and pray that you may not come into the time of trial; the spirit indeed is willing, but the flesh is weak" (Matt. 26:40–41 NRSV).

The power of the resurrection is great, but suffering really hurts. I need Jesus to join me in my deep places. But more so, I need to join Jesus in His deep places. It's so much easier to sleep. Ministry can be habitual and exhausting, people can be needy, sacrifice can be inconvenient, and death can be so . . . disruptive.

1. Is my goal to know Christ?
2. Do I honestly desire to be conformed to His death?

~

Dear Father, have my will show Your will so that I may know You better and love You deeper
through Your Son, our Lord Jesus Christ. Keep me awake and spare me from the time of trial.
And if You call me to the trial, help me endure by the power of the Holy Spirit. Amen.

Ronald A. Matthews, DMA
President
Eastern University, St. David's, PA

A Volunteer vs. a Calling

*That day David first **appointed** Asaph and his associates to give praise to the LORD in this manner: Give praise to the LORD, proclaim his name; make known among the nations what he has done. Sing to him, sing praise to him; tell of all his wonderful acts.*
1 Chronicles 16:7–9 (NIV, emphasis added)

It is clear throughout the Bible that God "appoints and anoints" worship leaders to serve as musicians. We must have a sense of calling on our lives to serve in music that is decidedly different from a volunteer community chorus, the PTA, Little League, etc.

Are you a volunteer or do you have a calling? Consider these statements as you answer.

Volunteers give up what they believe belongs to THEM (time, finances, etc.) to serve the organization. Called worship leaders are giving what they know belongs to GOD; He gave them their talent and love for musical worship in the first place.

Volunteers look at their schedule to see if their service *fits* their personal agenda. Called worship leaders adjust their schedule and personal agenda to *fulfill* their calling.

Volunteers seek to help and serve the cause of the organization or, sometimes, the leader of the organization. Called worship leaders are serving one person—Jesus Christ.

Volunteers move on to other activities when organizational change occurs or difficulties arise. Called worship leaders remain faithful to their calling no matter what.

Volunteers receive the satisfaction of knowing that they "did their part." Called worship leaders receive the deep spiritual blessing that only comes from being obedient to the call of God on their life.

1. Do I need to renew my calling as a worshiping musician?
2. Do I behave as a volunteer or as a committed and called worshiper?

~

O God, remind me each time I lift my voice to sing, or move my hands to play an instrument, that this is a gift and calling from You that deserves my very best.

Keith Ferguson
Associate Pastor, Worship Arts
First Baptist Church, Carrollton, TX

The Song of the Redeemed

But I will sing of your strength; I will sing aloud of your steadfast love in the morning. For you have been to me a fortress and a refuge in the day of my distress. O my Strength, I will sing praises to you, for you, O God, are my fortress, the God who shows me steadfast love.

Psalm 59:16–17 (ESV)

The other day I had a church member say to me, "I don't think I have a great voice, so I just don't sing." This was not the first person to ever say that to me and won't be the last. Often times, we can fall prey to thinking that because we may not be able to sing at a certain level of proficiency, we should refrain from doing so at all. But as believers, we have a song to sing, the song of the redeemed!

One worship leader writes, "The question isn't, *do you have a voice?* The question is, *do you have a song?* If you've turned from your sins and trusted in the finished work of Christ, if you're forgiven and reconciled to God, then you have a song. It's a song of the redeemed, of those who have been rescued from the righteous wrath of God through the cross of Jesus Christ and are now called His friends."[17]

As those who have been redeemed, we have the greatest song of all—the song of gratitude and praise for the Lord's grace and mercy toward us! Therefore, let us daily lift up thanksgiving and worship in response to the salvation we have through our Savior, Jesus Christ.

1. Take time to thank the Lord today for saving you and giving you a new song to sing.
2. Read through the passage above and put your name in the place of "I" or "me."

~

Most gracious Father, thank You for extending Your grace and mercy toward me and giving me a new song to sing. Help me to show gratitude daily for Your steadfast love and kindness, and to extend that grace to others. You are my refuge and strength. Amen.

Joshua McClain
Worship and Music Pastor
Central Baptist Church, Warner Robins, GA

Feast on the Lord

Oh, taste and see that the LORD is good!
Psalm 34:8a (ESV)

Growing up, we always had Thanksgiving lunch at my grandparents' house. Homemade applesauce was in abundance. Freshly carved turkey was on hand. Deviled eggs were a must. Mashed potatoes and gravy were a staple, followed by pecan and pumpkin pies. Is your mouth watering yet? Mine definitely is. The food was great, and the table looked as good as the food tasted. My grandparents knew how to set the banquet table for the family to come and feast.

The question comes: What are you feasting on? There are many things that can gain our attention. Maybe it is too much Facebook or working on cars in the garage all day. It could be that your eyes are looking at things they should not. Perhaps you feast on food to the point that it is an idol. Maybe your *feast* is sports.

Loved ones, the psalmist exhorts us to taste and see that the Lord is good. Jesus is better than anything. Period! Jonathan Edwards, the great American theologian, said about Jesus and His saving grace, that, "once you taste of the honeycomb you want nothing else." The woman at the well feasted on things other than the satisfying joy of Jesus Christ. Jesus invited her to drink of the soul-quenching living water that wells up to eternal life.

Feast on the Word day and night (Ps. 1). Set your mind, heart, and affections on the Savior. Drink of God's goodness displayed in His Son Jesus Christ, the atoning sacrifice for our sins, who gives to us life eternal. May you taste and see the Lord's goodness to you today.

1. How much time do you feast on the Word? What occupies most of your time on a given day?
2. What steps can you take this week to help you know God's goodness more fully?

~

Gracious God, I thank You for Your goodness in Your Son. I praise You for Your care for me. I praise You for Your faithfulness. Help me this day to taste and see that You are good. Amen.

Keith McMinn
Pastor of Worship
Bethel Baptist Church, Yorktown, VA

Perfect Peace

You will keep in perfect peace those whose minds are steadfast, because they trust in you.
Isaiah 26:3 (NIV)

D uring the Christmas season, as we proclaim "peace," we often recognize that there is a difference between "peace" and "*perfect* peace." As we sing about the "Prince of Peace," we long for "perfect peace." Like Henry W. Longfellow, who wrote the lyrics of "I Heard the Bells on Christmas Day" during the Civil War, we may agree that perfect peace seems impossible. *"For hate is strong and mocks the song, of peace on earth . . ."*

It's still so true! Our headlines are disparaging, and the reality of war and hate among nations continually hits close to home. However, something unseen seemed to nudge Longfellow's writing: *"Then rang the bells more loud and deep, God is not dead nor does He sleep . . . The wrong shall fail, the right prevail, with peace on earth, goodwill to men."* How can we more fully experience God's perfect peace?

1. Perfect peace comes when we acknowledge that God is all-sufficient. "And my God shall supply all your need according to His riches in glory by Christ Jesus" (Phil. 4:19 NKJV).

2. Perfect peace comes with the confident knowledge that our lives are in God's hands (Ps. 31:15).

3. Perfect peace comes from knowing that God is *always* with us. He is fully aware of every detail in our lives. Pamela Dowd once stated, "God sent a star to light the night for . . . the Prince of Peace. God has given us all the light we will ever need to find *peace* on earth."

1. What is causing me to feel restless or troubled during this season?
2. What steps can I take to experience God's perfect peace today?

〜

Lord, help me to listen anew to the song the angels still sing, "Peace on earth, good will to men!" Help me to rest in the perfect peace that only comes from You. Amen.

Dr. James L. Melton
Chair, Department of Music
Vanguard University, Costa Mesa, CA

Perspective Is Everything

In the year that King Uzziah died, I saw the Lord.
Isaiah 6:1a (NKJV)

We come to church for many reasons: Scripture commands it; parents require it; reputations depend on it; childcare is free. Not all of these are bad reasons, but what is the main reason to come to church? I believe Isaiah gives us the proper perspective regarding worship, regardless of our circumstances.

Isaiah saw the Lord in the year that the king died. This was not a joyful time; it was a season of devastating loss. Even in the most difficult of times, however, Isaiah's eyes were lifted. If we are truly worshiping God, He will be the center of our focus. If we are looking to Him, all other things line up and fall into place.

To See God—This should be our ultimate goal every time we worship. Getting a glimpse of the King on His throne changes everything about our perspective. I love the heart cry from these lyrics, "Open the eyes of my heart, Lord. I want to see you, I want to see You."

To See Myself—Only when I see God first can I get a proper perspective of myself. Isaiah saw God in all of His glory and then he saw himself for what he really was. "Woe to me, I am ruined" (Isa. 6:5, paraphrased). When compared to God's greatness, I realize how wretched I really am. Only by God's grace am I allowed into His presence. I don't deserve an audience with the King of kings. Jesus made a way where there was no way.

To See Others—God's question to Isaiah was, "Whom shall I send?" (Isa. 6:8). His answer to God was, "Here am I. Send me!" When we have an elevated view of God and a humble view of ourselves, then we see the world the way God desires us to see it. The result of my worship will be a life on mission for God.

1. When I come to church, am I desiring to see anything or anyone more than God?
2. Is my worship lifestyle resulting in others coming to know Christ?

~

Lord, help me see You, myself, and others in the right order.

Jason Breland
Worship Pastor
Immanuel Baptist Church, Little Rock, AR

Where Are You Aiming?

So whether we are at home or away, we make it our aim to please him.
2 Corinthians 5:9 (ESV)

A musician in the orchestra will wait for a glance from the conductor to get their approval. An employee might work extra hard to finish a job early or go an extra mile to get the approval from their boss. There are many times throughout your life that you make it your goal or aim to please someone. When my kids are playing sports, riding their bikes, or hitting a ball, they will always glance my way to make sure I'm watching. They want to please me. They want more than anything to make me proud of them.

In our walk with Christ, Paul reminds us that we must make it our aim, our goal, to please only our heavenly Father. Too many times we make it our aim to please only those around us. Aiming to please God takes daily focus and determination, but our ultimate goal should be to only please God.

1. Do you need to realign your focus or aim?
2. Are you trying to please someone other than God?

~

Father, please forgive me when I aim to only please others and not You.
Search me and know my heart, lead me in the way everlasting. Help me
today in making my aim to please You. In Jesus' name, Amen.

Jason Millsaps
Pastor of Music and Worship
Bell Shoals Baptist Church, Brandon, FL

Surprise!

I lift my eyes to the hills. From where does my help come? My help comes from the LORD, who made heaven and earth. He will not let your foot be moved; he who keeps you will not slumber.

Psalm 121:1–3 (ESV)

Some people love surprises. But there are, sometimes, surprises that are bad and blindside us, leaving us bewildered and sometimes very alone and dejected. The loss of a job, a loved one, or finding out that you have a terminal illness is something that often confounds and can be very shocking. Everyone handles these situations differently, but there is one person that's never surprised at our circumstances.

God is not surprised! He knows and is right there with us. He is our strength, our help, our comfort, and our solid rock and never sleeps. He knows what's coming our way and He's already got our back. So much so that the Scripture says, "He will not let your foot be moved."

So remember, when that "surprise" comes your way, you've already defeated the enemy. Breathe deep, take a step back, look to the hills and call out His name. He will give comfort, rest, and a peace that passes all understanding.

1. Can you think of times when you have been surprised?
2. How did you handle situations that seemed to blindside you?

~

Dear God, I pray that each moment of each day I would cast my gaze to You, the maker of heaven and earth. When life brings those challenging surprises, I will trust You and know that You are never surprised and know what the future holds. Amen.

Loren Minnick Jr.
Associate Pastor—Worship
Foothills Baptist Church, Las Vegas, NV

Does Jesus Care?

*Praise be to the God and Father of our Lord Jesus Christ, the Father of compassion
and the God of all comfort, who comforts us in all our troubles, so that we can
comfort those in any trouble with the comfort we ourselves receive from God.*
2 Corinthians 1:3–4 (NIV)

Does Jesus care when my heart is pained too deeply for mirth and song?
Frank Graeff wrote the hymn, "Does Jesus Care" in 1901, and it has been widely published over the last century. Recently, the song was brought to my attention during a conversation that I was having with my dad. You see, he was asked to sing this for a funeral service and was really struggling to keep his composure as he rehearsed the song.

"I just can't get through it," he said with a quiver in his voice.

After almost ten years of caring for my mom through her journey with dementia, his wife of fifty-three years was now in residential hospice care, nearing the end of her life and unable to communicate. *"Does Jesus care when I've said good-bye to the dearest on earth to me, and my sad heart aches till it nearly breaks . . ."* The lyrics were closer than ever.

And still, the swelling affirmation of the chorus consoled the most tender part of his wounded spirit: *"Oh, yes, He cares; I know He cares, His heart is touched with my grief."*

My dad persevered and was able to minister to those who attended the funeral service with both empathy and hope. It was diligent rehearsal that enabled him to internalize the message of this song and then effectively communicate it to others.

1. Can you remember a song that you struggled to "get through"?
2. How can you be more intentional to internalize the message of the songs you present?

*Lord, even during our rehearsal, use our songs to touch the
lives of those who need Your comfort today.*

Jonathan Ford
Minister of Worship and Arts
Forcey Bible Church, Silver Spring, MD

Move

"Perhaps the LORD will act in our behalf. Nothing can hinder
the LORD from saving, whether by many or by few."
1 Samuel 14:6b (NIV)

First Samuel 14 tells a great story that is full of suspense and ultimate victory. The story tells us that King Saul had been mentally paralyzed as a result of the situation in which the Israelite army found themselves, and he was sleeping under a pomegranate tree not doing anything.

On the other hand, young Jonathan decided that he had had enough, and the narrative tells us that Jonathan leaned over to his armor-bearer and said, "Let's go up to those Philistines and PERHAPS the Lord will move on our behalf."

Notice here what Jonathan did not say. He did not say, "The Lord has told me to go up to the Philistines and He will deliver our people." Jonathan did not know if the Lord would move or not, but he did know a couple of things.

First, he knew that God had made a covenant with His people and that God had been faithful to deliver, protect, and provide for His people. He knew the stories of God's saving acts through history, and He knew that God was a person of His Word.

The next thing he knew is that if they stayed in that valley, they were going to be killed. So, sitting under the pomegranate tree, sulking with his father, was not an option. If he was going to die anyway, he might as well go down with a fight.

1. I want to ask you what has hindered you from making a move? Have you been paralyzed because of your bad decisions? Are you stuck surrounded by your enemies (both physical and spiritual) because you have convinced yourself there is nothing you can do?
2. Or are you the young Jonathan ready at all costs to do something? Tired of sitting around waiting on something to happen?

～

Lord, give us the courage to make decisions to move as we trust in You. Help us to see
the world around us in need and make a move to bring healing and wholeness.

Brad Moffett
Director of Graduate Studies / Professor of Music
Lee University, Cleveland, TN

Priceless Treasure

*How can a young man keep his way pure? By keeping it according to Your word. With
all my heart I have sought You; Do not let me wander from Your commandments.
Your word I have treasured in my heart, that I may not sin against You.*
Psalm 119: 9–11 (NASB)

When I was in middle school, our church called a new minister for students and
music. Yes, that was a very long time ago. However, I still vividly remember many
of the things I learned under his teaching. He consistently emphasized that memorizing
Scripture was a key part of God's molding and shaping us into who He wanted us to be and
that having passages of Scripture in our memories would help us in our day-to-day lives.

Almost every time we got together as a group we would work on Scripture memory,
and almost every time I saw him, he would ask me what God was teaching me through His
Word. He made Scripture memory a priority for us. Psalm 119:9–11 was one of the first
passages we memorized.

When we miss a meal or two, we get hungry and find something to eat. The same
should be true with God's Word. Jesus said in Matthew 4:4, "It is written, 'Man shall not
live on bread alone, but on every word that proceeds out of the mouth of God.'" Don't
allow yourself to get so busy in the day-to-day "got to get it done" list that you are robbed
of the priceless treasure of God's Word.

1. What is the last Scripture passage you memorized?
2. Is spending time in God's Word a priority for you? Take time today to commit
   this or another passage to memory.

*Thank You, Father, for guiding us through Your Word. Help us to treasure it and
memorize it. Give us the strength to live in a way that causes others to see You.*

Michael Moore
Associate Pastor of Music, Media and Communication
Sarasota Baptist Church, Lakewood Ranch, Sarasota, FL

Thank You!

In everything give thanks; for this is God's will for you in Christ Jesus.
1 Thessalonians 5:18 (NASB)

Growing up in the South, you were always expected to say "thank you" when anyone did anything for you, said anything nice about you, or offered you something, even if you did not want it! I remember my parents telling me to say it even if I did not mean it because it was the polite thing to do. It was just a part of the "Southern Hospitality" culture.

God wants us to say "thank you" too, but with the expectation that the words come from a thankful heart.

During a particularly difficult time in our lives, my wife, Suzette, and I sat down and began to write on a yellow legal pad all the things we were thankful for. It did not take too long until we had several pages filled. Doing that helped us take our eyes off of our circumstances and keep our focus on God. It helped us to remember that we serve a mighty God who is in control regardless of our situation. It did not change the circumstances, but it changed the way we responded and enabled us to see how God was working.

A thankful heart will overflow to others. As people who represent Christ, we have the opportunity and responsibility to encourage and build others up. Saying "thank you" is a great way to start.

1. Who are some people that you are thankful for?
2. Why don't you take time today to drop them a note or make a phone call to let them know you are thankful for them?

~

Father, thank You for loving us and for caring for us. Open our eyes to those You place around us who need encouragement and guide us in the words we say.

Michael Moore
Associate Pastor of Music, Media and Communication
Sarasota Baptist Church, Lakewood Ranch, Sarasota, FL

Teamwork

Jonathan said to the young man who carried his armor, "Come, let us go over to the garrison of these uncircumcised. It may be that the LORD will work for us, for nothing can hinder the LORD from saving by many or by few." And his armor-bearer said to him, "Do all that is in your heart. Do as you wish. Behold, I am with you heart and soul.". . . Then Jonathan climbed up on his hands and feet, and his armor-bearer after him. And they fell before Jonathan, and his armor-bearer killed them after him.

1 Samuel 14:6–7, 13 (ESV)

Jonathan and his armor-bearer were going up against a whole garrison, twenty trained Philistine soldiers! The odds were 10–1. But they had a plan! They trusted the Lord; they trusted each other, and they had prepared. Notice how the armor-bearer responded! "Do all that is in your heart, I am with you heart and soul." He was ready! As they went into battle, Jonathan knocked them down, making them vulnerable, and exposing their weaknesses.

The armor-bearer finished them off with the kill shot! The armor-bearer didn't stab Jonathan in the back or run off and leave him exposed to a fatal attack. Jonathan did not duck and run on the armor-bearer or leave him exposed to attack from the enemy. He probably didn't even check to see if the job had been completed—he knew it would be! They took out the "whole" garrison. They took out twenty trained Philistines!

Godly teamwork is powerful! But like *any* relationship, it takes a lot of work, a lot of faith, a lot of trust and a lot of love. As powerful as this is with your team or ensemble, I think it is even *greater* with your spouse!

1. How can I better serve as an armor-bearer?
2. As a leader, do I trust and enable the armor-bearers God has given me?

Lord, help me be a faithful team member, to stand in faith and protect my leaders. As a leader, may I trust You and have the courage to do the things You have told me to do in leading Your people well. In Jesus' name, Amen.

Dr. Steve Bowersox
Chair, Department of Worship and Technology and Assistant Professor of Worship
University of Mobile, Mobile, AL

He Gives Me Rest

"Come to me, all who labor and are heavy laden, and I will give you rest."
Matthew 11:28 (ESV)

Rest is a fundamental part of life, and it is the counterpart to everything we do. It was designed by God and based off His image. In Genesis, God created and then on the seventh day, He rested. However, the verse in Matthew is gleaning a different understanding of the word *rest*. The rest that God is offering is not physical, but spiritual.

"For You made us for Yourself, and our heart is restless, until it rests in You."
—Augustine

The rest we find in our Creator when we align ourselves with His heart goes beyond any benefit we could gain from bodily rest. In fact, even when we cannot find rest for our body, our soul can find rest in the promise of God's faithfulness and in the steadfastness of His character.

If rest is the counterpart for everything we do, and God is everything we are, then, naturally, our soul must find its rest in the Almighty God.

1. What does "soul rest" feel like, in comparison to bodily rest?
2. What are the strongholds in my life that keep me from finding rest for my soul?

~

Search me, O God, and give me eyes to see Your faithfulness as it conquers my strongholds. Help me rest in the promise of who You are, and how You love me.

Austin Neal
Worship Pastor
Champion Forest Baptist Church, Jersey Village, TX

A Life Verse for Authentic Worship

*I appeal to you therefore, brothers, by the mercies of God, to present your bodies as a
living sacrifice, holy and acceptable to God, which is your spiritual worship. Do not be
conformed to this world, but be transformed by the renewal of your mind, that by testing
you may discern what is the will of God, what is good and acceptable and perfect.*
Romans 12:1–2 (ESV)

True, authentic worship is only expressed with the knowledge of who God is, the sacrifice made (on our behalf) by Jesus on the cross and the understanding of His role in our lives as Lord. It is only available because of the mercies of God for us. In other words, our worship has little to do with our abilities and everything to do with His mercies. What is a living sacrifice? The Old Covenant demanded animal sacrifices; the New Covenant was instituted with the shed blood of Jesus as the ultimate and final sacrifice. Our lives are to be lived in an aspect of complete surrender to the Savior's will and not our own. Our spiritual worship (lifestyle) is enacted in our transformation, not conformity.

Our lives and worship are transformed by renewal in Scripture daily. That is to say, treasuring His Word in our hearts that we may not sin against Him (Ps. 119:11). God's Word, treasured (or stored) within me, reminds me of God's thoughts concerning conformity to the ways of man. Memorize God's Word by putting it to a melody. Sing God's Word and, in the process, sing a new song (with ancient text) to the Lord. Our Creator created us to worship Him. He gave us humanity's "user's manual" in His Word. It is the how-to guide for authenticity in worship. After all, from Genesis to Revelation, it is ultimately all about worship.

1. Are you seeking to know God by memorizing Scripture?
2. Are you being transformed, not conformed?

～

*Heavenly Father, You give us the plan for worship. Today, I pray that You will
enable me to memorize Your Word, to treasure it in my heart, and to live by its
wisdom. I want to live in authenticity according to You. In Jesus' name, Amen.*

Jerry L. Newman
Executive Pastor of Worship and Media
Southcrest Baptist Church, Lubbock, TX

A Health and Wellness Checklist

I will praise you, LORD, with all my heart; I will tell of all the marvelous things you have done. I will be filled with joy because of you. I will sing praises to your name, O Most High.
Psalm 9:1–2 (NLT)

Thought of the day: in today's culture, we are bombarded with ways to be more healthy, fit, and aware of how we are treating our bodies. I submit that Scripture has much to say about being whole and healthy. Do you want to improve your health physically, mentally, and spiritually?

Then use this list right out of Scripture as your daily exercise:

- *Praise the Lord with all your heart.* No half-hearted worship or just going through the motions.
- *Tell of the amazing things God has done.* Be aware and conscious of God at work around you; talk about it!
- *Be filled with joy because of the Lord.* Joy is available constantly, so choose it!
- *Sing praise to the Lord.* Express your joy through singing. It is an outward expression of what is on the inside. The world needs to hear, so sing! It is great exercise!

1. So, will you? It is your choice today to praise, to tell, to express joy, and to sing.
2. Add these things to your "to do" list and make them a priority today. Then do it again tomorrow and the next day!

~

Father, may I be a healthy child of Yours as I worship You with all of my heart today, talk about You, find joy right where I am, and express that joy through singing!

Rocky Gillmore
Worship Pastor
Crossroads Baptist Church, The Woodlands, TX

What Is God Looking For?

*"But the hour is coming, and is now here, when the true worshipers will worship
the Father in spirit and truth, for the Father is seeking such people to worship him.
God is spirit, and those who worship him must worship in spirit and truth."*
John 4:23–24 (ESV)

God is inviting us to worship Him, but it's a choice we all have to make. God LOOKS for those who worship Him! This is a revolutionary thought! Worship is our ministry to the Lord. Other roles and responsibilities, including ministry tasks and goals, require energy and attention in our lives, but EVERYTHING begins with worship. Worship is not something to add to an overcrowded life.

The reason many sincere people struggle to mature in their Christian life is they don't make time for worship and devotion. Authentic worship requires permanent space in our lives, not random or temporary space. Second Chronicles 16:9a says, "For the eyes of the LORD run to and fro throughout the whole earth, to give strong support to those whose heart is blameless toward him" (ESV). Worship focuses our heart, mind, soul, and strength on loving God above everything else and thus becomes our ultimate priority. That is what God is looking for! God is seeking after true worshipers who worship Him in spirit and in truth.

1. How would a deeper life of worship make a difference in your community?
2. What steps can you take this week to make worship the ultimate priority in your life?

~

*Lord, thank You for the gift of knowing You. Help me to focus my
heart and mind on loving You above everything else. Help me to make
You, God, my ultimate priority, In Jesus' name, Amen.*

Andy Newsome
Music and Worship Pastor
Trinity Baptist Church, Ocala, FL

Same Difference

After this I looked, and there was a vast multitude from every nation, tribe, people, and
language, which no one could number, standing before the throne and before the Lamb.
They were clothed in white robes with palm branches in their hands. And they cried out in
a loud voice: Salvation belongs to our God, who is seated on the throne, and to the Lamb!
Revelation 7:9–10 (CSB)

All throughout the book of Revelation, we see people on their faces at God's throne. Do you think those people got into groups by skin color, or denomination, or age before they fell before the Lord in worship?

The answer is, of course, no. That would be senseless! Since that is the case, why are we so quick in this world to surround ourselves with only those who look like, act like, and think like us?

For me, this is one of the most beautiful things about worship. Our congregations should be places where we focus not on how we are different, but on what unites us: our love for God, our desire to worship Him, and our salvation through the blood of Jesus. As worship leaders, we can speak volumes to the congregation we lead when our team is made up of people who look different, are at different stages in life and have different preferences or comfort zones, but all of that has been cast aside so we can honor God together. What is the result of all of these differences coming together in unity? It is the same as what happens in music when we have many different types of instruments, all tuned together and playing the same song as one—we have the beauty of unity and harmony. It is a picture of heaven.

1. If God wants us to be united, why do we tend to focus so much on our differences?
2. What are some other ways that worship through music is a picture of the unity God desires for us?

~

God, in Your graciousness and creativity, You have surrounded us with people who are not
like us. Help us not to fear them, but to love them, to learn from them, and to paint a picture
of Your design for humanity as we worship You, and as we lead in Your worship together.

Clay Owens
Pastor of Worship Ministry
Emerald Coast Fellowship, Lynn Haven, FL

Firstfruits

But the king said to Araunah, "No, but I will buy it from you for a price. I will not offer burnt offerings to the LORD my God that cost me nothing." So David bought the threshing floor and the oxen for fifty shekels of silver.
2 Samuel 24:24 (ESV)

In 2 Samuel 24, King David is desperate for God to end the famine that David himself has brought upon Israel. David needs to make a sacrifice to the Lord. When David goes to buy a threshing floor upon which he can build an altar to the Lord, the owner of the threshing floor offers to give it to David free of charge, but David refuses, saying, "I will not offer anything that costs me nothing." Hello. My name is Conviction, have we met? If David had been without money and couldn't have done any better, he might have accepted the man's offer, but David knew that he had been blessed abundantly. Therefore, he knew that anything less than his absolute best wasn't good enough when it was being offered to the Lord, his God.

You've probably figured out where I'm headed with this. Those whom God has called to serve in the worship ministry have been given the *joy* and *privilege* to make music unto the Lord! Are we sometimes guilty of giving our best at home and work and then giving our leftovers to the Lord? Why do we expect the Living God to accept our "hand-me-downs"? Let me hasten to indict myself: I've been guilty of this, too. God does understand our human weaknesses and circumstances, and we do serve a God of mercy and compassion. I am so grateful that He is patient with me! But when we bring our gifts and offerings, we need to be ready to give our firstfruits to the Lord. When we come before the Lord with our musical offerings, let's be committed to giving out of the fullness of our hearts. Let's play and sing with PASSION. Let's be prepared to give God the very BEST we have.

1. What are some things that Christians often give to God as leftovers?
2. As a lead worshiper, what does it mean to you to "give God your very best"?

Father, help me to be aware of the specific areas of my life where I am offering less than my very best to You. Thank You for blessing my worship efforts with Your presence, despite my imperfections. May our worship convey that You are the ultimate priority and passion of our lives.

Steve Holt
Worship Minister
Central Baptist Church, College Station, TX

A Calling to Serve

"My sons, do not neglect your duties any longer! The LORD has chosen you to stand in his presence, to minister to him, and to lead the people in worship and present offerings to him."
2 Chronicles 29:11 (NLT)

It Is Your Calling

Although this was written for the professional worship leaders of the Israelites, it certainly can give insight to our understanding of who we are as volunteer and staff worship leaders today. In Ephesians 4, we learn that God calls out from within the church people to do the work of ministry. A sense of calling by God to build His kingdom is certainly more motivation to serve than just viewing yourself as a volunteer. This is something you were *made* to do; take your place as a called-out, gifted one in God's plan for His church!

Do It Now

The challenge to us all is to faithfully put the things of God before our schedules and self-imposed, filled-to-the-brim calendars. Matthew 6:33 says to seek Him first—all these (other) things will be added to us. A pastor friend of mine has said many times that "there is always time to do God's will." Don't wait until you get that degree; don't put off service to God until you *feel* like it. Run your life based on what you *know* to be true and *not* how you feel.

Do It Well

The call to be a disciple of Christ is a call to growth. It's a call to maturity. Understand that as a worship leader you should never stop learning. Make the disciplines of the faith, such as a daily time with the Lord, connection and accountability with others, service in your ministry, Scripture memory, evangelism, and spiritual growth a regular part of your life. Your worship leadership will become a natural overflow of the work that God is doing within your heart. Then, commit to grow your craft as a choir member, so that you can offer your very best every time you serve.

1. What are some steps I can take to become a better disciple of Christ, and thus, a better worshiper?
2. Is there anything on my schedule that I need to remove in order to serve God more effectively in my gifts and calling?

~

Lord, I commit my life to be a true worshiper. I commit to the process of becoming a mature follower of You by memorizing Your Word and developing my skills—however great or small, for Your glory and Your honor. Use me for Your kingdom's work today and for all of my days!

Jeff Askew
Worship Pastor
Liberty Baptist Church, Hampton, VA

Trusting God

Trust in the LORD with all your heart and do not lean on your own understanding.
In all your ways acknowledge Him, and He will make your paths straight.
Proverbs 3:5–6 (NASB)

Do you remember the feeling of watching a movie or a football game for the first time? There is an overwhelming, anxiety-filled surge coursing through your veins as you watch, hoping that it ends well. The second time you watch, you know how it ends, so you lean back and relax. It's easy to trust when you know the outcome. In Acts 20:22–24, Paul was arrested and beaten. He was bound in spirit and on the way to Jerusalem, not knowing what would await him.

The Holy Spirit earnestly testified to him in every city, saying that bonds and afflictions would be there. He didn't shy away or back down. Paul, instead, chose to be a man who walked by faith rather than by sight (2 Cor. 5:7). He trusted God at every turn and did not lean on his own understanding. The course, calling, and ministry that God placed before Paul overpowered and outweighed his fear of the unknown.

1. What is something that is hindering you from trusting God fully?
2. Would you have the faith, like Paul, to venture into the unknown if God told you to?

~

Lord, help us to trust You with our whole hearts and lean not on our own understanding. Let us walk by faith and go where You have called us to go, even when our eyes cannot see before us.

Tommy Quinn
Associate Pastor of Worship
First Baptist Church Tillman's Corner, Mobile, AL

Our Purpose Is for More Than Right Now

My days are like an evening shadow; I wither away like grass. But you, O LORD,
are enthroned forever; you are remembered throughout all generations.
Psalm 102:11–12 (ESV)

One of the most meaningful parts of the Psalms is that they show a contrast in who God is and who I am. Truthfully, we see how unlike God we really are and how much we need Him and are utterly dependent on Him. God has all strength and we are incredibly weak. God is sufficient in every way and we are dirt poor. God is mighty, and we are feeble. In the first eleven verses of Psalm 102, David, who many believe is grieving over his son, Absalom, admits his weakness, his loneliness, and his distress. As helpless as David is at this moment, God is all the more powerful.

From verse 12 through the end of this chapter, the reality turns from man-focused to God-focused. "But you, O LORD" is the exact quote. This is the turning point where David begins to see the reality of who God really is. He recognizes that God is feared and respected by all nations, that God hears his prayer, and that in God's completeness, He overcomes. The truth in this Scripture goes on to say that what David is going through at the moment has eternal significance. David states his desire for this to be recorded for a future generation . . . "so that a people yet to be created may praise the LORD" (v. 18).

So, whatever your situation in life, understand and acknowledge that God is sovereign and all-powerful . . . for you! Take your eyes off of yourself and put them on the God who created you and holds you. Your response to who He is will very well be significant in your present situation and a testimony for the generations that follow yours. Our faithful and dependent response is desired by our Creator and is eternal.

1. What possessions are you striving to attain?
2. In what situations in your life are you not trusting God and His sovereignty?

~

God, please help me to live in the shelter of who You are and not in the exposure of who I am. I trust You and depend on You in every life situation. Receive glory today from my response to my everyday situations. Take me and use me today! Amen.

Carl Setterlind
Worship Pastor
Biltmore Baptist Church, Arden, NC

Ready to Worship?

"But the hour is coming, and is now here, when the true worshipers will worship the Father in spirit and truth, for the Father is seeking such people to worship him."
John 4:23 (ESV)

Once in a while I have a dream that I am in college and about to take a final math exam. Of course, I am totally distraught because of the fact that I only attended the class on the first day of the semester. Regardless, I show up to take the test (in my pajamas) for which I am totally unprepared. (Oh, and by the way, as a vocal major, I was never required to take a math course! Crazy!)

As followers of Christ, it is our great privilege to gather each Sunday to worship and adore Him. The question is: *Are we ready to worship?* More specifically, is worship for you more about living for and loving God with your entire being, or is it an event you attend on Sunday?

Jesus clearly speaks to us as to the kind of worshiper He seeks . . . those whose heart and life are solely devoted to Him. Vance Havner wrote, "Our Lord approved neither idol worship nor idle worship but indeed ideal worship in Spirit and Truth."[18] Beloved, our Lord has, by His grace, poured out His life, forgiveness, and love for our salvation. How could we ever give Him less than a totally surrendered life? Oh, may you and I daily immerse ourselves in God's Word and commune with Him. May our lives and lifestyles permeate a fragrant offering of worship unto Him!

1. What does it mean to worship Jesus "in spirit and truth"?
2. Are there areas in your life in which Christ seeks victory?

~

Lord Jesus, I thank You for Your everlasting love and presence. Today, I surrender my life and heart as an offering of worship to You. In Your name, Amen.

John Griffin
Worship Pastor
Calvary Baptist Church, Beaumont, TX

God Is Able

Now to him who is able to do immeasurably more than all we ask or imagine,
according to his power that is at work within us, to him be glory in the church
and in Christ Jesus throughout all generations, for ever and ever! Amen.
Ephesians 3:20–21 (NIV)

What an amazing promise found in this conclusion of Paul's prayer. The same power that raised Jesus from the dead rests within us. Regardless of how bold our requests may seem, God can do all that we ask and so much more.

Through the years, I have seen God do more than I could have ever asked or imagined. Not just in my life, but in the lives of family, friends, and in His church.

God's means for accomplishing His work comes only through His strength. His work is accomplished by the Holy Spirit's power within us, rather than by our own human strength. Many times, God puts His people in impossible situations to display His power and glory.

God's ultimate purpose is to bring glory to His name. Give Him the praise! Declare His glory!

1. Do I truly believe that God is able to do more than I ask or imagine?
2. Am I willing to get out of the way so that God can work in my life, for His glory?

~

Father, You are all powerful. Help me to trust You to do more than I
can ever ask or imagine. May You receive the glory for it all.

Jon Skelley
Worship Pastor
Geyer Springs First Baptist Church, Little Rock, AR

Fog Finds Us

He took Peter, James, and John with him. He plunged into a sinkhole of dreadful agony.
Mark 14:33 (MSG)

It was a rainy drive from the East Tennessee mountains to my home in Charlotte, North Carolina. Every mile that passed, a dense and heavy fog began to form. As the fog swallowed the car, fear and insecurity engulfed me.

Life is just like the fog. In a moment's notice, worry, sickness, job loss, family crisis, or you name it can plunge the strongest believer into the abyss of fear and uncertainty. Like a fog, it swallows our every motion, thought, and waking minute. Yet, Scripture gives us a vivid picture of the Lord Jesus wrestling with the weight of His own deity and humanity. Taking a trip amid the twisted trees of Gethsemane, one will find a portrait of the Savior struggling. The sin of the world, the reality of death, and the hollow feeling of forsakenness weighed Jesus down. There alone, Jesus prayed and prepared for the climax of His earthly life—redemption.

The next time "the weight of this present suffering" pushes you into the "sinkhole of dreadful agony," remember Jesus. He cares, He understands, but most important, He prevails!

1. How does Jesus' Gethsemane experience comfort you in your own suffering?
2. When the fog of concern overwhelms you, what are some ways to rise above?

~

Heavenly Father, thank You that I am never alone, that You are with me, and, most important, that You understand me. Give me the grace and strength to face whatever is before me. I rest in Your prevailing resurrection power!

Matthew Slemp
Minister of Music
First Baptist Church, Indian Trail, NC

Hope's the Diploma, Not the Admission Fee

We rejoice in our sufferings, knowing that suffering produces endurance, and endurance produces character, and character produces hope, and hope does not disappoint us.
Romans 5:3–5 (RSV)

It's intuitive to think that one needs hope going into life's challenges. However, Paul expresses counterintuitively that hope is actually the result of a process that recognizes God's ability to turn our experiences of suffering into times of spiritual growth. Upon graduating from seminary, I was somewhat idealistic. I was ready to conquer the world for Christ, yet after just two short months of being on a church staff, the senior pastor suddenly resigned because of a moral failure, thus beginning my training in the school of hard-knocks. A year and a half later the next senior pastor suddenly resigned because of a moral failure. This was not what I signed up for, nor was it in my plan.

I was supposed to be climbing higher, but instead God had a different course and plan for me. The word translated *suffering* literally means "pressure," and it describes distress brought on by outward circumstances. The noun *endurance* is a compound word that consists of a noun meaning "staying" and a preposition meaning "under." The idea is one of having staying power under a heavy load. This is not passive endurance, but rather an attitude of overcoming. The word translated *character* describes the quality of being approved. I don't know about you but that's my desire: God's approval, Christ's character and a hope that does not disappoint me.

1. Recall a time in your life when this process of suffering/endurance/character/hope proved to be true.
2. Can you name a time when your plan did not end up being God's plan for your life?

~

Lord, help me to endure the sufferings and trials of life through the power of Your Spirit, giving me a hope that does not disappoint, as You build the character of Christ in me.

Todd Stearns
Pastor of Worship and Music
First Baptist Church, Naples, FL

God the Holy Spirit Sings in and through Us

*And do not be drunk with wine, in which is dissipation; but be filled with
the Spirit, speaking to one another in psalms and hymns and spiritual songs,
singing and making melody in your heart to the Lord, giving thanks always
for all things to God the Father in the name of our Lord Jesus Christ.*
Ephesians 5:18–20 (NKJV)

The Holy Spirit is the third Person of the Trinity and He completes the Trio of the Trinity in our worship. In the Old Testament the Shekinah Glory of God dwelt in the Holy of Holies above the Ark of the Covenant in the tabernacle and in the temple in Jerusalem. On the Day of Pentecost after Jesus' resurrection and ascent into heaven, the Holy Spirit came upon those in Jerusalem and dwelt in them. We, the blood-bought saints, are the temples of the living God! The Shekinah Glory of God dwells in us!

When we come together to worship with thankful hearts and voices of praise,

1. God the Father is singing over us and is enthroned on our praise,
2. Jesus is singing with us, always declaring the glory of the Father to us, His brothers and sisters in Christ, AND
3. The Holy Spirit is singing through us!

We supply the voice that carries the song of the Holy Spirit. Isn't this beautiful? God includes us in the song of the Trinity! He needs us! He has included us with himself to sing! All of history is the song of Redemption, "that God has sought us to reconcile us to Himself." He made us. Sin stole us. He bought us back through His own blood. Hallelujah!

There is a wonderful quote from *Worship: Rediscovering the Missing Jewel* by Allen and Borror: "When a non-singer becomes a Christian, he or she becomes a singer!"[19] When the church comes together to worship, no one can sing your praise for you. The Holy Spirit in you is waiting for you to open your mouth and declare your own praise! It doesn't matter what your voice sounds like. God wants to hear YOUR voice openly declaring YOUR love for Jesus! Isn't worship wonderful? We get to sing with the Trinity! Listen closely, you may hear them singing too!

1. Why does God want to hear our praise so strongly?
2. What is a good definition of the Trinity? (the Trinity is three separate Persons but one in nature, essence, and being. "God in three persons, blessed Trinity")

~

*Dear heavenly Father, thank You for including me, Your son/daughter in this
wonderful blessing of heavenly praise to You! Your plan is glorious, that You would
sing with us and over us and in us! "Blessing and honor and glory and power
be to Him who sits on the throne, And to the Lamb, forever and ever!"*

Jim Whitmire
Instructor in Music and Worship
Mid-America Baptist Theological Seminary, Cordova, TN

A Different Kind of Hero

Better a patient person than a warrior, one with self-control than one who takes a city.
Proverbs 16:32 (NIV)

The Bible is full of counterintuitive reversals. In its pages we read things like the meek will "inherit the earth" (Matt. 5:5 ESV), "Whoever finds his life will lose it . . ." (Matt. 10:39 ESV), "So the last will be first, and the first last" (Matt. 20:16 ESV). Here in Proverbs, we see another surprising statement about what it takes to be a hero according to biblical standards.

According to this passage, a patient person is better than a warrior. Excuse me? What?! To be a warrior is exciting and noble. To be patient is boring. The biblical author goes on to say that a person with self-control is better than one who conquers a whole city. How can this be? To conquer a city is incredible and admirable, but someone with self-control is weird and fanatical.

Here we see the truth from a biblical perspective. To be a conqueror of cities means nothing if you have not conquered yourself. If you have not learned to rein in your appetites and desires, no earthly achievement will ever satisfy—at least not for long. No amount of money or success will ever be enough. You will spend your life chasing the elusive wind of satisfaction just as a dog chases his tail. Using a similar metaphor, Proverbs 25:28 tells us, "A man without self-control is like a city broken into and left without walls" (ESV). This is a vivid and sorrowful picture of a ruined life. May we be more like the apostle Paul, who wrote, "I discipline my body and keep it under control, lest after preaching to others I myself should be disqualified" (1 Cor. 9:27 ESV).

1. What brings you satisfaction?
2. Are you praying about your ability to exercise patience and self-control?

Father, forgive me for placing value on the wrong things. Help me to bring my desires under Your control. Teach me what it means to take up my cross daily and help me to find satisfaction in living the cross-shaped life.

John Stegemerten
Worship Pastor
Hickory Grove Baptist Church, Charlotte, NC

Without Love . . . Nothing

And if I have prophetic powers, and understand all mysteries and all knowledge, and if I have all faith, so as to remove mountains, but have not love, I am nothing. If I give away all I have, and if I deliver up my body to be burned, but have not love, I gain nothing.
1 Corinthians 13:2–3 (ESV)

The musical was planned to a "T"! Each song had been rehearsed to near perfection. The lighting cues were checked and checked again. Instruments were tuned, vocalists warmed up and in their places. Anticipation was high, and all seemed ready for a great performance.

Now the director sets the tempo, stage lights come up, and the opening song begins. Following the beautiful instrumental intro, the soloist steps up to the microphone, opens her mouth with confidence, and . . . nothing. The soloist cannot be heard because no one checked to make sure there were fresh batteries in the wireless microphone. Regardless of all the good measures in place for a successful performance, without fresh batteries, there is nothing!

The apostle Paul writes in 1 Corinthians 13 that regardless of all the good measures a person may take, without love, all of their gifts and all of their efforts are useless. Without love, one's résumé is lacking the most essential component. Without love, any strengths, assets, or positive qualities a person may have result in no lasting value, no godly virtue, nor success of any kind. Love is everything! Without love, all you have is . . . nothing.

1. Are there any areas of your life in which you are functioning without love?
2. What are ways that you could love in these areas?

~

Father, I pray that today my words and actions come from a heart ruled by Your love and grace. Regardless of what is going on around me, may I always love You with all my heart, soul, and mind, and give me grace to love my neighbor as myself. Amen.

Jeff Stotts
Lead Worship Pastor
Central Baptist Church, Jonesboro, AR

Spirit and Understanding

I will sing with the spirit, and I will also sing with the understanding.
1 Corinthians 14:15 (NKJV)

Paul is teaching us about communication in corporate worship. Without going into the depths of word meanings, let's just look at the obvious. Our singing should be "with feeling," from the heart, not merely a perfunctory performance. However, neither should it be just a display of emotion. We are to engage our minds and sing "with the understanding."

First, let us sing with *the understanding of our message.*

We should be certain that our lyrics communicate truth that conforms to Scripture. Poetic license must not displace the biblical message. History reveals that doctrines of denominations have been changed by the texts of hymns sung by congregations.

Let us sing with *the understanding of the singing instrument.* Vocal technique can be picked up quickly by volunteer choir members without going into long and tedious exercises.

Let us sing with *the understanding of the music.* Again—no boring theory lessons, but over time people can become surprisingly literate in the language of music notation.

Let us sing with *the understanding of our purpose*, both ultimate and immediate. Our mission is to lead the congregation in worship and to recruit, train, and inspire people to lead in worship . . . to "teach and admonish each other through the use of psalms, hymns, and spiritual songs" (Col. 3:16, paraphrase).

The legendary conductor Toscanini has been quoted as telling his musicians that they should play with their brains on ice and their hearts on fire. It turns out that he was actually quoting Vladimir Lenin, who may not have realized that he was referring to Paul's biblical admonition.

1. In what other ways can we apply "singing with the spirit" to our worship experience?
2. Are there more areas in which we can "sing with the understanding?"

~

Lord, teach us to use all the gifts You have given us as we love and serve You with all our heart and with all our mind and to do it with all our strength. In Jesus' name, Amen.

O. D. Hall Jr.
Director
MUSICalifornia, Northridge, CA

Clean the Behavior

But you are not like that, for you are a chosen people. You are royal priests, a holy nation, God's very own possession. As a result, you can show others the goodness of God, for he called you out of the darkness into his wonderful light.

1 Peter 2:9 (NLT)

Malice, hypocrisy, slander, envy, and deceit. All of these words describe the behavior we exhibit when Christ is not the center of our hearts. We often ask God to remove these things from inside of us, but we never truly surrender them to the hands of a God who wants to make us whole. Have you ever asked God to clean out the bad behavior in your life? We sincerely believe that asking Him is the full process we must walk through, before we are magically cleansed of all unrighteousness.

The part we are missing, and often leave out, is *our* role in the process. We forget that we are holy! He calls us "chosen" in 1 Peter 2:9. We are set apart if we are a disciple and follower of Jesus Christ. We are not who we think we are, we are who He SAYS we are. In these moments of cleansing the indignation, we must focus on Him. God can definitely remove our filthy sin; He says we are chosen and holy, but we must play an active role in the cleansing of the darkness from our hearts and life. Don't replace bad behavior, but instead, let's rid ourselves of it by filling our hearts and minds with His Word. We are called to be light!

1. How do you show others that you live in light instead of darkness each day?
2. Is there hidden filth and sin in your heart that you're asking God to remove? Are you playing an active role in the cleansing of this sin in your life?

Jesus, we thank You for the gift of salvation! Thank You for dying so that the sins we commit and carry are removed when we fully surrender them to Your hands. Help us to trust and acknowledge You in our walk today and may our light shine bright to others so that they see a difference in us. Thank You for Your patience with us in our weakness. We love You! In Your name, Amen.

Josh Sullins
Worship and Creative Arts Pastor
Peachtree Corners Baptist Church, Peachtree Corners, GA

Boldly Speaking Your Story

Then they called them in again and commanded them not to speak or teach at all in the name of Jesus. But Peter and John replied, "Judge for yourselves whether it is right in God's sight to obey you rather than God. For we cannot help speaking about what we have seen and heard."

Acts 4:18–20 (NIV)

Following the resurrection and ascension of Jesus, the Holy Spirit came upon His disciples. Peter and John were living each day in God's Spirit. In Acts 3, they prayed for a forty-year-old lame beggar, who was then healed. Several people in Jerusalem noticed this miracle and went to hear these two disciples preach. Many who heard the message of Jesus, the Messiah, resurrected from the dead, believed. This worried the political and religious leaders of the day who wanted no uprisings or threats to their power and authority.

Peter and John were arrested and told not to speak of Jesus again. These two men, however, could not help themselves. They asked the authorities to make their own judgment about whether it was "right in God's sight to obey you rather than God." We are told these uneducated, ordinary men could not "help speaking about what we have seen and heard."

Are we bold and brave in speaking our story of salvation in Christ alone? Like Peter and John, authorities and leaders still tell us "not to speak or teach at all in the name of Jesus." Unbelievers still try to explain away our faith in Christ so they don't have to face their own emptiness without Him. Our world has always championed its peoples to listen to their leaders above God. But those who choose to follow Christ know that we are commissioned by God to boldly speak our story of salvation to all who will hear, just like Peter and John did.

1. How do we demonstrate the courage and bravery needed to overcome those who try to muffle the message of God?
2. Why are we so apt to forget that boldness comes from the Holy Spirit and not from inside of us?

~

God, give us the strength to hear Your voice, the discipline to follow You, and the love of Christ to share the gift of salvation.

David Thomas
Worship Pastor
Highland Baptist Church, Grove City, OH

Flying Blind? Or Right on Course

Trust in the LORD with all your heart, and do not rely on your own understanding;
in all your ways know him, and he will make your paths straight.
Proverbs 3:5–6 (CSB)

For three days, the astronauts of *Apollo 8* flew toward the moon. However, due to the flight path of the spacecraft, they had not seen their destination since they left the launch pad at Cape Kennedy. Though the journey to the moon was very dangerous, they weren't concerned, they didn't feel out of control, and they certainly weren't operating on blind faith.

The highly trained pilots fully trusted that the team of engineers, controllers, and instruments would navigate them safely to their final destination. Sure enough, at just the right time, the powerful service module engine fired. As they settled into Lunar orbit, the surface of the moon loomed large in their window, exactly when and where they believed it would.

Like the crew of *Apollo 8*, we find ourselves on a difficult journey, moving from one event to the next—hoping that we've chosen the right course. When we fully surrender to the will of Christ in our lives, we can have full assurance that He will place us on a course that will take us to destinations that we could have never imagined.

1. Are there moments in your life when you feel off course?
2. Have you given Christ complete control as the "navigator" of your life?

~

Father, I admit that there are moments where I have not given You full control of
everything that I do in my life. I pray, Lord, that You would give me the strength and
courage to fully depend on Your wisdom and Your plan and direction for my life. Amen.

Ken Van Cura
Worship Pastor
First Baptist Church, Plant City, FL

Good Advice

Let the word of Christ dwell in you richly in all wisdom, teaching and admonishing one
another in psalms and hymns and spiritual songs, singing with grace in your hearts to the Lord.
Colossians 3:16 (NKJV)

If one were to ask this author for the number-one piece of advice for Christian living,
it would be, without hesitation, "There is no substitute for a personal, daily walk with
Christ." That is the key to growing in Him—period.

The words *dwell in* mean "to live in a home." The Christian is admonished to be so
familiar with and obedient to God's Word that he or she feels at home when opening it
up. *Richly* means "abundantly," meaning that God's Word is to be abundantly at home in
our hearts.

The exhortation continues with the words *teaching and admonishing one another*,
which are in the imperative—"It must be done!" How is it to be done, you may ask? Here
it is, "in psalms [God's Word] and hymns [songs that speak of the character, attributes, and
work of Jesus] and spiritual songs [responses to who He is and what He has done]." God's
Word is to be taught in song!

When Moses had delivered the Law to the people of Israel, he put it to music
as God instructed: "Therefore write down this song for yourselves and teach it to the
Israelites; have them recite it, so that this song may be a witness for Me against the
Israelites" (Deut. 31:19 HCSB).

Dwell in God's Word. Do it with song!

1. Can you think of other biblical illustrations that express the relationship between
   God's Word and song?
2. What are some of your favorite psalms, hymns, and spiritual songs?

～

Heavenly Father, I rejoice that You have put a new song in my heart, even praise to You.
Teach me to dwell in Your Word, that I may rejoice in You all the days of my life.

Dr. Ron Upton
Minister of Worship and Creative Arts
Idlewild Baptist Church, Lutz, FL

No Holding Back

Shout joyfully to the LORD, all the earth; Break forth in song, rejoice, and sing praises.
Psalm 98:4 (NKJV)

Jim sits near the front of the worship center every Sunday. When the music starts, you don't have to look for him. You hear him. He sings loudly. So loudly, he sometimes is as loud in my ears as I am. He challenges me; not from volume but from his heart. He sings as one who celebrates his new birth in every song. God doesn't have to lean in to hear him. The joy and gratitude of his spirit cause him to "shout to the Lord." Do I have that same zeal and fervor? Am I as grateful to the God who sent His Son to save my sin-ridden soul? The sad truth is . . . not always, but Jim encourages me with his voice and his smile for me to lift my voice.

Jim is not the greatest singer. So, you can imagine my thoughts when he volunteered to go with us on a choir tour overseas. We, as you probably guessed, taught Jim to run sound. He did it with the same gusto with which he sang. Always in gratitude and with a heart to do his best for Jesus. Jim assisted with the setup and tear down with a servant's heart, never complaining. I have learned much from Jim. My heart is sometimes too stubborn, or pseudo-sophisticated, or full of myself to shout praises to God. May I be more like Jim.

1. What holds you back from giving God all your praise? Tradition? Fear of criticism?
2. What person in the Bible exhibited models for our praise?

⁓

God, You deserve the highest praise. You deserve my full praise. Rid me of the shackles of myself and self-consciousness and let me wholeheartedly lift Your praises. Let me only seek to please You. Shouting in the name of Jesus, Amen!

Pat Van Dyke
Minister of Music and Pastoral Care
First Baptist Church, Clarksville, TN

Detour

"For my thoughts are not your thoughts, neither are your ways my ways,
declares the LORD. For as the heavens are higher than the earth, so are my
ways higher than your ways and my thoughts than your thoughts."
Isaiah 55:8–9 (ESV)

Dad was a hardworking man. He was a tool and die maker, working from sunrise to sunset. Every year, the factory would shut down for two weeks. During the first week, we were out in the fields working, taking care of everything we wanted to grow. The first week was hard work, but the second week was our annual vacation. We would load up the station wagon and be off. Every year my dad would get a new set of maps. One of my favorites was the Rand-McNally travel atlas. Before the days of GPS, there was Rand-McNally. It was a big book that had all fifty states, Canada, Mexico, and sometimes Puerto Rico in it, and I loved it. My father would say where we were going on vacation, and I would immediately go to the map and plan out our trip.

One year, our destination was Myrtle Beach. I looked it up and plotted out every route that would get us to the beach. I had my boogie board, swimsuit, snorkel and was ready to go! The day finally arrived for our trip, and we loaded up the station wagon and set out on the long journey. Hours later, I asked where we were (to check my father's progress in the road atlas). He said, "We are in Gatlinburg headed up through the Smoky Mountains." To my shock, my father took a detour. I was furious! I wanted to get to the beach, but no! We had to go to the Smoky Mountains. So, I put my Rand-McNally atlas down and I stewed in anger in the back seat and got more and more angry with every twist and turn on the mountain road.

We finally parked at Newfound Gap and he said, "Let's get out and stretch our legs." He said, "Look son! Look at the view!" I looked. It was that moment that I fell in love with the mountains. I could see for miles across the lush valleys and majestic peaks of God's glorious creation. I was amazed!

We are on a journey. We may think we know where our life should end up. Many times, however, God takes us on a detour. We want to get to where we think we should go and God says, "Wait, I want to show you something."

Trust that your heavenly Father knows where He wants to take you. He has a map and has a route planned for your life. Enjoy the journey and pay attention. He may want to show you something amazing!

1. Has God taken you somewhere you didn't want to go? He doesn't make mistakes. He has you in this place at this time for His glory.
2. Where is God leading you now? Trust that He has the "map" and He is taking you exactly where He wants you.

~

Father, let me realize You have the "map" of where You took me, where You
have me, and where You want me to be. Give me a childlike wonder to enjoy
the journey and notice the amazing things that You want to show me!

Nathan Ward
Worship Arts Pastor
Woodland Community Church, Bradenton, FL

Criticism and Compliments

Who, when He was reviled, did not revile in return; when He suffered, He did not threaten, but committed Himself to Him who judges righteously.

1 Peter 2:23 (NKJV)

I was walking through our lobby after a service and someone stopped me and asked, "What was that song you did at the beginning?" I told them the name of it and they replied, "I'm going to download it. I loved it!" I walked a few paces and someone else stopped me and said, "I liked some of the songs you did this morning; well, except that first one. Don't do that one again."

Same Sunday. Same song. Completely different opinions.

One of the hardest parts of being worship leaders is the subjectivity of what we do. Everyone has an opinion, and many are convinced theirs is the right one. How should we respond to compliments and criticism?

Corrie Ten Boom was a holocaust survivor and a dynamic woman of faith. When asked how she handled compliments, her reply was, "I take each remark as if it were a flower. At the end of each day I lift up the bouquet of flowers I have gathered throughout the day and say, 'Here You are, Lord, it is all Yours.'" I think that's exactly right.

What we do isn't for people; it is ultimately for the Lord. Whether a compliment or a criticism, the best thing we can do is lay them all at the feet of Jesus.

1. Do you react to criticism? Sometimes the best thing we can do is smile, extract any truth from it, and lay it at Jesus' feet and move on.
2. How do you respond to compliments? Do you lay those at Jesus' feet too?

Lord, help me to not react to people's criticism or compliments,
but let me lay them all at Your feet.

Ken Hartley
Executive Pastor of Worship
Abba's House, Hixon, TN

Missing You

*"Call to me and I will answer you, and will tell you great
and hidden things that you have not known."*
Jeremiah 33:3 (ESV)

My wife and I have three grown, happily married sons. If you have grown children, especially sons, you know that sometimes (or most of the time) they "forget" to call home. I get it; I've been there. Going to school or starting a career or family takes a LOT of time and attention.

All of this came to a head one afternoon at church when I was in my office thinking about (missing) my children. Soon, I had the revelation that I was not a very good son either. Not toward my parents or in-laws but toward my Father in heaven, who wanted to receive a call from His Son. I prayed a lot for the church, my family, friends, and loved ones, but I had not talked to Him in a long while about me, how I was doing and asking His advice as my Father. I know that my ways are not God's ways or His thoughts my thoughts (Isa. 55:8–9), but I felt ashamed that what I wanted from my children, I was not giving to my Father in heaven. I determined that from that moment on, I was going to "call" my heavenly Father more often, especially anytime I felt lonely or missed hearing the voice of a loved one.

1. When was the last time you spoke with your parent(s) just because? What about God?
2. When you take the attention off of yourself and place it on God, how does that change the situation?

~

Heavenly Father, thank You for always being present and attentive to my prayers. Forgive me for not talking to You about my feelings, cares, and desires more often. Thank You for my family. Give me insight as a father in order to reflect Your work in my heart and life toward others that I have the opportunity to serve and know. In Jesus' name, Amen.

J. K. Weger
Minister of Music and Worship Arts
Ash Creek Baptist, Azle, TX

Cut It Off?

LORD, You have searched me and known me.
Psalm 139:1 (HCSB)

A couple of years ago, my son, who was seven at the time, was in class with a substitute teacher. The substitute gave the class an assignment. As students began to finish their assignment, my son decided he wanted to be finished so he could play with the other students. The problem was that he only had finished about half of the assignment. His solution was to pull out his scissors and cut off the rest of the page, pretending it didn't exist and turn it in.

His hope was that by mixing in with the crowd of students turning in their assignments, he wouldn't be noticed. Obviously, as the teacher graded the papers and judged his work, his actions were discovered.

How many times do we try to pretend our sin doesn't exist? We try to sweep it under the rug and hope it will never be discovered. This is not the correct action to take. Instead, we should deal with it honestly before the Lord. If we were to be honest, we could all dig around in our hearts and find areas of our lives that we've not surrendered to the Lord. God already knows the darkest secrets of your heart, so why not let Him deal with them? For some, these may be little items that God wants to purge from your life. For others, these may be large addictions that are consuming your heart and life. Ultimate freedom in Christ is found when we surrender our entire being.

1. What sin in your life are you pretending doesn't exist?
2. Why aren't you willing to surrender certain areas to the lordship of Jesus Christ?

~

*Heavenly Father, thank You for being all-knowing and perfect in all
Your ways. Lord, search my heart and reveal any wickedness in my heart.
Help me surrender my life to You today. In Jesus' name, Amen.*

Tim Whedbee
Senior Associate Pastor of Worship and Administration
Mobberly Baptist Church, Longview, TX

When It's Time to Quit

Therefore we also, since we are surrounded by so great a cloud of witnesses, let us lay aside every weight, and the sin which so easily ensnares us, and let us run with endurance the race that is set before us, looking unto Jesus, the author and finisher of our faith, who for the joy that was set before Him endured the cross, despising the shame, and has sat down at the right hand of the throne of God.

Hebrews 12:1–2 (NKJV)

Have you ever had one of those days when you feel like going and doing something else? If we're honest, we all have—even those of us who are in the very best work environments and situations. It is so easy to get caught up in the details of life that we lose sight of the bigger picture. We all need something in our lives that will bring us back to center—that will remind us why we do what we do. Remember, the race is a marathon, not a sprint; we must always approach it with endurance. The words of the song "Then and Only Then," written by Geron Davis and Joyce McCollough, always remind me of my calling and also, when it's okay to quit.

"When every broken heart has been mended
When every unbeliever believes
When every life that's bound and shackled is finally set free
When there's no longer a Savior who loves me enough to give His life for my
   own
Then and only then will I stop singing my song."[20]

1. Do you have something you use to help you refocus on your calling?
2. What are you doing to keep the distractions at a minimum?

Lord, help us to stay focused on You and You alone. Make us mindful that the enemy is trying to distract us from our calling and wants us to burn out and quit. Give us the endurance to finish strong and hear "Well done" when we stand before You. Amen.

Bradley White
Worship Pastor
First Baptist Church, Summit, MS

The Ministry of the Face

Wisdom brightens a man's face and changes its hard appearance.
Ecclesiastes 8:1b (NIV)

A re your facial expressions a testimony? Do they reflect Christ? Most of the time the face is the mirror of the heart.

> Now if the ministry that brought death, which was engraved in letters on stone, came with glory, so that Israelites could not look steadily at the face of Moses because of its glory, transitory though it was, will not the ministry of the Spirit be even more glorious? (2 Cor. 3:7–8 NIV)

In other words, the Law reveals sin, but no one can satisfy its demands and even with this, Moses' face reflected God's glory. How much more should we be reflecting the glory of the new covenant that brings salvation to all mankind!

When you are living for Jesus and controlled by His Spirit, you can't help but show it on your countenance. Proverbs 15:13 says, "A merry heart makes a cheerful countenance" (NKJV). What's in the heart comes out in the face!

"He has put a new song in my mouth—praise to our God; many will *see it* and fear" (Ps. 40:3 NKJV, emphasis added). Did you catch that? The song of the redeemed is SEEN!! The inner song becomes a visible testimony. The song in the heart is lived out for all to experience the glory of our God.

1. Can people "see" God's glory as I sing in the choir?
2. How important is it to evaluate our heart before we sing? Why?

~

Heavenly Father, strengthen my voice to sing Your praise, but tune my heart to hear Your message. Give me ears to hear the beauty of the music and more importantly, give me ears to hear the sermon in song. In Jesus' name, Amen.

Rick Stone
Worship Pastor
Whitesburg Baptist Church, Huntsville, AL

God the Father Sings Over and Surrounds Us!

"The Lord your God in your midst, The Mighty One, will save; He will rejoice over you with gladness, He will quiet you with His love, He will rejoice over you with singing."
Zephaniah 3:17 (nkjv)

There are beautiful verses in the Old Testament that tell us that God sings over us when we sleep, when we rise, and all day as we go about our work. He delivers us out of trouble with songs and shouts of victory!

This verse shows a Mighty One who laughs with us in gladness, quiets us with His peaceful presence and sings over us as we sleep like a baby! He is the total consummate Daddy! HE QUIETS US WITH HIS SONG!

Psalm 32:7 shows David speaking directly to God with, "You are my hiding place"! Our Heavenly Father is our protective hiding place. God our Father delivers us while singing loud songs that surround us and take away our fear, give us comfort, drive demons away and deliver us from evil. HE DELIVERS US WITH HIS SONG!

Psalm 42:8 (nkjv) says the word *lovingkindness*. It is used often to express God's love for us as a Father. A loving and kind Father is what every boy and girl needs. Our loving Father sings songs over us at night while we are going to sleep. Have you ever sung to your child as he or she was falling asleep or sick or scared? This is our Perfect Father teaching us all how to be the best father! It is interesting that the psalmist ends this verse with, "A prayer to the God of my life!" HE PROTECTS US WITH HIS SONG!

Jesus had a habit of rising early every morning to talk to His heavenly Father about His day's ministry. Jesus did nothing without the Father's direction! Nothing ever surprised Jesus, for God had already talked to Him that morning! That is what we should do. HE GUIDES US WITH HIS SONG!

Psalm 22:3 discusses how our Holy Father God inhabits the praises of His people. In the Old Testament, God inhabited the Holy of Holies of Israel's earthly temple. With the ultimate sacrifice of Jesus and His death, burial, and resurrection, we have become living temples where God dwells in us. God still today is enthroned on our praise just as He did in the Old Testament! HE SINGS OVER US AND INHABITS OUR PRAISE!

1. How have you heard God guiding you in your duties or in a crisis?
2. Can you name a time when you heard God speak to you clearly through a song (can you think of a time when you heard Him singing)?

~

Dear heavenly Father, I love You and trust Your Word. Cause me to HEAR Your voice of lovingkindness this morning as You sing over me! Give me direction for this day and deliver me from evil! In Jesus, my Lord's name, I pray. Amen.

Jim Whitmire
Instructor in Music and Worship
Mid-America Baptist Theological Seminary, Cordova, TN

The Battle

For he has rescued us from the dominion of darkness and brought us into the kingdom
of the Son he loves, in whom we have redemption, the forgiveness of sins.
Colossians 1:13–14 (NIV)

Narnia, Middle-Earth, Camelot; Aslan, the White Witch, Aragorn, Gandalf, Sauron, Merlin, Mordred, King Arthur. These characters and stories all bring to mind images of warriors and heroes fighting against evil and darkness. Battles to rescue and set free those people held captive and oppressed by the schemes of wicked rulers and kingdoms.

These are, of course, all fictional stories and accounts, but they perhaps give us a slight glimpse of the unseen but very real story of how each of us were held captive in the dungeon of sin and death. We were helpless until, through the battle at Calvary's cross and the victory at the garden tomb, Jesus rescued us—defeating Satan forever. He has brought us into the blessed realm of the kingdom of God!

The problem we sometimes have is that we do not act like we have been freed. We struggle with guilt and doubt and live under a cloud instead of rejoicing in the freedom that was won for us.

These are great verses to memorize. So, when fears and doubts assail us and we don't "feel" the joy of the Lord, we can repeat them over and over, letting their truth flood our hearts and minds with freedom and joy!

1. What is it in your life that is holding you captive today?
2. How can you verbally surrender that to Jesus right now?

～

God, thank You that You have already won the victory and rescued me
from the captivity of sin! Show me how to surrender my doubts and
fears to You and to live in the victory and joy of Jesus today.

John Williams
Worship Pastor
Hebron Baptist Church, Dacula, GA

Psalms, Hymns, and Spiritual Songs

*Let the word of Christ richly dwell within you, with all wisdom teaching
and admonishing one another with psalms and hymns and spiritual
songs, singing with thankfulness in your hearts to God.*
Colossians 3:16 (NASB)

What a joy and privilege it is to be called to ministry. At the age of fourteen, I felt
God calling me to music ministry, and I have not strayed from that calling. Does
that mean I do not go through discouraging times or periods of self-doubt? Of course not.
The truth is that when we trust Jesus as our Savior, He calls us to follow and trust Him
daily, despite our discouragements and doubts. He created us to worship and fellowship
with Him. One aspect I love the most about serving as a music minister is planning and
leading worship.

Paul's words to the people of Colossae apply to us as we seek to lead others to Christ
through music and corporate worship. We must heed Paul's words and let the words of
Christ dwell within us so earthly things, such as the style of music or the worship environment, do not distract our worship. God does not keep score of how many hymns or praise
songs we sing. He is looking for a heart that is in love with Him and seeks to worship with
gratitude and humility. Let us sing songs that teach God's Word and draw each of us into
His glorious presence so that we are changed to be more like Him. Worship is not reserved
for church services. It is meant for every moment of every day.

1. Have you become too busy to allow God's Word to dwell in your heart?
2. Do you desire to sing and worship with a heart of gratitude?

⁓

*Dear Jesus, thank You for calling us to serve You daily. May we allow Your Word to
dwell in us as we live for You and lead others to worship You. May Your Word dwell
within us as we sing psalms, hymns, and spiritual songs. In Your name, Amen.*

Mark Hill
Minister of Music and Worship
First Baptist Church, Garland, TX

The Abiding Presence

"Abide in me, and I in you . . ."
John 15:4a (KJV)

What does it mean to abide in the presence of Christ? Several years ago there was an ice storm in South Georgia that lasted for several days. South Georgia is not equipped to handle ice on its roads or power lines. Many across the state were without electricity for several days. There were no lights, mobile phones, computers, or other necessities of modern life. There was no way to cook or prepare a meal. For several days, we roughed it! We were completely powerless!

The apostle John reminds us that we don't have to be powerless when we abide in the presence of Christ. To abide means to remain or to stay. As believers we are plugged into the presence of Christ or we are not. There is no such thing as a spiritual power reserve that we are able to run on for days. This may be why so many Christians are spiritually weak today. The world has convinced many that their spiritual life can survive off of some sort of spiritual batteries. Not so! Power is produced when it is connected to the power source. Our power comes from being in the presence of the Lord Jesus.

Spiritual power is produced when we practice abiding in the presence of God. We practice abiding each time we read the Word and apply it to our lives. We practice abiding in His presence when we pray for and minister to others in His name. We practice abiding in His presence by having a consistent relationship with Him.

1. What area(s) of your life is keeping you from having fellowship with God? Surrender those areas and seek forgiveness today in order to get plugged into the power of the Lord Jesus Christ.
2. Are you relying on some sort of spiritual batteries to get you through the day, a relationship you may have had in the past, or are you relying on the relationship that you have today?

~

Father, help us to see the areas in our lives that are keeping us from being able to abide in Your presence. Help us, Father, to stay firmly connected to Jesus as the power source of our lives. Amen.

Dr. David Wilson
Assistant Professor of Worship and Church Music
Brewton-Parker College, Mt. Vernon, GA

Satisfaction Guaranteed

. . . for he satisfies the thirsty and fills the hungry with good things.
Psalm 107:9 (NIV)

"Blessed are those who hunger and thirst for righteousness, for they will be filled."
Matthew 5:6 (NIV)

Have you ever been so hungry you felt you would be willing to eat shoe leather or gnaw on your arm? You would make a great sacrifice just for a bite of food. This desperate hunger is the kind God desires for us to have for His presence.

Have you ever been so thirsty your mouth felt like it was full of cotton balls? You wanted a drink and would do anything to get it. This desperate thirst is what God wants us to have for His righteousness.

Here is a great truth: when we come to God, desperate for His presence, He doesn't merely give us a taste and send us away unsatisfied. He sets a banquet table before us, so we can enjoy a rich assortment of His graces (Ps. 23:5). He invites us to "taste and see that the LORD is good" (Ps. 34:8 NIV).

When we thirst for God's righteousness like a deer pants for water (Ps. 42:1), God does not merely satiate our thirst with a few drops of moisture. He invites us to stand in front of the open fire hydrant of His love and swim in the ocean of His mercy.

Hungry? Thirsty? Come to Jesus and be filled. Satisfaction guaranteed!

David wrote this prayer when he was in the desert in Judah, "Oh God you are my God, earnestly I seek you; I thirst for you; my whole being longs for you, in a dry and parched land where there is no water" (Ps. 63:1 NIV).

I have a friend, Erik Ngweya, who is a worship pastor in Lusaka, Zambia. Erik recently told me something that captured my heart, "The better I get to know my Savior, the more I experience new flavors of His mercy and grace." Wow! Be desperate to know the Savior better every day!

Write your prayer expressing your desperation for God's presence and His righteousness.

Dr. Herb Armentrout
Minister of Music
Broadmoor Baptist Church, Shreveport, LA

For Rainy Days!

"Remember not the former things, nor consider the things of old. Behold,
I am doing a new thing; now it springs forth, do you not perceive it? I
will make a way in the wilderness and rivers in the desert."

Isaiah 43:18–19 (ESV)

This day started out really rough—long story. Aw, who am I kidding, it's been a crazy month! Have you ever had one of those seasons? Years?

In this passage, after pronouncing Judah's captivity in Babylon, Isaiah comforts them with God's promise of deliverance. This salvation is based on God's love and will ultimately be realized in the coming of the Messiah. He encourages them not to dwell in the past but to look to the future and trust that God can and will do greater things to bring about their salvation.

Through this season, as I finally get to sit back in my chair and catch my breath, I'm reminded of the excitement I felt when I first read this passage. What refreshing verses! God has accomplished great things in each of us. It's exciting and faith-building to remember those things, but we cannot dwell there. God wants to do new and greater things to demonstrate His love for us.

How often have we said to God, "Oh, if only we could go back to . . ." or "If only things were as good as . . ." Even in our darkest times, our faith tells us that there are better things to come, "like rivers in the desert." I don't know what you are walking through today, but the God of Israel is saying to you, "Behold, I am doing a new thing; can't you see it?"

1. What in your life is causing you to doubt, to cling to the past?
2. Be encouraged. Ask right now for strength and faith to rest in the all-powerful God.

~

Father, forgive us when we struggle with doubt, and cling to the past. Give us courage
and faith to trust that You will create for us refreshing "rivers in the desert."

Ken Atkinson
Worship Pastor
First Baptist Church, Daytona Beach, FL

Songs Are a Weapon

*Jehoshaphat stood and said, "Listen to me, Judah and people of Jerusalem! Have faith in
the* LORD *your God and you will be upheld"... Jehoshaphat appointed men to sing to the*
LORD *and to praise him for the splendor of his holiness.... As they began to sing and praise,
the* LORD *set ambushes against the men of Ammon and Moab ... and they were defeated.*

2 Chronicles 20:20–22 (NIV)

Songwriter Michael Farren tells us that "songs are a weapon against the enemy. Songs are a sword of truth." I agree with Michael; there is great power in speaking and singing the Word. Words are nuclear—generating power to energize or to destroy. God's Word tells us there is a war going on around us against an unseen enemy who will stop at nothing to destroy us. Christian author and pastor John Piper says, "The Word of God is the most powerful weapon God has given us as it is both an offensive and defensive weapon—we use it offensively to attack the enemy, but also as a defense against his blows."[21]

Words based on biblical truth or the actual Scriptures themselves cut through the lies of the enemy like a sword and give us strength. Singing words of truth provides a weapon that can open doors, break chains, bring healing and deliverance, and defeat this enemy. When Jesus was being tempted, He used the Word of God, and the enemy had to leave. Paul and Silas prayed and sang praises while in a Philippian jail. The doors then flew open and they were freed (Acts 16). Martin Luther once said that music drives away the devil and makes us glad. I have found it to be so in my own life, and I venture to guess that many of you have as well.

God has provided us with two great weapons: The Word and song. So, let's use the authority of the spoken Word of God and ambush Satan with our song of praise and truth.

1. Do you have a feeling that God is working in and through you when you are singing Scripture and scriptural truth?
2. Have you ever felt oppression from Satan leave as you sang God's Word?

～

*Lord, often we don't recognize that the words we sing are powerful, yet Your Word says
it is so. Please help us to sing Your words in faith and believe that You will respond by
holding back the forces of the devil and give us the victory that is promised in Jesus.*

Don Marsh
Associate Professor of Music and Worship, Songwriting
Liberty University, Lynchburg, VA

Which Way?

This is what the LORD says—your Redeemer, the Holy One of Israel: "I am the LORD your God, who teaches you what is best for you, who directs you in the way you should go."

Isaiah 48:17 (NIV)

I've never been averse to asking for directions! In the days before GPS, I have been known to stop multiple times in my quest to get to a particular destination. But on a recent night, even with MapQuest at my fingertips, this was not the case; I thought that I knew better!

I had gotten word that my ninety-year-old mother was being transported by ambulance from her home in Kentucky to a hospital near me in Tennessee. Being familiar with the general location of the hospital, I set out, in a hurry, to be there by the time the ambulance arrived. It was late at night and a hard rain was falling.

I could see the hospital looming ahead and made a turn in that direction. With my destination clearly in sight, I took another turn onto a smaller road. With the hospital still visible, I thought this road, even though narrow, HAD to be the correct one! It didn't take me long, however, to realize that I was driving on the city's Greenbelt, a recreational WALKING trail!

How often do we begin a new project or determine a new goal and plunge headlong into it without first asking God for His guidance? In our enthusiasm, we're pretty confident we know where we're going, only to end up in a place God didn't intend for us to be! Today, determine to ask Him first and trust that He'll lead you safely there.

1. Do you have a funny story you could tell about being lost?
2. What are some factors that keep you from looking to God first for direction?

~

Lord God, help me humble myself and listen to Your voice to guide me. In Christ, Amen.

Tempa Bader
Music Minister/Women's Ministry
Crossroads Christian Church, Gray, TN

As for You . . .

As for you, you were dead in your transgressions and sins, in which you used to live when you followed the ways of this world and of the ruler of the kingdom of the air, the spirit who is now at work in those who are disobedient. All of us also lived among them at one time, gratifying the cravings of our flesh and following its desires and thoughts. Like the rest, we were by nature deserving of wrath. But because of his great love for us, God, who is rich in mercy, made us alive with Christ even when we were dead in transgressions—it is by grace you have been saved. And God raised us up with Christ and seated us with him in the heavenly realms in Christ Jesus, in order that in the coming ages he might show the incomparable riches of his grace, expressed in his kindness to us in Christ Jesus. For it is by grace you have been saved, through faith—and this is not from yourselves, it is the gift of God—not by works, so that no one can boast. For we are God's handiwork, created in Christ Jesus to do good works, which God prepared in advance for us to do.
Ephesians 2:1–10 (NIV)

My brother is nine years older than me, and so his teachers and coaches were, by the time I arrived, my administrators. On one very memorable trip to the junior high principal's office, I was subjected to a verbal excoriation, which began with the words "*As for you, young man . . .*" The principal reminded me that he knew my brother and my family and that I was a better person than I had been acting. This trip was my last trip to the principal's office for several years (but that is another story). That man cared for me enough to not let me continue on the same destructive path, but even more so, he helped change the course of my life. I experienced grace that day.

Ephesians 2, the grace chapter of the Bible, begins with "*As for you . . .*" In this chapter Paul reminds us of where we had once been, heading in a direction away from God. I love the fact that God loved us enough not to let us continue down the wrong path but made a way for us to experience salvation by grace through faith. I love how he ends with verse 10, reminding us that, ". . . we are God's handiwork, created in Christ Jesus to do good works, which God prepared in advance for us to do."

1. What has God prepared for you to do for His kingdom?
2. What can we do to demonstrate grace to others who need Jesus?

~

Father, thank You for demonstrating Your great love for me through Your grace. Help me to demonstrate Your grace in my life. Please show me the good works You have prepared for me to do and give me the courage and strength to do them. Amen.

Don Barrick
Worship Pastor
The Woodlands First Baptist Church, The Woodlands, TX

The Heart of a Worshiper

"God is spirit, and those who worship Him must worship in spirit and truth."
John 4:24 (HCSB)

In this familiar passage of Scripture, Jesus has a conversation with the woman at the well. Throughout the dialogue, we gain insight about this future worshiper of the Lord Jesus. She is not unlike the worshiper of today.

We all have many building blocks that contribute to who we are as worshipers. There are *external elements*, like our heritage or generational characteristics. There are *internal elements* such as our temperaments and heart instincts, and there are *eternal elements* such as our moral background and spiritual gifts.

These elements help us to understand ourselves, as well as others, in a corporate worship experience. Although the Samaritan woman spoke of most of these things, Jesus gently reminded her that worship was not about her or others; it was about Him. Note verse 7 in John 4; "*Give Me*" was His opening phrase. He established immediately that this was about Him. When we come with the heart to give to the Lord Jesus, we will worship in unity, spirit, and truth.

Consider these potential applications: First, respect one another—"esteem others better than [your]selves" (Phil. 2.3 NKJV). Second, repent for making the worship experience about you. Third, join me in asking God for a spirit of renewal or revival so that the entire body of Christ may be one in declaring that Jesus is Lord!

1. Illustrate how we make worship about us.
2. Discuss what a Sunday morning might look like if every child of God came with the attitude of giving and not receiving.

~

Heavenly Father, please forgive me for making worship about me. Forgive me for bringing my preferences and placing them as a higher priority than simply recognizing You as Lord of all. I worship You simply because of what You've done and who You are. In Jesus' name, Amen.

Dr. Ron Upton
Minister of Worship and Creative Arts
Idlewild Baptist Church, Lutz, FL

Render

What shall I render to the LORD for all his benefits to me? I will lift up the cup of salvation and call on the name of the LORD, I will pay my vows to the LORD in the presence of all his people.
Psalm 116:12–14 (ESV)

The Pharisees tried to trick Jesus by showing Him a coin and asking Him about paying taxes. Jesus said we should "render unto Caesar the things that are Caesar's, and to God the things that are God's" (Mark 12:17 ESV). What should we render to God?

To truly worship is to give our full allegiance to Christ. Oswald Chambers calls it *My Utmost for His Highest.*

What is keeping you from a life totally abandoned to Jesus? What gives you deepest joy? What absorbs your time and attention? Is it your job, money, possessions, or reputation? What sin has created a barrier between you and God? Is it pride? An unforgiving spirit? Envy, lust, or anger? What is keeping you from loving God completely?

God wants an undivided heart. Our response to "all his benefits" is to "bless the LORD" (Ps. 103:1–2). To *lift up the cup of salvation* is an act of remembering that we are saved by grace; our cup is spilling over with God's grace! We *call on His name* with every breath. We *pay our vows in the presence of all His people* by joining with other believers on a regular basis to proclaim the goodness and greatness of our God—together! There is a powerful witness in our worship!

1. Where does pride have a stronghold in your life?
2. Write down what is keeping you from full abandonment to Jesus. Will you lay that thing, that sin, that relationship, that barrier down and commit to a renewed walk with Him?

~

Lord, thank You for continuing to call me. Forgive me of all that has kept me from You. Help me leave those things here and now. Soften my heart toward You. Have Your way in me. Amen.

Kevin Batson
Worship Pastor
Taylors First Baptist Church, Taylors, SC

Keys to a Faith-Filled Life

Rejoice always, pray without ceasing, give thanks in all circumstances;
for this is the will of God in Christ Jesus for you.
1 Thessalonians 5:16–18 (ESV)

Take a moment and think about one of the most exciting moments of your life. Then, think of one of the greatest times you've had talking to the Lord in prayer. Now, think of a time throughout the course of your life that you were most thankful for all that God had done.

Do you remember how each of those instances made you feel?

When we read these verses all together, it may seem like overwhelming commands, though we can clearly recall different times in our lives when we've accomplished each of them separately. These commands are attributes that should mark our Christian walk.

Rejoice always—simply choose joy. Focus on God and keep Him at the center of your life.

Pray without ceasing—have a mental attitude of constant prayerfulness, remaining in fellowship with God throughout the day. Living with an attitude of prayer will cause us to approach our daily situations differently. I once heard a pastor say these words, "To be a Christian without prayer is no more possible than to be alive without breathing."

Give thanks in ALL circumstances—giving thanks when things are going well is easy, but to give thanks in the bad times is a conscious decision to trust that the Lord is sovereign and that the very trial that we are going through is the thing that will draw us to the cross of Jesus Christ.

1. How will you begin to practice this in your daily life?
2. Are there trials in your life for which you have not yet given thanks to the Lord?

～

Father, today I rejoice in You. Keep me in an attitude of prayer, and
thank You for all You are doing even when I don't understand.

Travis Blye
Worship Pastor
Longview Point Baptist Church, Hernando, MS

Look for Jesus on Every Page

And beginning with Moses and all the Prophets, he explained to them
what was said in all the Scriptures concerning himself.
Luke 24:27 (NIV)

Jesus is the central figure of *all* Scripture. Some believers think that God is the main object of the Old Testament, and Jesus, to save us from God's wrath, takes over as the dominant theme in the New Testament, but this is false. Jesus, His role, His mission, and His love is the principal and over-arching theme of all Scripture. In fact, when our resurrected Savior showed Himself "in all the Scriptures" to these two disciples in Luke 24, He only had the Old Testament to do so.

We too, in the same way, should look for Jesus, like one searching for priceless treasure on every page of Scripture. Whether it be Jesus in the beginning of creation as the Word (Gen. 1; John 1), the one door that God closed to protect Noah and his family (Gen. 7:16), the sacrificial lamb that God provided to Abraham to spare Isaac (Gen. 22:13), the blood that was placed on the door post that provided protection to God's people from the angel of death (Exod. 12:7), or the other countless examples, Jesus Christ can be found on every page.

1. What are some other places in Scripture that Jesus is found?
2. If Jesus can be found on every page of Scripture, should He be found in every page of our life story? If someone was reading the story of our lives, would they find Him on every page as well? What are some ways we show Jesus in our everyday activities?

~

Dear Lord Jesus, help me see who You are as the central figure and theme of all Scripture. As I open Your Word, let my heart passionately desire to find You. Let my eyes be sharp to see You, and let my ears be open to hear what You have to say to me. In Your name I pray, Amen.

John Bolin
Minister of Worship and Arts
Houston's First Baptist Church, Houston, TX

When Fear Comes My Way

*The LORD is my light and my salvation—whom shall I fear? The LORD
is the stronghold of my life—of whom shall I be afraid?*
Psalm 27:1 (NIV)

There were two kinds of light in biblical times: the sun and the lamp. The sun was very radiant, unable to be stared at, and like God, the sun gives light and life. From the beginning of creation, Day 1, "God said, 'Let there be light'" (Gen. 1:3).

We live in difficult times. There are things all around us that bring us fear and concern: job transfers, financial hardship, and even the safety of our children at school. We also live in a time when more people seek an inward light and strength to overcome fear.

God *is* light. He is the source of our confidence. He is a light to His people, to show them the way when they are in doubt. It is in this light that we walk on our way and our path burns bright.

God is salvation. Only He can save us from the darkness. In trusting Him, God becomes our comfort, joy, guide, and teacher.

God is the stronghold of my life. There is no part of my life that is excluded from His protective power. He is not the stronghold for a portion of my life; He is the stronghold *of* my life! That's why we can immediately ask the question, "Of whom shall I be afraid?"

1. Am I allowing God to be my light, salvation, and stronghold?
2. When fears return, do I seek the Lord through heartfelt prayer?

~

*Father, thank You for being my light and salvation. Help me to seek You more
when fear comes my way. Thank You for being the stronghold of my life.*

Jon Skelley
Worship Pastor
Geyer Springs First Baptist Church, Little Rock, AR

Rejected or Accepted?

"You whom I have taken from the ends of the earth, and called from its remotest parts,
and said to you, 'You are My servant, I have chosen you and not rejected you.'"
Isaiah 41:9 (NASB)

Rejection is awful! I'm sure anyone can quickly recall a moment when you experienced the devastating news that rocked you to your knees. "Spiritual people" can often be the worst to deliver such news! Heartache, pain, and despair are sometimes the only emotions you feel at that moment when another direction is proposed, another person is chosen, or you are not in control. Fortunately, the Lord knows how to connect with us if we will only pay attention.

God's promises are always true and timely. If beyond the shadow of a doubt He called you, His call is consistent and enduring. Just because you get knocked in the pit every now and then, God accepts you and chooses to use you for His glory. After all, it is all about Him anyway! The words following verse 9 simply say, "Do not fear, for I am with you; do not anxiously look about you, for I am your God."

1. Have you been in the pit? Are you still there? Can you trust God enough to bring you out?
2. Do you know someone who has been in despair for many years? Perhaps you are the one to encourage them today!

~

Father, we thank You for calling us to serve You and for giving us the gifts and influence to touch the lives of those around us. May Your spirit empower us to climb out of the pit or help someone in need today. For Your glory, Amen.

James Bradford
Minister of Music
Quail Springs Baptist Church, Oklahoma City, OK

The Purpose of Fruit

But the fruit of the Spirit is love, joy, peace, patience, kindness, goodness,
faithfulness, gentleness, self-control; against such things there is no law.
Galatians 5:22–23 (ESV)

Scripture often uses the idea of bearing fruit to communicate what we, as believers, should be doing in our Christian walk. Let us remember that fruit is not for the benefit of the tree; fruit is meant to be picked and enjoyed by something other than the tree. In fact, if left unpicked, the fruit eventually falls from the branches, rots on the ground, is wasted and leads to the likelihood of diseases and insects for the tree and root system the following year.

Did you know that bearing fruit is not only a command (Matt. 3:8), but is the very purpose for which we were created and redeemed? "For we are his workmanship, created in Christ Jesus for good works, which God prepared beforehand, that we should walk in them" (Eph. 2:10 ESV).

Don't let your fruit go to waste. Bear fruit for the purpose of reaching the lost, serving the church, and serving your Lord. As you grow in Christ, help others do the same. Let us be like Paul as he writes to Timothy: "And what you have heard from me in the presence of many witnesses entrust to faithful men, who will be able to teach others also" (2 Tim. 2:2 ESV).

1. When reflecting on good works in your life, are they self-serving by nature or do they have an outward focus?
2. Re-read Galatians 5:22–23. From this list, what is one of the evidences of the fruit of the Spirit that you could sharpen, refine, and make better this week in order that you might faithfully serve someone else?

~

Lord, let my life be marked with evidence of being filled with the Holy Spirit.
Draw me closer to You so that I may be fruitful and serve as the "aroma
of Christ to God among those who are being saved and among those who
are perishing" (2 Cor. 2:15 ESV) In Christ's name I pray, Amen.

John Brewer
Associate Pastor of Worship
First Baptist Church, Mustang, OK

In Spirit and Truth

All the Levites who were musicians—Asaph, Heman, Jeduthun and their sons and relatives—stood on the east side of the altar, dressed in fine linen and playing cymbals, harps and lyres. They were accompanied by 120 priests sounding trumpets. The trumpeters and musicians joined in unison to give praise and thanks to the LORD. Accompanied by trumpets, cymbals and other instruments, the singers raised their voices in praise to the LORD and sang: "He is good; his love endures forever." Then the temple of the LORD was filled with the cloud, and the priests could not perform their service because of the cloud, for the glory of the LORD filled the temple of God.

2 Chronicles 5:12–14 (NIV)

I LOVE CHOIRS! This account in 2 Chronicles is one of the greatest worship services ever held. It reminds us of what we will be doing for *eternity* in heaven . . . worshiping Jesus . . . in a *CHOIR!*

Whether it be Jehoshaphat going into battle with the choir leading the march or this account in today's Scripture, throughout the Bible we see the power and effectiveness of God's people joining together in authentic, genuine worship!

Every Wednesday night and Sunday morning, our worship centers and choir rooms should be a "microcosm" of what heaven will be like . . . millions upon millions of those who have been redeemed by the blood of the Lamb, from every tribe and tongue and nation and generation, all worshiping before the throne with abandon!

God gives us this awesome privilege and opportunity to experience a little bit of "heaven on earth" every time we gather to worship together here on the earth.

All throughout the Scriptures, we are admonished to worship in Spirit and Truth.

I guarantee you that this Sunday, behind all the smiles and handshakes, there will be a lot of hurting people in your congregation. Someone just lost a job; someone just received some bad news from their doctor; someone is going through some deep waters with their family.

Our job? Simply lead these people into the intimate, manifest presence of God where they can feel His presence and sense the power of God working in their lives.

As you prepare to lead your congregation in worship this Sunday, allow yourself to "flash ahead" to the heavenly choir where we will worship in spirit and truth for eternity! You'll have no trouble getting motivated to sing with abandon to our worthy Lord!

1. How can I be a more effective worshiper in both my private and public worship?
2. Who can I encourage this week that I know is going through a challenging time?

～

Lord, help me to worship with abandon in both my private and public worship as a true participant in authentic, genuine worship. May my worship be pleasing to Your ears. In the worthy name of Jesus, Amen.

Dr. Phil Barfoot
President / CEO
Celebration Concert Tours International / CCT Music, Franklin, TN

Stand Firm

Be watchful, stand firm in the faith, act like men, be strong.
1 Corinthians 16:13 (ESV)

When I was a younger boy in junior high school, I decided to play football. I can still hear my coach telling me to stand firm, hold your ground, and don't let them run over you. I did my best to do that, but it seemed like so many times I was the one getting run over by those who were a little bigger and older than me. Have you ever felt like folks were telling you just to stand up, stand firm, and hold your position?

Many years ago, my younger brother had taken our little aluminum fishing boat out to fish on the lake. He was only just a few feet off shore, but to him at that age it seemed like he was miles out. As he decided to open a lawn chair in the boat to sit in, he lost his balance, flipped the chair and boat over, and all went into the water, even all the fishing gear. As my brother was floundering in the water, a man on the shore yelled at him and told him to stand up. The water was only about two feet deep so he finally just stood up. It seemed so funny that he thought he was in water way over his head when he was only a couple of feet off the shore. All he needed was someone to tell him to stand up, stand firm, and you will be fine.

How about you today? Do you feel like you are in way over your head and just need for someone to tell you to stand up and stand firm? Do you need someone to let you know that it is going to be all right if you just hang in there and stand tall? Stand firm and, I promise, you will rise above the water in no time.

1. When has God called you to stand firm?
2. Has standing firm ever cost you?

~

Dear Father, I pray that as we face the trials and tribulations of this world that You would give us the strength to stand firm and hold fast. Help us to rely on Your strength and Your Word each and every day. Give us the power to rise above the water and stand tall.

Wayne Bridges
Traditional Worship Leader/Senior Adults
First Baptist Church, Ruston, LA

All You Have to Give Is You

I appeal to you therefore, brothers, by the mercies of God, to present your bodies as a living sacrifice, holy and acceptable to God, which is your spiritual worship. Do not be conformed to this world, but be transformed by the renewal of your mind, that by testing you may discern what is the will of God, what is good and acceptable and perfect.
Romans 12:1–2 (ESV)

In the Old Testament, before Jesus gave Himself for our sins, they would bring animals to be sacrificed for the sins of the people. The old system of sacrifice always had an ending . . . death. It was in the context of this system that the apostle Paul writes something very profound: "offer *yourself* as a *living* sacrifice." This is a significant departure from the previous requirement for death for the one sacrificing. Instead, Jesus has now paid the complete and total penalty for our sin on the cross. His death was and is sufficient.

Paul is saying that our sacrifice is a call to in-depth, internal, spiritual change through the power of the Holy Spirit and His victory over death. We now have the ability to be different, not what the world says we should be or how we should act or respond. We are being transformed! The Holy Spirit works from the inside of us to help us think and respond differently . . . renewing our mind. This powerful transformation only comes through the person and work of Jesus Christ and His Word. Change is possible when we allow Him to transform our thinking.

1. Ask the Lord to reveal the area of your thinking about Jesus Christ and how He works in and through you that is not consistent with His example in Scripture.
2. Ask the Lord to put under the microscope of His Holy Spirit your identity, decisions, and actions so that you can clearly see what does and does not line up with God's Word.

~

Lord Jesus, I present my body, mind, and spirit to You as a living sacrifice. I confess today that I desire to follow Your example. I want to think like You, act like You, respond like You, and love like You. I want to honor You with my life by knowing You more and understanding and applying Your truth in Scripture to my own daily life. Help me to follow after You and in the process, please transform my mind, my heart, and my life. Amen.

Jeff Brockelman
Worship Pastor
Anderson Mill Road Baptist Church, Moore, SC

It Just Makes Sense

He has put a new song in my mouth—praise to our God; Many
will see it and fear, and will trust in the LORD.
Psalm 40:3 (NKJV)

We can't *taste* the sunrise over the ocean. We don't *feel* Mom's homemade apple pie . . . that is, until we've had a third piece—then we feel it for hours. So how can one *see* the song in our mouth? I tell our choir often that if the audio in the room were to suddenly be silenced and the congregation is unable to hear our song, they should be able to see it.

The expression on our face and the exuberance of our worship should communicate our love and grateful devotion to Jesus, even in the midst of a less-than-best kind of day. This heart-song that was placed there by God Himself transcends our seasons of disappointment, loneliness, and fear. Perhaps that's what the songwriter had in mind when writing, *"This joy I have, the world didn't give it, and the world can't take it away."*[22] A heart that has been changed by the saving power of the gospel cannot be silent. It must sing! And when our heart sings, people see it.

1. Is my heart-song visible? Does it invite others to "taste and see that the LORD is good" (Ps. 34:8 NIV)?
2. Am I allowing my current circumstances to steal my joy and silence my heart-song?

～

God, I thank You for the song You've placed in my heart. Tune my heart today and
every day to sing Your praise so that others may see and know Your goodness.

Scott Bullman
Worship Pastor
Thomas Road Baptist Church, Lynchburg, VA

Anticipation of Worship

I was glad when they said unto me, Let us go into the house of the LORD.
Psalm 122:1 (KJV)

I'm sure we've all been in a place during our lives where it was challenging to repeat the words of the psalmist. I remember one particular time in my ministry when the relationships among the ministry staff were quite dysfunctional. Because of the many challenges, there were times, quite frankly, that I dreaded leading a worship service.

Perhaps some of you have had similar experiences. It may have been a time or a place when there was something in your life that robbed you of the joy of going "into the house of the LORD"—the loss of a loved one, a physical ailment, or a strained relationship. Regardless of what the challenge may be, I have found that healing can come by simply placing my focus on God (not on myself) and the outcomes that He can accomplish when He becomes the sole object of my worship.

Once our sole focus is on God and what He can accomplish every time we come together for worship, we will be filled with anticipation. I remember many times when choir members would share their excitement with me prior to our departure on a mission trip—the kind of excitement that children have prior to a trip to Disney World. The planning and the anticipation of all that we would experience made the trip all that more special. The same is true for worship. When we expect great things, great things will happen.

1. What are some challenges in your life that hinder you from having joy when you enter into corporate worship?
2. Do you expect something to happen as a result of worship?

~

Dear God, help me see You for who You really are when I prepare myself for worship. Help me expect great things because You are a great God. Amen!

Carlos Ichter
Minister of Music and Worship
Tallowood Baptist Church, Houston, TX

Jesus Loves Me

See how very much our Father loves us, for he calls
us his children, and that is what we are!
1 John 3:1a (NLT)

I t's really simple, yet we get so caught up in our lives that we forget. Our attention is focused on our work responsibilities, family issues, providing for our families, etc. We become distracted with what we sing in church, when that carpet will be replaced, the correct color paint for the walls . . . it goes on and on.

Is that man wearing shorts in worship? Is that person sitting in my seat? Should we have a choir and orchestra or just a band? What format will reach more people? That was way too loud. That doesn't sound like music for church. Those jeans are disrespectful. The church budget is just too big. Those people just don't fit here. Like I said, it goes on and on and on . . .

It's really so simple that we forget. A Civil War–era song states it all. We teach it to our children and take pride when they learn it and sing it. Oh, we don't sing it anymore, of course. It's for children . . .

"Jesus loves me, this I know, for the Bible tells me so." My pastor says often that the only thing that will matter in one hundred years is Jesus. How true! What will truly matter is what we have done with Jesus. When we remember this very simple truth, our lives will take on a whole new perspective, guiding everything we do. "Yes, Jesus loves me, the Bible tells me so."

1. Who can I tell about the simple love of Jesus today?
2. How do I need to change in order to let the simple love of Jesus show to others?

~

Lord, help me today to remember that I am loved by You and that
You love everyone I see today just as You love me. Amen.

Keith Clutts
Worship Pastor
Grand Avenue Baptist Church, Fort Smith, AR

What Do You Pursue?

One thing have I asked of the LORD, that will I seek after: that I may dwell in the house of the LORD all the days of my life, to gaze upon the beauty of the LORD and to inquire in his temple.

Psalm 27:4 (ESV)

When you really want something, you pursue it. You may want bacon in the morning but will settle for cereal if the refrigerator is empty. If you long for bacon, you will delay satisfying your hunger as you make a trip to the store. When you want something bad enough, you will do what it takes to satisfy your desire.

The psalm writer has a request: to dwell in the presence of God every day. His desire is strong enough that he not only asks for but seeks to have this close fellowship with our Creator. His active pursuit reveals that abiding with God is the most important thing in his life.

We should seek the presence of God every day. We need to take time to pray, to dive deep into Scripture, and to walk each moment aware of Him. Nothing should come before our desire for fellowship with God.

1. How can you actively seek to dwell in God's presence?
2. What are some things that can interfere with our pursuit of God?

~

God, please increase my desire for Your presence. Deepen in me a hunger for Your Word and a thirst for prayer. May I long after You.

Michael Cole
Associate Pastor of Music and Worship
Morrison Heights Baptist Church, Clinton, MS

How Can I Keep from Singing?

My heart is confident in you, O God; no wonder I can sing your praises with all my heart!
Psalm 108:1 (NLT)

I recently had the privilege of speaking at a friend's internment at Arlington National Cemetery, a place designated for men and women who have served our country in the armed forces. Scott's service was full of military honors and ceremony—a complete military band, a caisson with six white horses, and a twenty-one-gun salute. All of this celebrated his dedication and many years spent serving his country through military service, but none of this was as important as his devotion to his Lord and Savior.

Scott was a Christian above everything else and loved serving the Lord through music and worship. He played the piano, led choirs, and had a beautifully trained bass voice. When he received the devastating diagnosis of cancer, Scott chose to live out the remainder of his life testifying of God's greatness instead of giving up and feeling discouraged.

The psalmist David is a good example of one who trusted God in times of distress and pain. When he was faced with adversity, his confidence in the Lord triggered a response of great singing and worship. He testifies in Psalm 108 that God is in charge of the battles that lie ahead and that no earthly army comprised of men can defend him like God can. Scott and David knew that God was in control of their situations and that worship was the response to every circumstance, both good and bad.

1. What is your first reaction to a difficult situation? Is it to give God praise?
2. What are other ways to worship God during difficult times?

~

Heavenly Father, thank You for holding me in my times of weakness and for teaching me to worship You even through the storm. I pray that my life will be a testimony of a faithful follower and an obedient worshiper.

David Jones
Director of Music and Worship
Immanuel Bible Church, Springfield, VA

What Does God Sound Like?

And he said, "Go out and stand on the mount before the LORD." And behold, the LORD passed by, and a great and strong wind tore the mountains and broke in pieces the rocks before the LORD, but the LORD was not in the wind. And after the wind an earthquake, but the LORD was not in the earthquake. And after the earthquake a fire, but the LORD was not in the fire. And after the fire the sound of a low whisper.

1 Kings 19:11–12 (ESV)

Do you remember your grade school teachers? I sure do. If you are like me, you had many different kinds of teachers. I definitely remember teachers who I would call "yellers." In order to get our attention, they would yell over the sound of the whole class. But I also remember Miss Luttrell. If she really wanted to get our attention, she would whisper. When she did that, we knew she meant business.

I believe the Holy Spirit is a lot like Miss Luttrell. He's not going to scream in order to get my attention; He's simply going to whisper until I start to listen. I am told that I'm a good listener and consider that quite a compliment. Are you a good listener?

Are you in tune enough with the Holy Spirit to hear His voice? Would you know the voice of God if you heard it?

1. What is God whispering to you in this very moment?
2. What do you need to change in order to hear His whisper?

~

God, we live in a loud world! Help me to slow down enough in order to be able to not only hear Your whisper but to know what You sound like. Help me to turn Your whisper into obedience. Amen.

Chris Copeland
Worship Pastor
Central Church, Collierville, TN

Demonstrate Your Love

But God demonstrates his own love for us in this:
While we were still sinners, Christ died for us.
Romans 5:8 (NIV)

In that great bastion of theology, *My Fair Lady*, Eliza Doolittle breaks into song singing (in part):

"Words! Words! I'm so sick of words!
I get words all day through;
Don't talk of stars burning above;
If you're in love, show me!
Don't talk of June, don't talk of fall!
Don't talk at all! Show me!"[23]

I believe there is a world out there saying that very thing to Christians. "Don't talk of Christ's love, show me!" Throughout Scripture, there are so many examples of God demonstrating His love. When Adam and Eve sinned, God Himself made them coverings. Before Jacob's family even knew about the great famine, God showed His love by sending Joseph ahead to Egypt, arranging for him to be in charge of the entire grain supply. God had Hosea to be reconciled to Gomer, even though she was an adulteress. "Love her as the LORD loves the Israelites, though they turn to other gods" (Hosea 3:1 NIV).

As followers of Christ, we need to follow His example of demonstrating love. Jesus said in John 14:15, "If you love Me, you will keep My commands" (HCSB). In other words, "If you love Me, show Me by doing." When we pray for God to help someone, He may be waiting for *us* to help them. Ask God to give you a sensitivity to those around you.

1. What needs do you see around you?
2. In what specific ways can you demonstrate Christ's love to those around you?

Lord, give us a sensitivity to those around us. Help us to see what
we can do in Your name. Give us the courage to do it.

Glenn Crosthwait
Worship Pastor
Johns Creek Baptist Church, Alpharetta, GA

Let the Journey Begin!

"But seek first His kingdom and His righteousness, and all these things will be added to you."
Matthew 6:33 (NASB)

Have you ever been "stuck" in a long-term time of waiting? I'm not talking about a few days of waiting for a clear decision. I'm talking about years spent in prayer, fasting, longing, or possibly even some agonizing. Maybe you desire a spouse, a child, a job, healing, or a wayward family member to come home. The bad news is that these periods of life are never easy. The good news is you're not "stuck" there. God has a purpose and a plan!

In these situations it may be impossible to move the variables, but it is possible to move your focus. This verse teaches us to take our mind off what is going on around us, and to look to what God wants to do in us and through us. It's easy in these days to fixate on ourselves, but it takes strength to push past and look to God. The truth is it takes absolute surrender to say, "All I have right now is You, Lord." Once we're able to do this, the Bible says we will receive what He has for us! Sometimes, what we receive may be different from our original desire, but our focus on Him helps make His desires our desires.

1. What or who are you seeking after?
2. What can you do to better seek His will?

∼

Father God, we praise You for who You are, not just for what You have done.
We thank You for the merciful way You have met our needs. Please help
us to give today totally over to You. Help us to follow Your leading and to
make much of You in all we do. We pray this in Jesus' name, Amen.

Charles Darus
Worship Pastor
First Baptist Church, Kissimmee, FL

Identity in Christ

"But to all who believed him and accepted him, he gave the right to become children of God."
John 1:12 (NLT)

R onda Rousey was in the news a great deal in November of 2015. She was the bantam-weight boxing champion and was ranked #1 in the world. She dominated her sport. She was picked to win the UFC fight with contender Holly Holm. However, Rousey was knocked out by Holly Holm and lost the fight.

I am not a fight fan. I don't get it, but listen to this quote Ronda Rousey made during an interview with Ellen DeGeneres:

> I was like in the medical room and I was like down in the corner, I was like what am I anymore if I am not this and I was literally sitting there like thinking about killing myself and that exact second I am like I am nothing.[24]

It made me think about identity. Musicians and performers often deal with the same thing. Even worship leaders and church musicians are susceptible. Our musical skill or ability should not be what defines who we are. Our identity should be in Christ and Christ alone. Sure, we love music and enjoy playing and singing, but what happens when the lights go down?

As a follower of Jesus, I pray the music in us is only a reflection of the One who gives those gifts. Our identity should be rooted in the relationship we have with Jesus. Our peace, contentment, and joy should be consistently maintained because of Him and Him alone.

1. Is there anything more important than our identity in Christ?
2. How can we strengthen our identity in Jesus?

~

Father, thank You for adopting me into the family of God because of my relationship with Your Son, Jesus. May I never lose sight of my identity in Him. Amen.

Terry Hurt
Executive and Worship Pastor
Great Hills Baptist Church, Austin, TX

Is This All There Is?

"Man, who is born of a woman, is short-lived and full of turmoil. . . . If a man dies, will he live again? I will wait all the days of my struggle until my change and release will come."
Job 14:1, 14 (AMP)

Job surely had his struggles! He even came to the point in his life where he finally had to say, "Is this all there is?" If I die, is this the best it will ever be? Job's questions can be heard all around us today. Just turn on the radio to any station—pop, rock, country, or rap—and you will hear songs filled with this thought, that this is the best it will ever be! Songs of no hope or future. Listen to people on the talk shows and you will hear the same, but Job later saw the bigger picture. We know the "rest of the story," as Paul Harvey used to say! God has a perfect plan for our lives, but it is not accomplished apart from Him!

"The angel shall sound, The shout of His coming.
The sleeping shall rise, From their slumbering place.
And those who remain, Shall be changed in a moment,
And we shall behold Him, Then face to face.
We shall behold Him, Face to face in all of His glory.
We shall behold Him, Our Savior and Lord." —Dottie Rambo[25]

1. How easily are you discouraged about the events of "right now" in your life?
2. Imagine what God has in store for you tomorrow or in the future. Commit today to live for what you can't yet see.

~

Dear God, please forgive me when I am weak and only see today. I know that in Your perfect will there is a better day and time coming. Lord, please help me to be patient and to wait on You!

Paul Davis
Worship Pastor
Northcrest Baptist Church, Meridian, MS

Let Him Sing!

"The LORD your God is with you, the Mighty Warrior who saves. He will take great delight in you; in his love he will no longer rebuke you, but will rejoice over you with singing."
Zephaniah 3:17 (NIV)

Hearing four- to eight-part singing is a joyous event, especially when sung with excellence. Possibly the sweetest sound is that of young children singing in beautiful unison then breaking into two-part harmony!

However, there is a voice I have yet to hear, although I have read about it, but reading about it and experiencing it are two totally different things. Zephaniah 3:17 states that God, the Father, rejoices over me with singing! What a magnificent voice that must be!

Why would He sing over me? The Scripture is clear: He is with(in) me, He saved me, He greatly delights in me, He quiets me with His love. He, God our Father, has done all the work and He is overjoyed at my life in Christ!

We aren't much different from the Israelites. In Zephaniah, the Lord decided to send Israel's enemies against them because of their sin. They were defeated and sent into exile, but the Lord, once again, had compassion on His holy and repentant people and delivered them from the hands of their captors. Sound familiar? In our sin we were taken captive by Satan, held in bondage as slaves to sin. Then, we repent, and God's compassion comes overflowing like a river that washes us clean and removes our chains, and *He sings!*

Let Him sing! Let the song of love, compassion, freedom, and delight fill you with an everlasting song—Hallelujah! Our God sings!

1. Because He is with(in) me, He saved me. He greatly delights in me. He quiets me with His love. How do I sing over Him to thank Him for His never-ending love?
2. In the reading of God's Word, do I remain still long enough to hear His still, small voice singing over me?

~

Father, joy overflows within me just knowing that You sing over me! I pray for quietness within my soul so that I may hear Your still, small voice. In Jesus' name, Amen.

Dr. Mark Deakins
Worship Minister
Broadway Christian Church, Lexington, KY

What Is Missing?

"But it is a spirit in man, and the breath of the Almighty gives them understanding."
Job 32:8 (NASB)

The Spirit of God has made me, and the breath of the Almighty gives me life.
Job 33:4 (CSB)

"Behold, I will cause breath to enter you that you may come to life."
Ezekiel 37:5 (NLT, paraphrase)

The Lord Jesus will slay him with the breath of His mouth.
2 Thessalonians 2:8 (AMP)

We learn the music. We plug up the mics. We check the instruments. We put the lyrics in the presentation software. We have a sound check. Everything is ready. We start the service. The choir sings beautifully. The band is playing wonderfully. The transitions are flawless. The lights go on and off at just the right times. The lyrics all go on the screen perfectly. Everything seemed to just click. However, when we finish, we feel something was missing. We sense that there was an emptiness in the worship. It bothers us during the message. We leave for lunch, wondering what we missed.

Have you ever had those weekends? Have you wondered if you really made a difference? Have you ever left church feeling you missed the mark? For me, the answer is "yes," to all of the above. So, what happened? What went wrong? One thing I understand more every week is that, without God, I will fail. I need Him. I need His strength. I need His power. I need God to breathe His breath of life into our band, our choir, and me. His breath changes everything.

The breath of God created everything. That same breath gives life to us and power to our music.

1. Search the internet for "the breath of God." Write down what you find.
2. Read the words to the songs for this week's service. Ask God to breathe life into every word and every note.

~

Father, You tell me to "lean not on my own understanding." Today, I commit all of my gifts, talents and training to You. I ask You to breathe life into me, my church, and my worship. Give us the privilege of watching Your breath of life change the hearts of people, starting with mine. Amen.

Chip Leake
Worship Pastor
Thompson Station Church, Thompson's Station, TN

Humbled before the Exalted One

Oh come, let us sing to the LORD; let us make a joyful noise to the rock of our salvation! . . .
Oh come, let us worship and bow down; let us kneel before the LORD, our Maker!
Psalm 95:1, 6 (ESV)

Humility does not come easily. In a culture enraptured with ego, humility almost seems shameful to pursue. However, without humility, we cannot hope to truly worship Almighty God.

Searching for humility begins with the pursuit of understanding who God is. He is the Author of all living things, each uniquely created by His will. The Lord is also the Source of all life, giving all of His creations their next breath and heartbeat. Every living thing on the earth is here because God has chosen to make it so. He has a purpose for everything and everyone we see.

Our Lord is perfect. He has never sinned; never made a mistake; never forgotten to do something; never failed to accomplish anything. This is unfathomable because we are so prone to sin, mistake-making, and forgetfulness. God, however, is not like us. He is different from us; He is holy.

This perfect, powerfully creative God throws a curveball we cannot see coming: HE LOVES US! When we do not feel that we deserve love, He loves us. When we cannot feel or see the love of the Lord, it is still there. The undying love of the Lord was perfectly demonstrated by the salvific death of Jesus, God's Son.

We joyfully praise the Lord because we are humbled by the great love the Exalted One shows us.

1. Take a moment to reflect on God's perfection and authority.
2. Think of one or more ways God has demonstrated His love to you.

～

Almighty God, forgive me for spending so much time focused on myself. Help me to focus more on You, Your holiness, and Your love. I ask for Your help in the name of Jesus, my Savior. Amen.

Chris Diffey
Minister of Music and Worship
Lakeside Baptist Church, Birmingham, AL

Remembering to Surrender

Cast all your anxiety on him because he cares for you.
1 Peter 5:7 (NIV)

I cannot count how many times I had sung the hymn "I Surrender All" in my lifetime, and once again, I had picked this familiar hymn for our morning worship service. Five months earlier, I had accepted the position of Minister of Worship at First Baptist Church Tulsa. I had been living out of a hotel or commuting to my new church while my family lived in a different city. My wife and I had been searching for the perfect home, but we were constantly frustrated in that search. We had the best realtors showing us homes, but nothing was happening. I needed my family with me and they needed me with them.

That Sunday afternoon I was driving around Tulsa. I was tense, at a loss for what to do, and then, I was overwhelmed with conviction. I had just led our church in singing "I Surrender All," and yet, I was not surrendering myself or situation to Christ. I surrendered my house hunt to the Lord. Within ten seconds I saw an open house sign that led to a perfect house, a perfect school district, and a perfect location. I made an offer at the open house. The realtor had never sold a home at an open house event in her entire thirty-year career. I still live there today.

1. Is there an area in your life you have forgotten to surrender to the Lord?
2. Begin praying daily through that area, asking God to take control and lead you.

～

Father, forgive me for forgetting that I need to surrender all areas of my life to You. Please remind me of Your presence when I forget to include You in my life.

Jeff Elkins
Minister of Worship
First Baptist Church, Tulsa, OK

Are You Great?

Then his disciples began arguing about which of them was the greatest. But Jesus knew their thoughts, so he brought a little child to his side. Then he said to them, "Anyone who welcomes a little child like this on my behalf welcomes me, and anyone who welcomes me also welcomes my Father who sent me. Whoever is the least among you is the greatest."

Luke 9:46–48 (NLT)

Pride is huge. It is something we all have to deal with throughout the journey of our lives. Do you ever judge yourself against others and feel that you're a better person than they are? Try comparing yourself to Christ. As Christians, we are miserable replicas when comparing ourselves to Him. Do you ever complete a project and need or expect praise from someone? Do you ever look down on someone for not being as educated as you? For the musicians reading this, do you think you're really that good?

Imagine, for a moment, the disciples arguing about which one was the greatest and throw yourself into the mix? Could you be the greatest in the room? Being a musician, I can say I've had my struggles with pride. Jesus even spoke to the religious leaders about their pride in Luke 11:46, "What sorrow also awaits you experts in religious law! For you crush people with unbearable religious demands, and you never lift a finger to ease the burden" (NLT).

Pride is a tool that our enemy uses to keep us from true greatness. I remember one day needing some counsel from a friend about a certain situation. While I was right in the middle of the action I wanted to take, I was prideful in the way I was going to present my argument. As my friend walked out of my office he said to me, "A servant's heart ALWAYS wins!" That statement hit me like a ton of bricks. Now it hangs on a wall in my office to remind me to fight pride.

The Bible tells us that in order to be the greatest we must become less so that He becomes greater. We all must have a servant's heart, because a servant's heart always wins. Do you have a servant's heart?

1. Do you notice pride in your own life? Are you a servant?
2. Do you see that becoming a servant to others brings glory to God?

~

Lord, help me to have a servant's heart. Destroy the pride that is in me. Help me Lord to have the mind of Christ in all I do and think. Help me to become less so that You become greater. Amen.

Chris Ellenburg
Minister of Music
First Baptist Church, North Spartanburg, SC

A Hill to Die On

"If anyone wants to follow after me, let him deny himself,
take up his cross daily, and follow me."
Luke 9:23 (CSB)

In these days of social media, it seems everyone wants to be heard. One pastor friend of mine used to jokingly say, "This is my humble opinion which I highly regard," and then proceed with his thoughts about some issue. I'm sure he was kidding, but more and more we find examples of people who seem to really feel that way.

With the rise of the public opinion outlets, more and more "hills to die on" surface every day. Political issues, theological debates, and even smaller issues like sports and entertainment generate intense debate and argument.

It happens in the church as well. We are so convinced we are right, and that in many cases, we would rather win the argument than win our brother.

"Should the choir wear robes or not?"

"We need to sing contemporary songs!"

"Why don't we use the organ anymore?"

"The drums are too loud!"

It goes on and on . . .

Jesus actually did tell us about a hill we should die on—every day. That hill is our own pride. We should take our self-interests and ego to the cross every day.

It seems to me that if we would die on that hill every day, the rest of them would take care of themselves.

1. What current "hill to die on" could you let go of today, just by dying to self?
2. What issue in your church would evaporate if just a few leaders let go of their own pride? How about in your family?

～

Lord Jesus, thank You for dying in my place on the cross. I accept Your invitation to take up my cross and follow You. Help me die on this hill—every day—and leave the rest to You. Amen.

Mike Harland
Director of LifeWay Worship
LifeWay Christian Resources, Nashville, TN

Houston, We Have a Problem!

May the righteous be glad and rejoice before God. May they be happy and joyful.
Psalm 68:3 (NIV)

I love church-folk: Christians, Christ-followers, believers . . . whatever term you use, but let's be honest, many of us have a problem. It's not necessarily what I would consider a spiritual problem, although that *could* be at the root of it.

I've spent my entire adult life leading worship. I was taught that as I lead, I need to smile—to be an encourager to the saints. If I look happy, it will be contagious. I'm sad to report that often that concept hasn't worked.

Why do so many of us who name the name of Jesus look so sad? It's not only at church. It's in our neighborhoods, at our offices, and when we're home. Where is our joy? Why don't we smile?

I know we all have different personalities; not everyone is a "smiler" by nature, and yes, life has its difficult moments. But what if someone was watching you this week in worship, at work, in Starbucks—wherever? Think about a person who's hurting, looking for answers, or perhaps at the end of their rope. Would the simple expression on your face speak to them of the joy, hope, and happiness that Jesus offers? The Amplified Bible translates John 10:10 this way, "I came that they may have and enjoy life, and have it in abundance [to the full, *till it overflows*]" (emphasis added).

Years ago, I heard The Florida Boys sing a song on Sunday morning TV. I'll never forget the title: "If you're happy, notify your face . . . if you love Jesus, show it to the human race!" What a concept!

1. Have you ever been encouraged by having someone smile at you?
2. Will you make a conscious effort to encourage others with your smile today?

~

Father, use my smile to encourage someone who is struggling with life today. And may the abundant life of Jesus shine through me everywhere I go. In Jesus' name, Amen.

Joe Estes
Minister of Music and Worship
First Baptist Church, Trussville, AL

Does Your Life Reflect the Love of Jesus?

"A new command I give you: Love one another. As I have loved you, so you must love one another. By this everyone will know that you are my disciples, if you love one another."
John 13:34–35 (NIV)

The absolute most important thing God has commanded us to do is to love Him first and to love one another. Every decision we make either reflects the love of God or the love of ourselves. We cannot effectively show love to one another without first showing love to God. How different would things be if before EVERY decision we make, we first ask God? Then, we asked ourselves if this decision reflects love of God or love of myself? It is kind of scary; many times we think some decisions are not spiritual decisions, and we don't have to ask God. But if our life is to reflect love to God and others, then every decision matters.

Read 1 Corinthians 13:4–8a. This is the best way to measure whether the love you have is the love of God.

On our own strength, we are not capable of loving others in the biblical way described in this passage. We must ask the Holy Spirit to empty us of our selfishness and pride and to stir up the Holy Spirit who lives in us (if you are a follower of Jesus). Stirring up the Holy Spirit, who our Father in heaven has given us as a helper, can empower us with the love of Jesus.

"By this everyone will know that you are my disciples, if you love one another" (John 13:35 NIV).

1. Does everyone you come in contact with know you are a Jesus-follower based on your love for them?
2. Do people know you love God and love them more than you do yourself?

~

Father, empty me of myself, stir up Your Holy Spirit that is living within me. Allow me to be able to reflect the love of Jesus in my life, that everyone I come in contact with will see Jesus in me.

Matt Fallin
Associate Pastor of Worship
Santuck Baptist Church, Wetumpka, AL

See What I Did There?

The heavens are telling of the glory of God; and their expanse is declaring the work of His hands. Day to day pours forth speech, and night to night reveals knowledge. There is no speech, nor are there words; their voice is not heard."
Psalm 19:1–3 (NASB)

It's easy to think of worship as just music. The fact that we call ourselves "worship leaders" probably doesn't help convey the all-encompassing lifestyle of worship beyond church buildings. We worship by hearing, singing, saying, and doing (i.e., bowing or lifting hands). Rarely though do we talk in terms of worshiping with our eyes. Visual worship should be a vibrant aspect to both the corporate body and individual. Scripture says, "taste and *see,*" "the heavens are *telling,*" "lift our *eyes* unto the hills"; the Lord expects us to use our eyes to help our hearts grasp His greatness.

It is important to note, however, that God never speaks separate from His Word. For example, when the heavens "declare," it's not a separate message from Scripture; it is a reminder of Scripture. God has spoken everything in the Bible, so trying to add additional messages is bad news (Rev. 22:18). However, creation screams and reminds us of God's largeness, beauty, and mercy. We couldn't understand His infiniteness without the stars. The snow reminds me of Jesus' cleansing. Look at creation: birds, lilies, and grass (Matt. 6:26, 28, 30). Look around today, take in all that God has created and visually worship Him.

1. What are some aspects of creation that help you worship most deeply?
2. How can we visually help others worship each weekend during church services?

Lord Jesus, help me lift my eyes beyond the troubles of each day to behold Your testimony of faithfulness and grace in all Your creation (Col. 1:16).

Mark Maier
Pastor of Worship
First Baptist Church, Rogers, AR

Another Step Beyond

"But love your enemies, do good, and lend, hoping for nothing in return; and your reward will be great, and you will be sons of the Most High. For He is kind to the unthankful and evil. Therefore be merciful, just as your Father also is merciful."
Luke 6:35–36 (NKJV)

Walking with God is going another step beyond. Beyond what the world thinks. Beyond what we think. Walking with God seems to be opposite of all our natural inclinations. We tend to be selfish, while Jesus is selfless. We want judgment for others, but mercy for ourselves. We only have to check out social media for a little while to see cruelty and hate on display. Jesus is full of mercy and grace for all people. He is always compassionate and kind.

We are never more like Jesus than when we are kind to others. Kindness, mercy, and compassion, however, are just not valued in our culture today. So, when we are kind, we look very different from the world. When we are kind to others, we look more like Christ, and people will notice.

Is there someone you know that needs some kindness? Ask the Holy Spirit to open your eyes and give you an opportunity to be kind today. Ask God to help you go another step further in your walk with Him.

1. What would our churches look like if we were truly kind, compassionate, and merciful with people we encounter each week?
2. Could kindness and compassion be effective tools for evangelism?

~

Father, I don't want to keep doing the same old things the same old ways. Help me to step up my walk with You. Help me to be more kind and compassionate. Jesus, help me to be more like You. Amen.

Chason Farris
Worship Pastor
First Baptist Church, Hendersonville, NC

Run the Race with Faith

Therefore . . . let us also lay aside every encumbrance and the sin which so easily
entangles us, and let us run with endurance the race that is set before us, fixing our eyes
on Jesus, the author and perfecter of faith, who for the joy set before Him endured the
cross, despising the shame, and has sat down at the right hand of the throne of God.
Hebrews 12:1–2 (NASB)

The life we live is not a short sprint—a mere forty-yard dash. No, it is a marathon. It requires training, endurance, perseverance, and a steady gaze toward the long haul with our eyes on the prize. We live this life by faith, following the Word of God—the Lord's roadmap for life.

We march forward, one step at a time, with our eyes fixed on Jesus, even when we cannot see the road before us. Christ modeled endurance as He walked the Via Dolorosa. He was despised and rejected by man, well-acquainted with grief. He defeated death, hell, and the grave and victoriously reigns at the right-hand of God. We, too, are exhorted to walk by faith, not by sight (2 Cor. 5:7).

Although we may stumble and fall, we press on. Satan roars about as a lion, seeking those he may devour. Resist him and stand firm in the faith (1 Pet. 5:8–9). Remember that God is faithful and will not allow you to be tempted beyond what you are able, but with the temptation, God will provide a way of escape so that you will be able to endure it (1 Cor. 10:13). We trust, we obediently follow, and we run with determination the race marked out before us as to win the prize (1 Cor. 9:24).

1. How would you compare the life we live in Christ to the training, preparation, and running of a marathon?
2. What are you doing on a daily basis to prepare?

Father God, I am weak, but You are strong. Grant me grace and strength to run
this race. Forgive me when I fail You. Lift my head up, allow me to keep my
eyes focused on Jesus. Thank You for the example of Christ. Hold my hand and
guide my feet so that I run this race with faith. In Jesus' name, Amen.

Joe Fitzpatrick
Worship and Music Pastor
First Baptist Church, Nashville, TN

Don't You Know Who I AM?

And Jesus said to him, "'If you can'! All things are possible for one who believes."
Immediately the father of the child cried out and said, 'I believe; help my unbelief.'"
Mark 9:23–24 (ESV)

In Mark 9:17 we meet a father whose son is possessed by what the Bible calls an "unclean spirit." This spirit has made the child mute and full of violent seizures. It's very important to take note that when the child was brought to Jesus, the spirit inside the boy began to convulse. Yes, even the demon inside the boy immediately knew who Jesus was and feared Him.

Out of desperation and fear, the father looks at Jesus and says in verse 22, "If you can do anything, have compassion on us and help us." What this father didn't know is that Christ had seen the dawn of time and could change the outcome of any situation with a single word. With a holy confidence, Jesus says in verse 23, "If you can . . ." almost to say, "Don't you know who I AM?!!! All things are possible for those who believe." Scripture then tells us that the father cried out, "I believe, help my unbelief." WOW! What an incredible statement. The father knew in that very moment that Christ was the only hope for his possessed son, but his unbelief was just as prevalent moments before.

1. When has your unbelief caused doubt in your life?
2. Have you cried out to Christ to proclaim your belief in His Sovereignty?

～

Lord, help me to remain faithful and confident no matter what season I'm
currently in! Help my unbelief to dissolve into 100 percent belief!

Brett Fuller
Worship Pastor
First Baptist Church, Pelham, AL

A Tune in a Bucket

*Make a joyful noise unto the LORD, all ye lands. Serve the LORD
with gladness: Come before his presence with singing.*
Psalm 100:1–2 (KJV)

My father-in-law couldn't carry a tune in a bucket. When the congregation would sing in church, the best he could do was hum along. He said he couldn't even make a joyful noise!

It might interest you to know the original Hebrew meaning of that phrase is to sound an ear-splitting shout of joyful triumph. Most college football fans make a joyful noise when their team comes onto the field.

The next line of the psalm tells us to serve the Lord with gladness. Think how you might feel if you had the privilege of handing a microphone to the President of the United States as he begins a speech. Our service to the Lord should be done with that kind of joy and expectation.

Finally, we are instructed to come into God's presence with singing. John Wesley published his "Directions for Singing" in a 1761 hymnal. Some of them are humorous as he admonishes us to "sing lustily and not bawl, so as to be heard above the rest of the congregation." However, his last one encourages us to "sing spiritually and have an eye to God in every word we sing. Aim at pleasing Him more than ourselves or any other creature." If we are faithful to do this, I think even hummers can make a joyful noise.

1. Can you tell what is present in someone's heart by hearing them sing to the Lord?
2. Can you tell what is not present in someone's heart by hearing them sing to the Lord?

～

Father, thank You for showing us the condition of our hearts by our willingness to sing to You. We now ask You to tune our hearts, that we may sing Your praise.

Marty Hamby
Minister of Worship and Music
First Baptist Church, Roanoke, VA

The Dump Ground

And do not be conformed to this world, but be transformed by the renewing of your mind, that you may prove what is that good and acceptable and perfect will of God.
Romans 12:2 (NKJV)

As a young boy, my father had my brothers and I clean out the garage and then dispose of the "junk" at the local "dump ground" (a.k.a., landfill). The work was neither easy, nor fun. The reward for me, however, was being able to go to the dump ground to discover and collect "cool" stuff people had thrown away. Of course, the smell was horrible, but nothing would deter me from the excitement that this adventure held for me. I was a treasure hunter in pursuit of rare and valuable jewels. Thankfully, as I got older, I came to my senses and realized that I could not stand the way the dump ground smelled nor how it made me smell.

As Christ-followers, we have been delivered from the "dump ground" of sin and past failures. The stench of our sin has been eradicated through God's sweet aroma of forgiveness and love. We are "new creations" in Christ (2 Cor. 5:17)!

Brothers and sisters, we must daily put on God's full armor and live in holiness. Temptation and a visit to sin's "dump ground" can seem appealing at times, but every trip is costly and requires His cleansing power (1 John 1:9). May you and I, each day, be determined to pursue Christ in every area of our lives.

The "dump ground" is CLOSED!!

1. Ask God to search your heart regarding areas of unconfessed sin.
2. What Scriptures are you "hiding in your heart" (Ps. 119:11)?

～

Father, thank You for delivering me from the "pit" and stench of my sin by Your Son, Jesus Christ. Mold, fill, and use me today as a pure vessel of honor for You and for Your glory. In Your name, Amen.

John Griffin
Worship Pastor
Calvary Baptist Church, Beaumont, TX

Reeds Shaken in the Wind

I know that there is nothing better for people than to be happy and
to do good while they live. That each of them may eat and drink and
find satisfaction in all their toil—this is the gift of God.
Ecclesiastes 3:12–13 (NIV)

Johannes Brahms once said, "Without craftsmanship, inspiration is a mere reed shaken in the wind." The arts carry with them two ideas that often are thought of in dichotomy: nature or nurture. I would suggest, as Brahms would indicate, that they are complementary. Inspiration must be followed by steadfast craftsmanship to bring an idea to its strongest conclusion whether it be a sermon, a work of art, a building, or a song. Craftsmanship should begin with inspiration to bring meaning to design. Our Scripture today identifies the work God has given to us.

Ephesians 2:10 says, "For we are his workmanship, created in Christ Jesus for good works, which God prepared beforehand, that we should walk in them" (NIV). Those who abandon their work too soon or out of frustration are not following the example of Christ who completed His work on the earth. We are given work to do while we are on earth and it is our task to carry out that work, no matter how small or great the task. Often, the blessing of sanctification comes through the discipline and rigors presented by the task, and the lack of recognition to follow. Hardship can be used by the Holy Spirit to refine us, to make us more like Christ, to deepen humility, and to help us fix our eyes on the eternal.

1. What eternal task(s) has God called you to?
2. Are you a reed shaken in the wind or are you committed to fulfilling God's call no matter the circumstance? Where are you currently (on this day) in fulfilling His will in your life?

~

Dear Father, I pray You give me strength, wisdom, and perseverance to complete the tasks both great and small that You have for me this day. Thank You for Your calling on my life. Lead me in paths of righteousness not for my glory, not for my fame, but for Your glory. Amen.

Dr. David Hahn
Chair, Department of Commercial Music
Liberty University, Lynchburg, VA

But God

God, who is rich in mercy, made us alive with Christ even when we were dead in transgressions—it is by grace you have been saved . . . through faith—and this is not from yourselves, it is the gift of God—not by works, so that no one can boast.

Ephesians 2:4–5, 8 (NIV)

I recently heard our Liberty University campus pastor, David Nasser, speak on this amazing truth. I am quoting some of what he shared as he reminded thousands of students and faculty that *we were dead in our sins, completely without hope, but God made us alive with Christ!*

We can insert our own names into those words, as we all fit squarely into the condition of being "dead in our transgression and sins." This convocation came on the heels of the confession of another famous David Nasser who admitted to sexually assaulting hundreds of gymnasts as he served as their doctor. We would all agree that he should be held accountable for his terrible sin. Yet, in God's eyes, all of us are just as guilty as the worst molester or murdering dictator. We are all guilty . . . but God. John Newton, writer of the hymn "Amazing Grace," is said to have spoken the words, "I am a great sinner and Christ is a greater Savior." Praise God for that amazing grace.

Today you may have a loved one who feels there is no hope or a desperate problem that appears to have no solution—but let me encourage you with these words . . . *but God.* Jesus is the One with the power to forgive, to save, and to answer our prayers. This truth, spoken about a Savior who rose from the dead, is the basis for our joy, confidence, and hope in life's constant struggles and pains. No problem, no temptation, no heartache is beyond these words of hope . . . *but God.*

1. Do we ever feel that in the worship-leading process we do every week, we are holier than the ones that we are ministering to? How can we not have that attitude?
2. Is there something you are struggling with today where you need to apply the "but God" truth?

～

Lord, forgive me for ever thinking that I am more deserving of Your great salvation than another sinner. Help me to realize that my sins are as grievous to You as the worst sinner in the world and to thank You for saving me and raising me from death to life. May I proclaim through my music ministry that my life would be without hope or joy were it not for Your great work of salvation expressed in those two words . . . but God. May others be encouraged to have the hope You provide us when we trust You and believe that nothing is impossible with You.

Don Marsh
Associate Professor of Music and Worship, Songwriting
Liberty University, Lynchburg, VA

Who Is Your Delight?

Delight yourself in the LORD, and he will give you the desires of your heart.
Psalm 37:4 (ESV)

I have fond memories of growing up as a Baptist pastor's kid, and I loved being at church all the time. I was taught the importance of God's Word, and I was challenged to memorize Scripture once I became a Christian. There are many passages of Scripture that have blessed my life throughout my walk with Christ, but one of my favorite verses is one I encountered as a college student reading through the Psalms. "Delight yourself in the LORD, and he will give you the desires of your heart" (Ps. 37:4 ESV). I had not previously studied this verse or given it much thought, but the words spoke to me in a special way that day.

Since then, Psalm 37:4 has become my life verse. The passage reminds me that I should take great pleasure in my relationship with the Lord and that He is our joy! When I seek to please God, He makes His desires my own, and blesses me by granting those desires. I have experienced this truth time and time again throughout my life and have been reminded that I must delight in Him and not the temporary things of this world. This verse continues to speak to me. I encourage you to find your own life verse.

1. Have you taken the time to express the desires of your heart to God?
2. Do you delight yourself in Christ or in the temporary things of this world?

~

Heavenly Father, thank You for Your Word that gives life, and thank You for teaching us how to live for You each and every day. It is my desire to delight in You daily. Thank You for the many blessings you give Your children. In Jesus' name, Amen.

Mark Hill
Minister of Music and Worship
First Baptist Church, Garland, TX

What Do I Do?!

Do not be anxious about anything, but in everything by prayer and supplication with thanksgiving let your requests be made known to God. And the peace of God, which surpasses all understanding, will guard your hearts and your minds in Christ Jesus.
Philippians 4:6–7 (ESV)

D o the Next Right Thing.

Life and ministry can come with so many challenges. The saying, "when it rains, it pours" really does ring true at times. As leaders, especially those who lead others in worship, our character is tested when life continues to come our way bringing such troubles. We are tested on how we respond to these challenges and troubles. I'll be the first to admit I haven't always responded to these challenges the way I should. However, every decision I've made has directly shaped who I am and how others view me. So, I give you the advice my wife gives me consistently . . .

Do the Next Right Thing.

In our jobs, ministries, and relationships, things do not always go the way they should or the way we want. So then, how will we make lemonade to do what best serves God and His church? The passage above is such a great place to ground our hearts, tempers, and minds. Once we've been grounded in these things, do the next right thing. It's all we can do.

1. Are there problems in your ministry you can't seem to get over?
2. What's the next right thing you can do with these problems?

~

God, settle my spirit and give me Your peace and wisdom in this situation. God, let them see You in my actions and decisions. Let this not be about me but about You and Your church. Thank You for the opportunity to serve in Your kingdom. Amen.

Brad Jett
Worship Pastor
First West, West Monroe, LA

Recheck Your Work!

Now they told David, "Behold, the Philistines are fighting against Keilah and are robbing the threshing floors." Therefore David inquired of the LORD, "Shall I go and attack these Philistines?" And the LORD said to David, "Go and attack the Philistines and save Keilah." But David's men said to him, "Behold, we are afraid here in Judah; how much more then if we go to Keilah against the armies of the Philistines?" Then David inquired of the LORD again. And the LORD answered him, "Arise, go down to Keilah, for I will give the Philistines into your hand." And David and his men went to Keilah and fought with the Philistines and brought away their livestock and struck them with a great blow. So David saved the inhabitants of Keilah.
1 Samuel 23:1–5 (ESV)

"David inquired of the LORD" . . . once again, "David inquired" (vv. 2, 4). David inquired of the Lord concerning whether he should engage the Philistines in battle, and he got a "yes" from God. However, when he told his men, they were afraid because it did not seem to be wise or safe to do so. In Scripture, though, we see that David, instead of rebuking his men for not believing, checked himself again to make sure he was hearing from the Lord and not just leaning on his own understanding.

Sometimes in leadership, when we are convinced of something and have done the spiritual due diligence, we get insulted (if not even offended) by others who don't join us without question. David's response is instructional for us . . . "check yourself again to be sure!" God is not insulted when we want to ask a second time about His will in a situation or about new ideas. Our heart's desire should be to please Him, do the right thing, and "rightly" lead His people. The worst thing in the world is to be so driven by our sense of authority and rightness that we think we always get it right and always hear clearly from the Lord. Pray it through until we pray it true! That is, make sure that our motivation and hearing are not impaired. The best way to do that is to recheck!

Back in high school math class, I remember my algebra teacher constantly saying, "Before you turn in your test, recheck your work!" Our goal is not to hurry to get the work done, but rather to get it done right . . . with excellence! So, my encouragement to you is that if you have been guided by the Lord concerning a decision or a direction, make sure you have "checked your work!" Check His Word, check your heart, check it in prayer . . . and then do it again!

1. Have you ever had to make a decision and were not totally sure it was the best decision to make?
2. Have you inquired of the Lord a second, third, or fourth time in order to recheck your work?

~

Father, may we be diligent in rechecking our dreams, goals, and plans as we follow Your leadership. May we always pray it through until we pray it true! In Jesus' name, Amen.

Ross Johnson
Worship and Music Pastor
First Baptist Church, Madison, MS

The V.I.P. Choir

Making known to us the mystery of his will, according to his purpose,
which he set forth in Christ as a plan for the fullness of time, to unite
all things in him, things in heaven and things on earth.

Ephesians 1:9–10 (ESV)

We have a very diverse congregation. Whatever your mental image is when you hear that phrase, multiply it by ten and you will be getting closer to the tapestry of people that call our church in the suburbs of Washington, DC, their home. On a typical Sunday, there are close to forty nationalities represented in our worship services.

In 2016, our choir president, Abraham Ajenifuja, authored a book titled, *The VIP Christian*. It challenges believers to order their lives according to God's Vision, Intention, and Purpose. In Ephesians 1:9–10, Paul reminds us that God's *vision* is to unite all things in heaven and on earth; He is achieving this *intentionally* through Jesus Christ (and by extension, the body of Christ) for the *purpose* of glorifying Himself.

In recent years, racism, xenophobia (fear of people from other countries), and extreme nationalism (a feeling of superiority over other countries) have become prominent issues in our society. Clearly, the enemy of God thinks that he can destroy God's vision and rob Him of glory by sowing seeds of division, fear, and superiority on the earth . . . even in the church! As a multi-ethnic, multinational congregation, we feel the pain of those arrows hurled both from within and outside the church walls.

As a choir, we have a vision to model unity in our diversity and intentionally reconcile broken relationships through Christ, that we might purposefully glorify God.

1. How do issues of racism, xenophobia, and nationalism hinder the purposes of God?
2. How can we be more intentional to fulfill God's vision for all things to be united in Christ?

~

Father, thank You that unity in Christ will be realized. Use me, today, to advance Your cause.

Jonathan Ford
Minister of Worship and Arts
Forcey Bible Church, Silver Spring, MD

Grace for Life

Let us then with confidence draw near to the throne of grace, that we
may receive mercy and find grace to help in time of need.
Hebrews 4:16 (ESV)

I have been a regular church attender since before I was born. I grew up in the church, and I love the church. However, for most of my life, I was trained in a thought process that urged me to live in performance mode. I was never taught that my works would save me. For most of my life, I felt that I needed to live my life trying to win God's approval. There was this overriding theme in the teaching I heard that I needed to act right so God would bless me. Now don't get me wrong about this topic. I still believe that a true relationship to God through Jesus Christ will have an impact on your behavior. I also know it to be true that God is moved by our obedience and often rewards those who walk in that obedience, but there is a real difference in *living* for God and *performing* for God.

Grace is God's response to our deepest needs, our need for forgiveness. Grace is defined as the unmerited favor of God. My youth minister in 1972 defined grace as God's Riches At Christ's Expense. We do not deserve God's grace, but we desperately need His grace because the option beyond His grace is to go back to the Law. Our relationship to God is birthed by grace, kept by grace, and sustained by grace. His grace is undeserved yet absolutely necessary for life. His grace is sufficient for our every need and it will never fail. All of our good works should be motivated by His grace.

1. Does grace cover all our sin: past, present, and future?
2. How should I be different because of the grace of God?

⌒

God, Your grace was extended to me because of Jesus' great sacrifice. May my attitudes, actions, and responses be affected today by the grace You have extended to me. May the grace You give to me be given to all those who cross my path. Your love and mercy are my greatest tools. Make them sharp in my hands today. In Jesus' name, Amen.

Ray Jones
President and Founder
Radiance Ministries, San Antonio, TX

Sounds Good to Me!

My dear friends, don't believe everything you hear. Carefully weigh and examine what people tell you. Not everyone who talks about God comes from God.
1 John 4:1 (MSG)

Sometimes, while just having fun, I will tease people and tell them that my favorite Bible verse is Hezekiah 3:6, which says, "Lying is an abomination unto the Lord, but a ready help in time of need." (Of course, I'm just teasing; there's no book of Hezekiah in the Bible!) Most people catch it right away, but I have had a few people actually believe me!

Please rest assured that if someone does happen to believe this, even if just for a moment, I then assure them that it is all in good fun. I quickly explain that I'm teasing and tell them the truth. It's just interesting that making it "sound like" the language of a Bible verse (and a legitimate book of the Bible) seems to make it easier for some people to believe it!

Most of us have probably heard the lines "it's too good to be true," and "things aren't always what they appear," but is it easier to believe something that's false just because it "sounds good to me"?

1. Am I gullible, easily convinced, or led astray with false information? How can I overcome this?
2. How can I be more discerning about things I hear or read, testing whether or not they are truly "from God," instead of just "sounding good"?

~

Lord, help me learn to be more discerning about the things I hear, especially those things that sound just a little too good to be true. Help me to truly seek Your face, Your heart, Your wisdom, so I can know for sure when something is truly "from You."

Randy Kirby
Worship Pastor
First Baptist Church, Simpsonville, SC

It's Not Your Party!

So whether you eat or drink or whatever you do, do it all for the glory of God.
1 Corinthians 10:31 (NIV)

The story is told about a mom who took her son, Adam, to a kindergarten birthday party for Amy. Adam took his seat at one end of the table while Amy, the object of their "birthday blessings" was seated at the other end. Amidst the sound increasing with each gift being open, Adam, not being the object of the "birthday blessings," began to show distaste for the lack of gifts coming his way.

His face went from sadness to anger and his body language went from being engaged to being disgusted by the preferential treatment that Amy received. Mom was aghast at such behavior by her little angel Adam, especially when it became noticeable to the other parents. At that moment, Mom went over to Adam, cupped his face with both her hands, got face-to-face and said, "Adam, this is not your party!"

I wonder if there may be times when we are in a critical mood about the music style we sing, the choral director we watch, the pastor we hear, and God wants to come to us, hold our face in His hands and say, "This is not YOUR party!" God's glory is what we seek. As J. S. Bach inscribed at the end of each piece he wrote, SDG or *Soli Deo Gloria*, translated *"To the Glory of God, Alone."* May our participation in what we do as worship leaders always reflect this calling.

1. What interferes with doing all I do for God's glory alone?
2. How can I work on this?

～

Dear God, in my calling as a worship leader, help me always remember that it is for Your glory alone that I sing. Purify my heart, cleanse my motivation, and keep my focus on You. Amen.

Dr. Gary Matthews
Pastor of Worship and the Arts
Christ Memorial Church, Holland, MI

He's Got Your Back

"Be strong and courageous, and do the work. Do not be afraid or discouraged,
for the LORD God, my God, is with you. He will not fail you or forsake you
until all the work for the service of the temple of the LORD is finished."
1 Chronicles 28:20 (NIV)

These are some of King David's final words to his son, Solomon. He was passing along every bit of wisdom and encouragement he could so that Solomon would be equipped to build the temple where God would be worshiped. These words are also for you.

Do you realize you don't need to be afraid nor discouraged because the God of all gods is with you? He is the God who will never fail you. Sometimes you may think He has failed you because your prayers weren't answered in the way you desired. He knows what is best for you, and His answers are always perfect and perfectly timed.

God will never forsake you. Webster defines forsake as "to renounce or turn away from entirely." Stop thinking about your problems, hurts, difficult circumstances, and worries for just one moment. Instead, think about this: God will never, for even a second, turn away from you. Just breathe that truth in. Do you need strength? All-powerful God has it for you. Do you need peace? He has that for you, too. Do you need healing? He's the ultimate Healer. Do you need grace? He invented it. God's got your back!

1. In what areas of your life do you need to claim this truth?
2. Who around you is afraid and discouraged and needs to hear this? Share it with them.

~

Father, You are almighty and all-powerful. Thank You for never failing me or forsaking me.
I claim this truth against Satan, who wants me to live fearful and discouraged. Amen.

Ryan Krivsky
Worship Pastor
Greenwell Springs Baptist Church, Greenwell Springs, LA

The Formula for Contentment

But godliness with contentment is great gain.
1 Timothy 6:6 (NIV)

Commercials drive me crazy. Not only do they interrupt my favorite shows and ball teams on TV, but they are designed to make us feel discontented with our current life. Whether it is with the car we drive, the vacation we need to take, or the toothpaste we should use, the overarching message is always, "your overall life will improve greatly when you have *this*." While certain products can indeed enhance our lives, we need to be constantly aware of the pull in our heart that is always looking for the next thing or relationship that will finally bring us contentment or satisfaction.

The formula for a prosperous life is found by simply adding contentment to a godly life. That's it. There's no hidden secret under a mystic rock somewhere. We must be thankful for the story that God is writing for us instead of complaining inwardly that our lives would be so much better if God followed *our* plan for *our* lives.

1. Notice both parts of this formula: *godliness* and *contentment*. Why do both of these need to be present?
2. Think of the complete opposite of this verse: *ungodliness* with *discontentment* is great loss. How does reading the verse in this way put another light on this subject?

～

Father, You are good and wise in all that You do. Help me to enjoy the gain that comes by being content to live a godly life inside and out knowing that Your ways are best.

Clay Layfield
Associate Pastor, Music and Senior Adults
First Baptist Church, Eastman, GA

Consider the Shepherds

In the same region shepherds were staying out in the fields and keeping watch
at night over their flock. Then an angel of the Lord stood before them.
Luke 2:8–9a (CSB)

This was a normal night for the shepherds. Nothing was out of the ordinary, that is, until the angels showed up. At first, it was just one. Then, a whole multitude of them appeared and started talking and singing. What an incredible sight! The sight of the angels, however, was not the big news. The birth of Jesus Christ was the big news!

I wish I were one of those shepherds. No, not to be stuck on a hillside with smelly sheep, but rather, I wish that God would send His angels to tell me exactly what it is that He is doing in my life. Or maybe He could just write it in the sky for me. The shepherds got a clear message from God, so why can't I? I have wondered often what God was doing in my life and why I had to walk through certain circumstances. While I did not see angels or writing in the sky, it was during those times that I realized the amazing grace of God on my life. He was teaching me. He is constantly teaching me and maturing me.

You might be in a season of questioning. Why God? Why are You allowing this? What are You doing? Proverbs 3 reminds us to not lean on our own understanding but to completely trust Him. His ways are not our ways and His thoughts are not our thoughts. While it is okay to ask God "why," a better question might be "what?"

1. What is He teaching you?
2. In what ways is He maturing you?

～

God, I might not understand exactly what You are doing; but, I trust You. Help me
to understand what You are teaching me. Thank You for Your grace and mercy.

Robert Maddox
Worship and Missions Pastor
Spotswood Baptist Church, Fredericksburg, VA

Angels Never Sing?

Then I looked and heard the voice of many angels . . . in a loud voice they were SAYING: "Worthy is the Lamb, who was slain, to receive power and wealth and wisdom and strength and honor and glory and praise!"
Revelation 5:11–12 (NIV, emphasis added)

One of the great joys of my ministry was serving at the First Baptist Church, Dallas, TX. Upon my arrival in 1996, I met the legendary W. A. Criswell—the famous pastor of First Dallas for more than fifty years.

Upon a day—as "Dr. C" would say—I heard him say that in the Bible, angels *never* sing—only the redeemed of God. I had never heard or considered this!

At the website www.wacriswell.com I was able to find the sermon where Criswell further explains this, in his own inimitable style:

Never in the Bible do the angels sing . . . that was an astonishing thing to me! I got to reading, I got to studying . . . and this is the best that I can find: Always, the redeemed sing; God's blood-washed sing; God's children sing; angels don't sing. . . . He has put a new song in our souls and new praises on our lips. An angel has never been redeemed. An angel has never been saved. An angel has never fallen and then brought back to God. It's God's people who sing. . . . For it takes a lost and fallen man who's been brought back to God, who's been forgiven of his sins, who's been redeemed; it takes a saved soul to sing![24]

1. Renew your understanding that the only reason we have a song to sing is because we have been redeemed and now belong to God.
2. Give thanks, anew to God, for your salvation.

~

Lord Jesus, renew in me a joyful and grateful spirit for my salvation that overflows in songs of praise—songs that even angels cannot sing!

Keith Ferguson
Associate Pastor, Worship Arts
First Baptist Church, Carrollton, TX

Here I Raise My Ebenezer

When the Philistines heard that Israel had assembled at Mizpah, the rulers
of the Philistines came up to attack them. . . . The men of Israel rushed out of
Mizpah and pursued the Philistines, slaughtering them along the way to a point
below Beth Kar. Then Samuel took a stone and set it up between Mizpah and
Shen. He named it Ebenezer, saying, "Thus far the LORD has helped us."
1 Samuel 7:7, 11–12 (NIV)

I love monuments. I love looking at great sculptures or edifices whose purpose it is to cause us to remember a significant historical event or person. These "stones of remembrance" remind us that others have come before us, fighting battles, winning victories, and rising above defeat. They also remind us to praise and thank the God who granted the victory.

I have a friend who was a missionary in Africa. She had been going through a significant battle in her life. God, supernaturally, gave her victory over the dire situation. This happened to be during the very brief period of time when plums came into season in her village. Since this time, she always associates plums with God's victory in her life. She considers plums her "Ebenezer," her stone of remembrance.

1. What monuments do you have in your life that serve as a reminder of God's faithfulness and help?
2. Have you shared with others the victories God has granted you?

~

Father, thank You for Your faithfulness and help. Please help us to never forget Your
goodness and love. Let us be faithful in praising You for Your mighty works.

Kenneth Martin
Minister of Music and Worship
First Baptist Church, Milton, FL

Going from Glory to Glory

And we all, who with unveiled faces contemplate the Lord's glory, are being transformed into his image with ever-increasing glory, which comes from the Lord, who is the Spirit.
2 Corinthians 3:18 (NIV)

I love watching *Fixer Upper* on HGTV. I can read or work on something else and then come back to the show in the last six minutes and see the transformation that has taken place. The renewing of those old houses is incredible! As they reveal the house room to room, I marvel at its newly found beauty.

That's what our Scripture references here. We know we are already made in His image, but 2 Corinthians makes the statement that we are "being transformed into his image" (NIV).

How is that happening?

With His increasing glory! Unlike Moses, who hid his face from God's glory, we stand with *unveiled faces,* so all the world can see God's glory! As we experience Him and come into His presence with ever-increasing frequency, we are changed room by room. Our heart is made new; our mind is renewed by meditating daily on His Word and through our time of prayer. We are transformed into His image in many ways: through new actions, new language, new responses to Him and the people around us, new realization of the unseen world and living out "Christ in me!"

Second Corinthians 3:18 (NASB) states it this way: "But we all . . . *beholding as in a mirror the glory of the Lord*" (emphasis added). This transformation isn't just witnessed by those on the outside of our body. *We see it too!* Our countenance shines with the glory of the Lord. Why? Because "the Son is the radiance of God's glory and the exact representation of his being" (Heb. 1:3 NIV).

1. Think through the "rooms" of your life. Are there still transformations that need to take place? Identify those "rooms" and make a plan to re-new!
2. Am I realizing, when going from glory to glory, that I've been in the presence of the Lord?

~

Transform me, Lord, from glory to glory. Amen.

Dr. Mark Deakins
Worship Minister
Broadway Christian Church, Lexington, KY

Consider Others More Significant Than Yourself

Do nothing from selfish ambition or conceit, but in humility count others more significant than yourselves. Let each of you look not only to his own interests, but also to the interests of others.
Philippians 2:3–4 (ESV)

Maybe you're going to audition for the big Christmas event, or maybe you're trying out for the praise team. You might be interested in playing keys for the band, or maybe you've been taking guitar lessons. Your nerves are high, and you're wondering who else is chasing after the same position. "Are they better than me?" Auditions put us in a vulnerable place. They feel very personal, perhaps because our artistic expression is an intricate part of who we are. Does the Scripture address how we should handle this?

We are all sinners through Adam, partaking of the fall recorded in Genesis 3. We struggle with pride and conceit. We think too highly of ourselves, comparing ourselves with others. "Hey, I am better at electric guitar than that person!" We want the spotlight and fame that comes with being on the platform. In our best moments, we agree with the psalmist in Psalm 115:1, "Not to us, O LORD, not to us, but to your name give glory" (ESV), but sometimes we want a little glory too.

Philippians 2:3–4 implores us, "Do nothing from selfish ambition or conceit." Pray for God's grace in your life that you are not selfish with the opportunities in the church and ask God to break up the pride in your heart. James 4:6 reminds us, "God opposes the proud but gives grace to the humble" (ESV). Strive to be joyful and encouraging to others when they get the part. Encourage them as they serve. May we have the mind of Christ, walking in humility with Jesus and others.

1. Have you ever auditioned for something? How did it go and what was your response with the results?
2. What are some ways that you can encourage others in the ministry in which they serve?

~

Jesus, I thank You for giving me a gift to praise You and edify the church. You are a gracious God. Help me, Lord, to count others more significant than myself as I seek to honor Your bride and glorify You. Amen.

Keith McMinn
Pastor of Worship
Bethel Baptist Church, Yorktown, VA

The Simple Secret of Being Spiritual

And we, who with unveiled faces all reflect [contemplate] the Lord's
glory, are being transformed into his likeness with ever-increasing
glory, which comes from the Lord, who is the Spirit.
2 Corinthians 3:18 (NIV)

One of my dad's early heroes in the ministry was the preacher Dr. Manuel Scott. After hearing Dr. Scott preach one evening, my dad had the opportunity to have breakfast with him the next day. During the course of their conversation, my dad said, "Dr. Scott, it is so evident that you are a spiritual man. How does a man become spiritual?" Dr. Scott thought for a moment and said, "Well, Harold, when you wake up in the morning, start your day by reading and studying the Word of God, and then, throughout the day, continue to think about and meditate on what you've read. Then, as you pillow your head in the evening, allow the Scripture to continue sanctifying and cleansing your heart and mind 'with the washing of water by the word' (Eph. 5:26 CSB). Dr. Scott then paused, reached up to put his thumbs under his red suspenders, and with a smile said, 'If you'll do that every day, then one of these days, you'll just wake up . . . *spiritual!*'"

I love that! Being spiritual is not complicated; it is really quite simple. A man who is worshiping God in the context of His Word—reflecting and contemplating His glory—will be "transformed into the same image from glory to glory" (2 Cor. 3:18 CSB).

1. Based on the time you spend in God's Word every day, are you a spiritual person?
2. What are some tangible ways you can saturate your life with God's Word?

~

Father, help me to make spending time reading, studying, and meditating on Your Word the
priority of my life, so that I might minister from the overflow of Your Spirit in my life.

Dr. Gary Mathena
Director of Practica
Liberty University, Lynchburg, VA

My Identity

I have been crucified with Christ. It is no longer I who live, but Christ
who lives in me. And the life I now live in the flesh I live by faith in
the Son of God, who loved me, and gave himself for me.
Galatians 2:20 (ESV)

If we are in Jesus Christ, we are a new creation; the old has passed away. This means that there may be things that I think are critical to my identity that could be idols. Could my calling, my faith, my position, my skills, my relationships, my failures, my essential "me-ness" be idols?

Jesus reminds us that our lives are not our own. God has redeemed us. We lose our lives in Jesus. The creative and redemptive love of God is so great that we find in "losing our lives," we become more alive and more free—free to love, free to live, free to be holy, free to overcome, free to fail, free to serve, free to be rejected, free to be in the One who conquered everything. "For freedom Christ has set us free . . ." (Gal. 5:1 ESV).

1. Who am I in Jesus?
2. What idols do I have that are robbing me from the freedom Christ offers me?

∽

Our Father, may we not be content with anything less than Your freedom.
Please forgive us of our selfish contentment. Jesus, You are the way, the truth,
and the life. Help us walk with You all the way, in truth, forever. Amen.

Ronald A. Matthews, DMA
President
Eastern University, St. David's, PA

Freedom in Discipline

*For this very reason, make every effort to supplement your faith with virtue,
and virtue with knowledge, and knowledge with self-control, and self-
control with steadfastness, and steadfastness with godliness, and godliness
with brotherly affection, and brotherly affection with love.*

2 Peter 1:5–7 (ESV)

Watching a well-trained athlete is fascinating. The same is true with an extremely gifted musician or brilliant mathematician. The ability to perform at high levels requires discipline and hard work. Spiritual growth requires the same, though often times we think that it restricts freedom. We would do well to remember that discipline is the price of freedom.

Elton Trueblood writes,

We have not advanced very far in our spiritual lives if we have not encountered the basic paradox of freedom . . . *that we are most free when we are bound.* But not just any way of being bound will suffice; what matters is the character of our binding. The one who would be an athlete, but who is unwilling to discipline his body by regular exercise and abstinence, is not free to excel on the field or the track. His failure to train rigorously denies him the freedom to run with the desired speed and endurance. With one concerted voice, the giants of the devotional life apply the same principle to the whole of life: *Discipline is the price of freedom.*[27]

1. What area(s) of your life are lacking discipline and preventing you from spiritual growth?
2. Read 1 Corinthians 9:24–27.

~

Lord, help me daily to commit and discipline myself to the study of Your Word that I might not sin against You. As a well-trained athlete, help me to be self-controlled and ever growing in the spiritual disciplines as I grow closer to You. Amen.

Joshua McClain
Worship and Music Pastor
Central Baptist Church, Warner Robins, GA

Wonder and Worship

When I consider Your heavens, the work of Your fingers, the moon and the stars, which You have ordained, what is man that You are mindful of him, and the son of man that You visit him? . . . O LORD, our Lord, how excellent is Your name in all the earth!
Psalm 8:3–4, 9 (NKJV)

From creation and the time of Adam and Eve until a mere 400 years ago, all that we knew about our universe came through observations with the naked eye.

Then the astronomer Galileo turned his telescope toward the heavens in the year 1610. In an instant, so much that was hazy or questioned became clear! Saturn, we learned, had rings. Jupiter had moons. With each discovery, it changed how man looked at the world and the size and makeup of the universe. It created a revolution in science that has never really stopped.

With every advancement, our wonder of the created universe doesn't diminish; it *grows*. The more we learn about how God created the universe, the more we realize how much we still have to learn.

Did King David know all this when he wrote Psalm 8? Probably not, but he did know that it was a miracle that God, as the maker of all, still chose to take time to be concerned and involved with us, mankind. Even though we are so small in comparison, He lifts us up, blesses us, gives us charge over the creatures of this world and shows us care and love, and our response is worship!

"O LORD, our Lord, how excellent is Your name in all the earth!" (Ps. 8:9 NKJV).

1. In what other ways has God shown His benefits to mankind?
2. Name two things that prompt you to worship God in a deeper way.

~

Lord, I worship You for all that You are and all that You have made. Renew my wonder and help me to see each person as Your special and unique creation. Amen.

Tobin Davis
Minister of Music
Shadow Mountain Community Church, El Cajon, CA

Wait for the Lord

Wait for the LORD; be strong and take heart and wait for the LORD.
Psalm 27:14 (NIV)

W aiting can be difficult. Maybe you're at a traffic light, waiting for green, hoping to make your next appointment. Maybe it's the end of a long day and you've told your kids to get ready for bed, but they're moving at a snail's pace finding every excuse to slow down. Maybe you could even be in line for a big promotion at work, and you're expecting a call any moment. Perhaps you're waiting with an anxious heart for news from the doctor concerning the health of you or a loved one.

Everyone is familiar with waiting. Each day reveals new opportunities to exhibit patience. A difficult lesson in waiting is learned when we stop waiting on a set of circumstances and begin waiting on our Sovereign Lord. Will we surrender to the lordship of Jesus Christ and believe in His sovereign control over all things? Lending mental assent to the doctrine of God's sovereignty is much easier than being strong, taking heart, and waiting for the Lord as the psalmist exhorts. Is there a remedy, a way to provoke our hearts to wait for the Lord?

We must remember the works of the Lord! Recall God's faithfulness day after day. Are we worrying or growing impatient? Perhaps we have lost sight of God's constant provision over our lives. Jesus is a Good Shepherd. He cares for us. He keeps us. We serve an all-knowing, all-powerful God who is intimately acquainted with the details of our lives. Draw near to Him. Ask for grace. Hold tightly to Him and lean in; wait for the Lord. He is kind and compassionate.

1. How have you seen the faithfulness of God in your life?
2. In what areas of your life do you struggle with impatience?

~

Jesus, we thank You that You care for us. We praise You that You are sovereign and Lord over all things. You are faithful and never changing. Help me to trust Your work in my life. Amen.

Keith McMinn
Pastor of Worship
Bethel Baptist Church, Yorktown, VA

What Are You Listening To?

"Be strong and courageous. Do not be frightened, and do not be
dismayed, for the LORD your God is with you wherever you go."
Joshua 1:9 (ESV)

There are earbuds and headphones everywhere! Walking down the street you will see many people with earbuds blocking out the noise of life. Many athletes will wear headphones or earbuds as they warm up to block out all the noises and distractions. This helps them get in the winning mind-set. I always wonder what people are listening to; what song makes them tick. Is it classical, spoken word, rap, rock, Christian music? We all carry the desire to win and it starts with silencing out the noise and getting focused. What is your song? What gets you going? Joshua's song might have been Joshua 1:9.

I can imagine Joshua turning up his own Joshua 1:9 track really loud before heading out into battle or making leadership decisions. He knew that God would be with him every step. He knew He would provide all his needs. He knew God would guide and comfort him in every step, but sometimes we need to be reminded. God had called Joshua but reminded him, just as he reminds us every day, to be strong, to be courageous, and to simply trust Him!

1. Are you allowing God to lead and guide your every step?
2. What is your song in life?

~

Father, continue to guide and direct my every step. Help me to trust in You
completely and to know You will provide my every need. Thank You, God, for always
watching me and being with me every step of the way. In Jesus' name, Amen.

Jason Millsaps
Pastor of Music and Worship
Bell Shoals Baptist Church, Brandon, FL

Perseverance

Let us not become weary in doing good, for at the proper time
we will reap a harvest if we do not give up.
Galatians 6:9 (NIV)

Each of us can become weary at different times in our ministry year. Perhaps after a special Sunday, such as Palm Sunday or Easter, or it could be "just because." Life, family, and ministry are tough and even brutal at times. Recently, I asked a close friend in ministry when he knew it was time to retire. He quipped, "When Sunday seems to come every other day, rather than once a week!" There are times when we may feel the same, and we might be years from retirement!

We can also feel weary in doing good and may even want to give up—especially on Mondays! However, if we give up when we face opposition or experience hardship, we might miss His unique plan for us or fail to recognize what He desires to do within us.

Our ministry is full of ups and downs. High times of joy and low moments of disappointment. Don't give up! Don't allow your disappointments or failures to derail what God has planned for you. Stay faithful, and as Spurgeon once said, "By perseverance, even the snail reached the ark."

1. What is the greatest obstacle or current personal struggle that brings discouragement or disappointment to me and my ministry?
2. Who might be the best encourager for me to pray with today? Think of someone else who may have experienced what you are feeling right now!

~

Lord, help me this day to "throw off everything that hinders and the sin
that so easily entangles," so I may "run with perseverance the race marked
out" for me (Heb. 12:1). Remind me to let perseverance finish its work in
me so that I may be mature and complete (James 1:4). Amen.

Dr. James L. Melton
Chair, Department of Music
Vanguard University, Costa Mesa, CA

Wits End

And Jesus answered saying to them, "Have faith in God."
Mark 11:22 (NASB)

When you do everything right and one bad thing messes it up; when you're at your lowest point and don't know what to do or where to turn; when the kids have been at you non-stop and you're sick as a dog; when your employment is based on a one-time phone interview and your phone doesn't work for the call; when rent is due, the budget is tight, and you decide whether you will tithe or not this week, Jesus, take the wheel!

There are many more examples that could be used for times when we just need to "let go and let God." Jesus' answer to us is to have faith in God. Trust Him. Know without a shadow of a doubt that He's there at all times to help with the big things and the little things. Turn those situations over to Him and see what He does. Then, give thanks and celebrate the victories, blessing His name. Allow Him to build your faith.

1. What other Scripture passages come to mind when thinking about trusting God?
2. How can I allow God to build my faith in Him today?

~

Dear God, I know you love me and want what's best for me. Thank You for being with me even when I don't acknowledge You're there. I love You and will trust You with all things, big and small. Amen.

Loren Minnick Jr.
Associate Pastor—Worship
Foothills Baptist Church, Las Vegas, NV

Self-Love

"Love your neighbor as yourself."
Matthew 22:39b (NIV)

In this digital age of social media, we are able to portray an image of ourselves based on how we want others to perceive us. Are we getting our identity and understanding of ourselves based on what others think about us?

First, to understand self-love, we have to acknowledge that when God created us, He did so in His own image. While we are not God, we are an image of Him. Harold Best, in his book *Unceasing Worship,* says, "everything God is in infinity, we are a finite image."[28] As we consider self-love and the image of God, we must believe that God was completely satisfied in and of Himself for all eternity before He chose to create. He did not create us because He somehow needed us, He created us purely out of love, and at the end of the creation process of humanity, God said, "it was very good" (Gen. 1:1 NIV).

The second point is that while we have marred our original goodness, God has created a way for us to retain that original state in the birth, life, death, and resurrection of Jesus. Our lives have become dark and dirty since the fall of humanity. However, in Christ we are redeemed and made clean, ready to meet God when that day should come in our original state of His goodness.

When we think on these things, it becomes possible for us to think more highly of ourselves. We might even begin to love ourselves enough to make a difference in someone else's life. "Love your neighbor as yourself"—until we come to grips with biblical self-love, I am not sure we are able to love others the way Christ is calling all of us to love.

1. How many of us really love ourselves?
2. Maybe a better question is, "Do we only love the image of ourselves we have created for others to love us?"

~

*Lord, help us to see ourselves the way You see us, and help
us to see those around us the same way.*

Brad Moffett
Director of Graduate Studies / Professor of Music
Lee University, Cleveland, TN

The Manifestation of Jesus

*"The one who loves me will be loved by my Father, and I
too will love them and show myself to them."*
John 14:21b (NIV)

There are more than three thousand promises written in Scripture. In John 14:21, there are three precious promises just in this one verse!

The first promise is: *you will be loved by My Father.*

The second promise is: *I will love them.* In other words, *Jesus will love you!*

The third promise is: *I will manifest Myself to them.* In other words, *Jesus will show Himself to you!*

Have you ever had a really good thought come to your mind all of a sudden and you have said, either out loud or to yourself, "Where did that come from?" *That's Jesus showing Himself to you.* Have you ever been reading the Bible or a devotional book and literally had words *pop* off the page?
That's Jesus showing Himself to you.
Have you ever been driving somewhere, and you turn down a road not on your original destination because you "feel" like you're supposed to, and you end up helping someone along the way?
That's Jesus showing Himself to you.
Have you ever tithed, obeying the mandate in Scripture only to find out there's too much month at the end of the money? And then suddenly, in the mail, or in an envelope from a friend, a gift is given in the exact amount you need to pay your bills?
That's Jesus showing Himself to you.
The manifestation of Jesus is real! Our old mind wants us to think the term *coincidence.* But Jesus doesn't work in coincidence. He works in confidence and in keeping His promise to manifest Himself to you. Look closely, my friend. Jesus may just "show up" in your life this very day!

1. Have you thanked Him for His precious promises and for keeping them?
2. Do you know His three thousand plus promises? Why not know what He will keep and be faithful to do?

~

*Lord, manifest Yourself today! Let me delight in Your "showing up" in my life.
Don't allow me to miss knowing Your handiwork. In Jesus' name, Amen.*

Dr. Mark Deakins
Worship Minister
Broadway Christian Church, Lexington, KY

Don't Hold Back

The trumpeters and musicians joined in unison to give praise and thanks to the LORD. Accompanied by trumpets, cymbals and other instruments, the singers raised their voices in praise to the LORD and sang: "He is good; his love endures forever." Then the temple of the LORD was filled with cloud.

2 Chronicles 5:13 (NIV)

Have you ever heard a world-class drum and bugle corp perform live? It is an amazing sound. Trumpets are LOUD! Drums are LOUD! In the Scripture verse above, there were "other instruments," in addition to the trumpets and drums. Can you imagine how many voices it took to be heard over all of those instruments? (And remember, there were no sound systems back then!) What an extravagant celebration it must have been! After they had given praise to the Lord, His presence filled the place, stopping the priests from performing their duties because of God's overwhelming glory.

When we come together to give praise to the Lord, we need to bring our best; our all. DON'T. HOLD. BACK! We need to LOUDLY celebrate what God has done for us! When we give our all in surrender to the Lord, He will show us His power and presence, and His glory will be revealed. We will stand in awe and wonder at who He is. We worship an AWESOME God! Let's offer Him the praise He deserves.

1. What hinders you from giving your all when you sing praises to the Lord?
2. How have you experienced God's presence when you have truly worshiped Him?

God, I don't want to hold back when I praise You. I want to give You my all! May my praise be extravagant. You are worthy of all praise!

David Butler
Worship Pastor
First Baptist Church, St. Charles, MO

Real Prayer

*"When you pray, you are not to be like the hypocrites; for they love to stand
and pray in the synagogues and on the street corners so that they may be
seen by men. Truly I say to you, they have their reward in full."*
Matthew 6:5 (NASB)

Growing up, my mom and dad both worked, so after school, I would stay with my aunt Alice. She was one of the godliest people I have ever known, and I learned so much just from being around her. I will never forget how she prayed. Her prayers were always so respectful and genuine.

There was never any pretense or pride, only a heartfelt love for her Savior and for those she would pray for. Every time I saw her, even in her last years, every time, without exception, she would pray for me. I will never forget holding her hands as she prayed and feeling like I was being led to the very throne of God.

Jesus said we should never try to impress people with our prayers. He wants us to be real when we pray and not try to draw attention to ourselves. We don't need to pray things that we think God wants us to say rather than praying what's really on our hearts.

God loves us and knows us from the inside out. There's nothing we can hide from Him. So, why should we try to pretend when we pray?

We have the incredible privilege to talk to Him anytime! Don't miss the opportunity to grow your relationship with Him through time spent in prayer.

1. Do you let anything get in the way of your time alone with God?
2. Who do you pray for each day?

~

*God, thank You for loving us and caring for us as Your children. Thank You for always being
there for us. Help us to openly and honestly express our love to You and others as we pray.*

Michael Moore
Associate Pastor of Music, Media and Communication
Sarasota Baptist Church, Lakewood Ranch, Sarasota, FL

The God-Given Task

So I saw that there is nothing better than that a man should rejoice in his work,
for that is his lot. Who can bring him to see what will be after him?
Ecclesiastes 3:22 (ESV)

If you look carefully at Adam in the garden of Eden, you might notice something peculiar. Adam is tasked by God to work diligently on tending to the garden. Adam is working. Often, we can look at our work as a post-fall consequence. However, even before sin entered the garden, Adam was working. We were created to work. It's how we were designed, and our earthly work, though toilsome, has implications that lie beyond this world.

In Ecclesiastes, Solomon foreshadows such divine hope. He encourages us to rejoice in our work, not only because it is God-designed, but because it has a purpose and an eternal impact. We can enjoy our work on the earth, knowing that by the promises of God, that work will have a conclusion and we will be fully prepared for our God-given heavenly task.

1. Are there specific things in your daily work that God would change for His glory and kingdom?
2. What are some ways you could change the lens of your daily work to see it through a heavenly perspective?

~

God, give me the strength, stamina, and mental fortitude to always work my God-given earthly task as if I were preparing for my God-given heavenly task.

Austin Neal
Worship Pastor
Champion Forest Baptist Church, Jersey Village, TX

Trust

"Whoever can be trusted with very little can also be trusted with much, and whoever is dishonest with very little will also be dishonest with much."
Luke 16:10 (NIV)

The general principle of this parable is one of the core values of my musical ensemble. It undergirds how we prepare our music in the rehearsal room and in personal preparation. If we cannot be trusted with the small things, how can we be trusted with the big things? Now, in this parable, there is an eternal message being taught, but we can bring it down into everyday aspects of life as well.

For all of us, no matter our skill or talent level, it is a privilege to make music with our choirs, orchestras, bands, praise teams, or whatever type of groups we have in our churches. It is not an entitlement. As we offer ourselves to the kingdom, how we prepare our music week to week has the opportunity to make a big impact on those under our worship leadership.

A former music theory teacher often stated, "Music is supposed to sound good, and good music takes concentration." From a musical point of view, how we approach the preparation of the music, paying attention to the details of the music, and working hard to offer our best to God in worship are what matters. If we cannot play the right chords, or pay attention to releases, or hold the whole note the entire four beats with intensity and musical movement, how can we expect our music to make a difference in someone's life?

1. From a spiritual point of view, if we are not taking personal responsibility for our spiritual lives, how can we expect God to use us to lead others in a spiritual journey? The small things always matter.
2. How does your music preparation express your spiritual walk and discipline?

~

Lord, help us be aware of the importance of the small things in every area of our lives so You can trust us with the big things You are calling us to do.

Brad Moffett
Director of Graduate Studies / Professor of Music
Lee University, Cleveland, TN

Fill This Place! Fill Me, Lord!

And all the Levitical singers, Asaph, Heman, and Jeduthun, their sons and kinsmen,
arrayed in fine linen, with cymbals, harps, and lyres, stood east of the altar with 120
priests who were trumpeters; and it was the duty of the trumpeters and singers to
make themselves heard in unison in praise and thanksgiving to the LORD), and when
the song was raised, with trumpets and cymbals and other musical instruments, in
praise to the LORD, "For he is good, for his steadfast love endures forever," the house,
the house of the LORD, was filled with a cloud, so that the priests could not stand to
minister because of the cloud, for the glory of the LORD filled the house of God.

2 Chronicles 5:12–14 (ESV)

This has to be one of the greatest moments in worship history found in Scripture. Three thousand voices and instruments singing in unison concerning the steadfast love of the Lord. Can you imagine the power of that many voices and instruments in one accord? Two things need to be considered from this passage. First, the glory of the Lord filled the temple. In the Old Covenant, God dwelt in the physical location of the tabernacle in the wilderness and later in the temple.

In the New Covenant, God indwells His people. For those in Christ, we are the temple of God. Second, to have this type of unison, unity was required. Unity allows for authenticity, for worship that pleases our Savior, Redeemer, Creator, and Lord. It's easy to lose our focus, make worship about us and create division. It's also easy to seek a performance mind-set as worshipers and not fulfill the desired attitude of presentation in worship to our Father. This worship is not acceptable to God. Consider these questions today:

1. Lord, am I in right fellowship with You so that my worship is acceptable?
2. Is my temple (body) a place where You would happily dwell?
3. Am I in right fellowship with other believers to promote unity in spirit and present authentic praise to You?

Heavenly Father, I pray that our spiritual eyes would be open to the reality of Your greatness, enduring love, and desire to dwell in our midst. I pray that You will strengthen the unity of Your people and that what we present to You would bless You. In Jesus' name, Amen.

Jerry L. Newman
Executive Pastor of Worship and Media
Southcrest Baptist Church, Lubbock, TX

We Have Heard the Joyful Sound!

*Sing aloud, O daughter of Zion; shout, O Israel! Rejoice and
exult with all your heart, O daughter of Jerusalem!*
Zephaniah 3:14 (ESV)

We need to celebrate the Lord and what He has done for us. For the prophet Zephaniah, celebrating the Lord's deliverance of His people was the main event. Zephaniah issued four separate commands for God's people to obey. First, God's people must *SING ALOUD*. Regardless of whether you are trained in music or can't "carry a tune in a bucket," it is essential to worship with singing. Second, God's people are to *SHOUT*. Some believers may feel uncomfortable expressing a shout of praise.

A relationship with God is a profoundly personal experience. Yet, intense gratitude and overwhelming excitement are difficult to keep bottled up inside. If we can shout passionately at a football game, basketball game, or at a rockin' concert, can we not also express excited gratitude to our Lord? The third and fourth commands are knit together as one: *REJOICE AND EXULT!* When we take time to declare aloud God's blessings, we find it easier to keep an "attitude of gratitude" that stokes the flames of gladness and joy in our lives.

1. God addressed His chosen people as "daughter of Zion." What does this expression tell you of God's devotion to us?
2. How can you keep your relationship with God fresh and vibrant?

～

*Lord, thank You for so many reasons to celebrate Your goodness and
faithfulness. Help me to worship You with my whole life because You
alone are worthy of my devotion. In Jesus' name, Amen.*

Andy Newsome
Music and Worship Pastor
Trinity Baptist Church, Ocala, FL

Hard Work Always Pays Off

Whatever your hand finds to do, do it with all your might . . .
Ecclesiastes 9:10a (NIV)

In another church years ago, I was serving as a minister of music and youth. We were going through a somewhat difficult time in the youth area. I was really struggling—to the point that I really felt like giving up.

The pastor's wife was on my youth leadership team, and she was very much aware of the difficulty and that I was struggling. She was a very godly woman, a wonderful pastor's wife. She had a heart of gold and a beautiful spirit of encouragement. I deeply loved and respected both my pastor and her.

One day as I was sharing with her how I was feeling like giving up and walking away, she looked at me and said, "Randy, just get back to work." It didn't come across like a judgment or a command—it came across with love and compassion. She went on to say, "God always blesses hard work . . . HARD WORK ALWAYS PAYS OFF!" She climbed down into the trench with me and worked hard right alongside me.

Do you think the hard work paid off?

Yes, it did! I wish I could tell you about some of those youth who are now adults and how God is still working in their lives!

So, get back to work! God always blesses hard work!

Remember this verse (very similar to the one above): "Whatever you do, work at it with all your heart" (Col. 3:23a NIV).

1. What about you? Are you struggling? Are you ready to give up or walk away?
2. What are some ways we can encourage others who are struggling?

~

Lord, thank You for giving us a "work ethic." Remind us that You don't call
us to do something without equipping us to do it. Though we must learn to
let You work in and through us, may we never "grow tired of doing good"—
not for our own recognition or success but for Your glory. Amen.

Randy Kirby
Minister of Music
First Baptist Church, Simpsonville, SC

Jesus, the Light of the World

"I am the light of the world. Anyone who follows Me will never
walk in the darkness but will have the light of life."
John 8:12 (HCSB)

For light thinking, study Einstein's Theory of Relativity, $E=mc^2$. It presents some fascinating observations regarding light. There is a timeless element to light. If one could ride light, the distance traveled would have taken no time to do it.

There is a triune element to light. Light is comprised of three types of rays, none of which would be light without the other. The first originates and is neither seen nor felt (consider God the Father); the second illuminates and is both seen and felt (God the Son); the third consummates and is felt as heat (God the Holy Spirit).

Light appears to be the only unchanging or constant characteristic in the physical universe.

There is a triumphant element to light. In the absence of light, there is only darkness. Light extinguishes darkness. It *always* wins!

Be encouraged! Our eternal, triune, trustworthy, and triumphant God desires to shine through us to His glory. Remember He never fails, falters, or loses. Jesus, the light wins!

1. Take a moment and sing "This Little Light of Mine."
2. Discuss how light *rebukes* (or judges), *reproves* (or shows fault and error), *reveals* (or exposes), and *redeems*.

~

Heavenly Father, let my light shine before men, so that they may
see Your good works and give glory to You in heaven.

Dr. Ron Upton
Minister of Worship and Creative Arts
Idlewild Baptist Church, Lutz, FL

Power in Prayer

For this reason, I bow my knees before the Father, from whom every family in heaven and on earth is named, that according to the riches of his glory he may grant you to be strengthened with power through his Spirit in your inner being, so that Christ may dwell in your hearts through faith—that you, being rooted and grounded in love, may have strength to comprehend with all the saints what is the breadth and length and height and depth, and to know the love of Christ that surpasses knowledge, that you may be filled with all the fullness of God

Ephesians 3:14–19 (ESV)

One of the most powerful examples of prayer in Scripture is the example of Paul's prayer in Ephesians. In this passage, he states the reason for his prayer to God. It can be seen that phrases like *"according to the riches of His glory," "power through His Spirit," "to know the love of Christ,"* and *"to be filled with the fullness of God"* have a God-centered approach and not a "my situation" focus. It would be so easy for Paul's prayer to be focused on being delivered from oppression or attacks from enemies, but the foundation of this example is that Christ would be seen . . . that He would receive all glory. (Note the italics portions of Scripture above and the focus on Christ.)

There are three focal points to note:

1. Paul's prayer was aimed at spiritual maturity and growth.
2. Paul's prayer had a strong element of vision-casting and priority.
3. Paul's prayer focused more on other people and ultimately God.

In a culture of materialism that operates on a "my needs first" basis, let us always examine our motive when we pray. Is the desire for my situation and myself alone or is there a kingdom focus that directs our prayers to be Christ-centric? Of course, we should seek Christ in every life situation, but the example that Paul sets is that Christ's kingdom would be strengthened *and* that His people would be filled with the fullness of God.

When you pray, pray selflessly with vision for the church, recognizing God's strength and power, and giving Him glory in all things.

1. When you pray, are your prayers focused on yourself or on God's kingdom?
2. Do your prayers focus on your immediate need or on how God can use your current situation for His glory?

～

Dear God, please help me to learn to pray, focusing on my maturity in Christ, Your priority in each life opportunity, and that Your kingdom would advance through every situation. Thank You for every occurrence that allows me to be used by You for kingdom gain. In Your strong name I pray, Amen.

Carl Setterlind
Worship Pastor
Biltmore Baptist Church, Arden, NC

I Choose Joy

Rejoice in the Lord always. I will say it again: Rejoice!
Philippians 4:4 (NIV)

All of us will face various difficulties here on this earth. Outwardly, it may look different for each one of us, but we will all face challenges that will attempt to rob us of our earthly happiness.

This happiness can be a rollercoaster ride, fluctuating based on our circumstances and ability to have various things and experiences.

This word *rejoice* can't be understood properly when related to earthly happiness. Spiritual joy is a product of one's faith in Christ and can endure changing earthly circumstances. Paul did not enjoy good living conditions when he wrote "rejoice in the Lord." However, he had a constant joy because of his active faith in Christ.

God loves you and we must do our best to obey Him. Knowing and trusting Him will enable us to rejoice when our earthly circumstances become difficult. Hold on to the joy that is only found in God.

1. What things are occupying your mind and how do they affect your joy in the Lord?
2. Is your full faith in Him and your focus on His kingdom?

~

Father, help me give up my selfish pursuits and draw near to You so that I can experience true joy that only comes from You.

Jon Skelley
Worship Pastor
Geyer Springs First Baptist Church, Little Rock, AR

Becoming a King Maker

"Whoever wants to become great among you must be your servant, and whoever
wants to be first must be your slave—just as the Son of Man did not come
to be served, but to serve, and to give his life as a ransom for many."
Matthew 20:26–28 (NIV)

"Climb the ladder of success" is a well-known metaphor of our culture. Early in my ministry, my main goal was to position myself to be known as a great leader and one who leads the greatest ministry. I wanted the best, and I lived life in a way to make sure that I was the best. Ultimately, I was using others to make me the "king" of my own kingdom. We can all easily fall into this trap. In the book of Matthew, Jesus speaks about this very thing. The King of all kings tells His disciples that if you want to be a great leader, you must become a servant.

After many years of wrestling with the Holy Spirit on this matter, I began to realize that my success as a leader was not based on how great I could become, but instead about how I could make others great. So, I became a king-maker. I want to be someone who equips, encourages, and even positions others to do great things for the cause of Christ and His Kingdom. That's what we are all called to do! We're called to equip others to use their God given talents to fulfill the purpose for their lives. I encourage you to stop trying to be "king" but instead become a king-maker.

1. Like me, have you also worked hard to "build your career" so that you can be known as a great leader or musician?
2. Who are the people around you that you can serve by providing opportunities for their success?

Father, help me to have a servant's heart like Jesus. Give me eyes to see others as You see them and let me be someone who invests in the lives of others so that they can experience the fulfillment of living out their purpose like I get to. I lay aside my desire to be the "greatest" and devote my life to making others the "greatest" just as You taught us. In Jesus' name, Amen.

Daniel Morris
Worship Minister
Brentwood Baptist Church, Brentwood, TN

Perilous Prayers

*"But I will offer sacrifices to you with songs of praise, and I will fulfill
all my vows. For my salvation comes from the LORD alone."*
Jonah 2:9 (NLT)

In one moment, the blink of an eye, Jonah was tossed from a ship that was threatening his life into the sea that would most certainly claim it. Plunged beneath the water's surface and frantically fighting to find air, the great fish swallows him alive. In the most unseemly and uncomfortable environment, God interrupted Jonah's hot pursuit of his own ambition. Overboard and swallowed whole, Jonah was forced to make some major decisions. Jonah prays. Jonah's peril prompted his prayer, but it also changed his life. Getting right with God and realigning with God's call navigated the prophet from the digestive doom of the fish to the shoreline of destiny.

In our own peril, God may very well be using the storm to cultivate our obedience and change our ambition to His divine will and purpose. While His call may not line up with our preferences, it is the greatest place we can stand. Perilous times should drive us to prayer. The obedient response to God's call will be the catalyst to our greatest days in the future. Notice when Jonah got right with God, his song of praise returned.

1. In times of peril, are we driven to prayer or pursuit of disobedience?
2. Are you confidently standing in the place God has called you?

~

*God give me the strength to stand and heart to obey that which You have called me to do.
While peril is around me, I will choose to praise You and remember Your great faithfulness.
Accomplish Your great purposes in me and through me! To You be all the glory.*

Matthew Slemp
Minister of Music
First Baptist Church, Indian Trail, NC

The Context Matters

And when they saw him they worshiped him, but some doubted. And Jesus
came and said to them, "All authority in heaven and on earth has been
given to me. Go therefore and make disciples of all nations . . ."
Matthew 28:17–19a (ESV)

Every strong evangelical Christian that I know takes the Great Commission seriously as well as the Great Commandment. The heart of a true believer beats with Christ's command to GO and MAKE DISCIPLES of all nations. But have you ever thought about the context of the giving of the Great Commission? Where were the disciples at the time? What were they doing? Where in the Gospel narrative does this event take place? Remember that just three days earlier the disciples had experienced the agony of watching their Savior die on a cross. Now, they were at a mountain in Galilee where Jesus had directed them.

It's exciting to know that the posture of the disciples when they saw Jesus was that of WORSHIP! They had a post-resurrection worship experience that opened their hearts to the giving of the Great Commission. It certainly gives credence to the idea that worship is the catalyst that enables and propels the sharing of the gospel, fueling the flame of missions, evangelism, discipleship, and koinonia. Let me encourage you to begin each day in worship: reading God's Word, meditating, praying, praising, singing, and making melody in your heart to the Lord. You will find that by worshiping the Lord throughout the day, you will have a greater hunger to GO and TELL.

1. Does your personal and corporate worship empower you in the areas of evangelism, discipleship, missions, and fellowship?
2. Can you recall a few personal experiences that support this correlation between worship and other spiritual disciplines?

~

Lord, it is a joy to worship You and to be used by You in the making of disciples.
Lead me today to someone who needs to know Your grace, mercy, and salvation.

Todd Stearns
Pastor of Worship and Music
First Baptist Church, Naples, FL

A Life That Points to God

And they glorified God because of me.
Galatians 1:24 (ESV)

As the apostle Paul recounted the story of his conversion and described the ways that God had radically changed his life, he said that his incredible transformation had caused other people to glorify God. That's what grace does. Grace does not cause us to become fixated on the gift, no matter how magnificent it may be; rather, grace causes us to look beyond the gift and honor the Giver.

Living as followers of Christ will not always be comfortable and easy. Most people can honor God when their lives are comfortable and easy, but Paul exemplified what it means to honor God both in times of rejoicing and in times of sorrow. That's why he could sing from a prison cell (Acts 16:25).

Paul was constantly redirecting the attention of people away from their circumstances. He wanted them to look at Christ, and he lived his life in a way that would help them do that. He did not glory in his strength; instead, he gloried in his weakness, because the power of God is "made perfect in weakness" (2 Cor. 12:9 ESV). Paul's desire was to honor the Lord in both life and death. "For if we live, we live to the Lord, and if we die, we die to the Lord. So then, whether we live or whether we die, we are the Lord's" (Rom. 14:8 ESV).

1. So, what will people say about you? Will they say that you are nice? Successful? Talented? Or will they see that you live for a higher purpose and a greater person?
2. Does your life point people to God?

~

Gracious Father, my only desire is to glorify Your name. Give me strength to live in such a way that I honor You in both good times and bad. In both sorrow and rejoicing help me to know that You are always good. Give me an unshakeable confidence in the hope of eternal life and help me to live every day in light of that day.

John Stegemerten
Worship Pastor
Hickory Grove Baptist Church, Charlotte, NC

God Is Good!

For from Him and through Him and to Him are all things. To Him be the glory forever. Amen.
Romans 11:36 (NASB)

The final service of the day had just ended, and the tired, yet Spirit-filled, worship pastor was making his way to the back of the worship center to greet the congregation as they left. As he was walking, a young lady approached him saying, "I just love your voice!" Responding with a smile he said, "God is good!" As he walked on, another, a man in his early thirties, said "That first song was too high—I couldn't sing along." The worship pastor thanked the man for letting him know, shook his hand, and said, "God is good!" When he reached the back of the room, an elderly man approached and asked for prayer for his wife. She had just received a bad report from her doctor. After offering words of comfort, he prayed with the man. Following the amen, the worship pastor concluded with, "God is good."

The worship pastor knew that regardless of circumstance, God is constant and all good things come from Him. Anything good that we can do is God working through us. God gives our life meaning and purpose. God is worthy of all glory!

1. As God works through you, do you consistently give Him glory in all things?
2. Whether receiving praise or critique, are you able to stay centered on the task of pointing others to God, reminding them that if it's good, it comes from Him?

～

God, may I always give you the credit for anything good that is in my life. It is because of Your goodness and grace that I have purpose and happiness! Make me aware of opportunities to point others to You, regardless of my circumstance. In Jesus' name, Amen.

Jeff Stotts
Lead Worship Pastor
Central Baptist Church, Jonesboro, AR

Playing Offense

Don't just pretend to love others. Really love them. Hate what is wrong. Hold tightly to what is good. Love each other with genuine affection, and take delight in honoring each other.
Romans 12:9–10 (NLT)

Have you ever been ready to fight someone over how they've treated you? Being on defense is the position we take when we are hurt and wanting to defend ourselves or someone we love. We feel our heart racing, the tension rising, and we just want to reconcile it in anger. This Scripture is one that quickly comes to mind in those moments of displeasure and irritation. God calls us to love. If we are His, the love He has shown to us, through His death and resurrection for our sins, should overflow in our hearts for others. Listen, we all miss the mark. We say something we shouldn't or hurt others with our words, but this verse calls us to delight in honoring. We put on a smile and pretend in those moments, but God is calling us to more!

He wants us to hold our hands out to Him and place those that hurt us, even scar us, in His hands. He wants us to surrender our desire to be right or treated fairly for the sake of loving others. God wants us to take the field of life on offense. If Christ lives inside of us, loving others should be our act of service and gratitude to Him and His sacrifice. Without His love for you, where would you be? In those moments of anger and hurt, Romans 12:14 (NLT) asks us to "bless those who persecute you. Don't curse them; pray that God will bless them." God loves you and extends His grace to you each new day. Use this day to extend grace and love to someone who tries to steal your joy.

1. Is there someone in your life that needs your extension of love?
2. Are you sharing Christ's love with this person? Ask God to allow you to see them through His eyes.

~

Jesus, thank You for dying for us, and through Your blood, extending salvation to us. As we go through this day, help us to see others through Your blood. Help us to love as You have loved us and extend grace freely. We know in our flesh we can't love others that hurt us, but You give us the strength and courage to love them and honor them. We love You! In Christ's name, Amen.

Josh Sullins
Worship and Creative Arts Pastor
Peachtree Corners Baptist Church, Peachtree Corners, GA

God Answers the Earnest Prayers of Ordinary People

The prayer of a righteous person is powerful and effective. Elijah was a human being, even as we are. He prayed earnestly that it would not rain, and it did not rain on the land for three and a half years. Again he prayed, and the heavens gave rain, and the earth produced its crops.

James 5:16b–18 (NIV)

First Kings 17 and 18 tell us part of the great story of the prophet Elijah. He has more recorded miracles in the Bible than any other prophet of Israel. Perhaps that is why James tells his readers that Elijah had the same fallible, human nature as we do. He was an ordinary mortal. What we learn from him is earnest, passionate prayer. Prayer for Elijah was not a calm, laid-back request; he intensely poured out his heart to heaven.

For three and a half years, this prophet prayed with all his strength that it would not rain, and it did not. Then, the Bible says he climbed to the top of Mt. Carmel and asked God to make it rain again. Elijah "bent down to the ground and put his face between his knees" (1 Kings 18:42), and repeated this activity seven times before God answered his prayer with a heavy rainstorm.

Christians are not to manufacture passion, work themselves up into a frenzy of passion, or perform a certain number of rituals that cause God to decide that we've now reached "passionate prayer."

Instead, we should study the lives of Jacob, Hannah, Ezra, Nehemiah, Paul, and even Jesus to understand that true, passionate prayer must be energized by the Holy Spirit of God. Then, passionate prayer will be powerful and effective, coming from the heart of a righteous person.

1. Describe what your church needs to adjust to become a confessing church?
2. How can your church engage in a powerful prayer ministry of its own?

~

Father, humble our hearts to follow You passionately in prayer!

David Thomas
Worship Pastor
Highland Baptist Church, Grove City, OH

Do It with Freshness, Excellence, and Enthusiasm

Sing to him a new song; play skillfully, and shout for joy.
Psalm 33:3 (NIV)

It's often said, "As long as it's from the heart, it doesn't matter how well you do it." I humbly disagree. It matters a great deal what caliber of presentation you have as you deliver God's message. The difference between a poor performance and a great one is the difference between having your listeners be more concerned about you making it through the piece than they are about being set free to worship God.

This little verse encourages us by showing us what's truly important. Its opening line—*Sing to him a new song*—speaks to the *freshness* with which we should sing and play. Sure, it can mean that we should always be introducing *new music*, but it can also mean that even if we're doing a *repeat anthem*, we should do it as though it's the first time . . . with freshness and excitement!

It continues with *play skillfully*. This means that we're to bring our best efforts to the table as we prepare to make His praise *excellent*. Why would we do otherwise? I believe the chorus "We Bring the Sacrifice of Praise" speaks to this. Our musical offerings should cost us something, both in time and hard work.

And finally . . . *shout for joy!* These words remind us that all is made more effective by adding a generous dose of *enthusiasm*. And yes, it's a continual struggle to pull it off. I've heard choir members kiddingly respond to my request for them to smile as they sing, "I can either sing, or I can smile, but I can't do both at the same time." I say it's worth the effort to master doing both at the same time, for that added enthusiasm empowers our music!

1. Are we giving God our best as we prepare His praise?
2. How can we make *singing with enthusiasm* as essential as singing the right notes?

~

O God, spur us on to always approach our musical service to You with "wide-eyed" enthusiasm, and may we offer You nothing short of our best. Amen.

Bob Morrison
Minister of Music
First Baptist Church, Pensacola, FL

Sing as One Voice

How good and how pleasant it is for brethren to dwell together in unity!
Psalm 133:1 (NKJV)

A large choir singing in harmony is a wonderful thing to hear. Each member sings a unique and distinct part that creates a beautiful and interesting sound. Because each section is singing something different, one will often find the focus turning toward the beauty of the sound and not the message. In other words, the message has become unclear.

Most directors will admit that achieving a perfect unison is one of the hardest things for any choir. It may be difficult, but the result is breathtaking. When a choir sings together in perfect unison, breathing together, matching pitch perfectly, with no one individual standing out, the listener is led to lean in and listen intently. The message then becomes VERY clear.

As the body of Christ, we are each called to play a unique part. However, as hard as we might try, the contrary is that we may become enamored with ourselves and lose sight of the message. We may even sing or live our own part as loudly and boldly as we can. At this point, just like a choir, the message becomes muddled and unclear. We must always remember that even though we are unique, we are called to unite and sing as one voice with Christ so that the message can always be clear and unified.

1. Do you always seek to play or sing your own part first?
2. Do you listen for the voice of Christ in your life?

Father, I want to walk in perfect unison with You. I admit that there are times in my life where I have sought to place my uniqueness above Your will in my life. I pray, Lord, that You would remind me to walk, work, and sing in perfect unity with You. Amen.

Ken Van Cura
Worship Pastor
First Baptist Church, Plant City, FL

Imperfect Praise?

I will praise You, O LORD, with my whole heart; I will tell of all Your marvelous works.
I will be glad and rejoice in You; I will sing praise to Your name, O Most High.
Psalm 9:1–2 (NKJV)

Glenda was my favorite singer. I had known her all of her life. She was about ten years younger than me. She lived down the street. We went to the same church, and she LOVED to sing. She asked me to give her voice lessons. I did what I could to help her singing, but I could only do so much. You see, Glenda was born with Down syndrome. Her speech, and thus her singing, was not typical, but who said typical and conventional were the only approved singing methods?

Singing starts with the heart, and Glenda's heart was huge. She loved the Lord. She loved people, and like all of us, she enjoyed a bit of attention. She got mine. Glenda sang with a freedom that I could not . . . or would not. All of Glenda's personality, volume, and smile came out in her singing. Her favorite song was "How Great Thou Art."

When I served my first church, I asked Glenda to come and sing during a time of worship. She was beside herself at the opportunity. It thrilled her to sing for her Savior and to be in front of people who lovingly listened to her. We didn't hear just a person with Down syndrome. We heard God singing through His child. We heard the love of Christ reaching out in joy. We couldn't always understand the words, but we knew who gave her the voice of encouragement.

Glenda died recently. Her brother who had cared for her was by her side. She had been quiet the final couple of days, but just hours before she went to the arms of her Savior, her brother asked if she wanted to sing. The quietness disappeared as Glenda sang one last earthly time . . . "Then sings my soul, my Savior God to Thee, how great Thou art."

There was nothing imperfect about Glenda. She was God's child singing God's praise. *Forgive me, Father, when I put my standards on what singing is worthy of You. Help us all to see with Your eyes and listen with Your heart.*

1. Who is your favorite singer? Why? How do they inspire you?
2. What can you do to encourage others to sing praise to God?

~

To my Creator, Savior, and Sustainer, thank You for making each of us so uniquely.
Thank You for knowing everything about me and loving me anyway. Teach me to overlook
earthly differences and hear Your voice in all of Your creation. From Your children
so unique to our loving God, we sing how great You are. In Jesus' name, Amen.

Pat Van Dyke
Minister of Music and Pastoral Care
First Baptist Church, Clarksville, TN

It Is Enough

". . . it is enough . . ."
1 Kings 19:4 (ESV)

Elijah came off the victory of a lifetime at the end of 1 Kings 18. Through God's power, Elijah multiplied the widow's food supply, raised her son from the dead, stopped rain from falling, called fire from heaven, killed pagan prophets, outran the king's chariot and finally, made it rain again. Elijah should have been riding high, confident in the power of the God of the universe that just showed His servant how awesome He is. But he wasn't.

Elijah, instead, was afraid. You see, Elijah had a venomous couple named Ahab and Jezebel that were not happy with him. This couple just happened to be the king and queen of Israel and had the power to take his life. So, Elijah ran. He ran to the wilderness to hide from these villains who sought to end his life, but here's the thing: up to this point, he was following God's directions. He went; he saw; he obeyed . . . and he saw great victories. Even though there were some tough assignments, Elijah did what God wanted. Until now.

Elijah was so afraid that he didn't even bother to check with God. Elijah didn't even leave a note that said, "Went to the wilderness, be back when they're not trying to kill me!" No, he just ran. But then, God showed up.

God asked Elijah, "What are you doing here?" (as if He didn't know). God knew Elijah was deathly afraid. Even after all the miracles, things still looked dire to the prophet. "It is enough," Elijah said, and asked to die (1 Kings 19:4). But god was about to do something much greater. He was going to show Elijah something better than stopping rain, defeating false prophets, or raising a child from the dead. God was about to show Elijah Himself—the awesome glory of His very image.

How often do we find ourselves in similar situations as Elijah? We're serving God, seeing miracles happen and suddenly, the enemy takes notice and sends villains after us. We get so discouraged in our battles and frustrated when the villains seem to have the upper hand, but many times, that's when God is about to show up!

So, whoever your villains may be or however hopeless it may seem, God may be on the verge of showing up in a way you never imagined. Go where He sends you, do what He wants, and don't hide in the wilderness! He wants to show you something amazing!

1. Are you saying "It is enough" because you believe God has abandoned you, your family, or your ministry?
2. Do you trust Him with your life? Trust that God is guiding your life and protecting you in every circumstance. He may be asking you to do something that seems to go against the wisdom of practical thought but remember, "God chose what is foolish in the world to shame the wise; God chose what is weak in the world to shame the strong" (1 Cor. 1:27 ESV).

⁓

Father, help me to trust You when things seem bleak and hopeless. You are omniscient and see the "big picture"! Help me to know and do Your will in everything I do. Amen.

Nathan Ward
Worship Arts Pastor
Woodland Community Church, Bradenton, FL

Love Lifted Me

And everyone who calls on the name of the Lord will be saved.
Acts 2:21 (NIV)

As a worship pastor and minister of music for more than thirty years, I've had many occasions to sing the hymn "Love Lifted Me" by Howard E. Smith and James Rowe. Once, during the singing of this hymn, the Lord reminded me how true the words were. When I was seven or eight years old, my dad, three of my brothers, and I had been out fishing in Matagorda Bay, Texas. After a short while, our boat had engine problems. We walked the boat, in about thirty-inch-deep water, back toward our campsite. This took about half a day. Once we had the campsite in view, about 200 yards away, three of us went in a direct line to the camp. My dad and oldest brother took the boat by way of the water channel in a different direction.

After about 100 yards, my brothers and I found ourselves in very deep water. We sort of knew how to swim, but the shock of instantly being in water over our heads made us panic. Time and time again, we yelled for Dad to HELP. I remember slipping down past my brothers and looking up at them from the depths. I mustered all the strength I could to reach up and grab one of my brother's feet. I then crawled up his body to get some air. Dad did hear and came and saved us. I'll never forget the sheer relief as I clung to his neck and was rescued.

"But the Master of the sea heard my despairing cry. From the waters lifted me, now safe am I." Jesus offers life to all who ask. His love still rescues today.

1. Have you ever been rescued from drowning?
2. What do you need to do to be rescued? How has God rescued you?

~

Dear God, thank You for making a way for all of us because we need a Savior. Help those who are drowning in sin to look up and call out to You for help. Help us to cling to You as our Rescuer and to cherish the abundant life You give us in Christ. In Jesus' name, Amen.

J. K. Weger
Minister of Music and Worship Arts
Ash Creek Baptist, Azle, TX

Indescribable . . . Yet I Keep Trying!

Then the LORD came down in the cloud and stood there with him and proclaimed his name, the LORD. And he passed in front of Moses, proclaiming, "The LORD, the LORD, the compassionate and gracious God, slow to anger, abounding in love and faithfulness, maintaining love to thousands, and forgiving wickedness, rebellion and sin."
Exodus 34:5–7 (NIV)

I find the song "Indescribable," by Laura Story, to be powerful and ironic at the same time. Although it's entitled "Indescribable," we often try to describe God through a language and vocabulary that is woefully inadequate. So, why do I continue to try? As believers, there is an innate desire to express love and adoration to God because He is . . . (you fill in the blank). Different parts of His character and nature impact us in different ways.

Therefore, our expressions of worship vary from person to person. The psalmist described God through moments of joy and moments of despair. He used these descriptions as expressions of praise and worship. Some are very descriptive while others are more general in nature. As part of your personal worship time, I would suggest spending a few minutes trying to describe God. It's a great reminder of who God is versus who I am.

1. What words would you use to describe God today?
2. Does your perception of God match what is found in God's Word?

Heavenly Father, thank You for being more than words can describe. Thank You for being more than my mind can perceive. Because of who You are, I can trust You, completely, to work in every part of my life. I praise You for being the God of the universe . . . the I AM WHO I AM! In Jesus' name, Amen.

Tim Whedbee
Senior Associate Pastor of Worship and Administration
Mobberly Baptist Church, Longview, TX

The Battles Worth Fighting

For though we live in the world, we do not wage war as the world does. The weapons we
fight with are not the weapons of the world. On the contrary, they have divine power to
demolish strongholds. We demolish arguments and every pretension that sets itself up against
the knowledge of God, and we take captive every thought to make it obedient to Christ.
2 Corinthians 10:3–5 (NIV)

Do you ever type a response to someone on social media and, before hitting the send button, think better and delete the message? Too often we let issues that really don't concern us, consume us. At least they don't have eternal significance, but we want to persuade everyone to see things just the way we do. Our battles go beyond social media, politics, and personal preference, and abstaining from temporary concerns may give the opportunity to influence eternal concerns.

Pick your battles wisely and fight only those that have kingdom impact . . . that have eternal significance. One of my very favorite Scripture passages sums it up best: "Since you have purified your souls in obeying the truth through the Spirit in sincere love of the brethren, love one another fervently with a pure heart, having been born again, not of corruptible seed but incorruptible, through the word of God which lives and abides forever, because, 'All flesh is as grass, And all the glory of man as the flower of the grass. The grass withers, and its flower falls away, but the word of the LORD endures forever'" (1 Pet. 1:22–25 NKJV).

My friend Terry Williams recently spoke at a conference I attended. He said, "Life is too short to get caught up in water cooler conversations. The enemy is willing around the water cooler. Don't act like sheep. Live above them. Sheep can't lead sheep. This is not an opportunity; it is a responsibility."

1. What battles are you fighting that really don't matter in the eternal realm?
2. Does your desire to share your political and social views hinder your ability to share the gospel?

~

Lord, teach us to live in this world, but not be of the world.
Show us which battles are worth fighting. Amen.

Bradley White
Worship Pastor
First Baptist Church, Summit, MS

Where Should We Worship?

Jesus said to her, "Woman, believe me, the hour is coming when neither on this mountain nor in Jerusalem will you worship the Father. You worship what you do not know; we worship what we know, for salvation is from the Jews."
John 4:21–22 (ESV)

Authentic worship is not confined to a place. At first glance, it appears that Jesus was discouraging worship anywhere, when, in fact, He was encouraging worship everywhere. Jesus said that worship is not about places called sacred by religion. Jesus is unveiling a new age in which people will not have to travel to a physical temple in one city to worship but will be able to worship God in every place, because the Holy Spirit will dwell in them.

Worship isn't somewhere you go . . . worship isn't a place . . . worship isn't just an event on your calendar. Too often, devotion to God and church can become such a mundane part of our lives that worship becomes merely "something we do," like going to a restaurant or the grocery store. The apostle Paul said these folks only have a "form" or appearance of godliness, and they miss the miraculous power of God in their lives (2 Tim. 3:5). The "why we worship" is more important than "where we worship." The place of worship does not determine the authenticity of our worship. God wants worship to be a part of our DNA, a natural part of our daily lives.

1. One of my most memorable worship experiences occurred under a tree in the bush of Mozambique, Africa. Take some time to reflect on some of your most significant times of worship and thank God for His presence wherever you are.
2. If your worship is dry and routine, what steps can you take to revive your devotion to God?

~

Lord, thank You for the Holy Spirit that lives in me. Thank You that Your presence is with me everywhere I go. Help me to know You more and make worship a priority of everyday of my life, In Jesus' name, Amen.

Andy Newsome
Music and Worship Pastor
Trinity Baptist Church, Ocala, FL

Stop It!

LORD, my heart is not proud; my eyes are not haughty. I do not get involved with things too great or too difficult for me. Instead, I have calmed and quieted myself . . . like a little child. Israel, put your hope in the LORD, both now and forever.
Psalm 131 (HCSB)

The older we get, the harder it sometimes is to simply trust in the Lord. We go through experiences in life that cause our eyes to lose our spiritual focus on the Lord. We begin to focus on our own, or even other people's strength, cleverness, and abilities. Rather than trusting and hoping in the Lord, we put our trust in what we can do. We even start to inject our opinion into situations and things that really don't call for our input or control.

We need to STOP, quit struggling, "calm and quiet ourselves," become like a little child again, and simply trust God.

1. Is there a situation in your life—at work or at school or in your community— where you have gotten over-involved and are acting or reacting with less than Christ-likeness?
2. How can you become like a little child in that situation and let your hope in the Lord shine through what you say and do?

Lord, would You help me to keep my eyes fixed on You? Help me to become like that little child again—trusting in Your provision, Your strength, and in Your wisdom, both for today and for tomorrow!

John Williams
Worship Pastor
Hebron Baptist Church, Dacula, GA

Knowing the Will of God

I beseech you therefore, brethren, by the mercies of God, that you present your bodies
a living sacrifice, holy, acceptable to God, which is your reasonable service. And do
not be conformed to this world, but be transformed by the renewing of your mind,
that you may prove what is that good and acceptable and perfect will of God.
Romans 12:1–2 (NKJV)

As parents, we desire to teach our children based on our experiences of life. We do not want them to experience undue pain or misfortune. As Christians, we have a heavenly Father who wants us to know His will and direction for our lives. Psalm 32:8 says, "I will instruct you and teach you in the way you should go; I will guide you with My eye" (NKJV). God's desire is for us to know and carry out His will.

The apostle Paul urges us to present our bodies as a living and holy sacrifice to God. Warren Wiersbe says, "True Christian service and living must begin with personal dedication to the Lord. The Christian who fails in life is the one who has first failed at the altar, refusing to surrender completely to Christ."[29] True dedication is a surrendering of the heart, mind, and soul in relation to God's wants and desires for life.

As believers, we either conform daily to the world or we allow the Holy Spirit to transform us by the renewing of our heart, mind, and soul. The Greek word for transform is *metamorphosis*. Just like a caterpillar goes through a total transformation to become a butterfly, Christians must go through a transformation daily to avoid conforming to the world and its practices.

1. Are you failing at life? If so, why?
2. Do you know the will of God for your life? Why not? When we present our bodies and renew our minds in Christ Jesus, we can know the perfect will of God.

~

Father, transform my dead, lifeless heart into a beautiful sacrifice of
praise as I surrender and conform to Your will. Amen.

Dr. David Wilson
Assistant Professor of Worship and Church Music
Brewton-Parker College, Mt. Vernon, GA

Chosen . . .

*"You did not choose me, but I chose you and appointed you so that
you might go and bear fruit—fruit that will last—and so that
whatever you ask in my name the Father will give you."*

John 15:16 (NIV)

Back in the days before everyone got participation trophies for having a pulse and showing up, competition was a part of life. I remember being in the lineup against the school wall waiting to be picked for a team. Two eagle-eyed captains were sizing up the flock to pick the one who could help them win the game. It was always good to be chosen, and then assigned a position on the field.

Every time I think back on these experiences I remember a verse I learned as a youth. John 15:16 reminds us that we were chosen by Jesus and given a position on His team. We are chosen by Him to bear fruit—fruit that will last. I think it is interesting that Jesus promises that if we invest in His assigned task, bearing fruit, we end up tuning our hearts and desires to His heart and desires. The funny thing about fruit trees is that they don't bear fruit for themselves. You have never seen an apple tree eating an apple, or a blueberry bush eating blueberries. The fruit we bear for Jesus is for the edification of others. We bear fruit that will last to nourish and heal others. "But the fruit of the Spirit is love, joy, peace, forbearance, kindness, goodness, faithfulness, gentleness, and self-control" (Gal. 5:22–23a NIV).

1. What fruit is Jesus wanting to grow in you today?
2. How do others best benefit from the fruit growing from your life?

~

*Father, thank You for loving me and choosing me before I even knew
You. Thank You for challenging me to bear fruit so that others may see
You in me and be drawn to Your goodness and grace. Amen.*

Don Barrick
Worship Pastor
The Woodlands First Baptist Church, The Woodlands, TX

A Heart That Sings

Do not be drunk with wine, . . . but be filled with the Spirit, speaking to one another in
psalms and hymns and spiritual songs, singing and making melody in your heart to the Lord.
Ephesians 5:18–19 (NKJV)

Singing begins in the heart before it ever touches our lips. You've heard the old saying,
"What's down in the well will come up in the bucket"; whatever is in the heart will
eventually come out of the mouth. Every emotion is represented when we sing: joy, love,
sadness, anticipation, serenity, sorrow, etc.

There is something very distinctive about someone who expresses themselves by singing. I once heard Pastor David Jeremiah say, "The highest expression of praise our minds
can fathom is the expression of singing." Singing is very important to God. More than four
hundred times it is found in Scripture, not to mention, it is actually commanded at least
fifty times.

I think about all the ways we have to enter the presence of God: praying, teaching,
preaching, testimony, the reading of God's Word, and yet, according to Psalm 100:2, we
are commanded to enter His presence with singing. God gives everyone their own personal song of praise; it's a song that provides an opportunity for free, completely original,
personal, heartfelt expression. Find ways throughout the day to express yourself to God by
singing. Give your heart permission to speak; there's a really good chance it will come out
in song.

1. What keeps you from releasing your fullest expression of worship?
2. Are you willing to give God your deepest heartfelt emotion in song?

~

Father, I desire to offer my singing as a sacrifice of praise to You. May
my song bring honor to You and encouragement to others.

Terry Williams
Music and Worship Consultant
Florida Baptist Convention, Jacksonville, FL

Words on Fire!

So also the tongue is a small part of the body, and yet it boasts of great things. See how great a forest is set aflame by such a small fire!
James 3:5 (NASB)

Surely this verse is not talking about you and me! Is it? It didn't take much for me to remember when I was scalded by someone. I also shamefully remember the many times the younger me practically burned up someone's self worth! God jerked my chain at a stoplight when my toddler daughter said, "Move it, buddy!" She was reading a book and never looked up, but I had modeled a sense of road rage that bubbled right out of her. Twenty-five years later, I still try to be careful.

God desires each of us, in or out of ministry, to represent *HIM* in all situations. Even in the emotionally charged atmosphere of being criticized, we are to be like Christ. On the flip side, your words can breathe new life and encouragement into someone who is on the verge of giving up. You might be their last beacon of hope and not even realize it.

1. Can you think of someone who was scalded by your words? Is humbly asking forgiveness in order?
2. Who deserves your highest praise today? Could it be a family member, a colleague, a waitress, etc.? How about all of the above!

~

Father, give us compassion for those hurting around us. Give us patience with the intolerable and love for the unloved. Please take the reins of my tongue and lead me to a passionate lifestyle of speaking blessings and encouragement to those around me. I pray that people will notice a difference in my life today. For Your Glory, Amen.

James Bradford
Minister of Music
Quail Springs Baptist Church, Oklahoma City, OK

Amazing Grace

For from his fullness we have all received, grace upon grace.
John 1:16 (ESV)

I was watching a video of a service on Sunday morning and the preacher was talking about the song "Amazing Grace." He used the words of the hymn, and it really made me start to think even more about God's grace. The words are "amazing grace how sweet the sound that saved a wretch like me." Have you ever really thought about the words "how sweet the sound"? What is the sound that is so amazing that could save a wretch like me? I began to ponder this thought. Was it the sound of Christ on the cross when He cried out, "It is finished"? Was it the sound of angels singing when you and I were saved? Was it the sound of the angels at the empty tomb that Easter morning when they said, "He is not here, He is risen"?

Was it the sound of Jesus telling the lame man to get up and walk or when He called out to Lazarus to be raised from the dead? I am not sure what the sound of amazing grace would be, but I believe it is the sound of a sinner crying out to God for mercy and asking Him to come into their life to save them. I have to believe it is the sound of the redeemed praising God for all that He has done for them. Whatever the sound is, it is a sound that has been sung through the ages as people have come to know and trust Christ.

1. How has God given you grace?
2. When was a time that God's grace was very evident in your life?

~

Dear Lord, we thank You for Your love and grace and mercy. You have given to us the grace of everlasting life, and we stand to give You praise to the sound of "Amazing grace how sweet the sound that saved a wretch like me!"

Wayne Bridges
Traditional Worship Leader/Senior Adults
First Baptist Church, Ruston, LA

Living in the Light, Not the Spotlight

*Not to us, LORD, not to us, but to your name give glory because
of your faithful love, because of your truth.*
Psalm 115:1 (CSB)

We in worship ministry are walking a tightrope.

We know that God alone is worthy of worship, and we prepare praise offerings weekly to magnify His name.

As we are pointing attention to God, we are usually doing so while standing on a stage, with a microphone in front of us or perhaps with special lighting focused in on us.

How do we keep the attention off of us and on God?

First, let's make sure our heart and motives are pure (Ps. 51:10). Our motivation will shine through, whether it is to bring glory to God or to ourselves.

Second, we must make sure Jesus is living in and through us. Paul was so surrendered that he said, "I no longer live, but Christ lives in me" (Gal. 2:20 CSB).

Finally, stay humble. Don't get puffed up from all of the hot air people give you about how good you are! God will resist us if we are proud, but He lavishes grace on the humble (James 4:6).

When we have a pure heart, allow Jesus to live through us, and possess a humble spirit, we are vessels God can use to bring worship to Himself and draw others to Him.

1. Can you remember a time in worship when you wanted to take the glory instead of giving it to God?
2. How can we help others understand that our motivation is for them to see God and not us?

~

Father, our world tells us everything is all about us. Help us never to believe that, but to remember that our lives are only meaningful and effective when we are compasses aligned with our true north, pointing to you as the Giver of all answers and the Receiver of all glory.

Clay Owens
Pastor of Worship Ministry
Emerald Coast Fellowship, Lynn Haven, FL

Now You're Ready

He chose his servant David, calling him from the sheep pens. He took David from tending the ewes and lambs and made him the shepherd of Jacob's descendants—God's own people, Israel. He cared for them with a true heart and led them with skillful hands.
Psalm 78:70–72 (NLT)

We've all heard the statement, "Timing is everything." This is true in business deals, critical conversations, athletic competitions, etc., when we are strategically calculating our next move in hopes of being at the right place at the right time. In life, however, what we consider to be the "right place" and the "right time" may not be God's idea of what is best. Scripture tells us that God has a plan for us, and that He will be faithful to complete it. Yet, we often become impatient with His timing. The dreams that God plants in our hearts usually aren't fulfilled overnight. His calling becomes our journey that leads us through various seasons.

There are seasons of preparation and pruning that can seem like an eternity. David started out in the sheep pens, tending to ewes and lambs. It was there that God began molding his heart and sharpening his skills in preparation for greater things. I've learned that if we are patient in the process and faithful where we are planted, God will position us in the right place at the right time for His glory. Just know that where He has you right now is the right place for this season. If you are consumed by the dream and constantly focused on the next step, you won't be all you should be where you are. If you try to rush the Lord, thinking you're ready for what's next, you might just miss out on some of the greatest joys you could ever experience, right where He has you.

1. What about your current situation could be God's pruning and preparation for the next season?
2. Are you all in where God has placed you, or are you anxiously looking ahead to what's to come?

~

God, I know Your ways are higher than our ways. Help me to trust You more and know that You have my best interest at heart. Give me vision for the future, patience in the waiting, and joy in the journey.

Scott Bullman
Worship Pastor
Thomas Road Baptist Church, Lynchburg, VA

Unexpected Grace

Mephibosheth son of Jonathan son of Saul came to David, fell facedown, and paid homage. David said, "Mephibosheth!" "I am your servant," he replied.
2 Samuel 9:6 (CSB)

K ing Saul was dead! The custom of the day was that when a new king was installed, all family members of the old king were killed in order to prevent any of them from forming a coup to overthrow the new ruler.

David was now king. Years after his installation as monarch, David remembered a promise he had made to his best friend Jonathan, Saul's son, to protect any of his family members once he became the king. David inquired and found that Jonathan had a son by the name of Mephibosheth who was still alive.

Mephibosheth, who was crippled as a result of an accident, was brought to the king with full expectations of being executed. Instead, David showed pure and complete grace by giving him all that his grandfather Saul had possessed. To top it all off, David made him a member of his own household, telling him that, from now on, he would dine at the king's table.

Instead of death, Mephibosheth was elevated to the king's household as a son. What unconditional, unexpected grace! That's exactly what Jesus did for me! He lifted me from my depraved existence and gave me a seat at the King's table. I am Mephibosheth!

1. To whom should I show grace today?
2. How can I demonstrate grace to my family this week?

~

My dear Lord, I thank and praise You for grace freely offered to me that was so unexpected and undeserved! Amen.

Keith Clutts
Worship Pastor
Grand Avenue Baptist Church, Fort Smith, AR

Need a Lift?

But You, O Lord, are a shield about me,
my glory, and the One who lifts my head.
Psalm 3:3 (NASB)

Have you ever gone through a time where you were so emotionally burdened that you could barely lift your head? It probably seemed in that moment like the weight of the world, the weight of your family, the weight of your business, or the weight of a relationship rested squarely on your shoulders. Most folks have been there at some point in time. We know Jesus was also there as He prayed in the garden of Gethsemane with the weight of my sin and your sin about to be laid upon Him.

I have always loved the encouragement and imagery found in this verse. I first see God as a shield about us, protecting us from all sides. This leaves nothing vulnerable to the attack of the enemy. The second image I see is that of a hurt, embarrassed, or sad child coming to a parent for support. That parent then lovingly places their hands around the sides of that child's face and gently lifts their chin. When God does this for us, He redirects our focus from our temporary situation to our eternal reward. This also reminds us that we can go through whatever we're facing because of what Christ has already done for us!

1. What is burdening your spirit today?
2. How you can you encourage a friend who may need to be reminded of this verse?

~

Dear heavenly Father, You are our Glory and the One who lifts our head!
Help us to feel Your love and encouragement today. Help us, in turn, to show
Your love and encouragement to others. Please send us someone to minister to
and with whom to share the gospel. We pray this in Jesus' name, Amen.

Charles Darus
Worship Pastor
First Baptist Church, Kissimmee, FL

Where Is the Source?

We [who teach God's word] are from God [energized by the Holy Spirit], and whoever
knows God [through personal experience] listens to us [and has a deeper understanding of
Him]. Whoever is not of God does not listen to us. By this we know [without any doubt]
the spirit of truth [motivated by God] and the spirit of error [motivated by Satan].

1 John 4:6 (AMP)

Today, with social media, the internet, and other technology, we hear so much about "fake news." It is almost too easy to spread a certain narrative. Many are too quick to share the latest word based on numbers of "hits" or "shares" and not on the facts. Many times, we hit that "share" button before we even consider the source and whether or not it's even true.

Sadly, this is also true about many churches, religious movements, and trends in the modern church. We quickly jump to the newest trend or song or style, not based on prayer and God's leading, but on who else is doing it. The Word of God warns us in 1 John that there is both a spirit of truth and a spirit of error. Who will you follow today?

1. Today, in my worship life, will I follow the latest trend because everyone else is or because I have been led by God?
2. Will I seek the spirit of truth to guide my life and rebuke the spirit of error?

～

Lord, I pray You will give us all wisdom beyond our years and understanding.
Help us to hear Your Holy Spirit and let Him guide us daily. Amen.

Paul Davis
Worship Pastor
Northcrest Baptist Church, Meridian, MS

Is Your Gate Open?

The glory of the LORD entered the temple through the gate facing east.
Ezekiel 43:4 (NIV)

The glory of the Lord—the presence of the Lord—is something we all desire in our services, let alone in our personal lives. We look for His presence when the music is especially vibrant, the preaching is dynamic, the offering overflows or the communion is especially sweet, but I've never read those entities in the Bible as indicators of the glory of the Lord "showing up" in our lives.

Ezekiel goes on to say, "Then the Spirit lifted me up and brought me into the inner court [our heart], and the glory of the Lord filled the temple [me]. While the man [the Spirit of God] was standing beside me, I heard someone [God] speaking to me from inside the temple. He said: 'Son of Man, this is the place of my throne and the place for the soles of my feet. This is where I will live among the Israelites [you] forever'" (NIV paraphrase).

Can the glory of the Lord manifest Himself in our services at those particular times mentioned above? Of course, He can! But that means we have to wait from Sunday to Sunday for His presence to be known. The psalmist David wrote an answer for being in the presence of the Lord always! He wrote: "Lift up your heads, you gates; be lifted up, you ancient doors, that the King of glory may come in" (Ps. 24:7 NIV).

What are the gates and the doors? OUR EYES! He is telling us to keep looking to Him! The presence of the Lord is found by opening our eyes to what is unseen rather than what is seen (2 Cor. 4:18 NIV). Is your gate (eyes) lifted up? Are your doors (eyes) opened to Him?

1. What are those things in my life that are keeping my gate closed to Your presence?
2. When do I most often recognize the glory of the Lord—when I'm alone or in a group of people?

～

Father, my gates are lifted up, my doors are open to You. Fill this temple and dwell within me forever. Amen.

Dr. Mark Deakins
Worship Minister
Broadway Christian Church, Lexington, KY

Longing for the Lord

O God, you are my God; earnestly I seek you; my soul thirsts for you; my
flesh faints for you, as in a dry and weary land where there is no water. . . .
Because your steadfast love is better than life, my lips will praise you.

Psalm 63:1, 3 (ESV)

There are so many things in life that grab our attention. Some things should take our time—like family, friends, reasonable work and ministry, and some should not. However, nothing should be more important than spending time with the Lord. The psalmist shows us that we should long to be in the presence of God. We should find our life force and reason for living in Him.

Jesus puts it this way:

"I am the vine; you are the branches. Whoever abides in me and I in him, he it is that bears much fruit, for apart from me you can do nothing." (John 15:5 ESV)

Don't miss His point: we must earnestly seek the Lord. We must desire Him much like our bodies desire water. We are absolutely useless for His kingdom when we fail to abide in, rest in, and seek after Him.

You will likely still have a successful life, by the world's standards, if you ignore your thirst for the Lord. If you try to make it on your own, you may have everything you think you want, but you will still be empty. Your soul is designed for Jesus to fill it. You need the Lord in order to be completely you.

Surrender to the Savior. Abide in Him. Let Him lead you and give you everything you truly need.

1. What things stand in the way of you abiding and resting in the Lord?
2. Have you given your life to Jesus? If so, remember your commitment to Him. If not, ask Him to be your Lord and Savior.

Jesus, I want to abide in You each day. Help me to do so. Amen.

Chris Diffey
Minister of Music and Worship
Lakeside Baptist Church, Birmingham, AL

Abide in Jesus

"Abide in Me, and I in you. As the branch cannot bear fruit of itself unless it abides in the vine, so neither can you unless you abide in Me. I am the vine, you are the branches; he who abides in Me and I in him, he bears much fruit, for apart from Me you can do nothing."
John 15:4–5 (NASB)

As worship leaders, at times it is easy for us to lean on our talent, skill, and experience. You may be an incredible singer, instrumentalist, writer, arranger, and leader, but if you are not abiding in Christ, you'll be like a branch not attached to the vine; it will dry up and its fruit will amount to nothing.

The picture of a vineyard pruned is a crucial one for worship leaders. It is so important to cut off that which is dying and bear fruit that is attached to the life-giving vine: Jesus. Make it the priority of your life to abide (hold to, stick to, dwell with) in Christ. As you do, all of your gifts and talents will be infused with His life, His Spirit, His anointing—bringing light and life to all who come in contact.

1. What talents and gifts has the Lord given you?
2. In times where you have consciously been abiding in Christ, what difference have you noticed as you have led in worship?

~

Dear Father, may I do nothing apart from You! May my ministry be an overflow of what You are doing in my life as I abide in Christ. I lay all the gifts and talents You have given me at Your feet.

Gary Rhodes
Worship Pastor
First Baptist Church Woodway, Waco, TX

Overwhelmed by God's Peace

And the peace of God, which transcends all understanding, will
guard your hearts and your minds in Christ Jesus.
Philippians 4:7 (NIV)

My first job after graduate school was teaching at a university in Oklahoma. I absolutely loved my job. Every day I would look out my office window and watch college kids walk to class with their backpacks in tow. I was making music at a high level; I was spending quality time with family. Life was good. I was at peace.

I began filling in as a music director at a nearby church, and about three months later the church asked me to be their minister of music. I had no clue what a minister of music did all day. I wasn't trained for that job. I declined, but they persisted until I agreed to pray about it. My good and peaceful life was now rocked by the turmoil of decision-making and potential life change. I sought counsel from godly people and listened to advice from the dean and the president of the university. I was not sleeping. I was not eating. I was not at peace.

After a month of wrestling with God, while talking to a senior faculty member, I was overwhelmed by God's peace, and in that moment, I said "yes" to God! The unexplainable peace of God led me to my life's calling. I was not prepared for the journey ahead, but God knew that I was ready if I would step out in faith.

1. Is there an area in your life where you are not at peace?
2. Begin praying for God to reveal His plan for your life through His overwhelming peace.

~

Father, give me the courage to follow Your peace, even when it's not the easiest
path. Attune my spirit to the ways You might reveal Your plan to me, whether
it be through Your Word, others in my life, or my circumstances.

Jeff Elkins
Minister of Worship
First Baptist Church, Tulsa, OK

When Anger Rises Up

Human anger does not produce the righteousness God desires.
James 1:20 (NLT)

I want to pose a question for you to think about today. Do you believe it is okay for you to be angry? There are so many things in this world that could lead you and me to become angry. I understand, but I would like to give another perspective on anger. In Ephesians, the Bible tells us that we should not let the sun go down while we're angry. I think we can understand that this verse is telling us to deal with our anger when it rises up within us. If we are angry because of something someone did, something we did, or some other reason, the Bible tells us to deal with it quickly. Why? Because the anger of man does not produce the righteousness God desires from His children.

I understand that all of us from time to time get angry, but I want to encourage you to put off the anger and put on the fruit of the Spirit (love, joy, peace, patience, kindness, goodness, gentleness, self-control, and faithfulness). Several of the fruit of the Spirit can be put into action instead of anger. By using the fruit of the Spirit, we would be showing the righteousness of God rather than showing anger. Also in Ephesians, the Word tells us to put away "all anger." Why? Well, our anger does not produce the righteousness of God. We use all kinds of excuses to justify our anger. Don't justify your anger. Ask God to lead you to put on the fruit of the Spirit instead of anger.

1. Do you struggle with anger? If so, understand that your anger does not produce His righteousness.
2. Anger, if not dealt with, roots bitterness. Do you need to repent of anger in your own life?

~

Lord, thank You for being so patient with me. Help me today to live in a way that pleases You. Help me to deal with anger in a biblical way. Help me to put off anger and put on the fruit of the Spirit. Amen.

Chris Ellenburg
Minister of Music
First Baptist Church, North Spartanburg, SC

Hope through the Storms

More than the sounds of many waters, than the mighty
breakers of the sea, the LORD on high is mighty.
Psalm 93:4 (NASB)

Many times, trouble, stress, and heartache come in waves. The daily grind often seems too much to bear. The events in the news most days can be depressing. These are just a few of the "waves and thunder" to which the psalmist refers! Time and time again, these timeless passages from God's Word continue to encourage us of our need to put our hope, focus, and trust in Him every day. God's Word is greater than any flood we may face. He is mightier than any trial that comes our way. David prayed in faith, "May the flood of water not overflow me nor the deep swallow me up, nor the pit shut its mouth on me. Answer me, O LORD, for Your lovingkindness is good; according to the greatness of Your compassion, turn to me" (Ps. 69:15–16 NASB).

The bottom line is to turn to our Almighty God both in times of triumph and tumult. Praise Him because, "He heals the brokenhearted and binds up their wounds" (Ps. 147:3 NASB). Don't forget that we do live in a world where there is sin and darkness. God has promised, "When you pass through the waters, I will be with you; and through the rivers, they shall not overwhelm you" (Isa. 43:2 ESV). Saturate yourself with God's Word during these days. He is faithful and mighty to walk with us!

1. What are you doing to be able to hear God better each day?
2. Think of someone else who is going through a rough time, and try to encourage them with a call, text, or visit.

~

Father, I thank You for always being the calm from my storms. Thank You for the encouragement of Your Word and may You use me to encourage others as well! Amen.

Tom Tillman
Director of Music and Worship
Baptist General Convention of Texas, Dallas, TX

Go on a Little Farther

Then Jesus came with them to a place called Gethsemane, and said
to the disciples, "Sit here while I go and pray over there."
Matthew 26:36 (NKJV, also read through verse 39)

Let us recall when Jesus prayed in the garden of Gethsemane. Jesus came with all of His disciples and said, "Sit here while I go and pray over there." He took Peter, James, and John. As He became burdened and overwhelmed, even to the point of death, He asked them to take watch and pray. He went on a "little farther and fell on His face" (Matt. 26:39).

Imagine someone in a prominent position of authority, someone you look up to. Here in Alabama, for many that might be Nick Saban. Let's say he asks you to go with him to the National Championship game, but later asks you to stay in the tunnel and pray for the team and for safety for the team. There you are at the most important college football game of the year with your team playing. For whatever reason, Coach Saban has brought you but needs you to pray. You don't even get to watch even one minute of the game! It's halftime and here comes the team through the tunnel. They are down 13 points, and there you are taking a nap.

Were these disciples so caught up in their own world that they could not pray for Jesus, who they followed daily, witnessing Him perform miracle after miracle? They fell asleep when Jesus asked them to pray—not once, not twice, but three times.

Jesus showed us by example that before anything significant happens in our lives, we are to fall to our knees and pray, "not as I will, but as You will" (v. 39). Jesus went on a "little farther." Whatever you are going through or struggling with, go on a "little farther" and fall to your knees and pray as Jesus did. Don't be so caught up in your circumstances that you fall asleep when God has called you to pray.

1. Are you so caught up in your own world that you don't make time to pray?
2. What can you change in your life right now that will help you fall to your knees in prayer?

~

Father, help me not be so caught up in me that I fall asleep rather than
fall to my knees asking You to be the center of everything I do. Help me
do whatever it takes to go a little farther to make time for You.

Matt Fallin
Associate Pastor of Worship
Santuck Baptist Church, Wetumpka, AL

The Opposite Life

"Blessed are you when people hate you, when they exclude you and insult you and reject your name as evil, because of the Son of Man. Rejoice in that day and leap for joy, because great is your reward in heaven. For that is how their ancestors treated the prophets."
Luke 6:22–23 (NIV)

The Beatitudes would look very different if you and I wrote them. In our culture, you are blessed if you are rich, full, happy, loved, and accepted, but that is not what Jesus said. In fact, what Jesus said is the exact opposite. You are blessed if you are poor, hungry, sorrowful, hated, and rejected!

The Kingdom life is the opposite life. Humble yourself. Make yourself nothing and selflessly serve others. Do you want to really live the life God has for you? Take up your cross, deny yourself and follow Him. That's what Jesus did for you and me (Phil. 2:5–8).

To reach this world for Christ, we must truly become the "counterculture." We must embrace the life of the kingdom of God. We must keep our eyes fixed on Jesus, the author and perfecter of our faith (Heb. 12:1–3 NASB). He is our example of service and humility.

1. What are some practical ways we can be "countercultural" as Christians and churches today?
2. What are some steps we can take today to defer our preferences and put the needs of others first?

~

Father, I humble myself and surrender my rights to You. I ask for courage to live the opposite life of Your kingdom. Help me to serve, to love, to give, and to care. Help me keep my eyes focused on You alone. Amen.

Chason Farris
Worship Pastor
First Baptist Church, Hendersonville, NC

Singing Over You

"The LORD your God in your midst, the Mighty One, will save; He will rejoice over you with gladness, He will quiet you with His love, He will rejoice over you with singing."
Zephaniah 3:17 (NKJV)

It is a most awesome and humbling thought to comprehend that God would rejoice and sing over His people. Earlier, in Zephaniah 3:14 (RSV), we find the people of Jerusalem singing praises to God, "Sing aloud, O daughter of Zion," which, in turn, ignites the Lord's delight in His people to joyfully sing over them. It is a cause-and-effect response indicative of how God inhabits the praises of His children. He literally delights in the fact that we take delight in Him.

We take delight in the Lord through the very awareness of His presence in our midst. The Lord God is omniscient, omnipotent, and omnipresent. Psalm 139 beautifully expresses how God knows everything about us. He perceives our thoughts and is familiar with all our ways. There is no place in heaven or hell where we can flee from His presence. The Lord is the Lover of our souls and holds us close to His bosom in the good times and the bad.

Though we may walk through the valley of the shadow of death, we fear not because the Lord is on our side. He holds us in the very palm of His hand and quiets us with His love. Be encouraged today as you rejoice in Him. He will rejoice over you with loud singing.

1. What does it mean to you that God rejoices over you with singing?
2. How does this reality affect your worship?

~

Help me, dear God, to take delight in You today. I need not be anxious or worry because You are here. Thank you for meeting my every need. Thank you for saving my soul. I rejoice in You as You rejoice over me with joyful singing. In Jesus' name, Amen.

Joe Fitzpatrick
Worship and Music Pastor
First Baptist Church, Nashville, TN

Consider the Ox

*Where there are no oxen, the manger is clean, but abundant
crops come by the strength of the ox.*
Proverbs 14:4 (esv)

Ministry in general, and music ministry specifically, can be "messy." As I read this
Scripture, the phrase, "manger is clean," captured my attention, and I began thinking
about Christmas. After serving churches for thirty years in music ministry, I can attest to
the value of producing large-scale presentations for Christmas (Easter), which are musically
supported by choirs and orchestras.

I recently heard from a worship specialist that churches are dropping their choir and
orchestra ministries altogether for various utilitarian reasons:

- They are too expensive to run; a smaller team is more cost-effective and
  manageable.
- They are too much work, administratively, to maintain.
- They are too time-consuming on the church calendar, tiring out our people/
  young families (especially major productions).

I must admit that some of these reasons have a bit of truth in them IF your desire is a
"clean manger." However, I would say the benefits of being a part of something greater than
yourself like this far outweighs the negatives. Here are a few benefits:

- The community knows that you care for them.
- Personal discipleship is gained through participation.
- Multigenerational cooperation is displayed.
- Creative gifts/talents are utilized and appreciated.
- Spiritual decisions are made, and inspirational seeds are planted.

A healthy choir/orchestra/music ministry (ox) will produce an abundance of crops
that build the church and honor Christ. Let's roll up our sleeves and "get messy."

1. From your experience, name some other benefits of participating in choirs/
   orchestras/music ministries/church presentations.
2. How are you supporting your church's music and worship ministry?

~

*Lord, thank You for allowing me to use my gifts and talents to serve Your
kingdom and Your church. You are worthy of my devotion, my best, my all.*

Todd Stearns
Pastor of Worship and Music
First Baptist Church, Naples, FL

Proclamation in the Midst of Chaos

*He said to them, "But who do you say that I am?" Simon Peter
replied, "You are the Christ, the Son of the living God."*
Matthew 16:15–16 (ESV)

Traveling to the Holy Land will change you. To walk where Jesus walked is a humbling experience. In both of my Holy Land pilgrimages, Caesarea of Philippi was one of my favorite places to visit. It sits at the top of the state in the Golan Heights region near the base of Mount Hermon. The Jordan River finds its beginnings in this region, where its waters are crystal clear and cold! It's a breathtaking place!

Caesarea of Philippi was not a beautiful place during Jesus' time. In fact, it was a true "red light district," where many disgraceful acts took place. It was the site of worship for the pagan god, Pan. It was a sick and twisted place. The pagans believed that the main cave at Caesarea of Philippi was a portal to the underworld where fertility gods lived.

In Matthew 16, we find Jesus approaching Caesarea of Philippi with His disciples. The scene must have been chaotic. Pagan worshipers, sacrifices, deplorable sexual acts would have all been witnessed by the disciples. It's in this setting that Jesus asks His disciples, "Who do you say I am?" Simon replies with an emphatic statement of Christ's sovereignty!

Sure, it's easy to make such a statement when we're surrounded by like-minded believers, but how difficult is it to proclaim who Christ is when we are surrounded by the fallen world?

1. With chaos abounding, are YOU willing to proclaim Christ as the "Son of the Living God" when those around you say otherwise?
2. How can you be a light in a chaotic world?

～

*Lord Jesus, help me to proclaim You as the Son of the living
God no matter what situation I find myself in.*

Brett Fuller
Worship Pastor
First Baptist Church, Pelham, AL

The Blessings of God

And God is able to bless you abundantly, so that in all things at all times,
having all that you need, you will abound in every good work.
2 Corinthians 9:8 (NIV)

Hardship is difficult, but God's blessings can at times be even greater tests. Deion Sanders, football and baseball player, has said that if you want to see the true heart of a man, give him a million dollars. The test lies in the way we treat God's blessings and often reveals a heart centered in the flesh. Rather than giving God the glory, we often act as though we are the disseminator of all things bright and beautiful. What have you done with God's blessings, and what will you do with them as He continues to pour them on you?

Perhaps one of the hardest blessings is properly managing people who are better at some skill than you are. Do we stand as a barrier or as a facilitator between our people and their service in worship to God? Deuteronomy 31:3 gives warning to us of what can happen when God brings us into that place of blessing and we turn *from* Him rather than *to* Him. Human praise and fame are fleeting and will work to draw you away from what matters, but God's glory and His perfect will is everlasting. Endeavor to see God's glory in those in your care and draw it out of them as they minister to the Lord and to the wider church family. Often, those with skill become consumed with themselves and overwhelmed in their pride. Shepherd your flock and help them to develop the character required to sustain their wonderful talents.

1. Have you identified God's blessing(s) in your life? Spend time writing down ten ways God has blessed you. Write down ten people God has put in your life as a blessing.
2. Are you training up leaders and equipping them for works of service so that the body of Christ may be built up" (Eph. 4:12–13 NIV).

～

O God, help us to see the giftedness of those You have given us. Help us to see them
as blessings. Help us to serve them, to mentor them, to help them develop an ear
for Your Word and a sensitivity to hear the voice of Your Spirit. Amen.

Dr. David Hahn
Chair, Department of Commercial Music
Liberty University, Lynchburg, VA

Is He Worth It?

"Worthy are You, our Lord and our God, to receive glory and honor and power; for
You created all things, and because of Your will they existed, and were created."
Revelation 4:11 (NASB)

I had a pastor ask this question to me, "Is He, God, worth it?"
All homeowners go through the process of an appraisal. The definition of appraisal is, "an act of assessing something or someone" or "an expert estimate of the value of something." When a home is appraised, there are three steps to this process. The first approach is comparing other properties around your home to see at what amount you could price your home.

Think about it. What else compares to our God?

The second approach is inspecting the property to note the type and quality of materials used on the home. This allows the appraisers to assess how much it will cost to replace the property.

This concept gets me every time. Jesus' sacrifice on the cross is irreplaceable!

Last, the appraiser will assess what current or potential income this property can produce. When we walk daily with God, He produces the best "us" we could ever be. Today, as you prepare to lead others in worship, I want to ask these same questions about our God:

1. Are we showing our people who our God is in the songs we sing and ministries we lead?
2. How does God appraise in your life today? Is He the most valuable thing in your life?

~

God, always remind me that there is no one like You. There is nothing that can replace
You or what You've done for me. God, there is no one who cares for me like You do.
Father, keep my life and my worship to You Who is above all things. Amen.

Brad Jett
Worship Pastor
First West, West Monroe, LA

Road Rules

Paul's odyssey began in Acts 21, when he was falsely accused of defiling the temple in Jerusalem. This incited a series of horrific and terrifying events for Paul and his friend, Luke, the writer of Acts.
Acts 21–22 (ESV, paraphrased)

Here are a few "road rules" we can pick up from Paul's journey that will help us endure the struggles of our own life's journey:

- **Sometimes following the will of God will lead you into a storm.** God never promised health, wealth, and prosperity, but He did say He would never leave nor forsake us (Heb. 13:5).
- **God's power is made perfect in our weakness.** When the storms of life rage, the strongest thing we can do is to admit we are weak. Only when we acknowledge that God is in control do we find strength in Christ. As Paul himself said, when we are weak, then we are strong (2 Cor. 12:10).
- **Struggles in life present opportunities to testify to the faithfulness of God.** When life throws you a curveball, don't retreat inward, but look out to see who God is bringing into your path, and be prepared to witness (1 Pet. 3:15).
- **Spiritual formation and character development happen through trials.** The reality is that overcoming obstacles develops our faith in God, our resolve, and our character. That's why the Bible says to consider it joy when we face various trials. God uses storms to perfect us (James 1:2–4).
- **You don't have to walk this road alone.** God established the church precisely so that we wouldn't have to walk through the challenges of life alone (Rom. 12:15).
- **God has a purpose for your journey.** God will use every pain, every doubt, every failure, and every struggle to form you, shape you, teach you, and give you opportunities to speak into the lives of others around you.

1. What struggle are you facing today?
2. Are you running from or learning through that struggle?

~

Help me, Lord, to learn through the struggles that I am facing rather than running from them. Teach me through this and make my faith stronger for Your honor and glory! In Jesus' name, Amen.

Ross Johnson
Worship and Music Pastor
First Baptist Church, Madison, MS

Overcoming Your Offenses

If possible, as far as it depends on you, live at peace with everyone. Do not be
overcome and conquered by evil, but overcome [master] evil with good.
Romans 12:18, 21 (AMP)

We all have times when we have been desperately hurt by someone and find it difficult to move on. The enemy (Satan) wants us to stay offended, and wants to cripple us with anger, bitterness, and unforgiveness. We convince ourselves that forgiving is just too hard, and we end up hurting ourselves by disobeying God. How do we get past offenses?

Turn it over to God. It requires action on our part and a decision to "put on" our new nature in Christ. This can be difficult if you were raised in an environment of fault-finding, holding grudges, and finding pleasure in conflict. We can ask the Holy Spirit to renew our minds (Rom. 12:2).

Meditate on God's goodness and what He did for you on the cross. According to Isaiah 53, He bore ALL your sins. Unforgiving people tend to be self-righteous, but the truth is no one is perfect. If you expect people to be perfect, you will be sorely disappointed. Plan on forgiving others often, because those closest to you will disappoint you. "For if you forgive others their trespasses, your heavenly Father will also forgive you, but if you do not forgive others their trespasses, neither will your Father forgive others your trespasses" (Matt 6:14–15 ESV).

Believe the best about others! Instead of faultfinding, why not look for the good in others? God made us all unique. "Love bears up under anything and everything that comes, is ever ready to believe the best of every person . . ." (1 Cor. 13:7 AMP). This doesn't mean that we have to give up healthy boundaries.

Pray for those who have offended you. It is hard for us to remain angry and critical when we pray for those who have hurt us.

Make a choice and forgive. The benefits of forgiveness are endless. It is a command (not a suggestion) of God and it pleases Him when we obey. Jesus indicates in Mark 11 that our prayers are hindered when we do not forgive others. Refusing to forgive is like drinking poison and hoping it kills the other person. Make a choice to forgive.

1. Whom do you need to forgive today?
2. What will be your first step toward forgiving this person?

~

Lord, create a willingness to move from my unforgiving spirit to be an
overcomer through the power of forgiveness and love. As You forgave
me, I choose to forgive others. In Jesus' name, Amen.

Ray Jones
President and Founder
Radiance Ministries, San Antonio, TX

The Friend of the Bridegroom

"The bride belongs to the bridegroom. The friend who attends the bridegroom waits and listens for him, and is full of joy when he hears the bridegroom's voice. That joy is mine, and it is now complete. He must become greater; I must become less."

John 3:29–30 (NIV)

As the ministry of Jesus began to flourish, some of the disciples of John the Baptist began following Him. Those who continued following John came to him and asked him what he thought about those who were now following Jesus. The verses above are part of his response.

John compared his relationship with Jesus to the relationship between the friend of the bridegroom and the bridegroom. The friend of the bridegroom was appointed to arrange the events before the wedding, manage the wedding, and preside over the wedding feast. When he finished his job, he had to get out of the way to allow the bridegroom and his bride to do what everybody was there to see—a wedding.

In the same way, you must do everything you can in your life to prepare others to see Jesus and then get out of the way. We need to be diligent to prepare ourselves to lead worship (musically, mentally, and spiritually) EVERY week so that we are ready to set the stage for Jesus to do whatever He chooses to do. If we do our job the way we should, it won't be any problem for us to "get out of the way" because all anyone will be able to see is Jesus.

1. What are you doing to prepare yourself every week to be a worship leader?
2. Who do you know who has modeled this for you? Thank him or her.

～

Father, as Your worship leader, my greatest desire is that others will see You for who You are. Help me prepare myself in every way to be that kind of worship leader. Sing, play, and speak through me to show others Your greatness and goodness. Amen.

Ryan Krivsky
Worship Pastor
Greenwell Springs Baptist Church, Greenwell Springs, LA

Do They Match?

Set a guard over my mouth, LORD; keep watch over the door of my lips.
Psalm 141:3 (NIV)

The hearts of the wise make their mouths prudent, and their lips promote instruction.
Proverbs 16:23 (NIV)

Make sure your conversation matches your song. There is nothing worse than a Christian musician who sings the sweet songs of salvation then talks like a pagan. Our songs and conversations need to match. "You brood of vipers, how can you who are evil say anything good? For the mouth speaks what the heart is full of" (Matt. 12:34 NIV).

"A wise man's heart guides his mouth, and his lips promote instruction" (paraphrase). The heart and tongue are twins! The prayer, "create in me a clean heart" (Ps. 51:10) is critical. Why? "Out of the overflow of the heart the mouth speaks" (Luke 6:45).

Dear singer, guard your heart and your mind. Make sure your song matches your talk. Have you ever sung a song of blessing and shortly thereafter, spoken a curse? This should not be. We should allow the Holy Spirit to make not only our singing beautiful, but also our conversations. May this be our prayer: "Let the words of my mouth and the meditation of my heart be acceptable in Your sight, O LORD, my rock and my redeemer" (Ps. 19:14 NASB).

1. Who is the unseen listener of every conversation and song?
2. Would an encouraging word promote better singing in the choir?
3. Do we need to check our heart if it is difficult to sing a particular message in song?

~

O, God, may this psalm be my prayer before I sing or play a single note. "Search me, God, and know my heart; test me and know my anxious thoughts. See if there is any offensive way in me, and lead me in the way everlasting" (Ps. 139:23–24 NIV). In Jesus' name, Amen.

Rick Stone
Worship Pastor
Whitesburg Baptist Church, Huntsville, AL

Growing in Forgiveness

"Then his master summoned him and said to him, 'You wicked servant! I forgave you all that debt because you pleaded with me. And should not you have had mercy on your fellow servant, as I had mercy on you?' And in anger his master delivered him to the jailers, until he should pay all his debt. So also my heavenly Father will do to every one of you, if you do not forgive your brother from your heart."
Matthew 18:32–35 (esv)

It doesn't take long for us to experience pain when we have been sinned against. Sometimes that pain comes from the hands of those who should love us the most. We will often secretly nurse our pain by saying things like, "How could they do this to me?" or "I don't deserve to be treated this way," or "I'll never forgive them for this."

While the reality of being sinned against will never fade this side of eternity, we can become better equipped in granting forgiveness and reconciling with others. The key comes by frequently remembering how much we have been forgiven by our heavenly Father. No sin committed *against* us is greater than the sins committed *by* us against our Almighty God. Because God is infinitely good, all sins against Him are infinitely bad, and yet, He graciously offers to forgive us and calls us to pass this forgiveness along to others.

1. The pain involved in granting us forgiveness was absorbed at the cross. As you reflect on the cross, respond by becoming willing to absorb the pain required to forgive others.
2. Often professing Christians can become unforgiving of each other. How does this affect our witness as ambassadors of God's kingdom?

～

Father, You have forgiven me in infinite ways. Help me to pass along this forgiveness to others and help me find the sweet joy of reconciling more appealing than the bitter fruit of resentment.

Clay Layfield
Associate Pastor, Music and Senior Adults
First Baptist Church, Eastman, GA

Be Bold

*Then, along with many other exhortations, he proclaimed good news to the
people. But . . . Herod the tetrarch . . . locked John up in prison.*
Luke 3:18–20 (CSB)

John the Baptist had been preaching to the people that they must repent of their sin
and be baptized. He had encouraged them to live with each other fairly and not take
advantage of one another. He also told them to share their belongings if they had extra. His
message was very helpful and beneficial to society, but those such as Herod did not like to
be called out for their sin. Herod was so angered that he imprisoned John.

John was doing good deeds and was punished for it. The devil will try any tactics
necessary to distract and discourage those who are proclaiming Jesus to a lost world. Have
you ever felt like you were the only one who was doing right, and yet, you were the one who
was suffering? Maybe it was that you knew God was doing something in your life and you
were trusting God, but those around you were completely discouraging and critical of your
actions? The loneliness can be overwhelming.

We want to be liked and we seek the approval of others. While there is nothing
wrong with being liked and having others' approval, the caution here is when we seek man's
approval over God's.

Many times in Scripture God makes the point that, as believers, we will be at odds
with a lost world. The lost cannot discern spiritual things. It is craziness and foolishness to
them. So, what do we do? Take John's example. Be bold for the sake of the gospel and don't
worry about man's approval.

1. Have you ever been ridiculed for your faith?
2. Do those around you even know you are a believer?

~

God, please give me the boldness like John to proclaim the gospel to a lost world.

Rob Maddox
Worship and Missions Pastor
Spotswood Baptist Church, Fredericksburg, VA

Pot-Stirring Is Not a Spiritual Gift!

If it is possible, as far as it depends on you, live at peace with everyone.
Romans 12:18 (NIV)

I had the same pastor the entire time I was growing up. I was very close to his family and spent a great deal of time in their home. His wife was one of the godliest women I have ever known. She used to dance around the house, singing songs of worship, and sharing with us little truths that her mother taught her. One such phrase was: "Always tell the truth, but don't always be telling it!"

Certainly, everything we say should be true, but that in no way means we are to tell every truth we know at every moment. Scripture teaches, in Philippians 4:8, that we should think on things that are noble, right, pure, lovely, admirable, excellent, and praiseworthy. It is not a great stretch to believe we should speak of those things as well. It is important that we believers build up the body of Christ through our words and deeds. As we strive to live in unity and at peace with everyone, we should guard against the tearing down of one another.

1. How did you feel when someone shared a painful truth about you to others?
2. What are some practical ways you can focus your mind on building up others for the sake of the kingdom?

It is said that St. Francis of Assisi prayed this prayer; you may wish to pray it, also:

> *Lord, make me an instrument of your peace, Where there is hatred, let me sow love;*
> *Where there is injury, pardon; Where there is doubt, faith;*
> *Where there is despair, hope; Where there is darkness, light;*
> *Where there is sadness, joy;*
> *O Divine Master, grant that I may not so much seek to be consoled as to console;*
> *To be understood as to understand; To be loved as to love.*

～

> *For it is in giving that we receive; it is in pardoning that we are pardoned;*
> *And it is in dying that we are born to eternal life. Amen. (Public Domain)*

Kenneth Martin
Minister of Music and Worship
First Baptist Church, Milton, FL

Praying for Fellow Workers

Submit to one another out of reverence for Christ.
Ephesians 5:21 (NIV)

We all have to work with other people, whether on our jobs, at home, or in the church. Some are our coworkers. Some are our supervisors. In both cases, our work is interconnected with theirs. If the other person doesn't do a good job, our work is damaged. This is particularly true in music, as you have singers, instrumentalists, arrangers, and directors. The quality and effectiveness of our work is dependent upon others. That can be very stressful.

In dealing with such situations in my own life, the Lord has brought me back to what the Bible says about submitting to one another and praying for one another. I'm discovering that is great, practical advice. Instead of fretting about whether another person will do a good job or whether a supervisor will make the right decision, I'm learning to pray for them. I pray that God will guide them and work through them to accomplish His will. Then, having prayed for them and trusted the Lord to work through them, I can more easily rely on them and be submissive to them, and when I still feel I must disagree, I can do so in a non-defensive, non-territorial manner, remembering it is God's work, not mine, and He will accomplish it.

Sometimes, we feel that if everyone would just leave us alone, if we weren't so dependent on others, everything would be terrific. The Bible declares that simply isn't so. Each of us has a particular role to play. By ourselves, we are so limited. We were designed to work most efficiently and productively in our relationships. We are each like one part of the body that must work with other parts if the whole body is to function successfully. God created us to be dependent not only on Himself but on each other.

Prayer is the best way to make such relationships work. Through prayer, we lift up those on whom we are dependent. Through prayer, we maintain the right attitude toward them. Prayer for fellow workers fosters the unity and interdependence essential for all of us to be and do our best together. Through prayer, we keep our faith focused on God's will and on His ability to accomplish that will through us, not just through me.

1. Who in leadership needs my prayers?
2. How can I lead others to have a stronger prayer life?

～

Heavenly Father, I will be willing when asked. When I am not asked,
I will accept it joyfully as Your decision. You are always good, and I am
simply Your servant. Thank You for Your wisdom and love.

Chris Mason
Worship Pastor
First Baptist Church, Arnold, MO

Too Busy or Not Too Busy?

And God is able to make all grace abound to you, so that having all sufficiency
in all things at all times, you may abound in every good work.
2 Corinthians 9:8 (ESV)

Wait a minute! Is this true? Is grace greater than my finitude, my understanding, and my busyness? We know that in all labor there is profit. We know that the law of flesh confirms that if we are disciplined and talented, we will improve with instruction and practice. We may even find our sweet spot in life.

But what if we are inadequate? What if we fail? What if we are under resourced? God's grace is always sufficient. Our concept of good and bad, our standards, our sense of time—everything is subject to the grace of God. God's generosity surpasses our worst *and* our best. He can receive glory in ways we can't anticipate. Receive, exercise, and enjoy His grace.

1. Do I remember an event or experience that revealed God's grace to me in a significant, abundant manner?
2. Is there an area in my life where I doubt that the grace of God is fully sufficient?

~

Dear God, You give Your grace so that I can do anything You call me to do. I
ask that You enjoy yourself in my life and pour out Your grace in and through
me to encourage Your people and to be a witness to those who don't believe yet.
Thank You for doing this in the name of Jesus our Savior and Lord. Amen.

Ronald A. Matthews, DMA
President
Eastern University, St. David's, PA

Holy, Holy, Holy!

In the year that King Uzziah died I saw the Lord sitting upon a throne, high and lifted up; and the train of his robe filled the temple. Above him stood the seraphim. Each had six wings: with two he covered his face, and with two he covered his feet, and with two he flew. And one called to another and said: "Holy, holy, holy is the LORD of hosts; the whole earth is full of his glory!"
Isaiah 6:1–3 (ESV)

Throughout the Scriptures we see many attributes of God. Graceful, loving, just, and merciful are just a few, but there is one attribute that is emphasized over any other— God's holiness. In Hebrew literature, repetition is used to emphasize and draw attention to something important. Just as in our modern day we would underline or make something bold, ancient writers would repeat something to draw the reader's focus.

In Isaiah 6, the attribute "holy" is repeated not once, but twice. This is known as the *Trisagion*, or the "Thrice Holy." Of the many attributes of the Lord God stated in Scripture, this is the only one that is repeated twice (that is, stated three times). We know that the Lord is equal and perfect in all of His attributes; there is not one that transcends the other. We should take note here of what Isaiah writes about his vision and be reminded that the Lord our God is holy, holy, holy.

1. How many attributes of the Lord can you think of? Write a few down and pray to the Lord using those specific attributes.
2. In 1 Peter 1:16 the Lord tells us to "be holy, for I am holy." Are you seeking after holiness in every area of your life? Take time to examine that today.

~

Lord, I thank You for Your many attributes, and today I thank You specifically for Your holiness. Help me to strive for holiness in my life, and to be holy as You are holy. Through Your Holy Spirit, guide my life in Your ways of righteousness, that I would be more like Jesus. Amen.

Joshua McClain
Worship and Music Pastor
Central Baptist Church, Warner Robins, GA

Authenticity in Worship

And so, dear brothers and sisters, I plead with you to give your bodies to God because of all he has done for you. Let them be a living and holy sacrifice— the kind he will find acceptable. This is truly the way to worship him.
Romans 12:1 (NLT)

Following the yearly pilgrimage to Jerusalem for the Festival of the Passover, Mary, Joseph, and the family began the trip back home. Thinking Jesus was with them, they traveled for a day before noticing He was not. At this point I have a mental picture of Kate McCallister, Kevin's mom, realizing they left him "home alone." After three days of searching, they found Jesus in the temple courts with the teachers listening and asking questions. He was twelve years old!

If you have ever misplaced a child (I may or may not have), even for a few seconds, you know the worry, fear, and fret his parents were experiencing. Jesus' response is so innocent—*What . . . why are you worrying? You didn't know where I would be!? Why are you searching for Me?* "Didn't you know I would be in my Father's house?" (Luke 2:41–52 paraphrase).

As disciples of Jesus, I pray that would be said of us, and that we could confidently say that about ourselves. Regardless of what characteristic or quality people look at in our lives, I pray they see passion for Christ above all else.

My greatest desire is that our worship ministry will encourage and help people in their own pursuit of Jesus. I want us to disciple people with the authenticity of our worship. True worship is contagious, and I pray we infect them for Jesus. We have a saying in our worship ministry, "Live your song . . . sing your life!"

1. What does your devotional life look like?
2. How can we be more authentic?

~

Father, may people see the authenticity of my relationship in our worship. May we worship You in truth and spirit. Amen.

Terry Hurt
Executive and Worship Pastor
Great Hills Baptist Church, Austin, TX

Our High Calling

Praise the LORD, all you nations; extol him, all you peoples. For great is his love toward us, and the faithfulness of the LORD endures forever. Praise the LORD.
Psalm 117 (NIV)

This great missionary psalm and middle chapter in our Bible is a constant reminder to us as worship leaders. All nations and all peoples WILL praise the Lord! This daily reminder of our Lord's *hesed* love is two-fold:

1. God's loyal and constant love is extended outwardly toward us in unfathomable ways.
2. His faithful covenant love, *hesed*, will endure forever!

As John Piper has preached and written several times, "Worship is the goal and the fuel of missions. . . . Missions exists because worship doesn't." The great joy of knowing Jesus personally is not a private, cultural, national, or ethnic privilege. It is for all. Because we have tasted the joy of worshiping Christ, we want all families of the earth included.

Psalm 22:27 reminds us, "All the ends of the earth will remember and turn to the LORD. All the families of the nations will bow down before you" (CSB).

Praying for and seeking the worship of all nations and peoples is energized and fueled by the passion of our own personal worship. This is our high calling!

1. Am I passionate about involving and developing more leaders in my ministry that have a different cultural and ethnic background than myself or my current team?
2. How might our worship ministry more visibly support our missions' ministry?

~

Father, remind me that You desire for ALL nations to worship You. Give me a deeper love for our world and those that I serve daily, knowing that one day every knee WILL bow and every tongue WILL confess that You are Lord—to the glory of God! Amen.

Dr. James L. Melton
Chair, Department of Music
Vanguard University, Costa Mesa, CA

Becoming an Ironman

Forgetting what lies behind and straining forward to what lies ahead, I press on toward the goal for the prize of the upward call of God in Christ Jesus.
Philippians 3:13b–14 (ESV)

Have you taken a selfie and been surprised to see you've slowly gained a few pounds? That's exactly what happened to me. I had gained some weight and needed to get back in shape, so I set a big goal: to complete an Ironman Triathlon. An Ironman consists of swimming 2.4 miles, biking 112 miles, and running 26.2 miles, all in under 17 hours.

I didn't even own a bike at the time and only swam when we went on vacation. It was a lofty goal, but I was determined. Many obstacles came my way, but I strained forward to what I knew was ahead. I wanted to cross that finish line and hear the announcer say, "Jason Millsaps, you are an Ironman." After 13 months of training, I was 50 pounds lighter and was ready to compete in my first Ironman Triathlon. It wasn't easy, but I finished Ironman Arizona in 13 hours and 54 minutes!

In the race of life, our ultimate prize is the upward call of God in Christ Jesus. There will be things in life that will try to distract us from Jesus, but we must keep our eyes fixed on Christ. As a Christian, I can't wait to hear those words from our Lord when I enter heaven and cross the finish line and hear, "Well done, good and faithful servant."

1. What distractions in your life are keeping your eyes away from the ultimate prize?
2. What changes do you need to make in your life to reach the goal we are called to reach?

~

Lord, help me to continue pressing forward to what lies ahead. Forgive me when distractions get in the way of Your calling. I submit my life to You. In Jesus' name, Amen.

Jason Millsaps
Pastor of Music and Worship
Bell Shoals Baptist Church, Brandon, FL

Trials and Temptations as Good?

Consider it pure joy, my brothers and sisters, whenever you face trials of many kinds,
because you know that the testing of your faith produces perseverance. Let perseverance
finish its work so that you may be mature and complete, not lacking anything.
James 1:2–4 (NIV)

People who fulfill their God-given dreams aren't always the sharpest, not always the most talented, and not always the better skilled. They don't always have the best resources at their disposal. They're just people who refuse to let go of those dreams. They are people who persevered. God's will through the patriarchs, or any other saint, was not realized overnight. It took years of testing, molding, and refining.

But why do we have to be tested to realize God's will? Because God is working on us! Trials are part of every believer's life. The difficulties we face do have spiritual value. James is honest with us and encouraging when he says, "you know that the testing of your faith produces perseverance." We gain fortitude and toughness as we are tested and repeatedly prevail. The more we persevere, the more mature we become, and that maturity brings the completeness that God had in mind even before He began building His will into your life!

Sometimes we make it hard for God to speak clearly to us regarding His will. We are people whose minds are cluttered with other things. He needs our undivided attention. Our tests and trials are not meant to discourage us—they are meant to draw us closer to God.

1. Consider how Psalm 34:17–18 fits together with James 1:2–4.
2. Do you agree with the following statement? Why or why not? "It's doubtful God can use any man greatly until He's hurt him deeply." (A. W. Tozer)

Oh Lord, help me rejoice when testing is brought to my life, knowing it is for my good—to
be made spiritually tough—and for Your glory—as my life more completely reflects You.

David Thomas
Worship Pastor
Highland Baptist Church, Grove City, OH

Taking Hold!

*Not that I have already obtained all this, or have already been made perfect, but
I press on to take hold of that for which Christ Jesus took hold of me. Brothers, I
do not consider myself yet to have taken hold of it. But one thing I do: Forgetting
what is behind and straining toward what is ahead, I press on toward the goal
to win the prize for which God has called me heavenward in Christ Jesus.*

Philippians 3:12–14 (NIV)

Paul's letter to the church at Philippi is one of my favorite books in the Bible, and chapter 3 my favorite chapter. It's all about forging ahead and pressing on. It reminds us that we can't do anything about what's happened in the past, but we can do everything about what happens going forward.

It encourages us to "take hold of that for which Christ Jesus took hold of us." For our purposes as church musicians, let's acknowledge that we're all called to do what we do, but the thing that sets us apart is that we *answered the call*. At some point, we made the decision to "take hold" of the purpose for which God took hold of us.

This idea speaks of two actions: one by God and one by us. When God gifted you with a talent, either singing or playing, He did so for His glory. He was, in fact, *taking hold of you* by giving you that talent. That's *His* action.

Our action, though, is to respond to His action; and we do that by using the talent He's given us to His glory. To use Paul's words . . . our action is to *take hold*. It is that taking hold that drives us to be involved in choir, orchestra, praise team, or some other worship leading group.

As we press on toward the goal of taking hold, Paul tells us that we will win the prize for which God has called us. Now that's good news!

1. In what ways do you sense God's call on your life?
2. How can we encourage others who are called to take hold?

~

*Thank You, God, for placing a song in my heart, and for taking hold of me to
serve You through musical worship. I pray that my response will always be to "take
hold," faithfully serving You through music, and leading others to do the same.*

Bob Morrison
Minister of Music
First Baptist Church, Pensacola, FL

Delight in the Lord

His delight is in the law of the LORD, and in His law he meditates day and night.
He will be like a tree firmly planted by streams of water, which yields its fruit in
its season and its leaf does not wither; and in whatever he does, he prospers.
Psalm 1:2–3 (NASB)

What a wonderful picture it is to envision a tree planted by streams of water. I've seen many pictures and drawings of this over the years. Water, in many ways, determines how tall and healthy a tree will grow. It nourishes and cleanses as it travels from the roots, through the trunk and limbs, all the way to the leaves.

This psalm was the very first Scripture I memorized as a young believer. It encourages us to not only read God's Word, but to meditate on it day and night. When we do, His Word moves up every root in our lives and permeates our whole being. It continues through the branches of our lives, finally leading to the fruit that our lives yield (leaves that do not wither). As you spend time in God's Word today, memorize a verse or two and meditate on those verses throughout the day. As you continue in this practice, you will be like that tree planted by streams of water, living water.

1. How does God use His Word in our lives?
2. What difference does it make to go beyond just reading God's Word to actually meditating on it?

~

Father, I desire to be like that tree firmly planted by streams of water, yielding Your fruit in my life! Let Your Word continuously nourish and cleanse my life as I meditate on it daily.

Gary Rhodes
Worship Pastor
First Baptist Church Woodway, Waco, TX

I Want to Know You More!

For I desire steadfast love and not sacrifice, the knowledge of God rather than burnt offerings.
Hosea 6:6 (ESV)

The most important aspect of the life of a follower of Christ is to know and love God. In the garden, God created man to spend time with Him. In fact, we know that God walked with Adam and Eve. He spent time with them and enjoyed their fellowship. It is no surprise that God still desires that today. People place so much emphasis on their sacrifice and offerings and not enough of the simple premise of spending time with the Savior. That is still His ultimate desire. In our worship musically, if we bring an offering or sacrifice of praise to God without a heart that desires to know Him more and be more like Him, we do not fulfill His ultimate purpose for our Creation in the first place.

It is important to desire to know Him more and develop a steadfast love for Him. Rituals of religion fail in the attempt to express our total dependence on God. We must seek to be His children in right relationship with Him, on His terms. Mark 7:6–8 (ESV) states, "'This people honors me with their lips, but their heart is far from me; in vain do they worship me, teaching as doctrines the commandments of men.' You leave the commandment of God and hold to the tradition of men."

This passage speaks of worship that is from the lips, not the heart. The doctrines taught are traditional, not biblical. They are passed down from man and not from God's perfect idea of worship. It is religion at its worst. In our worship, we must seek God's purpose and plan. It must come from Him, not us. We must seek Him with our hearts by knowing and loving Him.

1. Is my worship acceptable to God or is it presented to Him out of ritual?
2. Do I seek to know Him more daily?
3. Is there evidence of my love for Him?

∼

Lord, today I pray the words penned by Steve Fry: "Lord, I want to know You more, deep inside my soul I want to know You. To feel Your heart and know Your mind. Looking in Your eyes, stirs up within me, cries that say I want to know You more."[30] *In Jesus' name, Amen.*

Jerry L. Newman
Executive Pastor of Worship and Media
Southcrest Baptist Church, Lubbock, TX

How Do We Praise?

From the mouths of infants and nursing babies, you have established a stronghold on account of your adversaries in order to silence the enemy and the avenger.
Psalm 8:2 (CSB)

As the worship music starts, she smiles broadly, lifts her hands in the air, and even begins to twirl. Her blonde hair swings out with the centrifugal force. Her dress swings in the breeze. Those around her smile at the joy in her heart. This is Sunday morning for Bailey, a precious four-year-old who is brought to church by her mother and father. Her father sometimes plays drums in the praise band. Anyone in viewing distance is uplifted by the joy exhibited by Bailey.

David spoke of the power of praise by the youngest of God's creation. Infants reflect the glory of God. How can one see a newborn baby and not praise the Creator of all life? We are fearfully and wonderfully made. The closer we are to our creation, the more we look to our God.

This young praise rebukes the adversary. Our praise silences those who are against our God. It is an arrow into the heart of detractors. Jesus told us, "Therefore, whoever humbles himself like this child—this one is the greatest in the kingdom in heaven" (Matt. 18:4 HCSB).

1. Since little children praise Him perfectly (Ps. 8:2), what can I do to praise God like a little child?
2. When did I grow out of praising God in this excellent way? How can I get back to that worship?

~

Father, teach me to praise You like a little child. Remind me of my beginning faith. Help me abandon convention that keeps me from fully praising You and thus, rebuking Satan. You are my Creator and Sustainer. I will praise You with my whole heart. In Jesus' name, Amen.

Pat Van Dyke
Minister of Music and Pastoral Care
First Baptist Church, Clarksville, TN

God's Perfect Timing

On his arrival, Jesus found that Lazarus had already been in the tomb for four days. Now Bethany was less than two miles from Jerusalem, and many Jews had come to Martha and Mary to comfort them in the loss of their brother. When Martha heard that Jesus was coming, she went out to meet him, but Mary stayed at home. "Lord," Martha said to Jesus, "if you had been here, my brother would not have died. But I know that even now God will give you whatever you ask." Jesus said to her, "Your brother will rise again." Martha answered, "I know he will rise again in the resurrection at the last day." Jesus said to her, "I am the resurrection and the life. The one who believes in me will live, even though they die."

John 11:17–25 (NIV)

On every tour we lead to the Holy Land, there are various biblical sites that are a "must" for every traveler to see. One of those is the Tomb of Lazarus. Although "off the beaten path," it is always worth the effort to go see this awe-inspiring landmark of God's healing power.

Imagine the anxiety, grief, and sorrow that Mary and Martha experienced as they waited four days for Jesus to come to the tomb. But after those grueling days of doubt, fear, grief, and sadness, Jesus simply says, "Take away the stone" and in an authoritative voice, says, "Lazarus, come out." Soon after, Lazarus walks out of the tomb in triumph over death, hell, and the grave.

Although it was God's perfect timing to bring Lazarus back to life when He did, all those involved must have thought God had forgotten them. Hundreds of stories in the Bible along with numerous firsthand testimonies from each of our lives can concur with the fact that God's timing is *always* behind ours, but He is *NEVER* late.

Maybe there is something in your own life today that you've been sincerely praying about, yet God seems to be looking the other way. There's good news. . . He's not! He's got your back!

Even Mary seemed to lose her patience with Jesus in verse 32 when she cries out in desperation: "Lord, if you had been here, my brother would not have died." Is there something in your life that you have been seeking the Lord and praying about and the answer seems light-years away with seemingly no response from the Lord?

You're in good company. Think of the disciples out in the storm in the middle of the Sea of Galilee. Think of Jonah in the belly of the whale three days and three nights. Think about the children of Israel wandering for forty years. Whatever the case, there's no doubt that the Lord is in control. Nothing surprises Him. He *allows* our faith to be tested to teach and strengthen us.

Let's allow the Lord to do His work in us during the storm, so when He comes through in His perfect time, He will receive all the glory for our deliverance.

1. What have you been praying about to which God seems to be silent?
2. How can you build your faith and have the patience to wait for His perfect answer at the perfect time?

～

Lord Jesus, give me the faith and patience to wait for Your perfect answer at the perfect time so that I can accomplish Your perfect will for my life. In the faithful name of Jesus, Amen.

Dr. Phil Barfoot
President / CEO
Celebration Concert Tours International / CCT Music, Franklin, TN

To Obey Is Better Than Sacrifice

Then the angel of the LORD called to Abraham a second time from heaven, and said, "By Myself I have sworn, declares the LORD, because you have done this thing and have not withheld your son, your only son, indeed I will greatly bless you, and I will greatly multiply your seed as the stars of the heavens and as the sand which is on the seashore; and your seed shall possess the gate of their enemies. In your seed all the nations of the earth shall be blessed, because you have obeyed My voice."
Genesis 22:15–18 (NASB)

Years ago, we decided to get a dog for our family. Our boys named him Biscuit. He is a very sweet and loving dog. Biscuit, however, is a beagle and beagles tend to be very stubborn. I spent a lot of time with Biscuit teaching him to obey. Finally, after several months of working with him, he began to follow and obey my commands. Our lives are so much more pleasant when Biscuit follows the commands of his master!

In Genesis 22, Abraham is a perfect picture of obedience to the Lord. God asked him to take his only son and sacrifice him as a burnt offering on a mountain God would show him. The Bible says the next morning, he got up, loaded his donkey, and headed to the place God had told him about.

The interesting part to me is that throughout the whole story not once did Abraham question God! He was obedient at every turn and did exactly what God asked him to do. As a result of his obedience, God told him that through his offspring, all nations on the earth will be blessed.

1. What blessings from God have you missed out on because of your lack of obedience in your life?
2. How has disobedience affected your life?

~

Lord, help us to obey You in all areas of our Christian lives!

Tommy Quinn
Associate Pastor of Worship
First Baptist Church Tillman's Corner, Mobile, AL

One Powerful Word: Hope

Surely a man goes about as a shadow! Surely for nothing they are in
turmoil; man heaps up wealth and does not know who will gather!
"And now, O LORD, for what do I wait? My hope is in you."
Psalm 39:6–7 (ESV)

What a powerful word picture in Psalm 39. David comes face-to-face with the reality of how temporary life is and what is truly important. He uses the term "shadow" in verse 4 and "breath" to show how fleeting life is. Both of these examples prove a point that no one really knows their longevity. Just as life is fleeting so are life situations. Man's inclination is to get as much in life as possible . . . to acquire as much stuff, knowing that in today's society, success is seen many times by what we have or earn. That, however, is not God's value system. So, what can we learn from this?

The question is posed in verse 7, "And now, O LORD, for what do I wait?" The question really is "What, really, do I anticipate and value?" When we wait, we trust. When we try, it *really* is about our effort. Waiting eventually yields a revealing of something. When we wait at a red light, it eventually turns green and we go. When we wait in a line at a ballgame for entry, we eventually get into the game. When we wait for a loved one to arrive from out of town, they inevitably arrive. In this passage he says, "And now, O LORD for what do I wait?" The reveal is powerful. Knowing the reality that life is brief, distress and turmoil surround, and evil is present, he says, "My hope is in You." No matter what happens in life, yielding to God is the most powerful response to the temporary, which will ultimately lead to the eternal.

So, when life happens, wait on God, trust His Word, yield your temporary, and trade it in for the eternal. That's how we give glory to God in every situation.

"Biblical hope not only desires something good for the future—it expects it to happen." —John Piper[31]

1. Is your well-being more important than what God desires in your life situation?
2. In life's "fast-food" and "quick-fix" mentality, are you patiently waiting for God's plan or hastily making your own life decisions?

Dear God, allow me today to trust in You in every life situation. Knowing
that I am temporary, and my life situations are temporary, allow me to wait
on You and by doing so, put all of my hope in You, O God. Amen.

Carl Setterlind
Worship Pastor
Biltmore Baptist Church, Arden, NC

Never Underestimate the Power of a Song

Let the word of Christ dwell richly among you, in all wisdom teaching and admonishing one another through psalms, hymns, and spiritual songs, singing to God with gratitude in your hearts.
Colossians 3:16 (csb)

Do you remember the first time you heard a song that changed your life? Have you ever been so moved by a song that every time you hear that particular song you feel a rush of emotions and you remember a significant event? That is the power of a song. It's amazing how a melody and a lyric can intertwine and have such great impact. It's astonishing that a motif can be so personal that it almost becomes "sacred" to us; it becomes "our song."

Singers sing, players play, and the whole earth can hear our song. From the time Moses' song was sung after God's people crossed the Red Sea, to the song Mary sang when Jesus' birth was announced to her, to the new song that is talked about in Revelation, songs have always had the power to move us. Do you think of the Billy Graham Crusades when you hear or sing "Just as I Am"? Nations and great causes have had songs that bring people together for a common purpose. In fact, bloodshed and war was averted in the late 1980s and early 1990s as "the singing revolution" brought people from Baltic States together to oppose rule by another country. Many times, I have told choirs or groups, "The right song at the right time can change a life forever."

1. Do you have a song that is "your song"? Why is it?
2. Is there a song from your youth or childhood that when you sing or hear it, it brings back memories?
3. Did you know the earth sings? Go to https://svs.gsfc.nasa.gov/11073.

~

God, thank You for the gift of music in our lives and for letting us use this gift to worship You. As I sing today, let my song be an offering of praise to You.

Dr. Randy C. Lind
Worship and Music Specialist
Baptist General Convention of Oklahoma, Oklahoma, OK

Leaving a Legacy

*Being confident of this, that he who began a good work in you will
carry it on to completion until the day of Christ Jesus.*
Philippians 1:6 (NIV)

This is possibly very strange to say, but I love a good funeral! Because I'm a music minister, I have probably attended more funerals than your average person serving as a pianist or directing the choir. As a result, I've heard many stories of people who lived their lives devoted to loving and serving God and other people. After these services, I've been left feeling inspired and encouraged to make my life count too!

But as much as I desire to live an exemplary life, I often feel that I'm failing miserably! Too often I let my mouth get the better of me. I let my busyness dictate my priorities and let relationships slide. Worst of all, I neglect the spiritual disciplines that would enrich my relationship with God.

I am so thankful, however, that His mercies are "new every morning." Each new day brings opportunities to renew my commitments, re-energize my efforts, and redirect my priorities. I'm also grateful for the promise that God is with me through it all. He will enable me and strengthen me to complete the work He has for me to do. I want my funeral to be one of the good ones!

1. What are some of the characteristics that stand out to you about a person in your life that left an eternal legacy?
2. What are some things you hope will be said of you when you die?

~

Heavenly Father, I want to finish well! At the end of my life, may I be worthy of hearing the words, "Well done, good and faithful servant." In Jesus' name, Amen.

Tempa Bader
Music Minister/Women's Ministry
Crossroads Christian Church, Gray, TN

Confidence and Reverence

But I, through the abundance of your steadfast love, will enter your house. I will
bow down toward your holy temple in the fear of you. Lead me, O LORD, in your
righteousness because of my enemies; make your way straight before me.
Psalm 5:7–8 (ESV)

The psalmist expresses both his confidence to boldly enter the presence of the Lord (Heb. 4:16) and the humble acknowledgment that he does not deserve to be there. He brings nothing of merit. He has done nothing to gain his acceptance from the Lord. He is able to come only on the basis of the incredible and faithful love of God.

And yet, as he confidently approaches, he remains in a posture of awe and fear. The love of the Lord is nothing to take for granted. He worships with equal parts confidence and reverence. He has the attitude of the hymn writer, "'twas grace that taught my heart to fear and grace my fears relieved."

This is the perfect combination for worship. God is our loving Father and He is also our sovereign and holy King. He is both grace and truth. We take courage in our unrestricted access into His presence while remembering that He has unrestricted access into our lives as well.

And so, just like the psalmist prayed in verse 8, we need God to lead us in a way that honors Him and conforms with His character. We need Him to make our way clear and free from obstacles, distractions, and temptations.

1. Do you think that you more often need more confidence in your standing with God or more reverence in your relationship with Him?
2. Are you living in a way that pleases God?

~

Heavenly father, thank You for Your unfailing love. I pray that You would
enlarge my vision of You. Lead me in Your righteous ways today, bringing
clarity to each new step I take. May I honor You in all that I do.

John Stegemerten
Worship Pastor
Hickory Grove Baptist Church, Charlotte, NC

Jesus the Son Sings
with Us and Around Us

Jesus' singing is described in 2 places in the New Testament:

In Mark 14:26 Jesus has just finished the Passover meal with His Disciples, *"And when they had sung a hymn, they went out to the Mount of Olives"* (NKJV). The song they sang was likely the 118th Psalm, which was the last of the six Egyptian Psalms and was always the last song of the Passover meal. It is wonderful to read this psalm and imagine the meaning that spoke to Jesus' heart as He sang this psalm one last time before His crucifixion. Jesus was so loved by children and the multitudes that it is hard not to imagine Him smiling and singing as He went about teaching. Singing was a huge part of Jewish worship, Israel's singing and music was known throughout the world. Even in Babylon after the Jewish people were captured, ". . . those who carried us away captive asked of us a song, and those who plundered us requested mirth saying, 'Sing us one of the songs of Zion!'" (Ps. 137:3 NKJV). Jesus was born into the race that created the "Song of Zion!" King David and his greater Son, Jesus, were master singers and musicians! The Bible says Jesus was in the synagogue every Sabbath and went to Jerusalem three times a year to present Himself as an obedient male Israelite to the temple priests to sacrifice and worship (Luke 4:16). A major part of this synagogue/temple worship was singing Scripture and playing instruments! GOD THE SON SINGS WITH US!

The next verse describing Jesus' singing is Hebrews 2:12—a direct quote from Psalm 22:22! Jesus stands in the midst of the church declaring the glory of God the Father to us His brothers! Here is what happens every Sunday when we sing in church. God the Father is enthroned on our praise (Ps. 22:3). He sings over us and with us (Zeph. 3:17). God the Son stands with us, singing around us and in us, as we sing together!

Our adult choir was singing the final session of the 1988 Southern Baptist Convention in San Antonio, Texas as over 100 banners paraded into the Spur's Arena! At the finale of the music, the Jesus Banner and the Cross came down the center aisle. The entire audience rose to their feet clapping and raising their hands! When our choir saw that, they started crying and began losing their volume in sound. I motioned to them to keep singing and stop crying. All of a sudden, this huge wall of sound came from the choir and ended with the best sound we had ever had! Afterward, as I thanked them for not crying and finishing the song well, they each turned to the others and said, "I wasn't singing, were you?" In that moment I just wondered if Jesus had stepped in and finished the song for us! GOD THE SON IS SINGING AROUND US!

1. Picture Hebrews 2:12 happening in your mind as you sing in a worship service.
2. What changes of attitude could you perceive in a worship service if everyone there realized that Jesus was singing with them?

～

Heavenly Father, thank You for Jesus and His death, burial, and
resurrection for my sins! I want to praise You with a joyful song and a
heart full of obedience to Your Word! In Jesus' name I pray, Amen.

Jim Whitmire
Instructor in Music and Worship
Mid-America Baptist Theological Seminary, Cordova, TN

I'm Not There Yet

Not that I have already obtained this or am already perfect, but I press on to make it my own, because Christ Jesus has made me his own. . . . But our citizenship is in heaven, and from it we await a Savior, the Lord Jesus Christ.
Philippians 3:12, 20 (ESV)

Rob had been approached numerous times to serve in different areas of the church. The student pastor thought Rob would be the perfect person to teach the Senior High Boys' Bible class. When asked, Rob replied, "Sorry, but I'm not there yet." When he was nominated by the church body to serve as a deacon, Rob returned his invitation to the senior pastor with a note that simply said, "Thank you, but I'm not there yet." Even though Rob was a devoted Christ-follower, he never considered himself quite ready to serve because he didn't feel like he was good enough. He knew he had been forgiven of past sins and was doing his best to walk with the Lord, but Rob never felt worthy because he knew there was a lot of room for improvement.

Paul reminds the church in Philippians 3 that because of Christ, we are now citizens of heaven, though we have not reached our destination. We are not there yet, but we must forget what is behind and press for what is ahead. In Hebrews 10:14, we are reminded that because of Christ's sacrifice on the cross, we have been made perfect in Him and are set apart for His purpose.

1. Do you ever feel unqualified to serve God, though you know in your heart that you should serve?
2. Realize today that you are God's child, and He has created you for His purpose—His purpose for you now.

~

Dear God, forgive me when I fail to do what I know I should. Help me to discern Your call, and to say "yes" when I hear it. Thank You for creating me for Your purpose. In Jesus' name, Amen.

Jeff Stotts
Lead Worship Pastor
Central Baptist Church, Jonesboro, AR

Walking Blindfolded

He will cover you with his feathers. He will shelter you with his wings.
His faithful promises are your armor and protection.
Psalm 91:4 (NLT)

Have you ever walked through a season of change, but had no clue how God was going to reconcile the end? It's difficult to walk forward when the season is ending without clear views of the horizon; you feel like you're walking blindfolded. You can smell the change, you feel the change, you can even hear the change . . . you just can't see it. As you are walking through the season, it's as if Jesus calms your spirit and says you must live it before you can see it. He gives us peace in the unknown and His promises are our protection. We know transition is coming and while our heart prepares, our mind questions everything. Will it hurt? Will we fall? The most daunting question . . . Will we survive? Those moments always bring us back to Psalm 91.

He covers us when we can't see and He shelters us in the unknown. Our job is to stay faithful. Obedience is the deciding factor on how this all ends. Do we trust Him enough to stay the course or are our senses being distracted by the grief and pain? He's calling us to daily surrender to His will as we lay down our own. Stand in the shadow of the Almighty and allow His faithful promise to be your armor and protection. He sees around the bend.

1. Are you trusting God in your season of change?
2. Are you walking in obedience or fighting for your own will in your transition?

~

Jesus, help us to trust You in the unknown. We lay our desires and will at Your feet today and surrender to Your will for our life. You see the layers we can't uncover and You know what is best for us. Give us a heart for You and protect us in the waiting. We love You! Amen.

Josh Sullins
Worship and Creative Arts Pastor
Peachtree Corners Baptist Church, Peachtree Corners, GA

God Is Singing Over You

"The LORD your God is in your midst, a mighty one who will save; he will rejoice over you with gladness; he will quiet you by his love; he will exult over you with loud singing."
Zephaniah 3:17 (ESV)

It breaks my heart when I hear my children or grandchildren tell me they aren't good enough, smart enough, pretty enough, or whatever it is they feel is lacking about themselves. I hug them tight and remind them about their worth to me and to God. I love them. God loves them. I speak comfort to them and show them how much they are valued. Sometimes, I even sing to them!

Did you know God is singing over you? The first time I heard that I immediately took to my Bible to see if someone was making that up or if it was real. Guess what, it's real! He is rejoicing over us! He quiets us with His love. He is singing over us LOUDLY. Can you even imagine how loudly God sings? He spoke the universe into existence, breathing life into Adam. Yet, He still sings over us. God loves you!

1. Have you ever had a time when you felt like God was distant? Super close?
2. What songs do you think God was singing over you during those times?

Dear God, thank You for loving me so much that You sing over me. Thank You for the comfort and closeness I feel in Your presence. Thank You for saving me. Amen.

Loren Minnick Jr.
Associate Pastor—Worship
Foothills Baptist Church, Las Vegas, NV

What Do You Depend On?

Our God gives you everything you need, makes you everything you're to be.
2 Thessalonians 1:2 (MSG)

Not long ago, as we were preparing for our move to our new church building, I found myself asking the question, "What is it that we really lean on?" As we went through the moving process, we had to remove several key technological elements from our old worship center to help facilitate the move to the new worship center. That created some significant challenges for our services during the transition period that made me think, "Do we lean on our own human strength, wit, and technology, OR do we lean on Jesus?"

We've got every tool and trick of the trade to make our lives easier and more "effective," and yet, when it matters most, we lean on those things rather than on the Creator/Sustainer God through whom all things are possible.

It didn't take me long to come to the conclusion that *the moment we lean on anything but Christ is the moment that we set ourselves up for failure.*

Remember that with tools or no tools, when we trust in Christ as our Savior and Lord, we put ourselves in the hands of the one who will give us the right tools to accomplish whatever task lies before us.

1. What do I really depend on?
2. Have I given Christ full reign in every aspect of my life?

~

Father, I am so grateful for all of the life, breath, intelligence, wit, and ability that You have placed in me. Even so, I pray that You would remind me each day that I need to depend on Your will and guidance in my life. Give me strength to depend on the fact that You have given me every tool that I need to accomplish Your perfect will in my life. Amen.

Ken Van Cura
Worship Pastor
First Baptist Church, Plant City, FL

Why?

*To each is given the manifestation of the Spirit for the common good. For to one
is given through the Spirit the utterance of wisdom, and to another the utterance
of knowledge according to the same Spirit, to another faith by the same Spirit,
to another gifts of healing by the one Spirit, to another the working of miracles,
to another prophecy, to another the ability to distinguish between spirits, to
another various kinds of tongues, to another the interpretation of tongues.*

1 Corinthians 12:7–10 (ESV)

It was one of those crystal-clear Florida days in mid-August when we arrived at my aunt and uncle's place in Clearwater. The sun just seemed brighter there, shining down on the white, powdery sand as the clear, blue-green water of the Gulf lapped gently upon the shores. I was ready to get in the water, but my mother was attempting to communicate the fact that I needed sunscreen on before I stepped out into the hot Florida sun. All her attempts were ignored, and I ran as fast as I could into the warm waters of the Gulf, paying no attention to her shouts.

Eventually, she stopped trying to warn me as she resigned herself to the fact that this hyper little ten-year-old boy would either come out of the water or learn a lesson the hard way. I chose the hard way.

Later that evening my skin was (you guessed it) bright pink and burning with the heat of that day's beach time. I complained and moaned about how bad the burn hurt and how it wasn't fair or right or good. However, my sweet mother lovingly calmed this sullen boy as she gently applied lotion to the "sunburn of the century." Her shouts, earlier that morning, were attempting to prevent my shouts that evening!

C. S. Lewis, who watched his beloved wife die of cancer, put it this way: ". . . pain insists upon being attended to. God whispers to us in our pleasures, speaks in our conscience, but shouts in our pains: it is his megaphone to rouse a deaf world."[32]

God is a shepherd and He attempts to guide His sheep (us) as we go through this life. Pain is a sharp, clear tool to achieve that purpose. Sometimes a needle may be necessary to prevent disease or infection. Nobody welcomes or enjoys the injection, but it prevents a far greater suffering.

What is God trying to shout to you? It may be something He wants you to do or something He doesn't want you doing. In your brokenness and pain, listen to His voice. Instead of asking God "Why?" ask Him "What?" as in "What do you want me to see in this trial?" He may be trying to say something to you!

1. What are you experiencing right now that seems uncomfortable or inconvenient? Is God trying to tell you something through this?
2. Are you walking close enough with Him to know what He is attempting to tell you?

~

Father, draw me closer to You so that I may hear Your voice and do Your will.

Nathan Ward
Worship Arts Pastor
Woodland Community Church, Bradenton, FL

Invitation Accepted

*"Go out quickly into the streets and alleys of the town and bring in the poor, the
crippled, the blind and the lame.' 'Sir,' the servant said, 'what you ordered has been
done, but there is still room.' Then the master told his servant, 'Go out to the roads
and country lanes and compel them to come in, so that my house will be full.'"*
Luke 14:21b–23 (NIV)

Invitations work. I know of a guy who was a senior in high school and had never stepped
foot in a church. For him and his family, Sunday was a day to work, to catch up on
chores, and if time allowed, to relax.

One Saturday, a friend invited this young man to go to church. Since he had the day
off from work, he was happy to take him the following day. An amazing thing happened.
This high school senior was completely blown away with the worship, music, and preaching. He couldn't begin to imagine that this whole religious "world" was going on around
him and he didn't have a clue. It affected him so much so that he asked his boss if he could
take every Sunday morning off from work and come in at 12:15 p.m. He also arranged to
be at every Wednesday night youth group Bible study in order to find out all he could about
God, Jesus, the Holy Spirit, and the church.

It took a while for all of the new information to be processed into his analytical mind.
Think, if you can, what it would be like to hear the real Christmas story for the first time.
Think on what it would be like to hear about the miracles, and His death, burial, and resurrection: not to mention, creation and all of the rest of the Old Testament. He felt like the
two guys on the Emmaus road did. "Were not our hearts burning within us while he talked
with us on the road and opened the Scriptures to us?" (Luke 24:32 NIV).

After a little more than four months of total immersion into Christianity, this teenager walked the aisle at that church and accepted Jesus Christ as Savior and Lord. Two years
later he surrendered to full-time ministry and was called a month later to serve on staff as a
minister of music at a church. All this happened because a simple invitation was accepted to
go with someone to church. That guy has recently completed thirty-seven years in full-time
Christian ministry. I am that guy.

1. How many non-church-goers do you know?
2. When was the last time you invited someone to go to church? What could happen
   if you invited someone to church?

~

*Dear Lord, help us to have a burden for the lost. Bring someone in our path
that we could invite to attend church. Give us the courage to invite them. Let
those who we invite hear from You and respond. In Jesus' name, Amen.*

J. K. Weger
Minister of Music and Worship Arts
Ash Creek Baptist, Azle, TX

It's Important Work!

*Let us not get tired of doing good, for we will reap at the proper time if we
don't give up. Therefore, as we have opportunity, let us work for the good
of all, especially for those who belong to the household of faith.*
Galatians 6:9–10 (CSB)

People who sing in church choirs and those who are involved in music ministry are frequently also Sunday school teachers, deacons, small group leaders, VBS coordinators, and much more. Choir members, and those committed to specific ministries in the church, are most often the backbone of their respective local body. Such dedication carries the ongoing burden of time and energy. Ministry, simply put, requires sacrifice—lots of it!

Be encouraged! The work that you are doing in your church is important. The Word of God and the Holy Spirit are watering every seed you sow in worship. Every song, every class, every board meeting, every Bible study, every nursery assignment, every hospital visit, every cup of coffee, every warm meal served, every phone call . . . it's all being carefully cultivated by the Lord and is never wasted—not one single moment!

Note that your work is particularly important for the good of those who "belong to the household of faith." You are enriching the lives of your family and fellow congregants in significant ways as you intentionally walk alongside and encourage them in their spiritual journey.

So, keep singing! Keep serving—anywhere and everywhere! Let your efforts remain consistent with the truth you proclaim each week. You are admonished by God's Word to remain relentlessly committed to the work God has for you to accomplish. Hold fast to the truth that the Faithful One will complete the work He began in you. He has promised to bring the harvest. He only asks one thing of you—to never give up!

1. Who are the people in your community of faith who give tirelessly of themselves in ministry to others?
2. What practical steps can you take to ensure that you will not grow weary in doing good?

～

Jesus, we thank You for the opportunity we have to sing and serve in this family and fellowship of believers. Humbly, we ask You to help us not to become weighed down by the work to which You've called us. May we never grow weary of doing good for all.

Craig Adams
Creative Director of LifeWay Worship
LifeWay Christian Resources, Nashville, TN

The Fight

Fight the good fight of the faith. Take hold of the eternal life to which you were called and about which you made the good confession in the presence of many witnesses.

1 Timothy 6:12 (ESV)

Eight years ago, my wife and I started the process of adoption. In the beginning, it seemed simple enough, but once we met the kids we felt God calling us to adopt, the challenges began to multiply. We faced battles with the state and threats from the kids' biological parents. It was an emotional, physical, and spiritual roller coaster. Because of these circumstances, we began to question if we should give up on this sibling group and start the process over. However, we knew God had set these children aside for us. We knew God had called us to adopt these kids.

Therefore, we had a choice to make. We could fight for what we knew was God's calling on our lives, or we could give up. By God's grace, we brought two girls and a boy into our family six years ago. We fought the battle and He brought us through.

First Timothy challenges us to fight the good fight because the road to eternity is filled with spiritual, emotional, and physical attacks. Satan is doing everything possible to deter us from accomplishing God's calling on our lives. We fight for that which is important to us. Nothing is more important than the gospel and our relationship with Jesus Christ. So, as we face obstacles in this journey we call life, we must stay vigilant, focused, and filled with God's Spirit in order to keep the faith and finish the race God has set before us.

1. What battles lie before you today?
2. Are those battles within the boundaries of God's calling on your life? Are they being surrendered to God?

~

Heavenly Father, thank You for being faithful in the midst of my battles and struggles. Help me to continually keep my focus on the prize of eternity. May I honor You through each and every battle I face, recognizing You will see me through. In Jesus' name, Amen.

Tim Whedbee
Senior Associate Pastor of Worship and Administration
Mobberly Baptist Church, Longview, TX

What Good Comes from Bad?

*"I have told you these things, so that in me you may have peace. In this world
you will have trouble. But take heart! I have overcome the world."*
John 16:33 (NIV)

So many times, in the midst of our heartache and struggle, we don't understand why bad things happen. For those of us who truly strive to live our lives for Him and be a daily example to others, the enemy seems to come at us twice as hard. We must look no farther than Job to realize that God will allow us to be tested.

Because of the rampant spreading of the "prosperity gospel," those with limited biblical knowledge are easily led astray. They are taught that if they follow the Lord, His desire is for them to be healthy and wealthy. When this fantasy life isn't realized, the result is a bitterness toward God and His church. It is time we stop pretending that everything is always wonderful in our lives, and admit the truth—that we are sinners, saved by grace. The old cliché, "The church is a hospital for sinners, not a showcase for saints," needs to be realized in our day.

His promise in Romans 8:28, that ALL THINGS work for our good, is true. It's just a matter of perspective—a matter of us realizing the good. One way we, as church musicians, can realize the good is to share our struggles with others going through similar situations.

My friend Joseph Habedank penned these lyrics for his song "Now I Know Him": "If my faith had not been tested by the flames, how could I have known these depths of grace?"[33] Think about that lyric for a moment; no further explanation is needed.

1. What struggle have you had recently where you are still looking for "the good"?
2. Who do you know that you could help by sharing how God brought good from your difficult circumstances in the past?

～

*God, help us realize the hurting world around us. Teach us to be encouragers through the pain
and to bear one another's burdens. Thank You for never leaving us or forsaking us. Amen.*

Bradley White
Worship Pastor
First Baptist Church, Summit, MS

Time

Teach us to number our days, that we may gain a heart of wisdom.
Psalm 90:12 (NIV)

Time keeps on slipping (slipping, slipping) into the future . . ."[34] These lyrics from the 1977 Steve Miller Band hit song talk about the same theme as Psalm 90—the inability to escape the relentless advance of time. We are all constrained by it. No one escapes it. Our time here on the earth is so very brief. Psalm 90:5–6 (NIV) describes it this way: "They are like the new grass of the morning . . . but by evening it is dried and withered."

Before you start to get too depressed about life, the psalmist goes on to describe God: "Before the mountains were born, before You gave birth to the earth and the world, from eternity to eternity, You are God!" (v. 2 HCSB). God is not affected by time! He stands outside of time. And the good news? God is our refuge (v. 1).

That brings us to verse 12. Because of the fact that we are very temporary and God is eternal, the verse teaches us to value each day as a precious gift from God and to use each day carefully, with wisdom, for the eternal glory of God our maker!

1. Read all of Psalm 90.
2. In light of Psalm 90, how will you live your life differently today?

～

*God, I thank You that You are eternal. I thank You that You made everything,
even me, for a purpose—to bring You glory. Would You show me how to live
my life today in such a way that I would do just that? Give me wisdom to see
with Your heart and with Your perspective. Satisfy us in the morning with Your
faithful love so that we may shout with joy and be glad all of our days!*

John Williams
Worship Pastor
Hebron Baptist Church, Dacula, GA

The Fragrance of Worship

Then Mary took a pound of very costly oil of spikenard, anointed the feet of Jesus, and wiped His feet with her hair. And the house was filled with the fragrance of the oil.
John 12:3 (NKJV)

Spikenard has been described as a fragrant ointment of the ancient world used for anointing. Nard is derived from an Indian plant, the Nardostachys jatamansi, which grows in the Himalayas. The plant of nard is a costly, but fragrant, aroma. Some believe that even a small amount could cost a year's wages. The spikenard oil was used as a perfume to refresh and exhilarate in dry and arid climates.

Mary, Martha, and Lazarus were hosting a dinner party for Jesus. Mary unselfishly takes a pound of spikenard and anointed the feet of Jesus. Mary gave of herself to worship and serve the Lord Jesus Christ. Once the spikenard was open, the fragrance filled the room and became part of those in attendance.

The fragrance of the oil permeated their clothes, hair, and everything in the room. I am sure the aroma of Mary's worship lasted for several days. I can imagine others asking about the fragrance and the reason it was used. Have you been to a wedding or a party? Have you been in the presence of royalty?

As I read the text above, I am filled with wonder and amazement.

1. Does my worship cause others to ask questions about what I have been doing?
2. Does my worship linger throughout the week or is it gone when the service ends?
3. Is the fragrance of worship refreshing and exhilarating to my life and others around me?
4. Does my worship point others to Jesus?

~

Father, we are changed as we encounter the fragrance of Your worship. Help me to spend time lingering in Your presence and meditating on Your Word. May the appearance and aroma of my life cause others to want to know more about You. Amen.

Dr. David Wilson
Assistant Professor of Worship and Church Music
Brewton-Parker College, Mt. Vernon, GA

Employ the Joy

Though the fig tree does not bud and there are no grapes on the vines, though the olive crop fails and the fields produce no food, though there are no sheep in the pen and no cattle in the stalls, yet I will rejoice in the LORD, I will be joyful in God my Savior.
Habakkuk 3:17–18 (NIV)

Because of its heavy saline and mineral content, the Dead Sea is denser than the human body. Therefore, if you go into those waters you will not sink, but rather, float on the top. That is a picture of biblical joy in the Christian life. Robert Morgan writes, "The joy of the Lord pushes us upward, keeps us afloat on choppy waters, refreshes us in desert places, and helps us resurface when pulled down by the undertows of life."[35] The Bible never promises that we will be happy, but it does promise that we can be full of joy. Before Jesus went to Calvary He said, "These things I have spoken to you, that my joy may be in you, and that your joy may be full" (John 15:11 ESV). You will have "sorrow now, but I will see you again, and your hearts will rejoice, and no one will take your joy from you" (John 16:22 ESV).

Happiness is based upon our outward circumstances, but joy comes from within and is based on our hope and trust in the Lord. The former is fleeting but the latter is permanent. "The joy of the LORD is our strength" means that even in the most difficult times in our life, we can faithfully endure because of joy. Everyone desires to be around a person who is genuinely joyful in his or her demeanor. If we are gloomy and pessimistic, then those around us will tend to reflect our negative attitude. Christians understand the power of employing biblical joy and they inspire confidence and optimism through their positive words and cheerful countenance.

1. What are some specific things you allow to keep you from living a life of joy?
2. What are your top three joy-builders, for yourself and for others?

~

In a world filled with difficulty and danger, Lord, it is easy for my heart to become weighed down with pressures and overwhelmed with problems. Thank You that Your strength is made perfect in my weakness, enabling me to rejoice in You at all times.

Steve Holt
Worship Minister
Central Baptist Church, College Station, TX

Are You Listening?

Just as they were leaving him, Peter said to Jesus, "Master, it is good for us to be here; let us make three dwellings, one for you, one for Moses, and one for Elijah.". . . Then from the cloud came a voice that said, "This is my Son, my Chosen; listen to him!"
Luke 9:33–35 (NRSV)

My high school English teacher began the year with something that I have always remembered. Mrs. Hall said there is a difference between hearing and listening. It is possible to hear something without really listening. Four people are standing in an elevator hearing the music, but only one of them is aware of the chord structure, the instrumentation of the orchestra, the harmonic rhythm, and the alternating piano and orchestral entrances. That person knows it's most likely a Mozart Concerto. They all heard the same music but only one actually listened.

In our Scripture, notice that God's voice on the mountain did not say, "This is My Son; worship Him, preach about Him, sing a song to Him, put a committee together to decide what to do next." He said, "Listen to Him."

How often we go to church, sit through Bible study, go through a worship service, sing songs, hear a sermon, and yet, never listen to God? How often do we read our Bibles and yet never listen to what God is trying to say to us?

If you'll notice, at the conclusion of some of His parables, Jesus said, "He who has ears . . ." He doesn't mean the ears on the side of our head. He means spiritual ears. Just as we have physical senses to relate to the physical world, if we are born again, we have spiritual senses. He must learn not only to hear but to listen to His voice. We must pay attention and listen.

1. What can you do today to be sure you are truly listening to God?
2. What difference does listening to God make in your life?

~

Lord, help us to hear Your voice and truly listen.

Glenn Crosthwait
Worship Pastor
Johns Creek Baptist Church, Alpharetta, GA

Tell Somebody!

". . . For the accuser of our brothers and sisters, who accuses them before our God day and night, has been hurled down. They triumphed over him by the blood of the Lamb and by the word of their testimony; they did not love their lives so much as to shrink from death."
Revelation 12:10b–11 (NIV)

One of the most powerful spiritual tools we have is the "word of our testimony." No one can argue with it; no one can debate it, and it can accomplish, in a few minutes, what we may never be able to communicate in any other way.

A changed life and a testimony of God's power being demonstrated in an individual's life has great potential to communicate the heart of the matter in a direct and dynamic way.

So often, we shy away from sharing our faith with others because we don't know how to get started or even open up the conversation.

Everyone loves a good story, and your testimony is unique to you and is proof of the truth of the gospel and the power of our Lord to change and transform a life.

Even if you came to Christ at an early age, and you feel your personal story is not dramatic enough, share it. It is more powerful than you think to realize the Lord has saved you, changed your heart, and kept you faithful to Him through the years.

As our Scripture today demonstrates, even Satan can't argue or stand up against the blood of the Lamb and the *word of your testimony!*

Let's be bold today to share our testimony and see how the Lord opens the doors to share the gospel.

1. Can I concisely share my testimony in five minutes?
2. Who can I share my story with today?

~

Lord Jesus, thank You for changing my life and giving me the promise of eternal life! Help me to be bold to share my personal story with someone today. In the loving name of Jesus, Amen.

Dr. Phil Barfoot
President / CEO
Celebration Concert Tours International / CCT Music, Franklin, TN

The "Be-Attitudes": Attitudes for Being a Disciple of Jesus, Step One

He opened his mouth and began to teach them, saying: "Blessed are the poor in spirit, for theirs is the kingdom of heaven. Blessed are those who mourn, because they shall be comforted. Blessed are the gentle, for they shall inherit the earth."
Matthew 5:2–5 (NASB)

The first step of discipleship is realizing that I am bankrupt in spirit! It is coming to God realizing that I have nothing to give Him that did not already come from Him. I need Him with every ounce of my being, but God, frankly, does not need me, and yet, He wants me, loves me, and created me for a relationship with Him.

We must not dare to think that God's process for growing disciples is a self-help program; it is far more radical than that. This first step means death to our sinful pride. Poor in spirit is not a state of depression but a place where our self-reliance is broken so that repentance and confession can flow daily.

Being broken by God hurts and we mourn, but God comforts us and develops a gentleness in our attitude and relationships as the Holy Spirit takes control of our lives. This world glorifies the brash and the loud, but God teaches us gentleness as we depend on Him and love others as ourselves. He calls it His Greatest Commandment.

This first step came at the greatest cost to God—He gave his Son. God took your debt and paid it forever at the cross. Because of that, the kingdom of heaven is yours through Jesus Christ.

1. How and when have you personally experienced brokenness through the crucifixion of your own sinful pride and self-centeredness?
2. Seriously consider your relationships. Do you demonstrate the attitude of gentleness to others?

O Lord, there are many great songs of brokenness. Overwhelm my life so that brokenness in You becomes not just a song but a real and active part of who I am.

Mark Powers
Worship Pastor
Riverland Hills Baptist Church, Columbia, SC

The "Be-Attitudes": Attitudes for Being a Disciple of Jesus, Step Two

"Blessed are those who hunger and thirst for righteousness, for they shall be satisfied. Blessed are the merciful, for they shall receive mercy. Blessed are the pure in heart, for they shall see God."
Matthew 5:6–8 (NASB)

Gentleness is only the beginning. As we grow in Christ, we hunger and thirst for a right relationship with our Father. An unquenchable hunger drives us to feel our Father's embrace and see His smile. Disobedience is disloyalty to the love relationship that we are building. Through the Holy Spirit, God Himself lives inside us and works His way from the inside out.

For those who have experienced God's mercy, we must run to the needs of others to share the mercy God has shown us. Mercy first offers *rescue* and *relief*, but godly mercy walks another person through relief into *recovery*. That mercy, however, is still not complete until we help them find *renewal* of purpose in God's plan for their lives.

We are making progress toward true discipleship, and yet, there is more to achieve. The next step is a purity of heart-focus on God and His will. Do you want to see God at work in your life? Focus totally on Him. Hear His words, "I love those who love me, and those who seek me find me" (Prov. 8:17 NIV). Wait on Him; talk to Him; trust Him totally, and you will see God at work in amazing ways all around you. It's a promise!

1. In what ways have you been reluctant to really hunger and thirst for God?
2. How do you think God might work in your life if you become a merciful person with a complete focus of heart on God and His will?

~

O Lord, I want to know an unquenchable hunger and thirst for You in my life. Help me focus my will today on trusting You totally. Who will I encounter today that needs mercy so they might know Your amazing grace?

Mark Powers
Worship Pastor
Riverland Hills Baptist Church, Columbia, SC

The "Be-Attitudes": Attitudes for Being a Disciple of Jesus, Step Three

"Blessed are the peacemakers, for they shall be called sons of God. Blessed are those who have been persecuted for the sake of righteousness, for theirs is the kingdom of heaven."
Matthew 5:9–10 (NASB)

There will always be those who will tell us that, if we just follow Jesus, we will have wealth and health. But Jesus, Himself, lived a perfect life and still endured horrific cruelty. If you truly follow Christ, you will endure tough times; follow Him anyway. If you are a Christian leader, you will be hurt by those who reject change; lead God's people anyway. If you love people with the love of Christ, they will hurt you; love people anyway.

In any combustible situation, we can choose what bucket we will "throw on the fire." Some choose a bucket of gasoline that ignites a wild fire and burns everything and everyone around. Some choose a bucket of cold water that causes everyone to recoil and run away.

True disciples choose a bucket of living water that applies God's viewpoint and His Word to situations that might otherwise explode. Be a peacemaker in the face of persecution and you will find that you have gone full circle to where we began in Step One. You will not only inherit the kingdom of heaven; you will embody God's kingdom in every way!

1. In volatile situations, what "bucket" do you usually "throw on the fire"?
2. What lessons have you learned in life when someone has hurt you because you were obeying or following God?

~

O Lord, help me to love and lead even when those around me reject and hurt me. Help me to be a peacemaker to everyone I come into contact with today.

Mark Powers
Worship Pastor
Riverland Hills Baptist Church, Columbia, SC

Think Big!

Where there is no vision, the people perish.
Proverbs 29:18a (KJV)

Helen Keller was once asked what would be worse than being born blind. She responded immediately, "To have sight and no vision." The old proverbs put it this way: "He who aims at nothing, hits it every time!" And, "He who fails to plan, plans to fail!"

Every single great invention, architectural design, idea, or accomplishment all started the very same way . . . with a vision. A vision motivates and encourages us to stay focused and "keep our eyes on the ball" until we realize and fulfill the dream or goal that started it all.

The Wright brothers envisioned humans being transported by "flying machines" literally around the world.

Steve Jobs dreamed of billions of people throughout the world holding a device that encompassed a phone that also played hundreds of songs, stored thousands of contacts, and served as a personal computer.

Paul the Apostle says in Philippians 3:14 (KJV): "I press toward the mark for the prize of the high calling of God in Christ Jesus." Paul's vision foresaw millions of people all around the world coming into a personal relationship with Jesus Christ in response to his tireless preaching of the gospel and training and mentoring believers wherever he went.

I encourage you to allow the Lord to help you "think outside the box" today and give you a vision to do something great for His kingdom. You might even start with a few small ideas first to build your confidence—something you could accomplish today . . . like writing an encouraging note to a friend with a Scripture that the Lord impresses upon you to send them.

When God gives you the vision, He will *always* give you the tools, people, and resources to accomplish the dream. So . . . pray for a fresh vision today and look forward to moving ahead by faith, and trust Him to supply everything you need to accomplish His purpose through the vision He plants in you.

Dream big today!

1. If you couldn't fail, what would you do for the sake of the kingdom of God?
2. What is a small idea that could serve as a "first step" toward a greater vision later?

~

Lord Jesus, give me Your vision today to accomplish Your purpose in my life. I trust You to provide all that I need to accomplish what You would have me do. Thank You, in advance, for the confidence You will give me to roll up my sleeves and move forward with the vision You plant inside of me. In the faithful name of Jesus, Amen.

Dr. Phil Barfoot
President / CEO
Celebration Concert Tours International / CCT Music, Franklin, TN

Contributors

Adams, Craig—*Creative Director of LifeWay Worship, LifeWay Christian Resources, Nashville, TN //* pgs. 24, 90, 353

Armentrout, Dr. Herb—*Minister of Music, Broadmoor Baptist Church, Shreveport, LA //* pgs. 31, 92, 208

Askew, Jeff—*Worship Pastor, Liberty Baptist Church, Hampton, VA //* pgs. 93, 115, 182

Atkinson, Ken—*Worship Pastor, First Baptist Church, Daytona Beach, FL //* pgs. 45, 95, 209

Bader, Tempa—*Music Minister/Women's Ministry, Crossroads Christian Church, Gray, TN //* pgs. 52, 211, 344

Barfoot, Dr. Phil—*President / CEO, Celebration Concert Tours International / CCT Music, Franklin, TN //* pgs. 1, 2, 62, 220, 340, 360, 364

Barrick, Don—*Worship Pastor, The Woodlands First Baptist Church, The Woodlands, TX //* pgs. 97, 212, 300

Batson, Kevin —*Worship Pastor, Taylors First Baptist Church, Taylors, SC //* pgs. 59, 99, 214

Blair, Mark—*Minister of Music, Bellevue Baptist Church, Memphis, TN //* pgs. 4, 34, 64

Blye, Travis—*Worship Pastor, Longview Point Baptist Church, Hernando, MS //* pgs. 85, 114, 215

Bolin, John—*Minister of Worship and Arts, Houston's First Baptist Church, Houston, TX //* pgs. 66, 102, 216

Bowersox, Dr. Steve—*Chair, Department of Worship and Technology and Assistant Professor of Worship, University of Mobile, Mobile, AL //* pgs. 73, 103, 175

Bradford, James—*Minister of Music, Quail Springs Baptist Church, Oklahoma City, OK //* pgs. 104, 218, 302

Breland, Jason—*Worship Pastor, Immanuel Baptist Church, Little Rock, AR //* pgs. 9, 80, 168

Brewer, John—*Associate Pastor of Worship, First Baptist Church, Mustang, OK //* pgs. 87, 106, 219

Bridges, Wayne—*Traditional Worship Leader/Senior Adults, First Baptist Church, Ruston, LA //* pgs. 107, 221, 303

Briscoe, Rick—*Associate Pastor of Worship, Prestonwood Baptist Church, Plano, TX //* pgs. 8, 17, 39

Brockelman, Jeff—*Worship Pastor, Anderson Mill Road Baptist Church, Moore, SC //* pgs. 101, 109, 222

Bugg, Dr. D. Doran—*Chair of Music Department, Belhaven University, Jackson, MS //* pgs. 5, 36, 65

Bullman, Scott—*Worship Pastor, Thomas Road Baptist Church, Lynchburg, VA //* pgs. 110, 223, 305

Butler, David—*Worship Pastor, First Baptist Church, St. Charles, MO //* pgs. 108, 161, 273

Clutts, Keith—*Worship Pastor, Grand Avenue Baptist Church, Fort Smith, AR //* pgs. 111, 225, 306

Cochran, Ron—*Former Executive and Music Pastor, Portland Christian Center, Portland, OR //* pgs. 38, 113, 154

Cole, Michael—*Associate Pastor of Music and Worship, Morrison Heights Baptist Church, Clinton, MS //* pgs. 100, 122, 226

Cook, Barry—*Minister of Music and Worship, First Baptist Church, Tifton, GA //* pgs. 116, 129, 147

Copeland, Chris—*Worship Pastor, Central Church, Collierville, TN //* pgs. 94, 117, 228

Crane, Greg—*Worship Minister, First Baptist Church, Hendersonville, TN //* pgs. 11, 40, 68

Crosthwait, Glenn—*Worship Pastor, Johns Creek Baptist Church, Alpharetta, GA //* pgs. 118, 229, 359

Darus, Charles—*Worship Pastor, First Baptist Church, Kissimmee, FL //* pgs. 120, 230, 307

Davis, Paul—*Worship Pastor, Northcrest Baptist Church, Meridian, MS //* pgs. 121, 232, 308

Davis, Tobin—*Minister of Music, Shadow Mountain Community Church, El Cajon, CA //* pgs. 140, 143, 266

Deakins, Dr. Mark—*Worship Minister, Broadway Christian Church, Lexington, KY //* pgs. 89, 233, 261, 272, 309

Diffey, Chris—*Minister of Music and Worship, Lakeside Baptist Church, Birmingham, AL //* pgs. 124, 235, 310

Duncan, Jon—*Lead State Missionary of Worship and Music Ministry, Georgia Baptist Mission Board, Duluth, GA //* pgs. 12, 41, 150

Duren, Cliff—*Arranger, Worship Pastor, First Baptist Church, Woodstock, GA //* pgs. 125, 133, 157

Dyer, Brent—*Lead Worship Pastor, Champion Forest Baptist Church, Houston, TX //* pgs. 6, 37, 67

Elkins, Jeff—*Minister of Worship, First Baptist Church, Tulsa, OK //* pgs. 127, 236, 312

Ellenburg, Chris—*Minister of Music, First Baptist Church, North Spartanburg, SC //* pgs. 128, 237, 313

Estes, Joe—*Minister of Music and Worship, First Baptist Church, Trussville, AL //* pgs. 26, 130, 239

Fallin, Matt—*Associate Pastor of Worship, Santuck Baptist Church, Wetumpka, AL //* pgs. 131, 240, 315

Farris, Chason—*Worship Pastor, First Baptist Church, Hendersonville, NC //* pgs. 132, 242, 316

Ferguson, Keith—*Associate Pastor, Worship Arts, First Baptist Church, Carrollton, TX //* pgs. 126, 164, 259

Fitzpatrick, Joe—*Worship and Music Pastor, First Baptist Church, Nashville, TN //* pgs. 134, 243, 317

Jones, David—*Director of Music and Worship, Immanuel Bible Church, Springfield, VA //* pgs. 146, 227

Jones, Ray—*President and Founder, Radiance Ministries, San Antonio, TX //* pgs. 148, 253, 323

Kirby, Randy—*Worship Pastor, First Baptist Church, Simpsonville, SC //* pgs. 149, 254, 279

Krivsky, Ryan—*Worship Pastor, Greenwell Springs Baptist Church, Greenwell Springs, LA //* pgs. 151, 256, 324

Lawrence, Jeff—*Executor Pastor, Lifebridge Church, Orlando, FL //* pgs. 18, 47, 72, 86

Layfield, Clay—*Associate Pastor, Music and Senior Adults, First Baptist Church, Eastman, GA //* pgs. 152, 257, 326

Leake, Chip—*Worship Pastor, Thompson Station Church, Thompson's Station, TN //* pgs. 77, 153, 234

Lind, Dr. Randy C.—*Worship and Music Specialist, Baptist General Convention of Oklahoma, Oklahoma City, OK //* pgs. 70, 136, 343

Maddox, Robert—*Worship and Missions Pastor, Spotswood Baptist Church, Fredericksburg, VA //* pgs. 155, 258, 327

Maier, Mark—*Pastor of Worship, First Baptist Church, Rogers, AR //* pgs. 63, 156, 241

Marsh, Don—*Associate Professor of Music and Worship, Songwriting, Liberty University, Lynchburg, VA //* pgs. 56, 210, 248

Martin, Kenneth—*Minister of Music and Worship, First Baptist Church, Milton, FL //* pgs. 158, 260, 328

Mason, Chris—*Worship Pastor, First Baptist Church, Arnold, MO //* pgs. 159, 329

Mathena, Dr. Gary—*Director of Practica, Liberty University, Lynchburg, VA //* pgs. 19, 48, 74, 88, 160, 263

Matthews, Dr. Gary—*Pastor of Worship and the Arts, Christ Memorial Church, Holland, MI //* pgs. 49, 162, 255

Matthews, DMA, Ronald A.—*President, Eastern University, St. David's, PA //* pgs. 163, 264, 330

Powers, Mark—*Worship Pastor, Riverland Hills Baptist Church, Columbia, SC //* pgs. 361, 362, 363

Quinn, Tommy—*Associate Pastor of Worship, First Baptist Church Tillman's Corner, Mobile, AL //* pgs. 7, 183, 341

Rhodes, Gary—*Worship Pastor, First Baptist Church Woodway, Waco, TX //* pgs. 21, 29, 311, 337

Setterlind, Carl—*Worship Pastor, Biltmore Baptist Church, Arden, NC //* pgs. 184, 281, 342

Shepherd, Scott—*Worship and Music Specialist, Tennessee Baptist Mission Board, Henry, TN //* pgs. 25, 53, 78

Skelley, Jon—*Worship Pastor, Geyer Springs First Baptist Church, Little Rock, AR //* pgs. 186, 217, 282

Slemp, Matthew—*Minister of Music, First Baptist Church, Indian Trail, NC //* pgs. 96, 187, 284

Stearns, Todd—*Pastor of Worship and Music, First Baptist Church, Naples, FL //* pgs. 188, 285, 318

Stegemerten, John—*Worship Pastor, Hickory Grove Baptist Church, Charlotte, NC //* pgs. 190, 286, 345

Stone, Rick—*Worship Pastor, Whitesburg Baptist Church, Huntsville, AL //* pgs. 105, 203, 325

Stotts, Jeff—*Lead Worship Pastor, Central Baptist Church, Jonesboro, AR //* pgs. 191, 287, 347

Sullins, Josh—*Worship and Creative Arts Pastor, Peachtree Corners Baptist Church, Peachtree Corners, GA //* pgs. 193, 288, 348

Thomas, David—*Worship Pastor, Highland Baptist Church, Grove City, OH //* pgs. 194, 289, 335

Tillman, Tom— *Director of Music and Worship, Baptist General Convention of Texas, Dallas TX //* pgs. 54, 79, 314

Tyner, Jonathan—*Minister of Music, Olive Baptist Church, Pensacola, FL //* pgs. 27, 55, 81

Notes

1. Martin Luther King Jr., "Letter from Birmingham Jail," April 16, 1963.
2. J. Oswald Sanders, *Spiritual Leadership: Principles of Excellence for Every Believer* (Chicago, IL: Moody Publishers, 2007), 102.
3. Donner Atwood, "Leaps of Faith," November 2016, http://access-jesus.com/illustrations_leaps-of-faith/.
4. Rory Noland, Heart of the Artist (Grand Rapids, MI: Zondervan, 1999).
5. https://worthilymagnify.com/2009/10/20/the-problem-with-postulating/
6. "Saved by Grace," words and music by Fanny Crosby (1891, Public Domain).
7. *The Charles F. Stanley Life Principles Bible* (Nashville, TN: Thomas Nelson, 2009).
8. "Turn Your Eyes Upon Jesus," words and music by Helen H. Lemmel (1922, Public Domain).
9. Watchman Nee, quoted in Don McMinn, *A Heart Aflame!* (Oklahoma City: NCM Press, 1993), 27.
10. Barbara Brown Taylor, *Leaving Church: A Memoir of Faith* (New York: HarperCollins, 2006), 102.
11. H. C. Leupold, *Exposition of the Psalms* (Grand Rapids: Baker, 1969), 152.
12. John MacArthur, "The Critical Elements of True Worship," August 19, 2007, www.gty.org/library/sermons-library/80-323/the-critical-element-of-true-worship.
13. George MacDonald, *Annals of a Quiet Neighborhood*, first published in 1865 as a serial in the *Sunday Magazine* in England.
14. Michael Short, Gustav Holst 1874–1934: A Centenary Documentation (London, UK: White Lion Publishers, 1974).
15. Vance Havner, *The Vance Havner Quote Book*, Dennis J. Hester compiler (Grand Rapids: Baker Book House, 1986), 65.
16. "What a Beautiful Name," words and music by Ben Fielding and Brooke Ligertwood, © 2016 Hillsong Music Publishing.
17. Bob Kauflin, "Words of Wonder: What Happens When We Sing" in John Piper's *The Power of Words and the Wonder of God* (Wheaton, IL: Crossway, 2009), 131.
18. Vance Havner, *Don't Miss Your Miracle* (Grand Rapids: Baker, 1984), 57.
19. Ronald B. Allen and Dr. Gordon Borror, *Worship: Rediscovering the Missing Jewel* (Eugene, OR: Wipf and Stock, 1982), 157.

20. "Then and Only Then," words and music by Geron Davis and Joyce McCollough, © 1996 DaviShop Publishing/ New Spring/ Joyce Martin/ McCollough Music/ Willow Branch Publishing.

21. John Piper source unknown.

22. "This Joy I Have," words and music by Shirley Caesar, © 1974 Capitol CMG Publishing.

23. "Show Me," words and music by Alan Jay Lerner and Frederick Loewe, Broadway musical *My Fair Lady* 1956.

24. Video clip from *The Ellen Show*. https://www.youtube.com/watch?v=iwCdv9iR8P8

25. "We Shall Behold Him," Words and Music by Dottie Rambo, ©1980 John T. Benson Publishing Company.

26. "The Songs of Heaven" (March 11, 1962); https://wacriswell.com/sermons/1962/the-songs-of-heaven/?keywords=angels+sing

27. From the book *Spiritual Disciplines for the Christian Life* by Donald Whitney, as quoted in *Leadership*, vol. 10, no. 3 (summer 1989) by Elton Trueblood.

28. Harold M. Best, Unceasing Worship (Downers Grove, IL: IVP Books, 2003).

29. W. W. Wiersbe, *Wiersbe's Expository Outlines on the New Testament* (Wheaton, IL: Victor Books, 1992), 399.

30. "Oh, I Want to Know You More," words and music by Steve Fry, ©1994 Birdwing Music (ASCAP) and BMG Songs (ASCAP) Birdwing Music Admin. by EMI CMG Publishing.

31. John Piper, Desiring God (Sisters, OR: Multomah, 1996).

32. C. S. Lewis, *The Problem of Pain* (New York: Macmillan, 1944).

33. "Now I Know Him," words and music by Joseph Habedank © 2014, Syntax Creative.

34. "Fly Like an Eagle" by Steve Miller, recorded by Steve Miller Band (Capitol Records, 1976).

35. Robert J. Morgan, *Mastering Life before It's Too Late: 10 Biblical Strategies for a Lifetime of Purpose* (New York, NY: Howard Books, 2015), 188, Amazon Kindle edition.